THE MURDER TRIAL OF WILBUR JACKSON

A HOMICIDE IN THE FAMILY

Second Edition

STONEHEAD
MANOR

4332　　　　4330

THE MURDER TRIAL OF WILBUR JACKSON

A HOMICIDE IN THE FAMILY

Second Edition

Professor of Law, Harvard University

WILLIAM H. KENETY
Adjunct Professor at Columbus School of Law,
Catholic University of America

WEST PUBLISHING COMPANY

St. Paul   New York   Los Angeles   San Francisco

COPYRIGHT © 1975 By WEST PUBLISHING CO.
COPYRIGHT © 1985 By WEST PUBLISHING CO.
50 West Kellogg Boulevard
P.O. Box 43526
St. Paul, Minnesota 55164

All rights reserved
Printed in the United States of America
Library of Congress
Cataloging in Publication Data
ISBN: 0–314–85315–4

1st Reprint—1985

Copy editing: *William Olson*
Text illustration: *Century Design*
Cover: *Jack Norman/Aqua Graphics Studio*

TABLE OF CONTENTS

CAST OF CHARACTERS

Wilbur Jackson	The defendant, accused of murdering his daughter and three young men
Mary Jackson	His wife, witness to the killings
Sandra Jackson	Their daughter, allegedly murdered by her father
Debbie Jackson	Their other daughter
Todd Wilson *Jonathan Carter* *Ricky Walters*	The three young men allegedly murdered by Wilbur Jackson
Joseph A. Gillis	Presiding judge
Leonard Gilman	Prosecuting attorney
Irvin Baranski	Police detective in charge of the case
Jerome Jasinski *James Caufield* *Leonard Fashoway* *and others*	Police witnesses
Carl Richardson	Manager of Stonehead Manor
Felipe Fernandez *Georgia Webster* *Mary Lee Von Allstein* *and others*	Residents of Stonehead Manor
Sally Jo Tucker	Sandra Jackson's best friend
Dr. Ames Robey *Dr. Lynn Blunt*	Prosecution psychiatrists
Oliver Nelson	Chief defense counsel

Emmett Tracy   His assistants
John Carney

Dr. Hubert Miller   Defense psychiatrists
Dr. Emmanuel Tanay

A map of Stonehead Manor may be found on page 146. The main entrance to The Manor is pictured on page ii. Photographs of the murder scene may be found on pages 116, 117, 118, 141, 149, and 150.

PREFACE TO THE SECOND EDITION

Since its first publication in 1975, *The Murder Trial of Wilbur Jackson* has served as an introduction to the criminal justice system for a half a generation of students. Hopefully that trend will continue.

In consideration of the book's continuing popularity, the authors, and West Publishing Company, decided that a revised second edition would be appropriate. This edition contains added explanatory material to help guide the reader through the workings of the criminal justice system. Indexes have also been added as has a comprehensive glossary that provides further explanation of various facets of that system. The trial of presidential assailant John Hinckley has heightened interest in the insanity defense and this subject has been given special attention in the glossary.

In the years since the book was written much has happened to the characters, particularly to Wilbur Jackson himself. Accordingly, a second epilogue has been added to close out the story. As the preface to the first edition notes, this book was originally written after Mr. Kenety, then one of Professor Heymann's students, took an interest in the case. Similarly, the current information concerning Wilbur Jackson was discovered only after Gordon Thomas, one of Professor Kenety's students, located Mr. Jackson.

During these intervening years the authors have not been idle. Philip Heymann served as Assistant Attorney General of the United States and William Kenety as Assistant Attorney General of Maryland. Hopefully those years have added perspective.

Both authors have been struck by the number of people who have contacted them to guess the city where this really happened and to inquire whether it is all true. It is. As the original preface notes, the location of the crime has been changed to protect the privacy of those involved. Likewise the names of Wilbur Jackson and his family, and those who lived at Stonehead Manor, have also been changed. Otherwise, as they say on the streets, this is how it went down.

Washington, D.C.
June 1984

William H. Kenety

PREFACE TO THE FIRST EDITION

Readers might be interested to learn how this book came about. Two years ago Professor Philip Heymann distributed a magazine article concerning the case to his students in first-year criminal law at Harvard Law School. The article had been written during the course of the trial and Bill Kenety, curious as to the outcome, made contact with Jackson's lawyer. As a result of that contact, and with the aid of a grant from the Center for the Advancement of Criminal Justice at Harvard, Kenety spent the summer of 1973 researching the case, reading the trial transcript, and interviewing the participants.

Out of that summer's work came a multilithed edition of the Wilbur Jackson case which Heymann used at Harvard Law School. The authors contacted West Publishing Company the following fall and West agreed to publish the book. Kenety returned to the scene of the trial in February of 1974, talked again to the participants, and acquired the photographs and exhibits included in this edition. Kenety and Heymann rewrote several sections of the book, extensively interviewed the trial counsel, and finally produced the present edition.

Wilbur Jackson is not the defendant's real name nor is Pittsburgh the site of the crime. To protect the privacy of the individuals involved, some of the other names have also been changed; otherwise this is as it happened.

The authors would like to express their appreciation to trial counsel Oliver Nelson and Leonard Gilman who spent many hours answering questions and who came to Harvard to be interviewed by the authors and by students who had read the preliminary edition. Judge Joseph Gillis, Sgt. Irvin Baranski, and Michael Mueller of the Prosecutor's Office were generous with their time and filled in important details of the story. Judge Robert Colombo and Jack and Sidney Kraizman provided needed information, while Betty and Paul Reinke gave unstintingly of their hospitality. Lastly, and probably foremost, the authors express their gratitude to Janet Johnson for countless hours of cheerful help and valuable advice in producing this book.

Cambridge, Mass.
January, 1975

Philip B. Heymann
William H. Kenety

INTRODUCTION

Early in the morning of 8 May 1970 Wilbur Jackson killed his daughter Sandra and three of her friends: Todd Wilson, Jonathan Carter, and Ricky Walters. Of that there can be no question—Jackson all but admitted the homicides, ballistics tests corroborated his statements, and his wife witnessed the killings.

At trial, Jackson's defense was that he had accidentally killed his daughter and then, temporarily insane as a result of grief and anger, proceeded to kill the young men he felt had led his once virtuous daughter astray. The evidence later brought forth showed that Jackson, born and raised in Tennessee, was in many ways a model "middle-American." A college-educated railroad engineer, he joined the Pittsburgh police reserves and proudly displayed an American flag over his livingroom mantel. He also kept a tight rein on his daughter Sandra, seventeen, a straight-A pre-med student at nearby Allegheny State.

Sandra Jackson tired of her father's rigid restrictions and eventually moved away from home, leaving no clue as to where she could be found. For a week Jackson spent almost every waking hour searching for his missing daughter. Finally, after paying a friend of Sandy's to reveal her new home, Jackson found his daughter. Less than an hour later he signed a confession at police headquarters admitting the killings. This is his story.

THE SETTING

To fully understand the case of Wilbur Jackson, one must realize the emotional climate that passed across America in the year 1970. It was the period in which the president of the United States termed student protesters "bums"; the time when the Black Panther Party and the Weathermen shocked the public consciousness; and an era of social upheaval when it frequently became difficult to tell right from wrong.

Panthers Fred Hampton and Mark Clark were the victims of an alleged police massacre in Chicago while Weathermen Mark Rudd and Bernadine Dohrn made the FBI's ten-most-wanted list, an honor previously reserved for criminals of a different sort.

On 15 February, 1970 Federal District Judge Julius Hoffman sentenced attorney William Kunstler to four years, thirteen days, for contempt of court. Three days later David Dellinger, Rennie Davis, Tom Hayden, Abbie Hoffman, and Jerry Rubin were found guilty of crossing state lines to incite a riot at the 1968 Democratic National Convention.

In March, 1970 a four-story brick townhouse in New York City was destroyed by several explosions. Three bodies were found. It would later be shown that the house had been a Weathermen bomb factory. Later that month the New York offices of IBM, Mobil Oil, and General Telephone & Electronics were rocked by mysterious explosions. Violence struck again in New York City when one man was killed, another critically injured, in what was believed to be the explosion of a Black Panther bomb factory. In an ominous portent of events to come, Prince Norodom Sihanouk was deposed as Cambodian ruler on 18 March.

In April, 104 Republican and Democratic representatives called for the creation of a select committee to consider the impeachment of Justice William O. Douglas. Harvard University suffered through two nights of demonstrations and trashings. The *New York Times* estimated that on 16 April the "rampage through the town of Cambridge" wrought one hundred thousand dollars worth of destruction.

In Detroit the school board approved a plan to achieve partial integration by extensive busing. The Michigan House voted 68–31 to nullify the plan. Tempers would flare to the point where, one year later, the school buses of suburban Pontiac, Michigan, would be fire-bombed by a group of self-described Ku Klux Klanners.

On 29 April South Vietnamese forces invaded Cambodia. One day later Richard M. Nixon committed U.S. ground forces saying, "I'd rather be a one-term president and do what I believe is right than to be a two-term president at the cost of seeing America become a second-rate power and see this nation accept the first defeat in its proud 190-year history."

On the first and second of May over fifteen thousand people demonstrated in New Haven over the indictment of Bobby Seale in a Black Panther murder case. On the second, the Hobart College Air Force Building was fire-bombed. Students charged that the incident and subsequent riots were incited by one Thomas Tongyai, a police undercover agent. "Tommy the Traveler" would later be cleared of charges of conspiracy to commit arson, criminal solicitation, and criminal facilitation and thereafter resumed his undercover role.

On 4 May panicky Ohio National Guardsmen shot and killed Allison Krause, Sandy Scheuer, Jeff Miller, and Bill Schroeder on the Kent State campus. Vice-President Spiro Agnew said the tragedy was predictable and unavoidable.

On 5 May the Senate Judiciary Committee acted to unanimously approve the nomination of Harry Blackmun to the Supreme Court seat for which Richard Nixon had previously proposed G. Harold Carswell.

On 6 May a Texas Court of Appeals upheld the extradition of Manson family member Charles "Tex" Watson to stand trial in California in the Sharon Tate murders. That same day Interior Secretary Walter J. Hickel sent a letter to the White House claiming that the Nixon Administration was turning its back on the mass of American youth. Later that year Hickel would be summarily fired.

On 7 May students at New York University seized a campus building and threatened to blow up a 3.5-million-dollar computer unless their demands were met. The *New York Times* of that day estimated that over eighty colleges and universities had shut down.

At 2:25 in the morning of 8 May, 1970 Wilbur Jackson murdered his daughter Sandra, and Todd Wilson, Jonathan Carter, and Ricky Walters.

The next day one hundred thousand people demonstrated in Washington, D.C. The next week fourteen people were shot at the Jackson State campus in what the president's Commission on Campus Unrest would later call an "unreasonable, unjustified overreaction."

The year would see even more tragic events, including a dramatic increase in terrorist bombings, ranging from the New York police headquarters to the senate chamber of the Louisiana state capitol. A research center at the University of Wisconsin would be destroyed and a student killed. Student demonstrators would clash with hard hat counterdemonstrators. The lurid Charles Manson murder trial would unfold. And, in a desperate bid to escape, black militant prisoners would kidnap a San Rafael, California, judge; when police officers opened fire on their escaping truck, they would all be killed.

THE BACKGROUND

It was against this backdrop of turmoil and chaos that seventeen-year-old Sandra Jackson left home. She did not leave her family her new address—only a letter detailing her mixed emotions. That letter is reproduced in Figure 1. It was introduced at the trial the following November as Defendant's Exhibit E.

Soon after Sandra left home, Wilbur Jackson searched relentlessly for her. What happened when he found his daughter is told in Figure 2, a reproduction of the front-page story carried in the May 8 editions of the *Pittsburgh News*.

Other front page headlines of that Friday were: "A Bid for Campus Truce: Students Get Nixon Plea," "Detroit Nun's Story Hints at Kent Sniper," "Shots Wound 4 in Buffalo Campus Clash," "Attack by Viet Reds Reach a High Point," and "GM White Collar Workers Face Layoffs Over Cutbacks." Also on 8 May the New York Knicks beat the Los Angeles Lakers 113–99 to win the National Basketball Association Championship.

Figure 1   Sandra Jackson's letter

Dear Family,   Deft: E

11-30-70 JR

I love you, everyone of you, very
dearly, and I know you love me.
I hope what I say doesn't change
any of your feelings toward me. I
feel I have to leave home again.
I'll be safe and I can take care
of myself. It's just that now since
I'm going to college I feel I'm
missing out a lot of the college ~~atmosphere~~
by living at home. So I've decided to
move to campus, where my classes will
only be in walking distance. In my
acquittance with fellow class mates I feel
inmature and irresponsible for taking
your money and living at home. I feel

Figure 1 Sandra Jackson's letter *(continued)*

like a parasite, and that I've spent
your hard-earned money ~~foolly~~ foolishly.
Please give me time to make up my
own mind about the uncaring world.
I'll probably be coming back home
soon finding it too much to cope
with. But I have to try. This has
been a very hard decision to make.
I've just gone away to school. Lots
of kids go away to college. I'll
just be another one. I'll call you
and write, this week, and as soon as you've
gotten ~~over~~ over the shock of me
leaving home I'll come back to visit
you. The place I'm moving into, is
already furnished. I'm moving in

Figure 1 Sandra Jackson's letter (continued)

with two other girls that go to ⟵③
school. We won't have a TV only a
record player ~~scribble~~ and a small radio.
I plan to block myself off from
the world and just study, study,
study. In an effort to improve
my grades. I'll be home on the
week-ends and I'll be alright.
Just remember that I love you
all very much and I always will.
I hope you'll be proud of me
when I make it on my own. And
I'll be proud of myself too. I'll
really be a person then.

Figure 1 Sandra Jackson's letter (continued)

And I know you'll really be
proud of me when I bring home
good grades. And we'll all be happy,
I know it will be hard at first
to adjust to me being gone and it
will be hard for me ~~to~~ not seeing
you as often. But there ~~j~~ comes a
time in every^(young) person's life that he
must make this big decision ~~Father~~, Thank
you very much for buying me the
car but I won't need it on campus
just walking to my classes. Mother,
you'll get more use out of it.
     I love you all. Please trust~~me~~
in me in this big decision. This

Figure 1   Sandra Jackson's letter   (continued)

is probably the biggest and only E-⑥

real decision I've ever made.

Love with all my heart,
   Your daughter and
      sister,
         Sandra *

* I'm going to be called
Sandra from now on. It's more
grown-up then Sandy which is
only my nickname

Figure 1   Sandra Jackson's letter   (continued)

E-E

P.S.

I'm sorry I couldn't tell you before that I was leaving that I had to tell you in this letter but I just couldn't. You would be surprised either way I told you and I felt it would be better in a letter. Not to face you. That's another problem I'm going to work on, facing my problems. I've lived too long in a fantasy and I hope moving away to campus will be reality. Because college is a reality. Don't bother calling my friends because no one knew that I was leaving, at least I don't think so. God bless you all.

I love you.

Figure 2 *Pittsburgh News* **article**

THE PITTSBURGH NEWS

Friday, May 8, 1970   SERVING PITTSBURGH SINCE 1842   Vol. 128, No. 128

Bodies Found in Bed

Dad Kills Daughter And Three Boyfriends

**By ADRIAN CRYSTAL and
PAT WILLIAMS
News Staff Writers**

A 45-year-old father is held by city police this morning after murdering his 17-year-old daughter and three 18-year-old boys she was staying with in a seedy apartment near the Allegheny State campus.

Held is Wilbur Jackson of 5755 Hill St., a railroad engineer for the Penn Central. Dead is his daughter Sandra, 17, and Todd Wilson, Jonathan Carter, and Ricky Walters, all 18. Police say the three youths rented a second-story apartment at 4330 Lincoln and Sandra had recently moved in with them.

(continued on page 17)

Father Kills 4

(continued from page one)

Witnesses said Sandra had left home a week ago and moved to the apartment, dubbed "Stonehead Manor" by its occupants. Jackson had been a frequent visitor during the past week, apparently trying to persuade his daughter to return home.

Inhabitants of the apartment building awoke sometime after midnight to the sound of gunfire as Jackson poured an estimated 50 rounds into the bodies of his daughter and her comrades. Jackson then drove to the second precinct station house where he surrendered himself and his weapons, a .38 revolver and a German Luger.

Police say the bodies, all nude, were found in the apartment's one bedroom and living room. The front door lock was found on the floor, leading police to believe that Jackson had forced his way inside. Several witnesses to the shootings including Mrs. Jackson were questioned by the police and later released.

Sandra Jackson was a 17-year-old sophomore at Allegheny State and the eldest of four Jackson children. A neighbor of the Jacksons, Mrs. Anthony Sherlouski, told reporters: "The Jacksons were a wonderful, kind family who were always very friendly. I never thought Sandra would get involved with men."

Young Wilson was the son of Norman Wilson of 17605 Francis. The elder Wilson owns a florist shop at 3206 West Hitchcock. He refused to talk to newsmen and asked his neighbors not to.

Carter, a minority group member, attended Cass Technical High School and worked part-time for Floral Bouquets, Inc. The shop's manager, Roger Wilson, told reporters: "Jonathan was a real hard worker that everybody liked. Why just yesterday he bought some flowers for his mother."

Nothing is known about Walters, although witnesses said he had just moved to the house at 4330 Lincoln.

ARREST AND PRE–TRIAL PROCEEDINGS

As in any criminal proceeding, a number of significant events took place between the time of the killings in May 1970 and the start of Wilbur Jackson's trial in November 1970, some six months later. During this time there were four important developments in the Wilbur Jackson case: (1) his arrest and confession, (2) the preliminary proceedings, (3) the competency examination, and (4) the change of venue hearing.

ARREST AND CONFESSION

The certificate shown in Figure 3 is known as a "Miranda form" after the famous 1966 United States Supreme Court decision in *Miranda v. Arizona*. A variation of this form is used by virtually every police department in the country.

As a result of that decision police officers questioning suspects must inform them of their "Miranda rights"—the five points listed at the top of the form. Any confession elicited without those rights having been given is considered to have been improperly obtained and will be "suppressed"—not allowed to be used in court against the defendant.

Hence defense attorneys frequently try to suppress confessions by arguing that they were obtained without the required warnings having been given. As a result police departments have developed Miranda forms. The use of these forms, particularly when signed by the defendant, helps to prove that the warnings were indeed given.

Wilbur Jackson did sign a Miranda form (see Figure 3) before Detective James Caufield elicited the confession shown in Figure 4.

PRELIMINARY PROCEEDINGS

Having surrendered himself in the early morning hours of 8 May, Wilbur Jackson was held in police custody until the next day when he was arraigned before Judge Cornelius J. Sullivan on a charge of first-degree murder in connection with the slaying of Ricky Walters. An arraignment is a brief proceeding wherein the defendants are formally informed of the charge(s) against them, informed of their right to an

Figure 3 Miranda form signed by Wilbur Jackson

CONSTITUTIONAL RIGHTS
CERTIFICATE OF NOTIFICATION

I understand that :

1 I have a right to remain silent and that I do not have to answer any questions put to me or make any statements.

2. Any statement I make or anything I say can be used against me in a Court of Law.

3. I have the right to have an attorney (lawyer) present before and during the time I answer any questions or make any statement.

4. If I cannot afford an attorney (lawyer), one will be appointed for me without cost by the Court prior to any questioning.

5. I can decide at any time to exercise my rights and not answer any questions or make any statement.

I understand that these are my rights under the Law. I have not been threatened or promised anything, and I now desire and agree to answer any questions put to me or to make a statement.

In the presence of :

WITNESS *Ptr. James Caufield*   ✗ *Wilbur Chester Jackson* SIGNATURE

WITNESS *Patr. Leonard M. Fashoury*   *5-8-70* DATE   *2:50 AM* TIME

☑ This certificate of notification was read to the suspect, and he/she had an opportunity to read it. Further, the suspect was given an opportunity to ask any questions that he/she might have concerning this certificate and his/her rights.

☐ Suspect is illiterate. He/she has had the rights under the law, as defined above, explained to him/her, and has agreed to answer questions or make a statement.

☐ Suspect can read and write. The rights, as defined above, have been explained to him/her, and he/she has agreed to make a voluntary statement but has refused to sign this certificate.

REMARKS : _____ *College Education* _____

_____

_____

5-8-70 DATE   *3:00 AM* TIME   OFFICER *Ptr. James Caufield Hamilton* P.P.D. UNIT

Holt Up Bureau PLACE   OFFICER *Patr. Leonard M. Fashoury #2* P.P.D. UNIT

Form C of D-78-CE (Rev. 3-69)   P.P.D. 342-8

Figure 3 Miranda form signed by Wilbur Jackson (continued)

INSTRUCTIONS FOR USE OF CERTIFICATE OF NOTIFICATION

When an individual is taken into custody or otherwise deprived of his freedom and subjected to questioning, procedural safeguards prior to any questioning must be employed to protect his privilege against self-incrimination.

The instructions listed below shall be followed in order to make proper use of the Certificate of Notification:

1. The interrogating officer shall read the Certificate to the suspect.

2. A copy of PPD 342-B shall be given to the suspect to read.

3. The suspect shall be requested to sign the certificate. Any witnesses who might be present during this process, such as an attorney, member of suspect's family, and other officers, also shall be requested to sign the certificate.

4. The officer(s) shall complete the remainder of the certificate as indicated.

5. If the suspect is illiterate, a summary of the explanation made to him shall be noted in the Remarks Section on the Certificate.

6. In the event the suspect refuses to sign the Certificate, a brief summary of the reasons for refusal, as given by the suspect, shall be noted on the Certificate. The interrogating officer(s) shall then complete the certificate and identify it by placing the suspect's name directly under the title.

7. If the suspect refuses to sign the Certificate, but is willing to answer questions or make a statement, the interrogating officer(s) shall proceed as usual with the questioning.

8. If the suspect takes advantage of his rights and refuses to make a statement and or requests to see an attorney, the interrogation must cease even though he may have answered some questions or volunteered some statements on his own.

attorney, and given an opportunity to plead guilty or not guilty to the charge(s) against them. The arraignment judge will also set bail and determine a date for a preliminary hearing.

Jackson pleaded not guilty and was remanded, without bail, to the Allegheny County Jail. Bail is the system whereby the court determines whether the accused should be released from custody pending trial and what, if any, security the accused must post in order to guarantee his appearance at trial. The security given to insure a defendant's appearance at trial may, in minor cases, merely be his or her promise to appear. In more serious cases the defendant may also have to pledge his or her money or home. Alternatively, the defendant may use a bail bondsman, an individual who, for a fee, puts up money to guarantee the defendant's appearance. If the defendant does not appear for trial, whatever security has been pledged is forfeited to the court. In theory, bail should be determined solely on the question of what guarantees are necessary to insure the defendant's appearance at trial, not by whether he may pose a threat to commit further crimes. As a matter of practicality, however, the judge will frequently consider the defendant's criminal record, and, as in the Jackson case, he may deny bail because the potential penalty in a murder case is so great that any defendant might logically be expected to flee.

At this time Jackson claimed that he was indigent and unable to afford an attorney. He was assigned, as his court-appointed counsel,

Figure 4 Wilbur Jackson's confession

May 8, 1970 3:05AM
Det. James Caulfield
Homicide Bureau

Statement from Wilbur Chester Jackson 45/wm
D.O.B. 9-21-24 of 5755 Hill 826-2734
Employed – Penn Central Railroad – Engineer
RE: Fatal Shooting

    I got off work 1:40AM and drove
home. My wife Mary 44/wf was waiting for
me. My wife told me she had gone to get
our 17 year old Sandra Jackson D.A.B 10-16-52
who works in a Dentists office. She had
our 13 year old son Paul Chester Jackson
with her. Our daughter left home last
Sunday with an 18 year old girl friend.
At the Dentists Office her Boy friend
Todd a red head was there with his
friend Ricky w/m and my daughter left
with them.

    I found out my daughter Sandra was
staying at 4330 Lincoln Apt # 9. At

Figure 4 **Wilbur Jackson's confession** (continued)

II

about 2:00 AM I armed myself
with my 38 Cal revolver and my
Luger and with my wife I drove over
to 4330 Lincoln. My wife and I
entered the Apartment bldg through
the unlocked front door. We went up
on the 2nd floor to apartment #9.
I knew my daughter was in there with
Todd. I broke the door down with
my right shoulder and went in.
Ricky was on the couch I went to
the bedroom on the left and saw my
daughter in bed with Todd. I was
carrying a flashlight in my right
hand. They were both nude. I put the
flashlight in my left hand and pulled
out my 38 revolver I had under my
belt and struck Todd over the head
with the gun as hard as I could
the weapon discharged killing my

Figure 4 **Wilbur Jackson's confession** (continued)

III

daughter who moaned and fell back. My wife screamed you killed my baby. I said it was an accident. After I knew my daughter was dead I shot Todd in the head Two or three times. I don't remember shooting a colored man named Jonathan who was in a bed in the same room. I remember thinking he probably had been taking Turns with my daughter. I remember seeing blood on Jonathan. I put the 38 revolver in my belt and pulled out the Luger and walked in the other room and shone the flashlight at Ricky on the couch and I shot him I believe through the forehead. I believe he was having intercourse with my daughter also. They all ruined my daughter.

I walked downstairs to apartment #3

Wilbur Jackson

Figure 4   *Wilbur Jackson's confession*   (continued)

$$IV$$

to find Sally Tacker 18/WF who
lived there with a colored man and
his mexican wife. I broke open the
door to Apartment 3 and Sally
wasn't there and I ran amuck
trying to get into other apartments
to find Sally. I had to drag my
wife out to the car but I wanted
to find Sally and get her because
she took my daughter from home.
     I got in the car and drove to
the Police Station and I got out
and kissed her goodby and told her
to tell the children to remember me
and I sent her home. I then went
into the Police Station and gave myself
up and surrendered my two weapons
and spare cartridges.
     When I went over to 4330 Lincoln
I armed myself because I planned on

Wilbur Jackson

Figure 4 Wilbur Jackson's confession (continued)

$$\underline{V}$$

going to the caretaker and get him
to open the door to Apartment #9
and I had heard he had 5 guns.
Also I had heard one of the boys
who lived with Todd had a rifle.

    When I went into the apartment
#3 the colored man and his wife were
in bed and I didn't want to harm
them and told them so. Another
white man was there and I told
him I wouldn't harm him. The
colored mans name is Eldrin and
I told him I would kill him if
he didn't help me find Sally. I
didn't intend to hurt him. Eldrin
went with me through the first
floor hallway looking for Sally.
We couldn't find her. We met
numerous tenants in the hall. I
remember yelling Sally, Sally, where

Figure 4 Wilbur Jackson's confession (continued)

VI

Are you.

X Wilbur Jackson

Interview over at 4:15 AM in presence of Patn. Leonard Fashoway

Det James Canfield Hm

X Patn Leonard Fashoway

Oliver Nelson, a respected and veteran criminal defense lawyer. Later, Jackson was assigned two additional attorneys.

On 18 May a preliminary hearing was held before Judge James H. McNally III. The preliminary hearing is a short proceeding wherein the judge reviews the charges against the accused to determine whether the accusations, if proved at trial, are sufficient to support the charges. At this point Jackson had only been charged with first-degree murder in connection with the death of Ricky Walters. First-degree murder is defined as murder intentionally committed with premeditation. Judge McNally found no evidence of premeditation and reduced the charge to second-degree murder.* He also determined that Wilbur Jackson should be released on a bail of two

---

* Prior to trial the prosecution appealed Judge McNally's ruling that reduced the charge against Jackson to second-degree murder. The Prosecutor's Office petitioned first the Recorder's Court, then an appeals court, for an order directing Judge McNally to reinstate the original charge of first-degree murder. These courts decided that it was within Judge McNally's discretion to reduce the charge. This issue was not finally resolved until November when the state's highest court declined to hear the matter.

thousand dollars. This sum was put up by a bail bondsman to whom Jackson paid a fee of two hundred dollars. Jackson was released shortly thereafter.

On 21 May Jackson was charged with three additional murders. The normal charging procedure in this jurisdiction involves three stages: (1) the police set forth all the information they have gathered in the form of a request for an arrest warrant (see Figure 5); (2) on this basis the prosecutor decides whether to request a local judge to issue an arrest warrant; and (3) if the prosecutor requests, and a judge signs, an arrest warrant, the steps of initial arraignment and preliminary hearing previously described are followed. If the defendant is bound over at the conclusion of the preliminary hearing, the prosecutor will then sign, and file with the court, an information, which constitutes the formal charge (see Figure 6).

The defendant is then arraigned a second time "on the information." At this stage, a copy of the information is given to the defendant, he is then asked to plead, a date is then set for pre-trial motions (generally within thirty days), and shortly thereafter a date is set for a pre-trial conference. These procedures were now followed as Wilbur Jackson was charged with three additional homicides.

On 21 May first-degree murder arrest warrants were issued for Wilbur Jackson in the deaths of Sandra Jackson, Todd Wilson, and Jonathan Carter. Jackson voluntarily surrendered to the police. He was arraigned before Judge Wayne Smith. Jackson was bound over on three first-degree murder charges and was denied bail. Recorder's Court Presiding Judge Robert DeMascio later affirmed Judge Smith's decision denying bail.

On 6 June another preliminary hearing was held, again before Judge McNally. This time Judge McNally did not reduce the charges, and Jackson was again bound over on first-degree murder charges in the killings of Sandra Jackson, Todd Wilson, and Jonathan Carter. Bail was again denied.

COMPETENCY EXAMINATION

On 9 June Judge DeMascio held a hearing on a prosecution motion to commit Wilbur Jackson to the State Forensic Center for a mental examination. The purpose of this examination was to determine if Wilbur Jackson was competent to stand trial. Competency to stand trial relates to whether defendants are mentally able to understand the proceedings against them and to assist in their defense. It does not concern whether they may have been insane at the time of the crimes.

Judge DeMascio granted the motion and Jackson remained in the Forensic Center from 2 July until 13 August. Figure 7 shows the Forensic Center's report.

On 25 September Jackson was released on bail by Recorder's Court Judge Joseph A. Gillis. Calling Jackson a "good risk," Judge

Figure 5 Request for warrant

PD 467 10 69.

THE PEOPLE OF THE STATE OF PENNSYLVANIA   PITTSBURGH POLICE DEPARTMENT
VS.   **REQUEST FOR WARRANT RECOMMENDATION**

(LIST DEFENDANTS NAMES AND ADDRESSES WITH ZIP CODE)

WILBUR CHESTER JACKSON
5755 Hill St.
Pittsburgh, Pennsylvania

AGE	SEX	RACE	D O B	IDENT NUMBER
45	M	W	9-21-24	282694

OFFENSE *Murder 1st degree*
TO BE FILLED IN BY PROSECUTOR

Det/Sgt. Irvin Baranski
Det/Sgt. Robert Wilson

OFFICER IN CHARGE D/S Irvin Baranski Homicide
PRECINCT/BUREAU

30080

DAY, DATE AND
TIME OF OFFENSE Friday, 5-8-70 2:15 AM
PLACE OF OFFENSE 4330 Lincoln, Apt. #9.

PERSON TO SIGN D/S Irvin Baranski, DS 529

ARRAIGNMENT ON WARRANT

COMPLAINANT SANDRA JACKSON   17 F W
                                         AGE SEX RACE

OFFENSE
NUMBER Hom 2-849510
                          IDENT. NUMBER

DATE OF COMPLAINT 5-21-70   5755 Hill St.
                                ADDRESS

DETAILS OF INVESTIGATION

1. On May 8, 1970 at approximately 2:00 AM the defendant Wilbur Jackson
forced open the door to apt. #9, at 4330 Lincoln by pushing it open
with his shoulder. Upon entry of the apartment he went in the bedroom where he found his daughter Sandra Jackson, in bed in the nude
with a Todd Wilson who occupied the apartment. The deft. went to
the bed and began to assault Wilson with a pistol, by striking him
over the head. During the assault on Wilson, the gun discharged
three times, striking Sandra Jackson in the chest three times, and
wounding her fatally. The deft. subsequently shot three male occ-
pants in the apartment, fatally wounding them all, and left the
premises.
Upon leaving the premises the deft. drove to the Second Precinct
Police Station, where he told the officer in charge that he wished
to turn himself in because he had just shot and killed his daughter, Sandra Jackson and three of her hippie friends over on Lincoln
street. The surrender occurred at 2:35 AM on 5-8-70. The deft.
also turned over two pistols to the officer at the time of his
surrender.

WITNESS #1. (Dr. John Hindeman, Allegheny County Medical Examiner)
Went to the scene where he examined the body of Sandra Jackson
and pronounced her dead, and ordered the body removed to the
Allegheny County Morgue.

WITNESS #2. (Dr. Clara Raven, Allegheny County Medical Examiner)
Performed autopsy on the body of Sandra Jackson at the Allegheny
County Morgue on 5-8-70 and gave the cause of death as a 3
gun shot wounds to the chest. Morgue File # 70-3798.

APPROVED _____
          SIGNATURE OF COMMANDING OFFICER   PRECINCT OR BUREAU
       Det. Insp. Delore Ricard, Homicide Bur.

FELONY – MISDEMEANOR

IN CUSTODY YES [X] NO [ ] PRECINCT NO. Homicide   5-21-70
                                                              DATE

I RECOMMEND THE ISSUING OF A WARRANT AGAINST   WILBUR CHESTER JACKSON   45 M W 9-21-24
                                                                        AGE SEX RACE D O B

NATURE OF OFFENSE *Murder 1st degree*
                  TO BE FILLED IN BY PROSECUTOR

SECTION 750,316 , CL1948

OFFENSE NO.

SIGNED _____
                          ASSISTANT PROSECUTING ATTORNEY

Figure 6 Information

WITNESSES:

IRVIN BARANSKI DS—529 HOMICIDE BUREAU		CHARLES HAYES
JOHN HINDMAN	SALLY JO TUCKER	JEROME JASINSKI
CLARA RAVEN	ALLISON FLETCHER	JOSEPH BECKER
CAROLINE VAN DEERLIN	SARAH JOHNSON	ROBERT JONES
ARTHUR BOHLING	ELDRIN JOHNSON	ANDREW PARKER
HOWARD IVES	MARY LEE ALLSTEIN	LYLE THAYER
GEORGIA WEBSTER	ALBERT SCULLY	JOSEPH ZISLER
JANET RIVERS	LESTER SCOTTIE	ROBERT WILSON
MARY MARTIN	MIKE KESSLER	
GARFIELD POWERS	EARL MONROE	

STATE OF PENNSYLVANIA—IN THE RECORDER'S COURT OF THE CITY OF PITTSBURGH

THE PEOPLE OF THE STATE OF PENNSYLVANIA
    –vs–

WILBUR CHESTER JACKSON

                                                    Defendant(s)

DATE OF OFFENSE _____ May 8, 1970 _____

LOCATION _____ 4330 Lincoln, Apt. #9 _____

                    City of Pittsburgh

COMPLAINANT _____ Irvin Baranski _____

COMPLAINING WITNESS _____ Irvin Baranski _____

            D/Sgt. Irvin Baranski

DATE WARRANT ISSUED _____ May 21, 1970 _____

OFFENSE _____ MURDER FIRST DEGREE _____

                P 7008041

STATE OF PENNSYLVANIA)
COUNTY OF ALLEGHENY } ss. **INFORMATION**
CITY OF PITTSBURGH)

IN THE NAME OF THE PEOPLE OF THE STATE OF PENNSYLVANIA, WILLIAM L. CAHALAN, Prosecuting Attorney in and for the said County of Allegheny, State of Pennsylvania, who prosecutes for and on behalf of the People of the State of Pennsylvania comes now here in said Court in the current term thereof, and gives the said Court to understand and be informed that the above-named Defendant(s), late of the said City of Pittsburgh, heretofore on or about the DATE OF OFFENSE set forth above, at the LOCATION set forth above, in the City of Pittsburgh, County of Allegheny, State of Pennsylvania.

feloniously, deliberately, willfully, with malice aforethought, and with premeditation, did kill and murder one SANDRA JACKSON, contrary to Sec. 750.316 C. L. 1948

and against the peace and dignity of the People of the State of Pennsylvania
Drafted by:

                                        William L. Cahalan
                                        Prosecuting Attorney

To: DEFENSE COUNSEL. Please take notice that the People intend to use in evidence in said prosecution the following confessions and admissions obtained from defendant(s) by law enforcing officers and persons acting in cooperation with such officers.

CONFESSION BY: _____   _____ DATE _____

Figure 7 Competency report on Wilbur Jackson

STATE OF PENNSYLVANIA

DEPARTMENT OF MENTAL HEALTH

CENTER FOR FORENSIC PSYCHIATRY
BOX 2060

FOX CHAPEL, PENNSYLVANIA

August 13, 1970

Sheriff William Lucas
525 Clinton Avenue
Pittsburgh, Pennsylvania

re: Wilbur Jackson
     CFP #91083

Dear Sheriff Lucas:

We are returning Wilbur Jackson who has been at the Center for Forensic Psychiatry for an evaluation in relation to his competency to stand trial.

We are aware that Mr. Jackson will be placed in custody within the county jail pending judicial proceedings. We are thus enclosing some information pertinent to his adjustment in a confinement setting.

We recognize the major responsibility your department maintains in the criminal justice system and are aware that patients who manifest emotional problems can be problematic in the jail setting. It is, thus, hoped that you or your representative will feel free to contact us in regard to management of this patient.

Sincerely,

Paul M. Isenstadt, A.C.S.W.
Director, Social Services Department

Fred Jones, Jr.
Forensic Services Coordinator

PMI/mjo

ENCL:

cc: Social Service Dept. - Allegheny County Jail

*Figure 7 **Competency report on Wilbur Jackson** (continued)*

CENTER FOR FORENSIC PSYCHIATRY   DATE: August 13, 1970

RETURN TO JAIL FORM

PATIENT'S NAME: Wilbur Jackson   COUNTY: Allegheny

ALLEGED CHARGE: Murder One (3 specifications) Murder Two (1 specification)

I. Brief review of the patient's adjustment as an inpatient at the
    Center for Forensic Psychiatry.

Mr. Jackson initially adjusted satisfactorily to the Center for Forensic

Psychiatry; however, on August 4, he attempted to escape while at a dental appointment. His attempt was of an explosive nature, and he has remained on escape pre-
cautions. Mr. Jackson is quite depressed because of the nature of the crime, and
his concern regarding return to the Allegheny County Jail.

II. Appropriate medication patient should be maintained on while pending
    trial.

_____ NONE _____

_____

    If there are any questions in relation to the use of medication by
    your jail physician, please feel free to contact the undersigned
    physician.

III. Physical problems which have been treated at the Center for
     Forensic Psychiatry and appropriate treatment recommendations:

    Mr. Jackson had five dental extractions but needs no follow up

    dental care.

_____

    If there are any questions in relation to any aspect of medical
    treatment by your jail physician, please feel free to contact the
    undersigned physician.

IV. Recommendations for treatment in county jail during the detention
    process:

    (1) Insure security with this patient, especially in transporting.

    (2) He should be reviewed periodically by the Social Service Department

    related to depression and possible suicidal tendencies, especially
                                         as the trial approaches.

                        Lynn W Blunt
                    Doctor: Lynn W. Blunt, M.D.

                        Paul M Isenstadt
                    Paul M. Isenstadt, A.C.S.W.
                    Director, Social Services Department

PI/llg
4/70
DMH-C660

Figure 7 Competency report on Wilbur Jackson (continued)

```
                    STATE OF PENNSYLVANIA

                    DEPARTMENT OF MENTAL HEALTH

                    CENTER FOR FORENSIC PSYCHIATRY
                    BOX 2060

                    FOX CHAPEL, PENNSYLVANIA

                            August 19, 1970
```

Honorable Robert E. DeMascio
Judge of Recorder's Court
Pittsburgh, Pennsylvania

```
              re:  Wilbur C. Jackson
                   5755 Hill
                   Pittsburgh, Pennsylvania
                   CFP #91083
                   Recorder's Court for the City of
                     Pittsburgh
                   Honorable Robert E. DeMascio
                   Docket Numbers:  70-03042; 70-03317;
                                    70-03318; 70-03319
                   Murder II; Murder I (3 Counts)
```

Dear Judge DeMascio:

I am enclosing the report of the psychiatric examination performed on the above-named patient who was committed by your order on June 15, 1970 for evaluation of his competency to stand trial, pursuant to 48 CL 767.27a(3).

The report contains, in my opinion, information which indicates that the patient may be considered <u>competent to stand trial</u>.

A copy of this report has been forwarded to the Prosecutor of Allegheny County, and to Defense Counsel, Oliver C. Nelson, 1851 Mercantile Bank and Trust Building, Pittsburgh, Pennsylvania.

Should it be necessary that I testify, please have your clerk notify me as soon as the date of a hearing has been established.

```
              Sincerely,

              Ames Robey, M.D.
              Director

              Lynn W. Blunt

              Lynn W. Blunt, M.D.
              Acting Clinical Director
```

LWB/lh

Enclosure

Figure 7 **Competency report on Wilbur Jackson** *(continued)*

```
                  REPORT OF PSYCHIATRIC EXAMINATION
                                 ON
                     COMPETENCY TO STAND TRIAL
                          70-03042;
NAME Jackson, Wilbur C. Docket # 70-03318;  CFP #91083    Date  8-19-70
                          70-03319
A.  Patient identification and court data.
```

This has been the first Center for Forensic Psychiatry referral of this forty-five year old, white, married, Protestant male who was born in Tennessee on September 21, 1924, the oldest of three siblings. Charged with One Count of Murder in the Second Degree and Three Counts of Murder in the First Degree, under Docket numbers 70-03042, 70-03317, 70-03318, 70-03319, in the Recorder's Court for the City of Pittsburgh, the patient was referred to the Center on an order for diagnostic commitment, dated June 15, 1970, pursuant to 48 CL 767.27a(3) by the Honorable Robert E. DeMascio.

B. Review of alleged crime and circumstances.

Review of the Pittsburgh Police Department Details of Investigation reveals that on May 8, 1970, at approximately 2:00 a.m., the patient allegedly forced open the door of an apartment at an address in Pittsburgh by pushing it open with his shoulder. Upon entering the apartment, he went into the bedroom where he found his seventeen year old daughter, Sandra, in bed with a white male identified as Todd Wilson, age eighteen, who occupied the apartment. The patient went to the bed and began to assault the young man with a pistol by striking him over the head. The gun discharged and struck his daughter in the chest three times, fatally wounding her. The patient then fired two shots into the head of a young man identified as Jonathan Carter. Both young men later died. The patient then left the bedroom and went to the living room, where Ricky Walters, a sixteen year old white male, was sleeping. He fired two shots, one of which struck the young man in the right temple and the other his right cheek, fatally wounding him. Allegedly, while he was leaving, the patient pointed the gun at several witnesses and asked one young woman where Sally, a girlfriend of the daughter's was, and stated that if he did not find her they were all going to die. One witness heard someone running in the hallway and heard two shots being fired into the door of another apartment, with the patient entering and asking for Sally. Another young woman observed the wife of the patient, Mary Jackson, who accompanied the patient to the scene of the crime, coming down the stairs from the apartment and screaming, "He shot my baby." The patient then left the apartment building and drove to the second precinct police station where he told the officer in charge that he wished to turn himself in because he had just shot and killed his daughter and three of her hippie friends. The surrender occurred at 2:35 a.m. on May 8, 1970. He surrendered two pistols to the officers at that time.

```
                                                        DMH 110
                                                        Rev 2/70
```

Figure 7   Competency report on Wilbur Jackson   (continued)

C.   Review of psychiatric examination.   *Includes mental status plus
     psychologicals, EEG, x-ray, and other studies as indicated.*

On examination, the patient appeared as a pleasant-looking white male of
about his stated age of forty-five who was overly polite with many uses of
"sir," and who was extremely careful to remember to use the interviewers'
names. He spoke openly an a general manner about the charges against him
and the terrible thing that has happened. He was quite circumstantial as
he answered questions which were asked of him about his background. For
instance, when asked about the small southern college where he had received
his bachelor's degree, he spoke in detail about the fact that Gary Powers,
the man who was shot down in the spy plane incident several years ago in
Russia, had gone to the school. He went on to talk about the fact that some
people thought Powers was a coward because he had not done away with himself
or voluntarily destroyed the plane. Except for breaking down on one occasion
into tears, the patient generally controlled himself very well and showed
little feeling as he talked about the circumstances surrounding his behavior.
He expressed considerable relief at having been able to leave the Allegheny
County Jail, talking about the poor conditions and poor food there. He seemed
to be confident that he would get "help" here. Everything he recounted was
done in detail with names and specific details. It was pointed out that he
seemed to have a good memory, and he told how he has a piece of paper with
him and writes down the details of everything he wants to remember. He said
that he had marked down how long he had seen his attorney at various times,
and other details of events during his court appearances and time im jail.
There was no evidence of a disorder of thinking. He appeared to be a rather
self-righteous man. The exact degree of the murder charges that were brought
against him seemed to have considerable meaning to him. There did not appear
to be any overt clinical evidence of organic brain dysfunction.

During the patient's hospitalization at the Center, he was taken to the
dental clinic at McKeesport State Hospital. At the time, he and two security
attendants were starting to return to the Forensic Center ward, and he
suddenly became very aggressive and an attempt at an escape was made. He
had one handcuff on and swung the loose end in a manner so that it struck one
of the security attendants in the face. He then attempted to kick the security
attendants repeatedly in the groin and ran into the kitchen area. He was
apprehended and returned to the ward. When talked to about his behavior, he
was very apologetic for what had happened, and said that he had attempted to
escape only on impulse and realized that it was a very silly thing to do.
This incident illustrates the very explosive tendencies present in this
usually passive, calm,and compulsive patient.

Psychological testing, including a Bender-Gestalt test, Thematic
Apperception Test, Draw-a-Person test, Rorschach test, and Minnesota Multiphasic
Personality Inventory, was administered. The testing was generally in
agreement with the clinical impression, and showed that the patient's way of
relating is through a massively constructed defensive system of denial,
within a strongly rigid religious structure. The patient demonstrated both
authoritarian and compulsive types of behavior. He wept repeatedly during
D.   Diagnosis: CONTINUED ON NEXT PAGE------

Personality disorder, obsessive-compulsive type, moderate (301.47), with
prominent passive-dependent and explosive features.

DMH 110
Rev 2/70

Figure 7 Competency report on Wilbur Jackson (continued)

Jackson, Wilbur

Continuation of Part C, page 2:

the psychological testing, but there was indication that this weeping
was partially hysterical and manipulative in nature.

Because the patient claimed essentially complete memory loss for
the events of the incident leading to the charges against him from the
time of the second shot to the time that he was leaving the apartment
building to drive to the police station in order to surrender, a
Sodium Brevital interview with Ritalin stimulation was performed.
It appeared that the memory loss was due to the use of massive denial
on the part of the patient, and this denial was able to be overcome
in the Sodium Brevital interview so that the patient could recall and
talk about his actions and feelings during that period of time.

In order to further rule out any possibility of organic brain
dysfunction, an electroencephalogram was performed. The results of
the electroencephalogram were completely within normal limits.

		YES	NO
E.	Competency Evaluation: *See comments below*		
1.	The defendant is able to participate in and cooperate with the medical and psychiatric examination.	x	
2.	The defendant is oriented as to time, place and events.	x	
3.	The defendant recognizes significant people in his current legal situation and their significance to him.	x	
4.	The defendant knows he is accused of a crime.	x	
5.	The defendant knows of what crime he is accused.	x	
6.	The defendant knows the potential penalties of such a crime.	x	
7.	The defendant is able to describe events of his life which happened in conjunction with or simultaneously with the alleged crime.		*x
8.	The defendant is capable of following and comprehending procedures and testimony which occurs in the course of trial.	x	
9.	The defendant is capable of cooperating with his counsel.	x	
10.	The defendant is capable of assisting his counsel in evaluating testimony of witnesses.	x	

Comments:

*7:   Although the patient is able to describe events of the incident
leading to the charges against him, up until the time the second shot was fired,
he did claim amnesia from that time until the time he was leaving the apartment
building and driving to the police station in order to surrender. However, in
a Sodium Brevital interview with Ritalin stimulation, the patient was able to
recall his behavior and feelings during the period of alleged amnesia. It appears
that the amnesia was most likely due to his use of massive denial, which is a
very characteristic defense mechanism used by the patient.

DMH 110
Rev 2/70

Figure 7 *Competency report on Wilbur Jackson* *(continued)*

		YES	NO
E.	(continued)		

E. (continued)

    11. Delay, length, arduousness of a trial would significantly alter the mental capabilities of the defendant.   ____   *x

    12. The defendant is receiving drug therapy for a physical or mental condition or illness.   ____   x

    13. The mental capabilities of the defendant have been altered or could be altered by current drug therapy.   ____   x

Comments:

*11.: Although the patient continues to express feelings that he is going to "break down" mentally, it appears that this is mainly a subjective feeling on the part of the patient, and a manifestation of his passive-dependency. It appears that he has a very strong characterological structure which protects him from stress. There does not appear to be any emotional illness present which would make it likely that he would undergo real decompensation under the stress of a trial.

F. Recommendations:

    1. It is recommended that the defendant be adjudicated (competent) XХИ̶д̶а̶м̶р̶а̶к̶а̶н̶к̶I̶ to stand trial.

    2. Commitment pursuant to 48 CL 767.27a(5) is (not) recommended.

Lynn W. Blunt

Lynn W. Blunt, M.D.
Acting Clinical Director

LWB/lh
References:

1. Order for Diagnostic Commitment, dated June 15, 1970.
2. Reports of Recorder's Court Psychiatric Clinic, dated May, 1970.
3. Pittsburgh Police Department Criminal Record.
4. Pittsburgh Police Department Request for Warrant Recommendation, dated May 9, 1970.

DMH 110
Rev 2/70

Gillis set bail at ten thousand dollars personal bond for each of the three first-degree murder charges. (Personal bond requires no security or collateral but only a signed statement that the money—in this case thirty thousand dollars—will be paid if the defendant fails to appear for trial.)

Figure 8 shows a *Pittsburgh Herald* report of Jackson's release on bail.

On Sunday, 4 October, the Sunday *Herald*'s "Pittsburgh Magazine" featured a ten-page story on the Jackson case. On the cover of the magazine was an artist's representation of the four murder victims surrounded by flowers. Across the top of the cover were the words "The People Wilbur Jackson Says He Killed."

The story contains life histories of the dead youths:

Ricky Walters came from a broken home. His father was a career Navy man and the town drunk. His mother had been married three times. At one point Ricky's father beat up his mother and stepsister and held a shotgun on the family until police arrived. Ricky was sent to a "training school" several times before running away to Pittsburgh in March. His mother, who had once told a court she didn't want Ricky home, said "Ricky was a good boy, he never hurt anyone. He was the only one of my kids who brought home a bird with a broken wing and kept it till it healed."

Jonathan Carter also came from a broken home and grew up with nine brothers and sisters from two marriages. He worked part-time at a florist's and a grocery store. Jonathan attended night school where he studied drama and screen writing. On the day after the murders Jonathan's mother received twelve long-stemmed roses and a card "To Mom on Mother's Day, Love, Jonathan."

Todd Wilson's mother died when he was six; his father, a florist, never remarried. Todd worked in the florist shop and hoped to attend college. He fancied himself a poet and intended to study creative writing. Todd was Jewish, had flowing red hair, and, according to his friends, spent much of his time with girls.

Sandra Jackson had been an honor student at high school and was taking pre-med courses at Allegheny State when she was seventeen. Sandy's best friend, Sally Jo Tucker, recalled that she and Sandy first began to call themselves "freaks" during their junior year in high school. Eventually the two girls graduated to hard drugs. However, Sally Jo remembered, "Sandy really loved her father and he really loved her."

The article noted that the pastor of the Erwin, Tennessee Baptist church, which Wilbur Jackson attended as a boy, said a prayer for Jackson every Sunday that ended with this wishful thought: "the Good Lord, according to His will, will direct the jury to the truth."

The article closed with this quote from Wilbur's father, Roy Jackson, age seventy-two: "Most folks down here don't see anything wrong with what he done. Most folks say they would have done the same thing. I feel sorry for the parents of the boys he killed, but I

Figure 8   Pittsburgh Herald article

Jackson Released in Multiple Murder Case

By Roger Lindburgh

Wilbur C. Jackson, accused of murdering his daughter and her three boyfriends, was released on bail by Recorder's Court Judge Joseph A. Gillis.

Jackson was released on $30,000 personal bond after it became apparent that his mental and emotional condition was rapidly deteriorating in the Allegheny County Jail. Gillis explained, "I had to get him out of that jail atmosphere." Jackson has been in either the County Jail or McKeesport State Hospital since the multiple murders last May.

Gillis explained that he released Jackson due to the particular facts of the case: Jackson's previously clear criminal record, his roots in the community, and the unlikely possibility that he might kill again while out on bail.

Jackson, however, was apparently reluctant to leave the familiar confines of the County jail. It was only after almost an hour of pleading by his wife Mary and his attorney, Oliver Nelson, that Jackson agreed to leave.

Jackson spent the weekend watching football on television with his family. His trial is tentatively scheduled for early December.

Pittsburgh Herald
9/28/70

don't see how hurting Willie will help them now. He will make himself suffer enough for what he did."

Wilbur Jackson was admitted to Mercywood Hospital on 6 October. Jackson voluntarily admitted himself to the mental institution after suffering prolonged periods of anxiety and depression. On 14 October psychiatrist Hubert Miller wrote defense attorney Nelson that Jackson had received three electroconvulsive treatments. Miller estimated three more would be required as well as a period of recuperation.

CHANGE OF VENUE HEARING

[On 27 October a change of venue hearing was held before Judge Joseph A. Gillis, now permanently assigned to the case.

A request for a change of venue may be made by either side and in this case was made by the defense. A motion for a change of venue requests that the site of a trial be changed, usually because of adverse pre-trial publicity. As will be seen, the defense request was based on the number of newspaper articles about the case which, the defense argued, would have prejudiced prospective jurors.

However, the defense also had an ulterior motive for this request. As will become obvious during the jury selection, defense attorney Oliver Nelson was seeking middle-aged conservative jurors who might identify with Jackson. The chances of finding such jurors would be substantially higher in a rural area removed from Pittsburgh than in the city itself.

Portions of the change of venue hearing transcript follow.]

The Court:	People versus Jackson.
Mr. Nelson:	In anticipation of being able to provide the court with substantive wherewithal of which we base this motion, if Your Honor please, we asked for and obtained from the court six days ago an order requiring the service of subpoenas duces tecum on the reference librarians of the *Pittsburgh Daily Herald*, the *Pittsburgh News*, *The Happening*, and the *Pennsylvania Chronicle*; which subpoenas, I understand, have been served.
	The record librarians of *The Happening*, the *Daily Herald*, and the *Pittsburgh News* are here.
	The reference librarian from the *Pennsylvania Chronicle* is not here, and I would respectfully request that Your Honor issue a bench warrant for that party at this time.
	Meanwhile, we will call Alison Schoenfeld from the *Pittsburgh Daily Herald*.

DIRECT EXAMINATION

Mr. Nelson:	**Q**	**Your name, pretty lady, is Alison Schoenfeld?**
	A	Yes.
	Q	**Where are you employed?**
	A	*Pittsburgh Daily Herald.*
	Q	**In what capacity?**
	A	I am a librarian.

Q   Is it within the nature and the scope of your duties as a librarian of the *Pittsburgh Daily Herald* to keep and maintain the morgue files of that paper?

A   It is.

* * *

Q   May I have what you brought with you, please.

These are the photostats.

A   There is a photostatic copy of the original if you wish to keep one.

Q   These are the originals?

A   Yes.

(Whereupon Defense Exhibit Number One was marked for identification.)

Mr. Gilman: Your Honor, we have no objection to the photostatic copies.

The Court: All right.

Mr. Nelson: **Q**   Now, witness, in this envelope, Miss Schoenfeld, is the entirety of everything that has been published in the *Daily Herald* from May 8, 1970, until this date, concerning Wilbur Chester Jackson.   Is that right?

A   To the best of my knowledge; this is what has been clipped and put in our clipping file.

* * *

CROSS–EXAMINATION

Mr. Gilman: **Q**   This is Miss Schoenfeld?

A   Yes.

Q   Is it true that the *Pittsburgh Daily Herald* is published throughout or distributed, throughout the state?

A   As I understand it, but this is not my area.

* * *

The Court: I am sure she can't tell us the daily circulation published in the last thirty days.

The Witness: I have it with me.

The Court: Fine, put it on the record then, a publisher's statement on what date?

The Witness: October 2, 1970.

There is free distribution in the amount of 6,445 for a total distribution of the daily paper of 590,341.

* * *

Q   How many separate articles are there?

A   Ten.

Q   Are you aware when the last article was published?

A   It would be October 6.

Q   Do you know, Miss Schoenfeld, how many of these articles appeared on page one of the *Pittsburgh Daily Herald*?

A   No, I don't.

Mr. Gilman: I have no further questions.

REDIRECT EXAMINATION

Mr. Nelson: **Q**   Of the circulation figures in the state, that is People's Motion Exhibit One here, Miss Schoenfeld, can you tell us what proportion of that total circulation for that particular day was distributed in Allegheny County?

A   No, I can't tell you that.

Q   Can anyone in the *Daily Herald* organization?

A   I'm not competent to say.

Q   I see.   All right.

(Whereupon Defense Proposed Exhibit Number Two was marked for identification.)

Mr. Nelson: **Q**   Miss Schoenfeld, I hand you Defendant's Proposed Exhibit Two and ask if you recognize that as being the *Pittsburgh Magazine Section* of the Sunday *Herald*, disseminated under the date of October 4, 1970?

A   I do.

Q   All right.   Now, I am going to ask you if you will compare that with the photostat of the clipping of that story in that particular magazine;   and see if they are the same.

A   They appear to be so.   How detailed, I don't know.   I would say yes.

Q   Okay.

The Court: You omit the cover, don't you?

The Witness: Yes, because this is a clipping file and we do not clip the cover for the clipping file.

Mr. Nelson: **Q**   The cover of the *Pittsburgh Magazine*, however, bears an artist's representation of some of the people involved in this prosecution, does it not?

A   Yes.

Mr. Nelson:	All right. I am going to ask that this be received in evidence, too.
The Court:	It is attached to the motion already?
Mr. Nelson:	Yes.
Mr. Gilman:	We have no objection.
The Court:	All right.
Mr. Nelson:	I have no further questions of Miss Schoenfeld.
The Court:	You are free to go.
The Witness:	Thank you.
Mr. Nelson:	Thank you very much.
	(Witness excused.)
Mr. Nelson:	We will call Ruth Braun, please.
The Court:	Is this witness from *The Happening?*
Mr. Nelson:	No.

(Ruth P. Braun having been called as a witness on behalf of the defense, having been first duly sworn, was examined and testified as follows:)

DIRECT EXAMINATION

Mr. Nelson:

Q Your name, young lady, is Mrs. Ruth Braun?

A   That's right.

Q Mrs. Braun, where are you employed?

A   I am employed as a librarian with the *Pittsburgh News.*

* * *

Q All right. Now, did this subpoena direct you to appear in this court today?

A   Yes.

Q Did it also direct you to bring anything in the way of documentation?

A   Yes.

Q What, if I may ask?

A   Yes, all news and stories with reference to Wilbur Chester Jackson printed from May 8, 1970, to the date thereof, in the *Pittsburgh News.*

Q Have you done so?

A   Yes, sir.

Q Have you done so in their original states as they are kept and maintained in the ordinary and usual course of the business of the library of the *News*?

A Yes, sir. I brought tear sheets of the original page or a microfilm where the tear sheets were no longer available.

* * *

(Whereupon Defense's Proposed Exhibit Number Three was marked for identification.)

Mr. Nelson: I move the receipt into evidence of Defense's Proposed Exhibit Three as Defense's Exhibit Three, if Your Honor please, purporting to be everything that has been published in the *News* with reference to everything published in regard to Wilbur Chester Jackson to this date.

The Court: Any objection?

Mr. Gilman: No objection.

Mr. Nelson: You may examine.

Mr. Gilman: Thank you.

CROSS-EXAMINATION

Mr. Gilman: **Q** Mrs. Braun, have you had the occasion to count these to see how many separate articles were published in the *News* regarding Wilbur Jackson?

A No, sir. I did not count them, but I will from the index card if you want me to.

Q Yes. Do you want to take your time?

A There are thirteen articles.

Q Do you know when the last article was published concerning Wilbur Chester Jackson?

A October 6, 1970.

Q Do you know on what page the article appeared?

A Section A, page twenty, column one.

* * *

Q Do you know how many articles among these thirteen appeared on page one of the *Pittsburgh News*, Mrs. Braun?

A One moment, please.

Q Sure.

A Two of the articles appeared in section A, page one.

* * *

Q With respect to People's Exhibit Two, Mrs. Braun, does this indicate the daily circulation of the *Pittsburgh News* throughout the state of Pennsylvania for the period ending March 31, 1970?

A It does. The daily circulation for the first quarter of 1970 was 637,962.

Q What was the Sunday circulation?

A The Sunday circulation 853,720.

Q Those figures are for the whole state of Pennsylvania?

A That is correct. This is for any circulation of the *Pittsburgh News*. It is not limited to Pennsylvania. It includes mailed copies out of the state.

Mr. Gilman: I have no further questions.

* * *

(Witness excused.)

Mr. Nelson: Gil Marks, please.

DIRECT EXAMINATION

Mr. Nelson: **Q** Your name, sir, is Gil Marks?

A That is correct.

Q Are you employed by a vehicle for the dissemination of information among the populus of the city known as *The Happening*?

A No, I am not. I am an independent contractor. I am the accountant, but I am not an employee as such.

The Court: Do you sign the statement of ownership and circulation as required by the United States laws as managing editor?

The Witness: That is correct, for purposes of that I am managing editor, but I am not an employee as defined by the Internal Revenue Code.

Mr. Nelson: Thank you for correcting me.

Mr. Nelson: **Q** As a matter of fact, in practice, and as a matter of function, are you the managing editor of this paper?

A Only when it is required, such as statements of ownership. Our paper is run on a communal basis and we have no bosses as such.

Q I see, communal basis is—I played on a football team that was run that way, and we didn't win a game for three seasons.

Does your paper keep and maintain a reference library?

A No.

Q How long has the paper been in publication?

A Since November, 1965. We are the second- or third-oldest paper of its type in this country. We never missed an issue and never been late.

Q Have you published continuously, without interruption, since May 8, 1970, until date?

A Of course.

* * *

Q Now, in the sense that this is ordinarily done, no morgue files as such is maintained by your paper? In other words, to obtain these articles and produce them here today, I assume that someone had to go through each issue of your paper printed between the dates of May 8, 1970, and to date?

A I did.

Q You personally did that?

A Yes, I did.

Q You personally are satisfied that the articles, copies of which you have here with you today, and which I am now perusing, have been in your paper regarding Mr. Jackson?

A Definitely.

Q All right.

(Whereupon Defense's Proposed Exhibit Number Four was marked for identification.)

Mr. Nelson: I move that Defendant's Proposed Exhibit Four be received in evidence as Defendant's Exhibit Four for the purpose of this motion; being all the articles produced by *The Happening* in reference to Mr. Jackson from May 8, 1970, to date.

I understand there are no objections.

Mr. Gilman: No objection, Your Honor.

The Court: All right.

Mr. Nelson: **Q Now, Mr. Marks, I am going to give you for the purpose of enabling you to refresh your recollection of what purports to be a circulation statement and a statement of ownership of *The Happening* appearing in the issue of that paper for October 15 through October 28, 1970; and what was the total circulation of *The Happening* as shown in that statement?**

A The most recent issue?

Q The most recent issue.

A Twelve thousand—excuse me—eleven thousand five hundred.

Q   **Where is your paper distributed?**

A   It is distributed all over the world.

Q   **All over the world. It is also distributed throughout the state of Pennsylvania?**

A   It is.

*   *   *

CROSS–EXAMINATION

Mr. Gilman: Q   **How is the paper distributed, Mr. Marks?**

A   It is distributed in two ways. We have mail circulation, which is distributed by the Post Office. Of course, we have a second-class permit.

  We, also, contract an outside firm to do the balance of distribution.

Q   **How many of your subscriptions are mail?**

A   I believe about fifteen hundred.

Q   **Are the balance sold on newsstands and street corners by different individuals?**

A   Yes.

Q   **All right. And there are a total of three articles?**

A   That's right.

Q   **The first article is totally about the Jackson case, is that correct?**

A   Yes.

Q   **That is a two-column article?**

A   Yes.

Q   **What page of the newspaper did that appear?**

A   To the best of my recollection, it was in the middle of the paper, around page ten or twelve.

*   *   *

Q   **Am I correct in saying that a small bit of the second article concerned itself with the Jackson case and the small bit of the third article concerned itself with the Wilbur Jackson case?**

A   That's correct.

Q   **Can you tell the court, Mr. Marks, who primarily reads your type of papers? Are you aware of that?**

A   We have a pretty rough idea just seeing people come in and buy the paper.

*   *   *

A   Oddly enough, it is males in the thirty—forty—and fifty—who usually come in to pick up the most recent want ads.

Q   **The most recent want ads?**

A   Right.

Q   **I see.   You have a variety of different types of want ads in your paper?**

A   We sure do.

Q   **Do you know anything else about the people that read the balance of the newspaper?**

A   Right.   It is generally young people under the age of twenty-five.

* * *

The Court: It is sold at music festivals?

The Witness: A number of judges read it also.

The Court: We have a limited control situation.   They won't let Judge Colombo subscribe, but they let me subscribe.

Mr. Gilman: I have no further questions.

Your Honor, I would like the circulation figures marked.

Mr. Nelson: I had it marked.

The Court: I wanted to find out who wrote "Pittsburgh Pipeline."   I wanted to correct a few statements in there.

There are thirteen judges on this bench, and we have individual dockets.   I have the least amount of individuals in the Allegheny County Jail of any of the thirteen judges—in fact, fifty percent of the least judge.

Secondly, I have never sentenced anybody in the county jail over ninety days.   I haven't sent in four years one over there for as much as ninety days.

Of the two thousand two hundred over there, only two belong to me as of today.

The Witness: I would suggest, sir, if you like, you can clarify that in a letter to the editor.

REDIRECT EXAMINATION

Mr. Nelson: Q   **Mr. Marks, on the last two of the three sheets of this exhibit, there are certain matters underlined.   Were those delineations there when they were printed or did you put it in there for the convenience of the reader?**

A   I put it there for the convenience of the reader.

Q   All right. Unless you want to tell me why you called me a fascist pig two years ago, I have no further questions.

The Court: You ought to see what they said about Judge Rock.

The Witness: Do we get a witness fee for this?

The Court: Yes you do. You get a half-day fee. The officer in charge will take care of it.

(Witness excused.)

The Court: Do you want to read what they said about Judge Rock?

Mr. Nelson: Is there anybody here from the *Pennsylvania Chronicle*? We subpoenaed them.

The Court: I know that. Today is Tuesday. I can get to him tomorrow.

Mr. Nelson: I suppose Mr. Gilman would be prepared to stipulate that everything they said—and that was probably every day—that it was inflammatory and derogatory and calibrated to create and stir up a lot of trouble.

Mr. Gilman: I haven't seen the *Pennsylvania Chronicle*. I wouldn't be prepared to stipulate to anything.

The Court: Mr. Marks, will I get 160 issues for my six dollars now?

Mr. Marks: For six months.

The Court: No, six dollars is two years.

Mr. Marks: That is correct.

The Court: Instead of it being 52 issues I will be getting 104?

Mr. Marks: That is correct. The next renewal will be increased, though.

The Court: All right. That is nice.

Anything else? I have clippings from the *Daily Herald*, the tear sheets of the *News*, the *Pittsburgh Magazine*, and a statement of ownership and circulation from the *Daily Herald*.

Mr. Nelson: I guess there should be seven exhibits in all.

The Court: Correct.

Mr. Nelson: All right. You have them all.

Well, it is our position, if Your Honor please, that the dissemination of all this material throughout the metropolitan area not—we are willing to concede—not exclusively throughout the metropolitan part of the city; but throughout the state—and almost methodically increasing intensity throughout the state—and particularly as you get further west in the state, there has been created by these vehicles from the eighth of May until as recent as last week, a climate concerning this case that it makes it impossible to impanel, we submit, an impartial jury in reference to this case.

Therefore, we submit one of two things should be done. The trial of this case should be adjourned under the authority of the Shepherd case, which is 384 U.S., page 333.

We feel it would not be inconsistent with justice, and in the best interest of the people and the defendant, that the matter be adjourned, and, therefore, as a matter of sound judicial discretion, Your Honor should change venue in this matter.

We particularly feel that the public climate to which I allude is a result of this—well, article—I can't think of a better way to characterize it. That is our Exhibit Two, appearing in the October 4 issue of *Pittsburgh Magazine*, distributed with the Sunday *Herald*, on the cover of which appears the legend in bold letters in caps "The People— Wilbur Jackson Says He Killed," and then artist's illustrations of these four young people appearing among a spray of flowers backed up by what would appear a moon or sun in which we submit is a most sympathetic treatment accorded these people.

A somewhat sympathetic treatment is accorded Jackson as well, but which I feel is particularly damaging in that it not only breathes life back into these people again but portrays them in a more sympathetic manner in which I believe we have every reason to believe has been not unusually necessary, but very generally throughout this community.

We feel, therefore, as a matter of sound judicial discretion, venue be changed in this case.

Mr. Gilman: Your Honor, the People oppose the motion to change venue in this case. We, of course, agree that the change of venue is within the sound discretion of this court.

We do not believe any sound grounds have been shown or presented by defense counsel by this motion so as to give the court the right to change venue in this case.

The statute provides that venue may be changed by good cause shown by either party, and I don't think good cause has been shown.

I think the law is clear, Your Honor, that before the court changes venue, an attempt should be made to impanel a fair and impartial jury.

Courts have also said that although a juror has an opinion on a case, that doesn't necessarily disqualify him, provided he can render a fair and impartial verdict; and the only way we can find that out is to ask the juror, in the city of Pittsburgh, the jurisdiction, it is alleged that Wilbur Jackson killed these four people and whether they can render a fair and impartial verdict.

Until it is established, we cannot draw a fair and impartial jury from the population of the city of Pittsburgh, I believe this court should not change venue.

With reference to the *Shepherd* case, I know the court read it, and I can only say that the weight of the pre-trial publicity and the publicity during the course of the trial in no way resembles the publicity that has occurred in the case of *People v. Wilbur Jackson*. In the *Shepherd* case there were editorials day in and day out, front-page articles, interviews with the defendant on television, interviews with the county coroner on television—all of these incidents occurred prior to the trial.

In that case, the Supreme Court did say that the defendant's due process rights were violated by the court holding the trial of that case in the city of Cleveland.

Wynn v. U.S., Supreme Court decision, 366 U.S. 717, says that the burden of showing a strong community feeling and a pattern of deep and bitter prejudice so as to deny the defendant due process is on the defendant.

I do not believe that Mr. Nelson has shown in his motion any strong community feeling or any strong bitter prejudices by the city of Pittsburgh against Wilbur Chester Jackson.

I ask the court to read the articles that Mr. Nelson has presented, a total of ten articles, in the *Pittsburgh Daily Herald* from a period of May 8, 1970, to the present time, considering the fact that the *Pittsburgh Daily Herald* publishes every day and publishes a Sunday edition, and considering the fact that the articles, as I read them, are objective. They do not give an editorial opinion, but merely state facts concerning the investigation or facts concerning the case as it is progressing.

I do not think in any way they amount to a strong community feeling or a strong feeling by anyone of the two newspapers concerning the guilt of Wilbur Jackson.

I don't believe that this court should change venue before the court tries to pick a fair and impartial jury. I think the court is obligated to do that.

We oppose an adjournment for that reason that we do not think the publicity, to this time, has been of any concern.

* * *

In a way there has been very little considering the population of the city of Pittsburgh, considering the circulation of the *Daily Herald* and *News* to outside areas, and considering the circulation of *The Happening*.

An attempt should be made, Your Honor, to pick the jury from the people of the city of Pittsburgh, the jurisdiction in which it is alleged that Wilbur Jackson committed the crime. We would oppose the motion.

The Court:	Any rebuttal?
Mr. Carney:	Well, Your Honor, I think that the court will find from the notations I previously supplied the court, 33 A.L.R.3d 17, a selection of cases

dealing specifically with the rights of the defendant to a change of venue, and a right to an impartial jury.

I think that the court will find upon pursuing that annotation that there are approximately four criteria which the court should use in ascertaining whether a change of venue—a motion for a change of venue—should be granted.

The first, I think, and the foremost, is the offense charged. Now, we have four separate cases here, three of which are first-degree murder, one of which is a second-degree murder.

The second is the nature of the offense charged. Did he not tell the court that the penalty for first-degree murder means mandatory life.

The third, the extent to which the pre-trial publicity has been disseminated. We have put testimony on the record here, and specifically with reference to the *Pittsburgh Magazine*, that the Sunday *Herald* has a circulation of 643,000 people—to which, I might add, that this magazine is appended.

* * *

The fourth criteria, which I think the court should use, is the time of the pre-trial publicity. We have here a magazine dated October 4, 1970, with the picture of the—or an artist's representation—of the victims in this matter, which preceded the set trial date by a matter of no more than thirty-five days, as the trial is set.

In other words, for the court to use its sound discretion, I think— it is our opinion, I would never argue by the way that the extent nor the weight of the pre-trial publicity is the same as *Shepherd*. This case would never match it. There is no question in my mind.

But, I think it is our contention that in the event the timing of the pre-trial publicity is directed toward a substantial number of people that could be sworn in as jurors in this jurisdiction, and might jeopardize the defendant's rights to an impartial jury. We have shown enough for this court to grant a change of venue.

* * *

Now, I think taking the total of circumstances here, that we have shown that the *Daily Herald* at least, and the *News*, the *Daily Herald* in particular, has a circulation of the Sunday edition of 638,000 at least; 643,000 in subscriptions and others.

This trial date is set for November 9. The trial is only thirty-five days subsequent to the selection of a jury in this jurisdiction, and that it may jeopardize the defendant's right to pick a fair and impartial jury in this jurisdiction.

I think that is all we have to show. In all cases cited by counsel, especially in *People v. Daily*, the nature of the offense is not as extensive. The pre-trial publicity for the most part, if I am not mistaken, were directed to the appellate court without regard to any motion made prior to trial.

Under all the circumstances of this case, I think that the court, and counsel, I believe, that the court either has to adjourn the trial date or grant a motion for change of venue.

The Court: Let's see. I find the *Pittsburgh News* ran three front-page stories, is that correct? May 8, May 10 and May 19, and never did make the front page of the *Daily Herald.*

Mr. Nelson: It made the front page of the *Pittsburgh Magazine.*

The Court: But that is buried in the back.

Mr. Nelson: But it is often read.

The Court: I think, overall, this is certainly not the *Shepherd* case.

No front page attention from Mr. Ricke or any writer such as Robert DeWolf. They do have a magazine section that came out on October 4 in the *Pittsburgh Magazine.*

I think, considering the total circumstances, that there is not enough here to prevent Mr. Jackson from getting a fair trial from a jury in Pittsburgh. If it appears differently at the selection of the jury, I may change my mind; but at the present time the motion is denied.

* * *

[Figure 9 reprints an article from *The Happening* in which Gil Marks describes his experience in court.]

Figure 9 The Happening *article*

Pittsburgh Pipeline
by GIL MARKS

Far freaked-out street people battled stolid "citizens" for almost an hour last Tuesday morning in an attempt to get seats in Pittsburgh Hall of "Justice." The stools were wanted so people could get a shot of (or take a shot at) Wilbur Chester Jackson, the newly created hero of the middle-class.

Jackson, you remember, broke down the door of a people's pad last May and blasted his young daughter apart as well as three equally innocent men who had dropped in to visit. The day was the same week as four (4) brothers and sisters at Kent State were murdered by the Ohio pigs.

The defense attempted to change the site of the trial to someplace out of sight (like Nashville). "Justice" (or convenience) prevailed and the pig Jackson will be tried before a "court." Pittsburgh Pipeline has been told that if he is acquitted there will be a People's Court to hand out justice.

The editor (i.e. myself) of Pittsburgh Pipeline was present for ten truly terrifying traumatic minutes. He was forced to explain tax laws to the court as well as endure a harassing harangue from Judge Joseph A. Gillis. Gillis accused The Happening of falsely fictuating facts concerning the amount of time innocent people languished in Pitttsburgh's pig's prison. The editor suggested the judge write a letter or take a flyer.

Jackson, himself failed to post due to the fact that he's locked up in a mental hospital for everybody's good. The Happening (or Pittsburgh Pipeline) hereby editorially declares that that is where he should be forever. The "trial" should start soon.

**POWER TO THE
PEOPLE
JOY TO THE
WORLD**

from The Happening
November, 1970

THE TRIAL

What follows is the actual trial transcript taken verbatim from the official records of the Recorder's Court. (See Figure 10.) The court reporter's comments are in parentheses; the authors' notes are in brackets.

JURY SELECTION

Monday 9 November

The Court:	Case of the *People* versus *Wilbur Chester Jackson.**
The Clerk:	Jurors please respond when your name is called.

Laura Blaess, Mary Flake, Velma Bradley.

Bolton Jones, Barbara Johnson, Isaiah Kelly, Charlene Johnson.

Dorothy Munger, Thomas Pfeifer, Ewald Nusbeitel.

Desaree Bell, Rudolph Kreus, Irene Durance, Martin Gluckstein.

(Whereupon all prospective jurors were duly sworn by the court clerk.)

[Jury selection procedures vary somewhat among jurisdictions. In the Recorder's Court it is conducted in the following way. A panel of up to one hundred jurors is called into the courtroom and, as soon as both the prosecution and the defense have indicated that they are ready to proceed, fourteen members of the panel are selected at random and asked to occupy the fourteen seats in the jury box. (During a major trial such as this, fourteen jurors are selected. Thus, if a juror must be excused because of sickness mid-way through the trial, the trial may go on. If fourteen jurors remain at the end of the trial, two are excused by lot from the group of twelve that attempts to reach a verdict.) The judge then reads the charges to the fourteen who have been selected, as well as to the others who are still waiting in the courtroom. The judge then asks the fourteen sitting in the jury box questions designed to determine whether they will fairly consider the evidence in the particular case. When the judge has finished with his or her questions, the prosecutor and the defense attorney ask any questions they wish to put to the fourteen prospective jurors.]

[At the conclusion of this stage, the prosecutor and the defense attorney are allowed to challenge any jurors "for cause" (i.e., on

---

* The case was tried before Judge Joseph A. Gillis of Pittsburgh recorder's court. Judge Gillis had first been elected to the bench in 1966. Previous to that he had served in the state legislature and had been in private practice. Judge Gillis ran unopposed for reelection in 1974.

Figure 10 Recorder's court document

STATE OF PENNSYLVANIA

IN THE RECORDER'S COURT FOR THE CITY OF PITTSBURGH

THE PEOPLE OF THE STATE OF PENNSYLVANIA,	Case Number
—vs—	70—03042
WILBUR CHESTER JACKSON,	70—03317
	70—03318
	70—03319
Defendant.	

VOLUME NO. I & II

PROCEEDINGS HAD and TESTIMONY TAKEN in the above-entitled cause, before the HON. JOSEPH A. GILLIS, a Judge of the Recorder's Court of the City of Pittsburgh, and a Jury, commencing on Monday, November 9, 1970, and continuing on Tuesday, November 10, 1970.

APPEARANCES:

LEONARD GILMAN

AND

RICHARD NELSON,*

Appearing on behalf of the People.

OLIVER NELSON

and

JOHN R. CARNEY

and

EMMET TRACY,

Appearing on behalf of the Defendant.

Glenn W. Rose,
OFFICIAL COURT REPORTER.

Typist: L. Besser.

* Richard Nelson was a young attorney who had recently joined the Prosecutor's Office. He was assigned as co-counsel to gain familiarity with court procedure and took little part in the trial.

Judge Joseph A. Gillis

grounds that they are legally disqualified from sitting as jurors in the matter before the court because of prejudice or bias). Following such challenges "for cause," the attorneys begin to exercise their peremptory challenges. They alternate in removing from the group of fourteen jurors sitting in the jury box any juror that one attorney wishes, for any reason at all, to have excluded from the jury. The prosecutor has fifteen peremptory challenges, the defense attorney twenty, in a homicide case. As each juror is challenged in this way, another is chosen at random from those sitting in the courtroom at large and takes the seat of the challenged juror in the jury box. The new juror is then asked questions by the judge and the attorneys. On the basis of the prospective juror's answers, the attorneys can move that he or she be excused "for cause." If a prospective juror is not excused in this way (and replaced by another from the courtroom), the process of exercising peremptory challenges continues.]

The Court:	Ladies and gentlemen of the jury.

This is the case of the *People v. Wilbur Chester Jackson.*

Mr. Jackson is charged with murder. There are actually four files that have been consolidated.

The information, or formal written charge, in the first file reads:

That on May 8 at 4330 Lincoln in apartment number 9, Pittsburgh, Pennsylvania, Wilbur Chester Jackson did feloniously, deliberately, with malice aforethought, and with premeditation, did kill and murder one—without premeditation, did murder one Ricky Walters.

Then file number two, at the same time and place, he is charged with murder of one Sandra Jackson.

File number three, at the same time and place, he is charged with murder of one Todd Wilson.

File number four, at the same time and place, he is charged with murder of one Jonathan Carter.

File number one is second-degree murder; the other three files are first-degree murder.

The four files have been consolidated for trial.

Now, the People of the State of Pennsylvania are represented by Assistant Prosecuting Attorney Leonard Gilman. He is being assisted by Assistant Prosecuting Attorney Dick Nelson. The officers in charge of the case are Detective Sergeant Irvin Baranski and Detective Sergeant Robert Wilson.

Now, the defendant is represented by his attorneys Mr. Oliver Nelson and Mr. John Carney.

Is Emmet Tracy in this case?

Mr. Nelson: Yes, Your Honor.

Now, the witnesses proposed to be called by the People in the four cases are:

[and the court then reads a list of forty-one names.]

Do any members of the jury now sitting in the jury box know any of the parties involved in this case, either the lawyers, the four deceased persons, or any of the witnesses or doctors that I have named?

Any members of the jury now sitting in the jury box have any friends, relatives, close friends, that have been victims of a homicide, that is, an unlawful killing?

Think back if you have ever had any friends, relatives, that have been killed.

Any members of the jury have any close friends or relatives engaged in law-enforcement work at either the federal, state, or local level?

Juror Munger: I have a cousin who is a Pittsburgh policeman.

Q How often do you see your cousin who is a Pittsburgh policeman?

A I don't.

Q What?

A   I don't.

Q   **When was the last time you saw him?**

A   About five years ago at a wedding.

Q   **Would that influence you at all from rendering a fair and impartial verdict, that you have a cousin who is a Pittsburgh police officer?**

A   No.

* * *

The Court: Anyone else?

Juror Nusbeitel: I have two brothers-in-law who are Pittsburgh policemen.

Q   **How often do you see your brothers-in-law?**

A   Quite often; they live nearby.

Q   **The fact that you have two brothers-in-law that are Pittsburgh police officers, would that influence you in any way from rendering a fair and impartial verdict for both the People and the defendant?**

A   No, sir.

The Court: Now, the defendant has filed a notice of insanity in this case, which is a proper defense, and I assume there will be some testimony about it. We get into an area here where it's not covered on the jury questionnaire.

Do any members of the jury have any members of their immediate family or relatives who are patients in any mental institution, state hospital, or otherwise?

Don't be embarrassed by this because I think statistics are one family out of three at one time or another has somebody that goes to a mental hospital. It may be a brain defect or something.

Juror Flake: Yes, my aunt—great aunt.

Q   **You have a great aunt who is confined to a state mental hospital?**

A   Yes.

Q   **Now, you have some knowledge of your aunt's condition. Do you think that you could keep a completely open, unbiased mind upon the psychiatric testimony, testimony of the doctors, in this trial and render any verdict that you may be called upon to render in regard to the sanity of the defendant at the time of the alleged homicide solely upon the evidence that you hear from the witness stand?**

A   Yes, I do.

The Court: Anyone else?

Only one out of fourteen.

Does anybody have any close friends that have ever been in a mental hospital that you are aware of, received psychiatric treatment?

The Court: Now, this is a homicide case; in fact, it's four cases. Mr. Jackson is charged with homicide of four different people at the same time and place.

Would any juror prefer not to sit on this case because of the nature of the case, the fact that Mr. Jackson is charged with three first-degree murders and one second-degree murder; would that influence you in any way; would you prefer not to sit on the case?

Do you think you could keep a completely open, unbiased mind?

Because you will be called upon to render a separate verdict in each case.

At the present time it looks like there will be about five possible verdicts in each case, although I don't know what the testimony will later develop.

Have any persons heard of this case before this? Any of the jurors now sitting in the jury box have any prior knowledge of this case from any source whatsoever, newspapers, TV?

Juror Flake: I read about it in the newspapers.

The Court: All right, we will start right through.

Q **Mrs. Flake, what do you know about this case, or where did you hear about it?**

A In the newspaper when it occurred.

Q **What paper?**

A *Pittsburgh News.*

The Court: How many regularly read the *Pittsburgh News* every day, get the *Pittsburgh News* every day?

All right, five jurors.

How many get the *Pittsburgh Daily Herald* daily?

All right, seven jurors.

The *Daily Herald* has got better circulation.

How many get the *Pittsburgh News* on Sunday only?

One juror.

How many get the *Daily Herald* on Sunday only?

Two jurors.

Q **All right, Mrs. Flake, you have read about this in the *Pittsburgh News*?**

A Yes, I have.

Q **The fact you have some prior knowledge of this case, do you believe you can decide this case solely upon the evidence that you hear**

from the witness stand, putting aside any prior knowledge you might have of this case?

A   Yes, I do.

The Court: All right, the next one is number seven, Mrs. Johnson.

Juror C.
Johnson: Yes.

Q   **Where did you hear about this case?**

A   I read about it in the newspaper, also, in the *Daily Herald* and the *Pittsburgh News*.

Q   **What *Daily Herald* article did you read about this?**

A   Well, I can't remember now, really; but I do remember reading about it.

Q   **How long ago?   This was supposed to have occurred last May.**

A   Well, it was about five months ago, I'd say.

Q   **Would you be willing to put aside anything that you may have read in the paper out of your mind and base any verdict you may be called upon to render solely upon the testimony you hear from the stand?**

A   Yes.

* * *

[After other jurors were questioned at some length concerning any newspaper accounts of the murder they might have read, court was adjourned for the day.]

[There then ensued a discussion between Judge Gillis and counsel concerning the number of peremptory challenges the defense would be allowed.   Pennsylvania law states "any person who is put on trial for an offense punishable by death or imprisonment for life shall be allowed to challenge peremptorily twenty of the persons drawn to serve as jurors."   Nelson, relying on an 1885 Pennsylvania decision, argued that the defense should be allowed twenty peremptory challenges for each charge of murder for a total of eighty.   Gilman, citing a 1969 Pennsylvania decision, countered that there was one trial, one defendant, and one jury and thus the defendant should be limited to twenty peremptory challenges.   Judge Gillis took the question under consideration.]

Tuesday 10 November

[Before the jury questioning continues, the court announces that it has decided to limit the defense to twenty peremptory challenges and the prosecution to fifteen.]

[The jury and jury panel enters.   The court "gives a couple more current events tests to the jury" and finds that jurors Munger, Pfeifer,

Nusbeitel, Kreus, Durance, and Gluckstein have read a recent article in the *Pittsburgh Daily Herald* concerning the trial, but still "keep an unbiased mind."]

The Court: Now, the next question:

Who goes to the movies?

How many have attended a movie in the last thirty days?

(No response).

The Court: All right, sixty days.

Juror Bell: (Indicating).

The Court: Just one hand, Juror eleven, goes to the movies. What movie did you see?

Juror Bell: *2,001 Space Odyssey.*

The Court: You waited until the price got way down. Did you like it?

Juror Bell: No.

The Court: I think sixty days is far enough back, as I recall.

The movie we are all thinking of—the night I went there were nineteen people in the theatre.*

Nobody has been influenced by any movies.

All right, I think we will let Mr. Gilman proceed.

Mr. Gilman: Thank you, Your Honor.

Ladies and gentlemen of the prospective jury.

Good afternoon.

As Judge Gillis indicated to you yesterday, my name is Leonard Gilman, and I am an assistant prosecutor, and I work for Mr. William L. Cahalan who is the prosecuting attorney for Allegheny County on behalf of the People of the State of Pennsylvania.

Judge Gillis also indicated to you that the charges in this case are the most serious charges known to the law.

Mr. Wilbur Jackson is charged with three counts of first-degree murder and one count of second-degree murder.

He is charged with the killings on May 8 of four separate individuals.

They all grow out of the same facts and circumstances, that is why they are going to be heard in one trial; but they are four separate charges, and you are to consider each of them separately.

Now, we are here—both of us, Mr. Nelson and myself—to insure that we get a fair and impartial jury, a jury which will base their

---

* *Joe* —a movie in which Joe, played by Peter Boyle, changes from a typical middle-class citizen to a gun-wielding hippie-killer.

verdict solely upon the evidence, that is, what you hear from that chair, not what you read in the newspapers, not what you hear on television, not what you hear from your neighbors, not what you hear from your children; what you hear from the witness stand is what you base your verdict on.

I think all of you will do that if you are chosen to sit on this case; is that correct?

How many of you are sitting on their first case?

(Jurors indicating.)

I'm sure all of you, even the ones that are sitting on their first case have been informed that in every criminal case the People have the burden of proof.

By the People I mean myself; I represent the state of Pennsylvania.

We must establish beyond a reasonable doubt the guilt of the defendant.

[Gilman proceeds to question the jurors to find out who has read about the case, who reads movie reviews, who watches television news, who wouldn't want to hear autopsy testimony, who (or whose spouse) owns guns, and who has served on a jury before.]

Mr. Gilman: We have had a chance, incidentally, to examine the jury questionnaires that all of you filled out before you were chosen as jurors.

Q   It indicates, Mr. Gluckstein, that you are a Ph.D.   Is that correct?

A   Yes.

Q   What was your major in college?

A   Chemical engineering.

Q   The psychiatrists that you know, have you had occasion to discuss with them the legal definition of insanity?

A   I have not.

Q   Have you had a chance to discuss with them the treatment of any of their patients?

A   No.

Q   Do you number among your close friends a psychiatrist?

A   Yes. I also have a sister who is a clinical psychologist.

Q   Does she live in the city of Pittsburgh?

A   She works for the city of Pittsburgh.

Q   Do you discuss her work with her?

A   In a vague—generally; not specifically.

Q Do you know whether or not she is involved in the treatment of people that are charged with crimes?

A I can't answer that. She deals with children.

Q From your contact with these psychiatrists, have you formed any opinion whatsoever as to the legal test or any test to determine whether or not a person is insane?

A I have not.

Mr. Gilman: Incidentally, in this case the defense has filed a notice of insanity; in other words, it is their claim that at the time of the alleged commission of these offenses, Mr. Wilbur Jackson was insane.

Will all of you listen to the testimony very closely on the defense of insanity?

Do any of you have any bias or prejudice against psychiatric testimony?

Will all of you abide by Judge Gillis' instructions at the conclusion of this case as to what the legal definition of insanity is; in other words, what the requirements are before a person is insane at the time of the act?

Mrs. Flake, you indicated yesterday you have an aunt who is presently confined to a hospital.

Juror Flake: Yes.

Q What hospital was that?

A It's in Columbia, South Carolina.

Q Where is that located, in what state?

A South Carolina.

Q Oh, I'm sorry. Have you had occasion to visit her in the past couple of years?

A No, I haven't.

Q I take it she is not in that hospital in regard to any alleged criminal conduct on her part?

A No, she is not.

Q She is in there in regard to a mental illness?

A That's right.

Q All right.

[After more questioning, Gilman states that he will not move to excuse any of the prospective jurors for cause.]

[The jury is then given to Mr. Nelson for questioning.]

Mr. Nelson: You realize, do you not, ladies and gentlemen of the prospective jury, that Wilbur Jackson comes before you charged with these offenses that Mr. Gilman alluded to already, clothed in what is known in the law as the presumption of innocence, by which is meant simply this:

That he, Wilbur Jackson, has no burden of proof in this case whatsoever, and that each and every element of the offenses that he is charged with and is about to go on trial before twelve from among your number here in this courtroom has to be proved by Mr. Gilman representing the People of this state, not by just a mere preponderance of the proof, not by that sufficient quantity of proof to kind of tip the scales of probability, but by what is known in the law as proof beyond a reasonable doubt, proof that is sufficiently convincing to create in your minds an abiding belief to a moral certainty of his guilt.

Now, are all of you—or to put it negatively—is there anyone in the box right now who either feels they can not, for whatever reason, or they will not accord both to the People of the state of Pennsylvania and to Wilbur Jackson the full weight and measure and intent and purpose of this presumption of innocence; is there anyone here?

Occasionally when objections are interspersed you will be asked to leave the room because they will involve legal argument that is no concern of yours as jurors. The province of your concern in this case and in any case is with the factual issues, the judge being the man who is endowed with the authority and the disposition to treat all legal issues.

And it will become tedious. Perhaps you will find yourself traipsing back and forth through that door into that juryroom six or seven times a day.

This is necessary to see to it that this case is tried according to the rules and procedures that have evolved through some eight centuries of trying cases; and I hope you can all understand that and forgive us all for our tediousness.

Can you all do that?

Now, Mr. Gilman has alluded to the fact that when a special defense such as alibi or as in this case insanity is to be invoked in a criminal trial, notice of that fact has to be given within a certain measure of time to the prosecutor, and such a notice has been given on behalf of Mr. Jackson; and it will be our endeavor to introduce proof during the course of this trial that will be of sufficient convincing propensity insofar as those twelve of you who will decide those cases or this case are concerned that will persuade you that in three of these deaths they resulted because he was insane; that in the first, the shooting was accidental.

This will, as Mr. Gilman has said, involve the submission both by myself and my colleague in behalf of Mr. Jackson, and by the People as well, of a considerable amount of highly technical and abstruse medical-psychiatric testimony.

It's going to be difficult to follow. It is going to involve the use of a terminology, nomenclature of vocabulary, that ordinarily, working folk like myself, for example, aren't familiar with or conversant in.

Are you going to be able, ladies and gentlemen of the prospective jury, to accord to all the witnesses in this case that measure of attention that is required to be able to follow thoroughly and fully and completely the nuances so as to do your best to arrive at here and give a verdict that is fair to both the parties in this case, the People and Mr. Jackson?

* * *

Mrs. Blaess, is that the way you pronounce your name?

Juror Blaess: Yes, sir.

Q   May I know what your maiden name was, please?

A   Trombly.

Q   Are you still working at Kaufman's? [Pittsburgh's largest department store.]

A   Part-time, yes.

Q   In what department are you a salesperson?

A   Usually in the ready-to-wear dresses and coats.

Q   How long have you been working at Kaufman's?

A   Eighteen years.

Q   You are an east-sider, is that correct, Mrs. Blaess?

A   Yes, sir.

Q   When you did jury service twenty-some years ago, Mrs. Blaess, did you ever encounter the judge's father, the senior Judge Gillis?

A   I don't remember.

* * *

Q   You are probably a grandmother then.

A   I'm a grandma and a great- one, too.

Q   Good for you. Mrs. Blaess, Mr. Gilman has alluded to the fact that one of the people that Mr. Jackson shot on the eighth of May in the Stonehead Manor was his daughter. Now, the other three of these individuals are young men, all in their teens, if I'm not mistaken.

Are you sure that your sensibilities are such that you are going to be able to audit this case and come through it at the end and deliver a fair and impartial verdict in view of that fact that the man is charged with shooting and killing his own daughter, with premeditation and malice, and three other people as well?

A   I think so.

* * *

Mr. Nelson: Well, things are liable to—I'll tell you right now. Mr. Gilman is going to get things just as gory as he can in this courtroom before we get done. Do you think that's going to bother you?

Juror B.
Johnson: No.

Mr. Nelson: How about you, Mr. Kelly; you indicate, among other things, you get a stomach ulcer, in your return on the jury questionnaire here.

Juror Kelly: Yes, sir.

Q   **Do you feel that the rather unpleasant character of a good deal of the testimony that is going to be introduced here would render you disposed not to sit on this case if you were otherwise excused?**

A   Well, I don't think that would bother me so much because I've had the ulcer now for ten years, I've been taking medication, and I've heard some pretty bad things.

* * *

Q   **How do you feel about deciding the fate of a man who is charged with four murders, Mrs. Munger?**

A   Well, I feel that this man is innocent until it is actually proven beyond a shadow of a doubt that he is guilty, and I feel that it's my privilege and duty to sit on this jury if it's your will.

Q   **Do you feel it's kind of an awesome responsibility that is being kind of thrust upon you by the law?**

A   Well, I'm not sure if I know what you mean by awesome. Of course, it is because this is a big case, you know.

Q   **Do you have any strong and pronounced feelings about runaways, young children that leave home, go off and live communally with other children, independent of their parents, independent of their family?**

Juror
Pfeifer: A   I've never given it much thought. I don't know anybody like that. It's never crossed my mind.

Q   **What are your feelings, Mr. Pfeifer, about drug addiction and drug use?**

A   I don't like it.

Q   **You are not a hunter, are you?**

A   No, sir.

Q You don't then have any reason to believe that you can't listen to the testimony in this case and, solely and exclusively on the basis of the testimony in this case, arrive at an honest and fair, evenhanded decision in this case, do you?

A I believe I could arrive at a decision, yes, sir.

Q You have indicated that you own a deer rifle—

Juror
Nusbeitel:

A Right.

Q —and a handgun?

A Two of them.

Q One is a .22.

A One is a .22.

Q What is the caliber of the other one?

A The other is an 8-mm Japanese.

Q Were you in the service?

A Yes, sir.

Q What branch?

A Signal Corps.

Q Where did you see service, in the Pacific?

A All over.

Q Were you in both theatres?

A Yes.

Q This was during the second war?

A Yes.

Q Do you belong to the American Legion now?

A No, sir.

Q Do you belong to the Veterans of Foreign Wars?

A No.

Mr. Nelson:

How about you, Mr. Pfeifer, do you belong to any veteran's associations or organizations?

Juror Pfeifer:

No, sir.

Q Mr. Nusbeitel, do you belong to any veteran's organizations at all?

A No.

Q Do you go deer hunting?

A   When I can.

*   *   *

[Court is adjourned until Thursday.]

Wednesday 11 November

[Veteran's Day.]

Thursday 12 November

[Nelson continues his questioning. He asks the jurors about their family background, their children, maiden names, education, jobs, religion, military service, and political aspirations.]

[Nelson then passes for cause. Gilman again passes for cause and for peremptories. Nelson then peremptorily excuses jurors Mary Flake (great aunt in a mental hospital), Isaiah Kelly (stomach ulcers), and Martin Gluckstein (the Ph.D.). Three more jurors enter and are questioned.]

Mr. Nelson: Miss Strong, on your jury questionnaire you indicate that you have bad nerves.

Juror Strong: *(Nods.)*

Q   **Are you under treatment by a doctor for a nervous condition?**

A   No.

Q   **My wife tells me that I make people nervous; I make her nervous, anyhow.**

A   I get nervous.

Q   **Would you prefer, as a result of your nervousness, not to sit on this case?**

A   Yes.

Q   **If you do, Miss Strong, just say so.**

A   Yes.

Q   **That is nothing that should bother you very much.**

A   I will get nervous.

Q   **You will get nervous?**

A   I will get nervous, yes, I will.

Mr. Nelson: May Mr. Gilman and I approach the bench?

(Conference at the bench between the court, Mr. Gilman, and Mr. Nelson; outside the hearing of the jury and the court reporter.)

The Court: All right, the court will excuse you.

*   *   *

Q Well, Mr. Taylor, in the course of the presentation of the proofs in this case it's going to be developed testimonially from that witness stand that Wilbur Jackson is a native of Tennessee, born and raised in Tennessee, southeastern Tennessee, went to school down there, went to college down there, received an education directed toward a teaching career down there, went on after he got out of the service and attended for a while the University of Tennessee, where he did some graduate work there.

Nonetheless, for reasons that also will be developed here, I assume, he came up here to Pennsylvania some twenty-five, thirty years ago and went to work for the Penn Central Railroad.

Now, he shares many of the philosophies, many of the beliefs, many of the prejudices that are existent in the state of Tennessee.

I would assume that you are probably familiar with some of these because you come from the state of Mississippi, don't you?

A That's correct.

Q Now, is that going to affect your thinking through your disposition toward a verdict in this matter?

A Absolutely not.

Q You can't think of any reason why you can't sit in fair and impartial judgment on this man?

A No.

* * *

The Court: Let me talk to Mr. Przydzielski.

Would you rather not sit on a murder case? Let's put it that way, is it the fact that this is a murder case that is going to bother you?

Juror
Przydzielski: Yes, Your Honor.

Q How about the fact that we are going to have a lot of doctors—several doctors and psychiatrists—testifying, will that cause you any difficulty understanding?

Of course, we are all going to have trouble understanding psychiatrists; but some will have more difficulty than others.

A It might be.

Q Do you think you could handle other jury cases such as a stolen car, a bad check, or a breaking and entering?

A Yes.

The Court: All right, the court on its own motion will excuse you.

(Whereupon juror number fourteen, Wojciech Przydzielski, left the jury box.)

Mr. Gilman:	Incidentally, among the witnesses called in this case by the People will be the people that were living at 4330 Lincoln on the morning of May 8, 1970. Among the people that will testify, perhaps, will be some young men with long hair, perhaps with beards, perhaps with a goatee.

Is there any person on the jury who would not believe a witness under oath just because they have long hair?

I want you to look into your hearts and answer this question honestly and openly.

All right, I take it all of you will judge a witness with long hair the same way you judge any other witness; is that correct?

And does the same follow:

If that person has a beard or a goatee, or if a witness is wearing a miniskirt or any kind of dress, does that also apply?

Will you judge all the witnesses independently, judge their testimony as individuals, and not put them in some classification such as hippies or yippies or yappies or whatever you read about in the newspapers?

Will you judge them all as individual witnesses and give the testimony of each witness the weight you feel it deserves?

[Gilman excuses jurors Dorothy Munger (who felt a man innocent until proven guilty) and Ewald Nusbeitel (who has a deer rifle and two handguns at home).]

[Nelson excuses Charlene Johnson and another.]

[Gilman excuses Irene Durance and another.]

[Nelson excuses two more.]

[Gilman excuses Thomas Pfeifer (who didn't like drug use).]

[Nelson excuses Barbara Johnson and Desaree Bell.]

[Nelson excuses another.]

Friday 13 November

[Gilman excuses two jurors.]

[Nelson excuses two jurors.]

[Nelson excuses Velma Bradley and another.]

[Nelson excuses another juror.]

(Proceedings held outside the presence and hearing of the jury panel.)

The Court:	You may proceed.
Mr. Gilman:	Your Honor, I would request at this time that any available jurors who are on the tenth floor be called down for purposes of selection in this case.

I noticed that there were approximately sixteen people—prospective jurors sitting out there. I believe only two of these individuals were Negroes.

The record should indicate that I have excused eight individuals, all of whom have been white; Mr. Nelson has excused twelve people peremptorily, eleven of whom have been black, and one of whom has been white.

Mr. Nelson: I guess maybe you don't count Mr. Gluckstein as being a white man.

Mr. Gilman: I said eleven Negroes and one white.

Mr. Gilman: Your Honor, this isn't a racial case. I am just asking for a representative group.

I am asking to get all of the jurors available down here, and I will abide by whatever is left.

I don't see the prejudice of that.

The Court: Mr. Nelson.

Mr. Nelson: I think the push is just about as bad as the tug.

I say he isn't asking for anything.

I'd say he's doing a little bit of whining now.

Mr. Nelson: I would like to make one more point.

I resent the implications of these remarks.

I don't think they are fair and I don't think they are fairly taken.

I think he is trying to try this case in the papers; he is trying to make me and my client out as some kind of racists.

I think he is grossly unfair.

It just so happens there's still about half that panel in there that are Negroes.

Mr. Gilman: Your Honor, I am not claiming there is any systematic exclusion of Negroes from the jury panel.

The Court: We have fifteen potential jurors in the hall. We have twelve peremptory challenges left.

Mr. Gilman: I agree. All I am saying is I would like all the jurors from the tenth floor. I know they are not trying any cases this afternoon.

The Court: I don't know that. Judge DeMascio criticized my holding jurors unjustly.

He is at a budget hearing at City Hall and won't be back for an hour.

We have five attorneys tied up here.

I think we will go along with his order and select from what we have here.

Bring in the jury panel.

(Whereupon the jury panel entered the courtroom.)

* * *

[After more questioning, several jurors are excused including Laura ("I'm a grandma and a great- one") Blaess. Two jurors now remain of the original fourteen.]

The Court:	Any peremptory challenges, Mr. Nelson?
Mr. Nelson:	We are satisfied.
Mr. Gilman:	The People are satisfied, Your Honor.
The Court:	Will anybody be inconvenienced if we run over your normal jury term?

The sexes are mixed so we won't have to lock them up; so there is no problem there. We do have a rule: if we have a jury all the same sex, we have to lock you up overnight. It's an old law that runs back to the days before they gave women the right to vote. They have never taken it off the books.

Can anybody else think of any problems before we swear them?

Mr. Gilman:	I have no problems in regard to this case. I have a million problems, but not in regard to this case.
The Court:	All right, once the die is cast, you will have this jury; and you will get to know each other very well in the next few days.

All right, swear the jury.

(Whereupon at 3:35 P.M. the jury was duly sworn by the court clerk.)

The Court:	Ladies and gentlemen of the jury.

We are going over our schedule for the coming two weeks.

We will probably work from nine until four, four-thirty each day.

It is a difficult case. We have five attorneys involved.

You will have Thanksgiving Day off.

We will expect the jury to come back on Friday after Thanksgiving.

Then December it will be Monday through Friday if we go that long.

I don't want the jury discussing the case among themselves until all the testimony is in. Do not discuss this case among yourselves.

At the proper time we will want all twelve—at that time your number will be reduced to twelve—and you will hold a frank discussion.

Prior to that time, we don't want a discussion among two or three of you at lunch tomorrow or anything else.

Next, if anyone else tries to talk to you about the case—witnesses, attorneys, or anybody in the world tries to discuss this case with you—I would like that reported to the court.

I don't think anybody in the box now has seen a movie in the last sixty days. I doubt whether any of you will be going to the movies in the next three weeks. There is a movie that is playing in the Pittsburgh area, and we will tell you about it after the trial is over.

If you want to go to the movies, tell me what you are going to see ahead of time.

We will let you wonder about that movie, and you can go see it afterwards.

I think the court and counsel have seen it. It's not very popular. The night I saw it there were only nineteen people in the theatre.

It could influence you one way or the other.

Is there anything else?

Mr. Gilman: May we approach the bench?

(Conference at the bench between the court, Mr. Gilman, and Mr. Nelson; outside the hearing of the jury and the court reporter.)

The Court: From time to time there may be some articles in the paper about this case.

We prefer that you do not read those articles.

The reason for this is that you are here firsthand hearing the testimony from the witnesses. You might get a different version in the newspaper of what that reporter thinks a witness says.

So if you see the articles in the paper, we would like you to skip over them.

If it's on television, go and get a glass of milk or something and don't watch the television.

We prefer you not to read any articles about it, listen to any radio or television stories on this particular case.

Is there anything else from the lawyers?

Are there any questions from the jury?

Juror West: You said Wednesday we don't come in?

The Court: I will be working; but we won't be taking up this case. You make your definite plans to be off Wednesday.

Juror West: Where I work, I'm supposed to go back to work. Would it be better if I didn't go back to work that day?

The Court: Let your conscience be your guide in your relationship with your employer.

Any other questions from the jury or the attorneys?

All right, the jury is excused for the weekend.

[Figure 11 reprints a *Pittsburgh Herald* article that discusses the jury selection in the Jackson case.]

*Figure 11 Pittsburgh Herald **article***

Jackson Trial to Try Murder Victims

A News In-Depth Analyis

by Roger Lindburg

It has become increasingly apparent that the main issue in the Wilbur Jackson murder trial will not be whether Jackson killed his daughter and her three boyfriends but whether he had the "right" to kill the four youngsters.

Jackson is currently standing trial in Recorder's Court before Judge Joseph A. Gillis for the murders which occurred last May in an apartment house near the Allegheny State campus. Jackson is defended by a trio of attorneys—Oliver Nelson, Emmet Tracy, and John Carney—while Leonard Gilman is representing the Allegheny County Prosecutor's Office in the proceedings.

During the week that it took to select a jury, attorneys on both sides questioned potential jurors about their attitudes towards communal living, long hair, and drug use. For once the roles were reversed. Normally prosecutors seek middle-aged, law-and-order jurors who are generally inclined towards conviction. However in this case it was the defense who wanted the law-and-order jurors—those who would hopefully identify and sympathize with Jackson.

Prosecutor Gilman excused older, conservative, white jurors including gun collectors, veterans, retirees, and a Baptist Bible school teacher. "I threw out jurors I would love to have in any other case" stated Gilman. "I wanted the type of jurors who would normally tend to acquit, not convict."

On the other hand, the defense excused all the young potential jurors as well as a Ph.D. and a psychologist. Twelve of the fourteen individuals excused by defense were black. Explained Oliver Nelson, chief defense counsel, "To tell the truth, I didn't want anyone on that jury who would identify with the victims. We wanted older, more mature, established people with roots in the community."

It was not until after 47 prospective jurors had been questioned that a jury of 14 was finally selected. Of those 14 nine are white and ten are men. The actual trial is slated to begin Monday.

Pittsburgh Herald 11/14/70

SUPPRESSION HEARING

Monday 16 November

In the morning the court held a hearing on the defense's motion to suppress the statements made by Wilbur Jackson to the police shortly after the killings. A suppression motion asks the court to rule that some item of evidence—perhaps a confession or a gun or a lineup identification—cannot be used at trial because it was illegally obtained by the police. Suppression hearings are always held outside the presence of the jury, for the very logical reason that if the evidence is suppressed then the jury should not hear of its existence.

A confession may be suppressed for either of two reasons. First, as described previously, because it was obtained in violation of a suspect's Miranda rights in that the police did not give the suspect the required warnings. Second, because the confession was involuntary in that it involved force, coercion, or threats. A confession could fully comply with the Miranda requirements, yet be suppressed because it was obtained as a result of a physical beating.

In the present case, the defense will argue that the Miranda requirements were violated. Note that a suspect may waive his Miranda rights if that waiver is intelligent and voluntary. For example, a drunk person could not waive his rights because he would lack the capacity to intelligently do so. By the same token, the defense will argue, Wilbur Jackson was so emotionally distraught that he did not know what he was doing.

Note also that Miranda applies only when the police *question* a suspect. The police are under no obligation to give Miranda warnings to an individual who *volunteers* statements, as happened in this case. Hence, even the defense will concede that Jackson's initial statements should not be suppressed.

* * *

Mr. Gilman: **Q Would you state your name, please, sir.**

A Jerome Jasinski.

Q What is your occupation, Mr. Jasinski?

A I am a police officer in the city of Pittsburgh.

Q To what bureau or precinct are you presently assigned?

A Second Precinct.

Q Were you on duty at the Second Precinct, Sergeant Jasinski, on the early morning of May 8, 1970?

A I was.

Q To what part of the Second Precinct were you assigned on that morning?

A I was assigned to the desk in charge of the station.

Q At about 2:35 in the morning, Sergeant, did something take place in the Second Precinct?

A Yes, it did.

Q Would you tell the court what happened, please?

A I was behind the desk, and a white male walked in.

Q Can you identify that man?

A I can.

Q Do you see him in court today?

A He's seated next to Mr. Nelson,—

Mr. Gilman: Let the record show the witness has pointed to and indicated the defendant Mr. Wilbur Jackson.

Q Did you speak to him at that time, or did he speak to you?

A He spoke to me first.

Q What did Mr. Jackson say at that time?

A He said, "I want to turn myself in."

Q What happened then, Sergeant?

A I asked him, "What for?"

Q What did he say?

A He said, "For murder; I just murdered my daughter and her hippie friends."

Q What happened then, Sergeant?

A I asked him, "Where?"

Q What did he say?

A He said, "On Lincoln."

Q Did you ask him any further questions at that time?

A Not at that moment, no.

Q Had you placed him under arrest up to that moment?

A No.

Q After he said, "On Lincoln," what happened then?

A Patrolman Becker, who was on the other side of the desk, walked over to him; and I believe he asked him if he had a gun, and he raised his jacket, and he had a gun tucked in each side of his waistband.

*   *   *

Q When you observed these guns, what happened then?

A Patrolman Becker removed the guns from his waistband, and I motioned Patrolman Becker to lead the man back to the registering room. . . .

Q When you indicated to Patrolman Becker to take Mr. Jackson back to the registering room, what happened then?

A I walked from behind the desk back to the registering room.

*   *   *

Q **What happened then?**

A When I got back there, he [Jackson] was taking live bullets and empty casings out of his pocket and setting them up on a half door with a ledge on it. . . .

Q **What happened then?**

A When I walked up to him, he said he saw his daughter having intercourse in bed with a man; he struck the man on the head with the gun, and it went off, killing his daughter.

Q **Now, had you asked him any questions before he made that statement?**

A No. . . .

Q **Now, after Mr. Jackson made this statement, what happened then, Sergeant?**

A I went to phone the homicide bureau to tell them that Mr. Jackson was in the station and I was going to send him straight downtown.

Q **Was Mr. Jackson sent straight downtown at that point?**

A That's right.

* * *

Q **At the time you first encountered Mr. Jackson at your desk in the Second Precinct, would you describe the way he appeared to you at that time, his outward demeanor?**

A He was crying, tears were flowing, he seemed rather excited, his clothes were not orderly, they were in disarray.

Q **Was he crying throughout the time he was in the Second Precinct, or did there come a time that he stopped crying before he left?**

A All the while I saw him, he was crying.

Mr. Gilman: I have no further questions, Your Honor, of Sergeant Jasinski.

CROSS–EXAMINATION

Mr. Carney: Q **Sergeant Jasinski, you say that Mr. Jackson was crying. Was he visibly upset? Was he shaking?**

A He was excited. He wasn't slow and calm.

Q **Was he excited to the extent—was he shaking?**

A He wasn't shaking or jerking. He was crying.

Q **Did he appear to you to be lucid at that point?**

A Excited, I would say.

Q Excited to the extent he didn't know what he was saying or didn't know what he was doing?

A I couldn't say for sure to that.

* * *

Q When he walked in, he said something to the effect that he murdered his daughter?

A Yes.

Q Could he have said he shot his daughter, or do you remember?

A I put down exactly what he said, "murdered."

Q You made that report out within an hour of the occurrence, is that correct?

A Approximately an hour.

* * *

Q The last time you saw Mr. Jackson, he was visibly upset and excited?

A Yes.

Q At the time you saw Mr. Jackson that night, what were the configurations of his face? Besides the crying, was he stern, excited?

A Excited—not calm, he wasn't calm.

Q Was his face drawn?

A It's hard to describe. He was crying. That's all I would be able to really say for sure on that.

Q Was he sobbing, weeping?

A No.

Q He was not?

A He was crying; the tears were falling.

Q Was he pacing up and down?

A Not in my presence. He had just walked up to the desk, and from there he was led in the back.

[Figure 12 shows Sergeant Jasinski's report.]

* * *

Q His speech at the time that you saw him, did he speak rapidly?

A A little.

Q Was it clear?

A Yes.

Figure 12 Sergeant Jasinski's report

REPORT ON		ASSIGNED TO			M.O. FORM PREPARED?	COMPLAINT NO.
CMPT HOMICIDE					☐ YES ☐ NO	

PLACE OF OCCURRENCE	CENSUS TRACT	SCOUT CAR AREA
☐ CHECK IF ON STREET 0901 W. VERNOR	04-004	2-3

TYPE OF BUSINESS	TIME	DAY	NIGHT	UNKNOWN
	2 AM (35)	☐	☒	☐

TYPE OF BUILDING	DATE
	5-8-70

PERSON REPORTING OFFENSE (AGE SEX COLOR)	TITLE	ADDRESS	DAY OF WEEK FRIDAY	TELEPHONE

COMPLAINANT'S NAME	ADDRESS	PHONE BUS. RES.	AGE SEX COLOR

RECEIVED BY OFFICER JEROME JASINSKI	TIME 9 AM DATE 5-8-70	VICTIM AND PERPETRATOR ARE ☐ RELATED ☐ ACQUAINTED ☐ STRANGERS	RELATIONSHIP ☐ UNKNOWN

METHOD OF ENTRY	METHOD OF ESCAPE	DESCRIBE WEAPON ☐ UNKNOWN

STATE NUMBER OF PERPETRATORS HERE OR ☐ CHECK BOX IF NUMBER IS UNKNOWN	IF ONLY ONE PERPETRATOR, DESCRIBE HERE	☐ MALE ☐ FEMALE ☐ UNKNOWN	☐ JUVENILE ☐ ADULT	☐ WHITE ☐ NEGRO ☐ OTHER ☐ UNKNOWN	TOTAL VALUE $

☐ COMPLAINANT AVAILABLE ANYTIME ☐ OR AT	OTHER UNIT NOTIFIED	NAME OF PERSON NOTIFIED	TIME DATE

IMPORTANT: PRIOR TO BODY OF REPORT BELOW, GIVE NAME, AGE, COLOR, ADDRESS, AND CHARGE OF EACH PERSON ARRESTED. (IF NONE, CHECK BELOW.) GIVE ADDITIONAL DETAILS OF OCCURRENCE, PERSONS, AND PROPERTY NOT INCLUDED ABOVE. IF MORE THAN ONE PERPETRATOR, DESCRIBE BELOW.

☐ NO ARRESTS

ON 5-8-70 AT 2 AM (35) WHILE IN CHARGE OF THE 2ND PRECINCT DESK A W/M LATER IDENTIFIED AS WILBUR JACKSON WALKED IN THE FRONT DOOR & UP TO THE DESK. BEFORE I COULD ASK IF I COULD HELP HIM HE SAID, "I WANT TO TURN MYSELF IN." I ASKED WHAT FOR & HE SAID, "FOR MURDER I JUST <u>MURDERED</u> MY DAUGHTER & HER HIPPIE FRIENDS." I ASKED WHERE & HE SAID, "ON LINCOLN." AT THIS TIME PATR. JOS BECKER TOOK FROM THE MAN'S WAISTBAND A B&A, & A B5.38 REV & ESCORTED THE MAN TO THE REGISTERING ROOM.

IN THE REGISTERING ROOM HE SAID HE SAW HIS DAUGHTER HAVING INTERCOURSE IN BED WITH A MAN. HE STRUCK THE MAN

SIGNATURE OF OFFICER RECEIVING REPORT SGT *[signature]* Jasinski	BADGE NO. 5-363	PRECINCT 2	ASSIGNMENT

NAMES OF OTHER OFFICERS INVOLVED	BADGE NO.	PRECINCT	NAMES	BADGE NO.	PRECINCT

SIGNATURE OF RANKING OFFICER CHECKING REPORT	RANK

P.P.D. 108   C of D-783 RE Rev. 6.67   **PRELIMINARY COMPLAINT RECORD**   (FOUR COPIES TO BE MADE ON EACH REPORT PLUS EXTRAS AS NEEDED)   PITTSBURGH POLICE DEPARTMENT

MAN ON THE HEAD WITH A GUN & THE GUN WENT OFF KILLING HIS DAUGHTER. AT THIS TIME I PHONED HOMICIDE & NOTIFIED THEM THE MAN WAS AT #2 & I TOLD PATRS BECKER & FASHOWAY 2-15 TO CONVEY HIM TO HOMICIDE.

Q **Was he in any way—was he jerking—**

Mr. Gilman: Your Honor, I think he is asking that question—the question has been asked and answered.

The Court: I don't think on jerking.

Mr. Gilman: Okay.

A Not jerking. I'm trying to picture him, and it's hard. I wouldn't say he was jerking.

Q **Wasn't he a little bit spastic?**

A Well, he was moving a little; but not a jerk or not a shake. More or less—I'm trying to think how to put it—in an excited state. His arms would be moving a bit up and down.

*   *   *

Mr. Gilman: **Q** **State your name, please, sir.**

A James Caufield.

*   *   *

Q **On the early morning of May 8, 1970, Sergeant Caufield, were you assigned to the homicide bureau?**

A Yes, I was. . . .

Q **Did you have occasion on that morning to see an individual named Wilbur Jackson?**

A Yes, I did. . . .

Q **What was the first time that you saw him on May 8?**

A Approximately 2:45 A.M.

*   *   *

Q **Would you describe for the court Mr. Jackson's demeanor when you first observed him; how did he look to you?**

A Upset.

Q **How could you tell he was upset?**

A He was nervous, in a little nervous condition.

Q **Was he crying when you first saw him?**

A I don't recall, when I first saw him, if he was crying or not. I don't believe he was when I first saw him, no. . . .

Q **Do you recall what you said to Mr. Jackson when you first saw him?**

A I asked him to sit down in a chair opposite me at one of the desks . . . .

Q **Did he do that?**

A   Yes, he did.

Q   **Did you introduce yourself to Mr. Jackson?**

A   Yes, I did.

Q   **Was anyone else present . . . when Mr. Jackson took a seat . . . ?**

A   Patrolman Fashoway.

Q   **After Mr. Jackson took a seat, what happened then, Sergeant Caufield?**

A   I told the defendant he was under arrest on an open charge of murder, and I told him before I talked to him I would have to advise him of his constitutional rights.

Q   **When you said that to Mr. Jackson, was Mr. Jackson crying?**

A   No, he wasn't.

Q   **Did he appear as nervous as he did when you first encountered him, or less or more nervous?**

A   At times during the interview, he would get more nervous, and then he would relax. At this time he appeared more relaxed when I had him sit down.

Q   **Exactly what did you say to him? I don't want to restate something you didn't say.**

A   I told the defendant he was under arrest on a charge of murder and before I talked to him I would have to advise him of his constitutional rights.

Q   **After you told him that, did you proceed to advise him with respect to his constitutional rights?**

A   I did.

Q   **What did you say to Mr. Jackson, Sergeant?**

A   I had in my possession a Pittsburgh Police Department Constitutional Rights Certificate of Notification. I showed it to the defendant. Then I read it to him.

* * *

Q   **Did you ascertain prior to reading that form to him the extent of Mr. Jackson's education?**

A   I did.

Q   **What did he indicate to you regarding his educational background?**

A   He stated that he had a college education.

Q   **After you read him that form, Sergeant Caufield, you indicated you handed it to him?**

A   Right.

Q   What, if anything, did Mr. Jackson do at that point?

A   He looked at the form. I signed the form. Patrolman Fashoway signed the form. The defendant Wilbur Chester Jackson signed the form.

Q   Did he sign the form in your presence?

A   Yes, he did.

Q   Did he indicate to you that he didn't understand any of the rights that you had read to him?

A   I asked the defendant if he understood these rights that I had given him. He stated he understood his rights.

    I also explained to him before I started talking to him after giving him this form, I asked him:

    "Do you want to make a statement to me now without having an attorney present to represent you?"

    He said:

    "Yes, I want to make a statement; I want to tell the truth, what happened, and why."

Q   You asked him that after you had read him that constitutional rights form, is that correct?

A   That's correct.

Q   And then he indicated he did indeed want to make a statement, he wanted to tell the truth?

A   Yes, he did.

Q   After that, Sergeant Caufield, did you take a statement from Mr. Jackson?

*   *   *

A   I didn't write down the statement right away. I asked Mr. Jackson to tell me what happened that evening in his own words.

    Mr. Jackson went through the complete story of what happened that evening before I started writing. I heard the whole story once.

    Then I told him that we would start over, and I would write and would ask him questions to make sure that everything I was putting down was as he said.

Q   Now, you indicated that throughout the course of this interview with Mr. Jackson he appeared at times to be nervous; is that correct? . . .

A   Distraught and crying.

Q   All right.

A   There were a couple of times I asked him if he was all right; he stated, "Yes."

Q   During the time that you have been a member of the homicide bureau, you have had occasion to interview other defendants, have you not, at the homicide bureau?

A   Yes, I have.

Q   It is a usual occurrence for a defendant being interrogated at the homicide bureau to be nervous?

A   Oh, yes, sir.

Mr. Nelson: Oh, really, now—

Mr. Carney: Wait a minute, now—

The Court: The objection is sustained.

Mr. Gilman: I would like to get some ground rules as to who can rise and make a protest here. Mr. Carney spoke, and Mr. Nelson spoke. . . .

The Court: Each witness can have only one defense attorney. Whoever rises first, he's the attorney for that. They came up together; so I thought it was a tie.

Q   During the entire time that you spent with Mr. Jackson, was Patrolman Fashoway there?

A   He was with us at all times.

Q   Did he participate in any of the questioning?

A   No, he didn't participate in the questioning; but he did sign the constitutional rights certificate after I had advised Mr. Jackson of his rights, and he also signed the statement that I took.

Q   Did Mr. Jackson sign the statement that you took?

A   Yes, he did.

Q   Did he sign each page of it?

A   Yes, he did.

Q   Did he sign at the bottom of the last page?

A   Yes, he did.

Mr. Gilman: Your Honor, I have no further questions.

CROSS–EXAMINATION

Mr. Carney: **Q   Detective Caufield, how was Mr. Jackson dressed when you first saw him?**

A   If I remember correctly, I believe he had work clothes on. I'm not quite sure, sir. . . .

Q   **Did they appear dirty?**

A   Unkempt.   .   .   .

Q   **Did he look like a man who just came home from work?**

A   Yes, sir.

Q   **What about his facial configurations at the time you first saw him?**

A   Distraught look on his face, red in the face, bloodshot eyes, hair was—

Q   **Unkempt?**

A   Unkempt.

Q   **He appeared agitated?**

A   Not agitated.

Q   **Excited?**

A   At times excited.

Q   **At the time you presented the constitutional rights certificate, did Mr. Jackson read it?   .   .   .**

A   Yes, sir; after I read it to him, I handed it to him, and he read it.

Q   **He read it, or appeared to read it?**

A   He may not have read it; but he looked at it like he was reading it.

Q   **How much time did it take him?   I am not trying to be facetious here.**

A   Three or four minutes, a couple of minutes.   He stated that he understood it.

Q   **At the time you gave him the constitutional rights certificate, was he nervous at that time, or excited?**

A   No; he was all right then.

Q   **At what point did he become excited?   .   .   .**

A   When he hit a certain incident that happened, that's when he got upset.

*   *   *

Q   **And at certain times, you stated, he became a little more excited and cried; is that correct?**

A   Yes, correct.

Q   **Did he appear to you to be lucid?   Did he know what he was doing?**

A   Oh, absolutely, yes, sir; no problem there.

Q   **Even though he was excited?**

A   Even though he was excited, and he even got angry a couple of times.

Q   At whom?

A   At something he was explaining about what happened; not at me.

* * *

Q   Was there any particular reason why Mr. Jackson should be taken to the holdup bureau, or did it just happen?

A   No, sir; he was taken there for a specific reason.

Q   What was that?

A   Because we had witnesses from the scene of the crime in the homicide bureau itself.   We did not want the witnesses to be confronted by the defendant.

* * *

Q   How many murders have you investigated in your period with the homicide bureau?   I think you indicated it was three years.

A   I've been with them two years.   Possibly thirty, thirty-five.

Q   You are fairly familiar, then, with the modus operandi of the homicide bureau?

A   Yes, sir.

* * *

Q   In the investigations conducted by the homicide bureau, is there a general time span between the reporting of an incident or bringing someone in on a charge and taking of statements?

Mr. Gilman: Your Honor, I am going to object to that question.   I don't think that is material.

The Court: Yes, I think we have to keep to this case.

We know that the courts have ruled that if you hold them too long to take the statement—and, depending on the circumstances, as little as twenty-four hours can be too long.

I haven't heard any case where they have ruled taking a statement too fast is improper.

Mr. Carney: Your Honor, my point here is that the killings alleged and alleged statements were all taken within a period of less than fifteen minutes.

The Court: Is this objectionable?

Mr. Carney: No, ordinarily; but we are going into whether or not Wilbur Jackson knowingly voluntarily waived his rights.

He has come from a set of tragic circumstances, he is at the police station, and they take him downtown and take a statement all within a period of fifteen minutes.

I think that is very unusual.

The Court: Well, I think it's very efficient.

I don't see any objection to it.

The only objection we have had is where they have taken it twenty-four hours after the crime.

No, I will sustain the objection.

* * *

Q **Over what period of time did you question Mr. Jackson and write the statement?**

A Approximately 2:45 A.M. when I first saw Mr. Jackson; advised him of his rights, approximately 2:50 A.M.; we talked about his rights for approximately ten minutes, at 3 A.M. I signed the constitutional rights; I started questioning Mr. Jackson at 3:05 A.M., and this interview went on up until 4:15 A.M.

Q **Now, you advised Mr. Jackson of his rights at the beginning of this meeting with you; is that correct?**

A Yes, sir.

Q **Did you tell him at any time during that subsequent hour and ten minutes that he had a right to stop at any time?**

* * *

A Yes, sir.

Q **Did you at any time, Detective Caufield, attempt to take Wilbur Jackson to the prosecutor's office and have a stenographic statement taken?**

A No, sir.

Q **Was there any particular reason why you didn't?**

Mr. Gilman: Well, Your Honor, I am going to object to that. I don't think that is material.

That doesn't go to whether or not he was advised of his constitutional rights.

The Court: We will take the answer to that, if there is any.

A At that time we were what we call very busy in the homicide bureau. We had myself and my partner working and one man out at the scene. We had no other men in the office.

If he was to be taken up to the prosecutor's office, this could be done the next morning by the officers assigned to this case.

It didn't enter my mind. I didn't see any reason for it.

Q **The statement, in fact, was not written by Wilbur Jackson; was it?**

A   No sir. When I read the statement to Mr. Jackson and asked him if he understood, he said, "Yes," and there was one reason why he said he understood better than most other people would.

Q   But he didn't write the statement?

A   No, sir.

Q   And the statement is in your handwriting, is that right?

A   Yes, sir, the statement is in my handwriting and signed by him with his signature on all pages.

Mr. Carney: I have nothing further of this witness, Your Honor.

[Patrolman Robert Jones of the Pittsburgh Police testifies next. He states that while on duty 8 May he observed Wilbur Jackson in the Second Precinct Station. Jones testifies that Jackson was crying, appeared dazed, and remembered striking a man he had found in bed with his daughter.]

Mr. Gilman: **Q   Will you state your name, please, sir?**

A   Ptm. Leonard Fashoway.

*   *   *

Q   On May 8, 1970, . . . did you have occasion to see a man that was later identified to you as Wilbur Jackson?

A   Yes, sir.

*   *   *

Q   Did there come a time when you took physical custody of Mr. Jackson for the purpose of taking him down to Pittsburgh Police Headquarters?

A   Yes, sir.

*   *   *

Q   Was Patrolman Becker with you at this time?

A   He was.

Q   During the ride from the Second Precinct to the homicide bureau, did you or did Patrolman Becker in your presence attempt to question Mr. Jackson?

A   No, sir.

Q   Did Mr. Jackson say anything at all that you can recall in the ride in the scout car down to Pittsburgh Police Headquarters?

A   Yes, sir.

Q   Did you ask him any questions before he made statements to you?

A   Well, no, sir, not before he started making statements, no.

Q Where was Mr. Jackson seated in the scout car?

A He was in the center of the rear seat. I was on his left.

Q Patrolman Becker was driving the car?

A Yes, sir.

Q Was Mr. Jackson handcuffed at this time?

A No, sir.

* * *

Q When you were in the scout car conveying Mr. Jackson to police headquarters you indicated that Mr. Jackson said something, is that correct?

A Yes, sir.

Q Prior to his saying anything, had you asked him any questions regarding the incident at 4330 Lincoln?

A No, sir.

Q What did Mr. Jackson say to you, if anything, in the back seat of the scout car?

A He stated, "I just killed my daughter," and he made a reference to killing some other hippies. He stated he did not want to—he did not intend to hurt anyone originally, but after killing his daughter he went berserk. And I think I'm using words I believe he said, either berserk—I believe later on he even said he ran amok through the house, in his statement.

* * *

Q Well, what did you say to him?

A Well, I believe I said nothing. Patrolman Becker turned around before we left the parking lot, and he told him that he did not have to say anything to us; and he was attempting to give to the defendant his constitutional rights, but I believe Mr. Jackson insisted on speaking. So he kept on talking, regardless.

Q Did you hear Patrolman Becker ask Mr. Jackson about the events at 4330 Lincoln?

A No, sir.

Q You can recall Patrolman Becker, though, indicating to Mr. Jackson that he had a right to remain silent?

A Yes, sir.

* * *

Q How long did it take to get from the Second Precinct to Pittsburgh Police Headquarters?

A   I believe it would have been about a five-minute ride.

*   *   *

Q   **Were you present throughout the time Sergeant Caufield allegedly advised the defendant of his constitutional rights and took a long-hand statement which Sergeant Caufield took down?**

A   Yes, sir.

Q   **Did you question the defendant at any time?**

A   No, sir.

Q   **When you first saw the defendant in the Second Precinct, was he crying?**

A   At one time or another he may have been, yes, sir.

Q   **Did he cry at any time while Sergeant Caufield interviewed him?**

A   Yes, sir, I believe he did.

Q   **Was this throughout the course of the interview, or at one time or another during the course of it?**

A   I believe he was actually crying toward the end of the interview.

Mr. Gilman: Thank you.

CROSS–EXAMINATION

Mr. Carney: Q   **Patrolman, what do you have in your hand?**

A   The statement I made at homicide.

Q   **Can I examine it, please?**

A   Yes, sir (producing instrument).

[Figure 13 shows the instrument produced, Patrolman Fashoway's report.]

*   *   *

Q   **What was his demeanor in the police car at the next time you saw him?**

A   He was extremely nervous and, I would say, agitated; very talkative.

*   *   *

Q   **Now, he was nervous and agitated, I think you testified—**

A   Yes.

Q   **—when he got into the police car. Did that condition prevail throughout the trip downtown?**

A   Yes, sir. .   .   .

Figure 13 Patrolman Fashoway's report

PITTSBURGH POLICE DEPARTMENT
Detective Division
HOMICIDE BUREAU

Date _8 MAY 1970_

TO:

SUBJECT: REQUEST FOR INFORMATION

Please forward to the Homicide Bureau, at the earliest possible date, a resume listing events in the order of their occurrence, of the individual action taken by you at the scene of:

MULTIPLE SHOOTING   -   4 DEAD

which occurred at: _4430 LINCOLN_

on: _8 MAY 70_ , at: _2:15_ APPROX. (A.M.) P.M.

Also please include a complete summary of your conversation with the defendant and/or witnesses. The return shall be written in the first person, i.e. "I saw", "Italked to", ect. The signature must be in your own handwriting. This information is necessary for the proper preparation and presentation of the case in Court.

Attention: _____

(Officers in Charge of the Case)

Delore Ricard
DELORE RICARD
Detective Inspector
Homicide Bureau

Homicide File # _____

DETAILS: I was assigned to Scout 2-15 with Patr. Joe Becker and was writing a report at the Verner station when Wilbur Jackson turned himself in to the station stating that he had just shot & killed four people. We were assigned to convey him to Homicide Bur. While in the wagon, Jackson stated that he accidentally killed his daughter when striking "Todd" WM on the head with his .38 revolver. He was advised of his rights (BY PATR. BECKER) and proceeded to detail killing additional persons, and he did not intend to murder, but "went insane" after seeing his daughter dead, she had "become a hoar" after being raised

Gerard M. Fashoway
Signature

If Necessary, please use reverse side as indicated.

Figure 13 *Patrolman Fashoway's report* *(continued)*

Officer's Name: _LEONARD M. FASHOWAY_ 484
(Please Print)

Partner's Name: _JOE BECKER_
(Please Print)

Assignment: _2-15_

DETAILS: (Continued)

by the family properly and was led astray by friends. I was asked to escort Jackson to be questioned by Sgt. Caufield who advised him rights, interviewed him, prepared a statement, and we took him to Scientific Bur. for a Nitrate Test, where he signed the statement. I prepared a fingerprint card and escorted him to 9th fl.

Leonard M. Fashoway
Signature

Q   What was his demeanor at police headquarters?

A   He was still very nervous but very cooperative. He just seemed to be very anxious to do anything that we thought necessary for him to do.

From the little experience that I had, he was almost overcooperative; because the contact I've had with the normal person that I would convey to downtown isn't usually quite that agreeable.

Q   Did his demeanor change during the course of interrogation by Detective Caufield?

A   I would suppose that as the conversation went on, I would imagine that he became more calm, perhaps, more relaxed.

*   *   *

Q   Patrolman Becker was driving the car?

A   Yes, sir.

Q   Patrolman Becker was directing conversations to Mr. Jackson?

A   He directed a few remarks toward him.

Q   Well, all right, remarks. Did those have to do with his constitutional rights?

A   I distinctly remember him turning around before we had left the vicinity of the Second Precinct Station and telling Mr. Jackson he did not have to speak.

Q   Did Mr. Jackson make a response?

A   Yes, sir; he responded right away and said, "I know; but I want to—" I can't recall the exact words, but in essence "—I want to talk, I want to say what is on my mind."

*   *   *

Mr. Gilman: Mr. Carney indicated, for the purposes of this hearing, anyway, he does not require Patrolman Becker's presence.

The Court: All right.

Let me advise Mr. Jackson of his rights again.

I told you last week, Mr. Jackson, that you may take the stand and testify for the limited purpose of making a record of the facts and circumstances under which these admissions were obtained.

By so doing, you do not waive your right to decline to take the stand on the trial, nor do you waive any of your other rights stemming from your rights not to testify before the jury.

The sole issue here is the voluntariness of the confession.

Mr. Carney: Your Honor, we have discussed this matter with Mr. Jackson; and at this time he will take the stand.

Mr. Carney: **Q   What is your name, sir?**

A   Wilbur Jackson.

*   *   *

Q   Mr. Jackson, you remember the events that took place on or about May 8, 1970?

A   Yes, sir, some of them.

Q   Do you remember those events that have brought us here today, specifically, the killing of your daughter and three other people?

A   I was in a shock. I remember some things; some I don't.

Q   **Do you remember what happened at 4330 Lincoln?**

A   Yes, sir.

Q   **What happened at 4330 Lincoln?**

A   Well, the young people were slain.

Q   **Did you have anything to do with that?**

A   Yes, sir.

Q   **Now, after the events that transpired at 4330 Lincoln, do you remember what you did?**

A   I was in shock. I remember some of the things I did.

Q   **Well, you tell us, to the best of your recollection, what happened after leaving 4330 Lincoln.**

A   When I came to my senses, I was driving the car down toward the railroad tunnel. I thought about catching a freight train, I guess, to Canada.

Q   **Was anyone with you, Mr. Jackson?**

A   Yes, sir; my wife was along.

Q   **What kind of a car do you drive?**

A   Volkswagon, sir.

Q   **Who was driving the automobile?**

A   I was.

Q   **After you thought about going to Canada, where did you go then?**

A   I decided not to go. I thought about going down south, too, I guess; but I went to the police station. . . .

Q   **You knew where it was?**

A   Yes, sir.

Q   **Do you remember walking into that police station?**

A   Yes, sir, I believe I do.

Q   **Do you remember talking to someone at the desk, a certain Sergeant Jasinski that you have seen here this morning?**

A   I believe I do remember.

Q   **Do you remember what you said to him?**

A   I surrendered myself.

Q   **Do you remember making any statements to him?**

A   I think I told him I had just killed some people.

Q **How did you feel at that point?**

A I was in shock, dazed, extremely upset.

Q **Do you remember whether you were carrying any firearms?**

A Yes, sir; I was carrying two, I believe. . . .

Q **Do you remember making any statements in the presence of other officers . . . .**

A I remember saying something. I can't remember details.

Q **What was the gist of the statement that you made that you remember?**

A Well, I think I told them that I had shot some people.

Q **Do you remember if anybody at this point had advised you of your constitutional right to remain silent?**

A Well, I'm sure the officers didn't lie about this. . . .

Q **Do you remember them advising you of your constitutional rights to remain silent?**

A Not at this time I don't believe I did.

Q **Do you remember proceeding from the Second Precinct to the First Precinct . . . in a police car?**

A I remember I was in shock; I wanted to do a lot of talking.

Q **Do you remember going down in the police car in the company of Patrolman Fashoway?**

A I believe I recall a portion of it. I can remember certain things. Some things, I can't.

* * *

Q **Do you remember Patrolman Becker advising you of your rights in the car, as testified to by Patrolman Fashoway?**

A I don't believe I do. If he said he did, he probably did.

Q **Do you remember or don't you remember?**

A I'm not positive. I don't think I remember.

Q **Do you remember walking into the First Precinct downtown?**

A No, sir, I don't remember walking in. . . .

Q **Do you remember conversations with Detective Caufield?**

A I remember parts of this with a plainclothesman. I remember a lot of talking. I don't know exactly what I said—all of what I said.

Q **Do you remember making a statement to Detective Caufield?**

A No, I don't remember a detailed statement. I guess I told him what I did.

Q **Do you remember signing a statement?**

A Maybe somewhere I signed one. I don't remember just where it was.

Q **Do you remember being advised of your constitutional rights?**

A I don't recall where it was. Seems like I remember somebody telling me, and I interrupted him—I wouldn't let him keep talking or something.

Q **Do you remember signing a certificate on the constitutional rights?**

A Could I see a copy of that?

The Court: That hasn't been marked yet. That's the one Detective Caufield testified to. Let's get it marked as an exhibit.

* * *

(Certificate of Constitutional Rights Form was marked as People's Exhibit No. 2; Longhand Statement of Wilbur Chester Jackson was marked as People's Exhibit No. 2–A.)

* * *

Q **Mr. Jackson, I show you now this constitutional rights certificate of notification** *(producing instrument).* **Do you remember reading that statement?**

A *(Examining instrument)* No, sir, I don't; but that looks like my signature. . . .

Q **Is it your signature?**

A It appears to be.

Q **When you were talking to Detective Caufield, do you remember him reading that statement to you?**

A No, sir; but if he said he did, I guess he did.

Q **Just answer the question, Mr. Jackson. Do you remember signing that statement?**

A No, sir; but it looks like my name.

Mr. Carney: I have nothing further, Your Honor.

CROSS–EXAMINATION

Mr. Gilman: Q **I just have a few questions, Mr. Jackson.**

A Yes, sir.

Q **Mr. Jackson, do you remember, do you not, getting back into your VW at 4330 Lincoln?**

A   I don't remember getting into the car. I remember a portion of the drive.

Q   You were driving the car, is that correct?

A   Yes, sir, that's correct.   .   .   .

Q   You keep saying you were in shock. You were driving the car, weren't you?

A   Yes, sir.

Q   It is a stick-shift VW or an automatic?

A   It's an automatic, sir.

Q   Now, you indicate when you arrived at the Vernor Precinct you said something to your wife, is that correct?

A   Yes, sir; I advised her to take the car and take it home and look after the children and forget about me.   .   .   .

Q   Do you remember walking into the Second Precinct?

A   Yes, sir, I remember walking in.

Q   And you indicate that when you went in something made you want to do a lot of talking, is that correct?

A   Yes, sir.

Q   Why did you want to do a lot of talking, Mr. Jackson?

A   I just felt compelled to talk; I had a guilty conscience or something.

Q   A guilty conscience?

A   Yes.

Q   Did you want to get it off your chest?

A   I wanted to talk to someone.

Q   So you did, in fact, speak to that sergeant that was here; do you remember that?

A   I'm not sure; but I guess I did.

Q   Now, you do remember, however, taking these guns out and putting them up on the counter; is that correct?

A   I believe that is correct.

Q   And then do you remember the drive in this police car down to Pittsburgh Police Headquarters?

A   I think I remember a little of it.

                                        *   *   *

Q   Do you remember, however, talking to Sergeant Caufield?

A   I don't know whether I could tell their images apart or not. I spoke to some uniform men and some plainclothesmen. . . .

Q   **Did you also feel at that time like—did you feel like talking at that time, the same way you had felt earlier in the Vernor Precinct?**

A   I think I did.

Q   **Mr. Jackson, you have had a chance to look at this exhibit, have you not, this morning?**

A   Yes, sir.

Q   **And you indicate that does look like your signature, is that correct?**

A   Yes, sir, it appears to be.

*   *   *

Q   **After you had talked to the man that was not in uniform, where did you go then, Mr. Jackson?**

A   Well, I believe they led me over to the Allegheny County Jail.

Q   **Do you remember spending the night at the Allegheny County Jail?**

A   Yes, sir, I do. I slept on a bench without a mattress.

Q   **Did you get much sleep that night?**

A   No, sir, I didn't sleep any at all.

Q   **How did you spend the night?**

A   Crying, I think, sobbing.

Q   **Were you thinking about what you had done?**

A   Yes, sir; and what was going to happen.

*   *   *

AFTER THE NOON RECESS

The Court: You may proceed, Mr. Gilman.

Mr. Gilman: It's our position that all the statements made by Mr. Jackson, both to the uniformed officers at the Second Precinct and to Sergeant Caufield at the homicide bureau, were made freely and voluntarily and therefore should be admitted by the court into evidence.

The statements made to Sergeant Jasinski, the officer who was working the desk at the Second Precinct, are threshold statements made by a person coming in from the street.

Sergeant Jasinski had no idea whatsoever that Mr. Jackson was about to confess or about to state that he had just murdered his daughter and some other people; therefore, how could the sergeant have advised him of his constitutional rights at that time?

Well, the statements made to Patrolman Jones in the booking room or fingerprinting room, the People would contend are also admissible because the officer could not prevent Mr. Jackson from speaking.

As Mr. Jackson said himself from the stand, he wanted to talk, he wanted to say what was on his mind, he wanted to tell the officers what had happened.

The officers testified that they made an attempt—Officer Fashoway indicated at one point that Officer Becker made an attempt to advise Mr. Jackson of his constitutional rights.

Mr. Jackson indicated he knew he had a right to remain silent, but he wanted to tell about it, he wanted to talk.

It's our position that the officers should not have to shut their ears to incriminating statements—allegedly incriminating statements—by a person in custody.

No doubt Mr. Jackson was in custody at the time he was in the fingerprint room and at the time he was in the police car on the way to the homicide bureau.

However, at that point, Mr. Jackson was volunteering information to the officers, and I think it should be admitted into evidence.

Furthermore, the statement made to Detective Caufield at the holdup bureau, we feel, met all the requirements set down in *Miranda v. Arizona.*

The officer indicated that he advised Mr. Jackson fully of his constitutional rights.

He further indicated that Mr. Jackson indicated he understood his rights, he didn't have any questions concerning his rights.

He indicated, although Mr. Jackson did cry at one point or another during the time he spoke to him, I don't think this in any way makes the statement an involuntary statement.

Sure, he was emotional; but that doesn't mean he was under duress or forced to speak against his will or the statement in any way was involuntary.

Detective Caufield further indicated that he ascertained Mr. Jackson was a college graduate, he had a college education.

Mr. Jackson freely admitted on the witness stand he remembers speaking freely to an officer in uniform; he doesn't remember making a full statement, but he remembers telling him some things.

He says he can't remember who he talked to because, as he said several times, he was in shock; and I put that in quotes because I don't know what he means by that.

Officer Caufield stated that he read him his rights, showed him his rights, asked him if he understood what his rights were.

Mr. Jackson indicated he did.

The officer asked if he wanted an attorney present.

Mr. Jackson indicated he didn't want an attorney present.

He signed it, Officer Fashoway signed it, Mr. Jackson signed it.

Mr. Jackson's signature does, in fact, appear on the constitutional rights form and on each page of the five-page statement allegedly given by Mr. Jackson.

Mr. Jackson admits that that indeed does look like his signature on the constitutional rights form and on each page of the statement.

For all of those reasons, Your Honor, we believe that the statement made to Sergeant Caufield was also given freely and voluntarily, as Mr. Jackson had been fully apprised of all his constitutional rights as in *Miranda v. Arizona,* and the statement was freely and voluntarily given and should be admitted into evidence.

The Court: Mr. Carney.

Mr. Carney: Initially I think the statements to Sergeant Jasinski, to Officer Fashoway, to Patrolman Becker, are probably threshold statements within the purview of *United States v. Perry* [342 F.2d 813, cert. denied 382 U.S. 959] and other cases, in that the defendant Wilbur Jackson did volunteer statements at that point. He was in custody, not under arrest.

I think another matter is the alleged statement to Sergeant Caufield.

We have heard testimony that initial contact with Mr. Jackson was made at or about 2:35 A.M. of that morning.

A constitutional rights certificate of notification has a time noted thereon of 2:50.

The alleged voluntary statement has a time noted thereon of 3:05 A.M.

I believe, and it is our contention, that the circumstances surrounding these shootings, the admittedly excited, agitated state of the defendant at that time—at the time of making a statement to Sergeant Caufield—render that statement inadmissible.

The fact is that some less than an hour earlier Mr. Jackson had shot and killed four people.

He says he didn't know they were dead, went down directly to the police station, made those threshold statements.

But, in fact, he was so agitated that our position is that he couldn't intelligently waive his rights when he made that statement to Sergeant Caufield. . . .

I think we would all agree that the statements to Sergeant Jasinski, probably those to Officer Fashoway and Officer Becker, are admissible. . . .

When the purpose of the interrogation begins—when its focus is on the accused, and its purpose is to elicit a confession—*Miranda* applies.

He must voluntarily, intelligently, knowingly, waive his constitutional rights against self-incrimination.

It is our contention here that Mr. Jackson's state of mind, as testified to by most of the officers, the impact of his deeds, conversing forth within a period really of less than thirty minutes after he first went to the Second Precinct, was not in a position to intelligently, knowingly waive his constitutional rights against self-incrimination, and thus makes the statement involuntary. . . .

The Court: Any reply, Mr. Gilman?

Mr. Gilman: Yes, Your Honor.

I would only point out that the . . . sergeant who did take the statement, Sergeant Caufield, has indicated that in no way was Mr. Jackson so agitated or so upset or so insane that he didn't know what he was doing at the time that he made this statement.

Detective Caufield indicated there were times that Mr. Jackson started to cry, that he appeared nervous, and that's about all.

He indicated that Mr. Jackson was coherent throughout, that he understood the questions that he asked him, that he understood his constitutional rights when read to him, and that he proceeded to make a statement to him at that time.

If Mr. Jackson were spoken to at nine o'clock in the morning, I believe Mr. Carney would be up here just as strenuously telling the court that Mr. Jackson was placed on the ninth floor of Pittsburgh Police Headquarters for the purpose of a confession being sweated out of him.

These officers acted promptly in this case.

He was placed under arrest at the Second Precinct, immediately conveyed to the fourth floor of the Pittsburgh Police Headquarters, and immediately questioned by Sergeant Caufield.

I don't think there is any law that indicates that a prompt questioning of a suspect is illegal or is bad.

Detective Caufield testified that he advised Mr. Jackson fully of his constitutional rights.

He further indicated that Mr. Jackson has a college education.

Mr. Jackson corroborated this on the witness stand.

It's interesting to me to note that Mr. Jackson recalls many things about that night, but he doesn't recall talking to Detective Caufield.

That is the most important part of this hearing, and that is what he doesn't recall; and he doesn't recall writing his name down, although he indicates that this looks like his signature.

He can't deny what he can't deny, Your Honor. We have his signature, and he can't deny that that is his signature.

So we believe that, although Mr. Carney's statement of the law is correct, it doesn't apply to this factual situation at all because this factual situation in no way resembles a situation where a defendant is so out of it, so to speak, that he just simply doesn't know what he's doing; and those are not the facts in this case.

Mr. Jackson obviously knew what he was doing.

He proceeded from Stonehead Manor to the Second Precinct and gave himself up, turned over the weapons to the officers, was taken over to the fourth floor where he proceeded to get the things off his chest that he wanted to get off his chest at that time; and he said so from the witness stand.

We would, once again, urge the court that everything that had to be done under the law was done with respect to Mr. Jackson, and the statement should be admitted into evidence.

The Court:	This *People v. Perry* that you are talking about, where is that?
Mr. Carney:	I can get that for you, Your Honor. . . .
The Court:	Is it the United States Supreme Court?
Mr. Carney:	Yes.
The Court:	When was it decided?
Mr. Carney:	It's in the advance sheet.
Mr. Tracy:	Give me a second, and I'll get it for you.
The Court:	All right.
	(Whereupon about a five-minute recess was taken while law books were examined.)
The Court:	All right.
Mr. Carney:	Mr. Tracy apparently went back to get the citation.
The Court:	We have waited five or ten minutes. I have researched everything the Supreme Court has done for years. I have not found this case.
	I will grant the prosecution's motion to admit the confessions— Well, here comes Mr. Tracy. Let's see what you have got.
Mr. Tracy:	It was affirmed by certiorari.
The Court:	Well, it isn't the law.
Mr. Gilman:	I have no objection to the court reading the case.
The Court:	Let me see the case.
Mr. Tracy:	The case really affirms the fact that the first statements come in.
Mr. Gilman:	Well, all right.

| Mr. Carney: | That's what I said, we didn't argue as to that. |

Mr. Carney: That's what I said, we didn't argue as to that.

Mr. Tracy: It's an opinion of Justice Warren Burger.

Mr. Carney: There is no suspect in this case except Mr. Jackson.

The Court: Well, just reading the summary—

The court of appeals held that where a defendant after a shooting went to the police station and surrendered himself and the pistol saying that he shot the victim, refusing to say more, the defendant was taken to the scene and so on, it was affirmed.

They had confusion getting to the police station there, too. This was six o'clock in the morning; it took them from six to six-thirty. They had thirty minutes to make the statements. It all occurred within twenty to thirty minutes.

Why didn't you find this case, Mr. Gilman?

Mr. Gilman: I wasn't looking for it.

The Court: Everything happened within twenty to thirty minutes in the police station. The police were all confused. It was six o'clock in the morning.

Mr. Gilman: Your Honor, I think the *Miranda* case is it.

The Court: All right, I will admit the statements.

I will find they were given free and voluntarily.

* * *

THE PROSECUTION'S CASE

[At this point, the jury returned to the courtroom and Leonard Gilman made his opening statement.]

[Before the start of the trial, each side has a chance to speak to the jury about the case. The prosecution speaks first. The defense attorney may then speak or may reserve his opening statement until the start of the defense's case.]

[The opening statement gives each attorney an opportunity to outline his case by briefly summarizing what he expects to prove during the trial. An opening statement, unlike a closing argument, is generally not argumentative. It is meant more to inform than to persuade.]

Leonard Gilman

OPENING STATEMENT

Mr. Gilman: *

Ladies and gentlemen of the jury.

As you all know, this portion of the proceedings is an opening statement.

What I tell you at this point is a guide to what I feel the People can present as testimony in this case.

Evidence is what you hear from that chair, and that is all you can consider in arriving at a verdict in this case.

Now, during the long course of selecting a jury in this case, there were many times in which there was laughter in the courtroom.

I want you to remember throughout the course of this trial that on the early morning of May 8, 1970, four lives were taken.

The People have the burden of proof.

We must establish beyond a reasonable doubt that Mr. Wilbur Jackson is guilty.

In these cases, in each and every one of them, we propose to meet that burden.

---

* Leonard Gilman, a Pittsburgh native, attended Allegheny State University. He graduated from Allegheny State Law School in 1966 and went to work for the National Labor Relations Board.

As he explains it, "I worked for the Labor Board for a year and a half. We just didn't get any trial experience there. Three of us at the Board figured after the '67 riot there would be a lot of activity at the Allegheny County Prosecutor's Office. The first week I was there I was trying a sodomy case by myself, and I didn't even know what the hell sodomy was. I looked into the law books, and I said, "my God! That carries fifteen years?""

We propose to prove that in the deaths of Sandra Jackson, Todd Wilson, and Jonathan Carter, Mr. Wilbur Jackson acted wilfully, feloniously, with malice aforethought, and with premeditation, as he proceeded to shoot each of these three young people and kill them.

We propose to prove beyond a reasonable doubt that Wilbur Jackson committed second-degree murder when he shot and killed a young man named Ricky Walters.

We propose to do that by calling many, many witnesses to the stand.

I ask you to give these witnesses your closest attention, as well as any witnesses that the defense might call.

Now, we propose to call witnesses that will testify that on the early morning of May 8, 1970, a young lady named Sandra Jackson was living at 4330 Lincoln, and that address will be referred to as the Stonehead Manor, and that she and another young lady named Sally Tucker, moved in together into apartment number 3 of the Stonehead Manor.

There will be testimony that Sandra Jackson had a boy friend, a young man that she was going with, and that boy friend's name was Mr. Todd Wilson, and Mr. Todd Wilson was eighteen years old, and Mr. Todd Wilson lived in apartment number 9.

The testimony will indicate that he lived with another young man, a seventeen-year-old young man named Jonathan Carter.

There will be testimony that on the fourth day of May, 1970, some four days before these four young people met their deaths, the defendant in this case, Mr. Wilbur Jackson, and his wife Mary, came to 4330 Lincoln looking for their daughter.

There will be further testimony by the People's witnesses, and this testimony will involve what actually took place on the early morning of May 8, 1970.

The testimony will indicate that Mr. Jackson proceeded up the stairs of 4330 Lincoln, which is a two-story building, and he proceeded directly to apartment number 9; and that at that time Mr. Jackson broke the door of apartment 9 and entered into that apartment, and at that time Mr. Jackson killed four people.

Suffice it to say that Mr. Jackson, the testimony will indicate, shot all four people, including his daughter, while each and every one of them were sleeping.

Then the testimony will indicate that Mr. Jackson left the apartment, proceeded with his wife Mary, who had accompanied him, on to the Second Precinct where he indicated to the officers working at the desk that he had just murdered his daughter and her friends, and he was there to give himself up.

Now, that, ladies and gentlemen of the jury, in substance, is our case.

You will be asked at the conclusion of this case to decide whether or not Wilbur Jackson was legally sane or legally insane at the time he committed these acts.

If we have established beyond a reasonable doubt that Mr. Jackson was sane and committed these acts on May 8, 1970, I simply ask you to do your duty as jurors to this state and find him responsible for his conduct and find him guilty.

Thank you.

[The defense reserved its opening statement until the start of its case.]

[When the prosecution discovered that its opening witnesses had gone home for the day, court was adjourned.]

Tuesday 17 November

PATHOLOGISTS' TESTIMONY

[At the start of a murder trial, the prosecution customarily first introduces evidence of the death of the victims. This is generally done through the testimony of the pathologists who conducted the autopsies on the victims. In this case, three different pathologists conducted the autopsies, so the prosecution was forced to call all three as witnesses.]

[Before an expert witness can testify, he or she is examined as to qualifications—i.e., whether the expert, be it a doctor, handwriting analyst, or psychiatrist, has sufficient expertise in a specialized field to qualify him or her as an expert able to give an opinion. Frequently, a party will "stipulate" as to qualifications—i.e, agree that a witness is an expert and thus qualified to give an opinion.]

[The reader will note that all three pathologists are questioned concerning any indication of sexual activity or drug use. Defense Counsel Nelson is already revealing his own strategy, which is to attack the morals of those who lived at Stonehead Manor. This theme will be repeated throughout the trial.]

(Dr. Gilbert Corrigan, was thereupon called as a witness on behalf of the People, and after having been first duly sworn by the court clerk, testified upon his oath as follows:)

DIRECT EXAMINATION

Mr. Gilman: **Q Will you state your name, please, sir.**

A Gilbert Corrigan.

Q What is your occupation?

A I am a pathologist for Allegheny County.

Q Are you a doctor of medicine?

A   Yes, sir.

Q   **Are you licensed to practice medicine in the state of Pennsylvania, Doctor?**

A   Yes, sir.

Q   **Where did you attend medical school?**

A   Allegheny State University.

Q   **When did you graduate from Allegheny State University?**

A   1962.

* * *

Q   **What exactly is an autopsy, Doctor?**

A   That is the examination of a body after death to determine the manner and nature of the person's death.

Q   **During your career as a pathologist, about how many autopsies have you performed?**

A   I don't count. I'd say, roughly, one a day.

Q   **One a day?**

A   My specialty is autopsies.

Q   **When did you begin doing autopsies?**

A   In 1963. I qualified for forensic pathology.

Q   **What is that?**

A   That is the performance of autopsies on people who die in public deaths, people who die as the result of homicide or suicide, people who die at work, these kind of deaths, which are of importance to the public at large.

[After questioning, Nelson stipulates that Dr. Corrigan is a qualified forensic pathologist.]

Q   **Dr. Corrigan, pursuant to your duties as a pathologist at the Allegheny County Medical Examiners Office, on the eighth day of May, 1970, did you perform an autopsy on the body that was identified as that of Ricky Walters?**

A   Yes, sir.

Q   **Would you describe the apparent age, height, and weight of the body of Ricky Walters?**

A   Yes, sir.

The body was that of a well-developed, well-nourished white male; the body appeared to be the stated age of sixteen; weight was 139 pounds; height was five foot nine.

Q Now, when you examined the body externally of Ricky Walters, did you observe any indication of trauma or injury to the body?

A Yes, sir.

Q Would you tell the ladies and gentlemen of the jury what you observed?

A Well, it's, very simply stated, that Mr. Ricky Walters had two gunshot wounds of entry in his head and two gunshot wounds of exit.

The gunshot wound of entry in one instance was in the left cheek, and the other one was in the right forehead.

The wounds were characterized by having a hole with an abrasion collar, which is the mark the bullet makes as it goes through the skin, and there was no powder or tatooing or anything to indicate that the firearm was close to the skin.

Q Tatooing would indicate that the firearm was close to the skin, and there was no tatooing present as to either entrance wound; is that correct?

A That's correct, sir.

Q You indicated that one wound entered the left cheek and one wound entered the right forehead, is that correct?

A Yes.

Q Did both wounds pass through the head?

A Yes, sir.

Q Did both bullets exit the head?

A Yes, sir.

Q So you did not recover any bullets from the body of Ricky Walters, is that correct?

A No, sir, nothing was recovered.

Q Did you observe any other trauma or injury to the body besides those two gunshot wounds?

A No, sir; the body was otherwise unremarkable.

Q Did you perform an internal examination of Mr. Walters's head?

A Yes, sir.

Q Would you tell the ladies and gentlemen of the jury what your findings were as to that?

A I will just read the paragraph or so that I have that described in:

"The intact scalp is reflected to reveal diffuse subgaleal hemorrhage in the right and posterior portions of the scalp."

Which means there was hemorrhage between the bone and the scalp underneath it.

Q **What is hemorrhage?**

A When the blood leaves the vessels and comes out under the surface.

"There is complete fracturing of the right lateral posterior portions of the calvarium."

Which is the skull bone.

"Numerous bone fragments are present. Typical outshoot wounds are present—"

—on the right posterior head.

"The wound from the right forehead passes in a near horizontal position, whereas that of the left cheek passes slightly superiorly at approximately a thirty degree angle."

Q **Let's go back to that. The wound to the right forehead, you indicate, passed in a right posterior direction?**

A Yes; and went out almost the back of the head.

Q **And it went straight?**

A Yes.

Q **"—passes slightly superiorly at approximately a thirty degree angle." What does that mean?**

A It came up from his cheek and went up through his head. This was, roughly, a thirty degree angle.

Q **It traveled in an upward direction?**

A Yes.

"The cerebrospinal fluid—"

That is the spinal fluid that is in the brain.

"—is grossly bloody. The right cerebral hemisphere—"

That is the upper half of the brain.

"—is torn and lacerated by the penetrating gunshot wounds, one passing from the right forehead through the anterior and lateral portions of the cerebral hemisphere. The other wound of the left cheek entering into the cranial cavity directly through the pituitary fossa—"

Right in the center of our head where there is a little pituit gland.

"—in the basisphenoid bone and shatters and destroys the right basilar portion of cerebral hemisphere—"

The one bullet pellet destroyed the right hemisphere of the brain, and the other came up through the under half and destroyed this side of the brain.

There was massive hemorrhage of the right Willis, and this circle of Willis is the major blood supply route to the brain.

The right, middle, and posterior cerebral fossa were fractured.

That means the base of the skull was broken.

"—diffuse hemorrhage of the right cerebral hemisphere. There is destruction of the hypothalamus and right hypothalamus and thalamic areas. The remainder of the brain section is unremarkable."

Q   Did you notice anything else that was remarkable about the remainder of Mr. Walters' head?

A   No, sir.

Q   You examined the other organs of his body, is that correct?

A   Yes, sir.

Q   Based upon your experience, Dr. Corrigan, as a pathologist, based upon your findings after performing an autopsy on the body of Ricky Walters, are you able to present to the jury your opinion as to the cause of Ricky Walters's death?

A   Yes, sir.

In my opinion, Ricky Walters died of gunshot wounds of the head.

Q   Now, if Mr. Walters would have just suffered any one of these two wounds, would either one have been fatal?

A   Yes, sir; they are both very severe injuries to the brain and the head.

Q   Was a toxicology examination performed on Mr. Walters's body fluid to determine the presence of any drugs?

A   Yes, sir.

Q   What were the findings, if any, as to that?

A   Toxicology is negative for ethanol, barbiturates, carbon monoxide, and cyanide.

Q   Ethanol would be alcohol?

A   Yes, sir.

Q   And what other?

A   Barbiturates, carbon monoxide, and cyanide.

The ethanol reading is 0.01, which in our lab is negative.

Q   That is such a small amount that you term it negative?

A   That's right.

Mr. Gilman: I have no further questions of Dr. Corrigan, Your Honor.

*   *   *

[Nelson is cross-examining Dr. Corrigan.]

Q **Did you examine this young man's genitalia in an effort to determine if he had recently engaged in an act of intercourse?**

A I examined the man's genitalia. There was no evidence of anything abnormal about the man's genitalia at all.

Q **Now, what if any effort was made on your part or on the part of Dr. Weatherall, Doctor, to determine whether this young man immediately prior to his death had ingested any heroin?**

A None.

Q **Marijuana?**

A No examination was made for marijuana.

Q **Any of the so-called dangerous drugs?**

A Hallucinatory drugs or narcotic drugs, we didn't examine for that.

Q **Did you examine this young man's arms in the course of your gross examination, and particularly in the course of your external examination?**

A Yes, sir.

Q **Were there any needle tracks on his arms—**

A No, sir.

Q **—or his legs?**

A No, sir.

Q **In other words, you just made no effort at the morgue to determine whether there had been any recent ingestion of any hallucinatory or narcotic drugs?**

A It wouldn't be fair to answer you with a yes or no. We perform examinations when they are indicated. And under these circumstances, we didn't feel as though they were indicated.

Q **Did you make that judgment?**

A Yes, sir.

Q **You personally made that judgment?**

A And Dr. Weatherall made a judgment also.

Mr. Nelson: Thank you.

(Witness excused.)

* * *

(Proceedings held outside the presence and hearing of the jury.)

Mr. Gilman: Your Honor, it came to my attention that yesterday when I began my opening statement, and today I had a chance to look at Mr. Jackson, the defendant in this case.

It seems to me that as soon as Sandra Jackson's name is mentioned or the fact that Mr. Jackson is charged with killing four people is mentioned, Mr. Jackson begins to cry.

Mr. Jackson just now began to cry profusely.

I was just wondering if Mr. Jackson isn't in control of himself, perhaps we could take a recess in order for him to gain control of himself.

This isn't a trial based on tears or sympathy or anything like that.

The jury—all they have seen is Mr. Jackson's tears.

Mr. Nelson: I quite agree, Your Honor; and I think the problem can be very simply solved.

Simply order Mr. Jackson to stop crying.

Mr. Gilman: Your Honor, perhaps Mr. Jackson could take some time and gain control of himself.

The Court: We are not going to do that, Mr. Gilman. We are going to continue this trial. We have dealt with a lot more obstructous defendants than Mr. Jackson. I think I can run the courtroom.

Mr. Gilman: I am not saying the court can't run the courtroom.

The Court: We are going to continue this trial. It's running very slowly now, and I am not going to slow the trial down any more.

Mr. Gilman: All right.

The Court: Bring out the jury.

(Whereupon the jury entered the courtroom.)

[*Dr. Clara Raven* is sworn and qualified as a forensic pathologist. Mr. Gilman examines.]

Q Did you perform an external examination of the body of Sandra Jackson?

A Yes, I did.

Q Would you describe for the ladies and gentlemen of the jury Sandra Jackson's age, height, and weight at the time you performed your autopsy?

A She was a well-nourished white female, about seventeen years of age, height five foot three, weight 107 pounds.

External examination of the body showed a number of gunshot wounds of the chest.

* * *

Q I will show you People's Proposed Exhibit No. 3, held on evidence tag number 923950, and I will ask you if you can identify that object?

A   Yes. This is the bullet which I removed from the spine, and it has my initials at the base.

Q   **Now, the two bullets that entered in Miss Jackson's chest and passed through the body, did they cause any damage to any of the organs of her body?**

A   There was massive hemorrhage from all the wounds described to the chest.

> The first two also destroyed the aorta and the heart.
>
> This one passed through the lungs.
>
> And both were associated with massive hemorrhage.

Q   **What is the aorta?**

A   The largest artery—artery that carries blood from the heart through the entire system.

Q   **Did you examine the other organs of Miss Jackson's body?**

A   Yes; I examined all the organs.

Q   **Would you give your findings as to the organs that you found remarkable in some way?**

A   There were no additional injuries other than I have already described.

> There was no evidence of any hemorrhage or any tear in the vagina or the external portions of the entrance to the vagina.

Q   **From your examination, doctor, and based upon your experience as a pathologist for many, many years, are you able to present to the jury your opinion as to the cause of Sandra Jackson's death?**

A   Yes. The cause of death was multiple gunshot wounds of the chest.

*   *   *

Q   **And you found no evidence in the pelvic region of this young woman of any injury?**

A   No, sir. In the pelvic organs, no, sir.

Q   **Did you yourself do any kind of a semen test?**

A   No, sir.

Q   **Do you know whether the laboratory did?**

A   I don't believe that there was any secretion—there was no secretion there; and there was no moisture around that area to indicate that there was any moisture or any fluid.

Q   **Did you see anything in your examination of this young woman's pelvic organs that would have indicated to you that she, prior to her death, had recently engaged in an act of intercourse?**

A   I could not determine that. There was no—

Q You couldn't determine that?

A   No. There was no evidence of that.

Q Is that what you said, you could not determine that?

A   No. There was no evidence of any entry, no evidence of any injury.

Q Now, what if any toxicological tests were made upon the various fluids and organs removed by you from this woman's body and submitted to the morgue laboratory for that purpose to determine whether there had been by this young woman during her lifetime, ingestion of any narcotic or hallucinatory drugs?

A   Well, the narcotics were tested for, and they were negative. The laboratory—

Q What narcotics?

A   Basic drugs would include all opiates and derivatives.

Q Morphine and derivatives?

A   All narcotics.

Q Morphine and narcotics, is that not correct?

A   Yes, morphine; that's in the same category.

Q Those are generic drugs, are they not?

A   Yes, sir.

Q What about LSD?

A   We have not had much luck in the office of the medical examiner to have a reliable test for hallucinogens such as marijuana and LSD.

Q Well, did you try in this case?

A   It's routine for them to examine for those.

Q You don't know whether they did or not?

A   There is no record here that they did; but they usually do.

[See Figure 14 for the autopsy report on the body of Sandra Jackson.]

*   *   *

[*Dr. Taisja Tworek* is sworn and qualified as an expert pathologist. Dr. Tworek performed autopsies on the bodies of Todd Wilson and Jonathan Carter. She describes Wilson's cause of death as two gunshot wounds in the head penetrating the brain, while Carter's death resulted from one gunshot wound penetrating the brain. Dr. Tworek also discovered a laceration on Wilson's forehead, which Nelson brings out on cross-examination is consistent with Wilson being struck by the butt of a pistol. Neither body was expressly examined for signs of recent semen ejaculation or for drug use.]

Figure 14   Autopsy report on Sandra Jackson

Bakowski

SANDRA JACKSON , AKA UNKNOWN WOMAN #32   Case No. 3798-70
May 12, 1970   Autopsy No. A70-680

REPORT OF AUTOPSY

Autopsy on the body of   SANDRA JACKSON , AKA UNKNOWN WOMAN #32.
Autopsy was performed May 8, 1970, at 12:45 PM, at the Allegheny County
Morgue , Pittsburgh, Pennsylvania.

EXTERNAL DESCRIPTION

The body is that of a fairly well developed, well nourished white
female, about 17 years of age.   Height 5'3" and weight 107 pounds.

External examination of the body shows multiple gunshot wounds
of the chest, which are described as follows.

Number 1 gunshot wound of the right side of the chest, measuring
4/16" in size with a slight abrasion on the right side and this is located
1" beneath the suprasternal notch, and 1" to the right of the mid-sternum.
This wound penetrates into the chest cavity.

Number 2 is a 4/16" gunshot wound just to the left of the above
described, and is ½" left of the sternum, 1" beneath the suprasternal notch
and this wound, likewise, penetrates into the chest cavity.

The third wound is a 4/16" gunshot wound by 6/16" of the right
posterior axillary line with a large area of abrasion surrounding it and
this wound penetrates with fracture into the chest wall. This latter wound
approximates an exit wound of the left anterior chest wall, which measures
6/16" in size and is located 7½" beneath the anterior left shoulder and
3½" to the left of the mid-sternum and beneath the left nipple. This
wound is irregular and is slightly everted.

The organs are removed separately.

HEART:

The heart weighs 210 grams. The penetration of the right auricle
and the arch of the aorta has been described. There is massive
hemorrhage into the pericardial sac, as well as both chest cavities
Otherwise, the heart shows no additional abnormalities.

Figure 14   Autopsy report on Sandra Jackson (continued)

LUNGS:

> The right lung weighs 150 grams, the left 200 grams. There are
> multiple gunshot wounds of the right lung and a grazing wound of
> the medial portion of the left lung. The right lung is markedly
> engorged and has hemorrhages along the course of the bullet wounds
> described. The left lung is subcrepitant. The bronchi and
> bronchioles contain small amounts of blood.

LIVER:

> The liver weighs 1180 grams and is not unusual grossly. The
> gallbladder is distended with bile.
> The pancreas is firm.
> The adrenals are not unusual.

SPLEEN:

> The spleen weighs 150 grams and is moderately congested.

KIDNEYS:

> The kidneys together weigh 250 grams and are moderately congested.
> The gastro-intestinal tract is not unusual.

HEAD:

> The usual mastoid to mastoid incision is made, scalp retracted,
> calvarium removed. There is no evidence of any injuries or
> trauma. The brain weighs 1390 grams. Coronal sections of 1 cm.
> intervals is not unusual.

CAUSE OF DEATH:

> Multiple gunshot wounds of the chest.

GROSS DIAGNOSES:

> 1. 4/16" gunshot wound of right upper chest wall, 1" beneath
>   the suprasternal notch and 1" to the right of the mid-sternum,
>   with passage between the 1st and 2nd ribs, through right
>   auricle, rightlung and between 8th and 9th ribs, right of
>   spine, with exit 9" beneath the right posterior shoulder,
>   ¼" long.

Figure 14 Autopsy report on Sandra Jackson (continued)

2. 4/16" gunshot wound ½" to left of sternum, 1" beneath the
suprasternal notch, passage between the 1st and 2nd ribs,
through the arch of the aorta, through right lung and with
bullet fracture of 10th thoracic vertebra and the bullet
lodged in soft tissue level of 12th rib to the rightof the
spine, with marked localized hematoma.

3. 4/16" gunshot wound of right posterior axillary line, 7½"
beneath the shoulder, with fracture of the 7th rib, passage
through the right lung and with fracture of 6th rib and exit
6/16" irregular in size, 7½" beneath the anterior left
shoulder, beneath the left nipple and grazing inner portion
of left upper arm, with abrasion 3/4" x 1/2" in size.

4. Massive bilateral hemothorax.

STATUS:

Homicide.

Signed: *Clara Raven*
CLARA RAVEN, M.D.
DEPUTY MEDICAL EXAMINER

CR:ec

[Figure 15 shows the autopsy report on the body of Todd Wilson.]

CARL RICHARDSON'S TESTIMONY

(Carl Richardson was thereupon called as a witness on behalf of the People.)

Mr. Gilman: **Q Would you state your name, please, sir.**

A My name is Carl Richardson.

Q How old are you?

A Twenty-two.

Q Where were you born, Mr. Richardson?

A Poughkeepsie, New York.

Figure 15 Autopsy report on Todd Wilson

TODD WILSON , AKA JOHN DOE #243   Case No. 3800-70
May 12, 1970   Autopsy No. A70-682

<u>REPORT OF AUTOPSY</u>

Autopsy on the body of   TODD WILSON , AKA JOHN DOE #243. Autopsy
was performed May 8, 1970, at the Allegheny County Morgue, Pittsburgh, Pennsylvania.

<u>EXTERNAL EXAMINATION</u>

The body is that of a well developed, well nourished white male,
estimated age 18 years, weighing 103 pounds and measuring 5'8½" in length.
The head is normal in configuration. The hair is long and red in color.

The head exhibits two gunshot wounds of entry and one gunshot
wound of exit.

The #1 gunshot wound of entry is on the left side of the forehead
(front), being 2½" from the top of the head and 2" from the midline. The
wound exhibits an abrasion collar and measures ¼" x ¼". The pathway of
the bullet is through the left frontal bone, through the brain, crossing
the midline, passing through the skull on the right side, with bullet
recovered in the right occipital lobe of the brain. The overlying scalp
is intact. <u>The bullet is labeled with "TT".</u>

Number 2 gunshot wound is at the forehead (front) on the right
side, being ¼" from the midline and 4½" from the top of the head. The
wound measures ¼" x ¼" and exhibits an abrasion collar. The skin surrounding the wound exhibits gunpowder tattoo in diameter of 4 3/4" x 3". The
pathway of the bullet is through the frontal bone, toward the left side in
the back, in the occipital area with the exit through the occipital bone and
overlying scalp. The brain in this area (left occipital lobe) contains
two metallic fragments.

The skin of the forehead, as outlined in attached diagram,
exhibits a laceration measuring 3/4". The underlying skull is intact.
The nose, ears and oral cavity are not remarkable. There is slight
bilateral ocular hematoma present.

Figure 15 Autopsy report on Todd Wilson (continued)

The neck, chest and abdomen are not remarkable, except old surgical scar, as outlined in attached diagram. The external genitalia are those of adult male. The penis is circumcised. The extremities are symmetrical, exhibiting no sign of violence.

INTERNAL EXAMINATION:

The body is opened by the usual "Y" shaped incision. The ribs and sternum are not remarkable, exhibiting no fractures.

The organs of thorax and abdomen are normal in position and relationship. The pleural surfaces and peritoneal surfaces are smooth, exhibiting no excess fluid. The mediastinum is in t he midline. The pericardial cavity contains normal amount of clear yellow fluid.

The larynx, trachea and thyroid gland are not remarkable.

HEART:

The heart weighs 250 grams. The epicardial surface is smooth. The myocardium is firm and tan, being normal in thickness on the right and left side. The valve circumferences are within normal limits. The respective valve leaflets are not remarkable. The foramen ovale is closed. The coronary arteries are widely patent. The aorta and its main branches are normal in size and shape.

LUNGS:

The right lung weighs 250 grams, the left lung weighs 200 grams. The pleural surfaces are smooth and glistening. The cut surfaces are tan, exhibiting no areas of consolidation. The bronchial tree is not remarkable.

LIVER:

The liver weighs 1100 grams. The capsule is thin and smooth. The cut surfaces are tan. The gallbladder is not remarkable. The pancreas is not remarkable.

Figure 15 Autopsy report on Todd Wilson (continued)

SPLEEN:

> The spleen weighs 110 grams. It is not remarkable grossly.

> The right and left adrenal glands are not remarkable grossly.

KIDNEYS:

> Each kidney weighs 120 grams. The capsule strips with ease from
> the external surface of each kidney, which is pale tan and smooth.
> The renal parenchyma is not remarkable.
> The right and left ureters are not remarkable.
> The urinary bladder is not remarkable, containing clear yellow
> urine.
> The prostate gland is not remarkable.

GASTRO-INTESTINAL TRACT:

> The esophagus is not remarkable. The stomach, in the area of the
> pylorus, exhibits old surgical sutures. The lumen of the
> stomach contains semi-digested food particles. No specific odor
> is noted. Loops of small and large intestines are not remarkable.
> The appendix is surgically absent.

HEAD:

> The head, as described above, exhibits two gunshot wounds of entry
> and one gunshot wound of exit. The skull exhibits diffuse
> laceration, involving frontal, both parietal bone, occipital and
> sphenoid bone. There is subdural hemorrhage present. The brain
> weighs 1500 grams, exhibiting diffuse subarachnoid hemorrhage.
> The cut surfaces exhibit diffuse laceration and hemorrhage in-
> volving both parietal and occipital lobes. Particles of bone
> are present within the brain matter. The cerebellum exhibits
> diffuse subarachnoid hemorrhage. The pons, medulla oblongataan
> and upper spinal cervical cord are not remarkable grossly.

Figure 15 Autopsy report on Todd Wilson (continued)

CAUSE OF DEATH:

Gunshot wounds to head (2) penetrating brain.

GROSS PATHOLOGICAL DIAGNOSES:

1. Gunshot wounds to head, #1 entry on the left in front with bullet recovery on the right, in the back. Number 2 entry in front on the right, with exit on left, in the back.

2. Massive laceration of brain.

3. Fractured skull.

4. Status post operative laparotomy ? Pyloroplasty and appendectomy, old.

5. Laceration of forehead.

Signed: *Taisja Tworek*

TAISJA TWOREK, M.D.
Prosector – Pathologist

TT:ec

Q Did you attend school in Poughkeepsie, New York?

A Yes, sir, grade school.

Q Where did you attend grade school?

A Boysville of Pennsylvania.

Q What type of institution is Boysville of Pennsylvania?

A It's a Catholic boarding school; it's run by the Brothers of Holy Cross.

Q Did you graduate from Boysville of Pennsylvania School?

A Yes, sir.

Q When did you graduate from high school?

A 1966.

Q Following your graduation from high school in 1966, what did you do then, Mr. Richardson?

A I enlisted in the U.S. Army.

Q How long did you serve in the army?

A   Two years and ten months.

Q   **As part of your service in the army, did you have occasion to go to Vietnam?**

A   Yes, sir.

Q   **How long a time did you spend in Vietnam?**

A   One year and one day.

Q   **Did you get an honorable, or dishonorable, discharge from the army?**

A   I received a bad-conduct discharge.

Q   **What year did you get out of the army?**

A   1969—excuse me—1968.

Q   **Did there come a time, Mr. Richardson, when you came to the city of Pittsburgh?**

A   Yes, sir.

Q   **When was that?**

A   I came in 1969, February.

Q   **Are your parents still living in Poughkeepsie, New York?**

A   No, sir; they are both deceased.

Q   **Did there come a time, Mr. Richardson, when you undertook residence at 4330 Lincoln?**

A   Yes, sir.

Q   **Is that address located in the city of Pittsburgh?**

A   Yes, sir.

Q   **When did you begin to live at 4330 Lincoln?**

A   In February, sir.

Q   **Is that February of 1969 or February of this year, 1970?**

A   February of this year.

Q   **February of 1970?**

A   Yes, sir.

Q   **What apartment at 4330 Lincoln were you living in?**

A   Apartment 6.

Q   **Is apartment 6 of that address located on the first, or on the second, floor?**

A   On the second floor.

Q Now, at the time that you began to live at 4330 Lincoln, did you hold some title in connection with that structure?

A Yes, sir; I was assistant manager.

Q Did you have any duties as the assistant manager?

A Yes, sir; I cleaned the building.

Q Who was the manager of the building when you undertook residence there?

A Mr. Felipe Fernandez.

Q Did he live in the same apartment as you—apartment 6—or a different apartment?

A Different apartment.

[Richardson testifies that Sandra Jackson and her friend Sally Jo Tucker moved in about a month before the murder, but that Sandy moved out a day later, taking her belongings. Richardson states that Sandy and Sally Jo's apartment cost seventy dollars a month. Richardson describes Todd Wilson, Jonathan Carter, and another youth * renting apartment 9 on the second floor.]

[Richardson testifies that on 4 May Mr. and Mrs. Jackson arrived at the apartment house with the parents of Sally Jo Tucker.]

Q When you came out of your apartment, you observed Mr. Jackson speaking with Ricky Walters; is that correct?

A Yes, sir.

Q Could you hear what they were saying at that point?

A No, sir.

Q What did you do then, Mr. Richardson?

A I came down and stood on the landing on the second floor.

Q Is that the same area that they were standing in?

A Yes, sir.

Q At that point did Mr. Jackson speak to you?

A I don't recall how I entered the conversation; but somehow I entered the conversation.

Q After you had entered the conversation, did Mr. Jackson speak to you?

A I believe he was addressing both Ricky—Ricky and myself.

Q What did he say?

---

* The other unnamed youth will dramatically "reappear" at the close of the trial.

The living room of apartment 9, Stonehead Manor, on 8 May.   [Official police photo]

A   I don't recall the exact conversation.

Q   **Do you recall anything of what he said?**

A   Yes, sir.

Q   **What do you recall that he said?**

A   He said that he was a very desperate man and that he wanted Sandra back and that he would do anything, he would even go to New Castle [the Pennsylvania state prison].

Q   **Did he say anything else?**

A   Not that I recall.

Q   **How long did Mr. Jackson speak to you and Ricky Walters?**

A   About five or ten minutes.

Q   **Now, as you were walking down the second-floor landing, what happened then, sir?**

A   We walked down, and we continued talking, and we went outside, and Mr. and Mrs. Tucker and Mrs. Jackson walked ahead.

The kitchen of apartment 9.   The bedroom is through the beads underneath the "Express" sign.   The back of the door into the outside hall has a "No Parking Friday" sign.   (See map in Figure 19.)   [Official police photo]

At that point Mr. Jackson offered me fifty dollars if I would call him and inform him when Sandra arrived at Stonehead.

*   *   *

[Richardson testifies that on May 8 he and Felipe Fernandez went out to eat at approximately one-thirty A.M.   Upon returning, they found the apartment swarming with police.   Richardson went to police headquarters to make a statement and to the morgue to identify the bodies.]

*   *   *

Q During your lifetime, Mr. Richardson, have you ever been convicted of any crime?

A Yes, sir.

Q Would you tell the ladies and gentlemen of the jury what those are?

A I was convicted of forgery, fraud, grand larceny, and conspiracy against the government.

Q When was that?

The bedroom. The kitchen is through the beaded curtain at right. [Official police photo]

A   1969.

Q   1969?

A   Yes, sir.

Q   Anything else, sir?

A   Yes, sir.

Q   Would you tell the jury?

A   Possession of an unregistered firearm and possession of stolen property under one hundred dollars.

Q   When were those convictions?

A   1970.

*   *   *

[Mr. Nelson is cross-examining Richardson.]

Q   And you are the recipient of a bad-conduct discharge?

A   Yes, sir.

Q **Is that as a result of all these charges that you have described for us as having been promulgated against you and concerning which you were found guilty back in 1968?**

A For the fraud, forgery, grand larceny, and conspiracy.

Q **Would you speak a little slower, please.**

A Fraud, forgery, grand larceny, and conspiracy.

Q **Forgery—**

A Right.

Q **—fraud—**

A Right.

Q **—grand larceny—**

A Yes; and conspiracy against the government is why I received the bad discharge.

* * *

Q **Did you do any time in the stockade as a result of these charges?**

A I did, I believe it was approximately thirty days in the stockade—army stockade in Okinawa. The remainder of the nine months I did in Leavenworth—Fort Leavenworth, Kansas.

Q **As an army prisoner, is that right?**

A Yes, sir.

Q **Now, you say, some time this year—last part of last year—you were probably pleaded guilty to what?**

A Possession of an unregistered firearm.

Q **Was there something about possession of stolen property, too?**

A Yes, sir; that was another case.

* * *

Q **With whom, if anyone, do you live there? [at Stonehead Manor]**

A I live with my wife.

Q **When did you marry?**

A It's a common-law marriage.

Q **Did you live with this lady for any period of time at all at the Stonehead Manor?**

A Yes, sir.

Q **What is her name, please?**

A Nancy.

Q What is her last name?

A McTighe.

Q Does she use that name now?

A No, sir.

Q Does she hold herself out to the public as being Nancy Richardson?

A Yes, sir.

* * *

Q How did you support yourself?

A My mother died while I was in Leavenworth, and I received a small insurance benefit from it.

Q So I gather then from your answer, you didn't undertake any kind of gainful employment?

A No, sir.

Q And you lived out in Carnegie Heights until some time between the end of October '69 and whatever date it was in February that you moved into the Stonehead Manor, you lived out there in Carnegie Heights?

A No, sir; I lived in Castle Shannon for about a month after I got out, until November.

Q Did you live in some kind of communal surroundings in Castle Shannon?

A No, sir; I lived in a boarding house.

Q Well, then you moved from there to 4330 Lincoln?

A Yes, sir.

Q When in February did you move into 4330 Lincoln?

A I don't recall the exact date.

Q How did you come to find out about the availability of an apartment at 4330 Lincoln?

A Two friends of mine from Royal Oak moved in 4330 Lincoln.

Q Who were they?

A They were two girls; one is a witness.

Q What is her name?

A Allison Fletcher.

Q And the other girl's name?

A I believe it was Denise McLain.

Q **You believe that?**

A Yes, sir. I don't recall exactly what her name was.

Q **So they introduced you to—did you go down there to visit them?**

A Yes, sir.

Q **Did you ever have occasion, let us say, to stay there overnight prior to your moving in?**

A Yes, sir; I spent the night there several times.

Q **I assume that you came to know some of the other people that lived there as a result of probably being introduced to them by one or the other of these two girl friends of yours?**

A Well, sir, they weren't—they were friends; they weren't girl friends.

Q **Well, they were girls, weren't they?**

A Yes, sir.

Q **I didn't mean to suggest anything. Forgive me if I gave you that impression. Did you get to meet, as an example, Felipe Fernandez?**

A Yes, sir.

Q **Was he when you met him the caretaker of this establishment?**

A Yes, sir.

Q **He had been endowed with that position and authority by whomever owned the building?**

A Yes, sir.

Q **As the caretaker of the building, would it be fair to characterize Mr. Fernandez, as well as being kind of chief-among-equals in this communal society down there—**

Mr. Gilman: I am going to object to that, Your Honor. There has been no testimony at all—

Mr. Nelson: We have had all kinds of testimony about who lived where and when, and everywhere else in this place. I think I am entitled to develop what kind of life went on down there, if Your Honor please.

Mr. Gilman: I am interested in making a legal objection, if Your Honor please.

There has been no testimony this is a communal life style, and I think Mr. Nelson is characterizing the testimony.

The Court: Yes. I think you can just develop who is in every room and how they moved around and who lived there. The jury can draw their own conclusion.

Mr. Nelson: Very well. I'm sorry.

* * *

Q   **All right, now this place had come to be dubbed Stonehead Manor some time before you moved into it; is that right?**

A   Yes, sir.

Q   **As a matter of fact, that name was printed or lettered on a sign, and the sign was hung on the front porch prominently displayed; was it not?**

A   Yes, sir.

Q   **Well, among your age group, Mr. Richardson, does the term _stoned_ or _to be stoned_ have some particular significance?**

A   Yes, sir.

Q   **What is the significance of that term.**

A   It means to be high.

Q   **On what.**

A   Whatever you prefer, sir.

Q   **The galaxy of choice there running all the way from heroin to aspirin and Coca-Cola, is that right, including alcohol and all the various generic dangerous drugs?**

A   Well, sir, if you consider alcohol and wines and liquors dangerous drugs; because being high also includes them, sir.

Q   **But it's a term that is specifically used ordinarily among your peer group to refer to people who are high as a result of ingestion of either a narcotic drug or a dangerous drug?**

A   Yes, sir.

Q   **And a stonehead is someone who ordinarily stays in that condition as long as he can ordinarily afford to do so, is that right?**

A   No, sir. A head is for a good person. Stonehead, on some occasions, refers to a person that is exceptionally good.

[Richardson wants to read a statement he made at a preliminary hearing, and Judge Gillis explains to the jury what a preliminary hearing is.]

(Proceedings held outside the presence and hearing of the jury.)

Mr. Nelson: Rather, regrettably, Your Honor, I feel I am in a position where I have to move for a mistrial.

I think that by telling the jury that an examination is a filtering process, that the measure of proof is somewhat less sophisticated than required here, and that this man Wilbur Jackson was bound over for trial; you, in effect, told them there has already been a finding by someone sitting in a magisterial capacity here that he is guilty.

Regardless what you tell them about this regarding that, they are still going to think in these terms.

You have left me with no alternative in this matter.

[The court denies the motion and adjourns until Thursday.]

Wednesday 18 November

[There is no court because Judge Gillis had a commitment to a local high school to give a talk, and in the afternoon he had his monthly Judge's Meeting.]

Thursday 19 November

[Carl Richardson is still being cross-examined by Mr. Nelson.]

Q Now, have you at any time during that period of your life beginning, let's say, the first of May, 1970, self-administered any narcotic drugs?

A Yes, sir.

Q What drugs?

A Marijuana and amphetamines.

Q During May of 1970, if you know, did any of the other inhabitants of 4330 Lincoln habitually use or ingest drugs?

A No, sir.

* * *

[Nelson asks questions concerning the various people who lived in Stonehead Manor, apparently emphasizing the sharing of apartments.]

Q Did you not neglect to mention, in this list of people, Mary Lynch?

A Yes, sir; but she wasn't living there.

Q When she was there, where was she?

A She was usually with Miss Rivers.

Q And Miss Rivers was living in apartment zero with Mr. Fernandez?

A Yes, sir.

Q You also forgot to mention a Mary Lee Von Allstein.

A I believe she was living with Allison Fletcher.

Q Who was living with a Garfield Powers, is that right?

A Yes, sir, in apartment 1.

Q What about Howard Ives?

A I believe he was one of Miss Tucker's guests.

Q One of Miss Tucker's guests?

A   Yes, sir; there was another man there, but I don't recall his name.

Q   Who is Georgia Webster?

A   She was a guest of Miss Wendell in apartment number 10.

Q   Virginia Wendell in apartment 10 is a girl, is that right?

A   Yes, sir.

Q   Now, in May of 1970, was there not a kind of house rule that was in practice and in effect in the Stonehead Manor that any girl down there had to sleep with any boy who also lived there?

A   No.

*   *   *

[The witness is finally excused.]

STONEHEAD MANOR WITNESSES

[*Janet Rivers*, nineteen, testifies that she had been living with Felipe Fernandez in apartment zero, but that she is now back in high school and separated from Felipe. She states that she heard Wilbur Jackson "tell Felipe that he would get Sandy back dead or alive" and that she had "heard" that Sandy was "dating" Todd Wilson, although she had seen them together only once.]

[Janet Rivers says that at 2:00 A.M. on May eighth she was lying on a couch in apartment zero when she heard noises sounding like firecrackers. She got up and saw Wilbur Jackson leaving Todd Wilson's apartment.]

Q   Now, what happened then, Janet?

A   Then he come back out, and he stopped; and he looked at us, and he goes, "Where's Sally?" and I said I didn't know, and he says—he says—"Well, you better find her, or else I'll kill you all."

Q   Now, at this time could you still see whether or not Mr. Jackson had this gun?

A   Yes.

Q   And did he have the gun at that time?

A   Yes.

Q   How was he holding the gun at that time?

A   He had it pointed in front of him.

Q   Was it pointed at anyone when he came out of the apartment?

A   Yes; it was pointed toward Mary and I.

[She further testifies that she saw Jackson searching all over for Sally Jo Tucker, and then she ran outside and got a bus driver to call the police.]

[On cross-examination, Nelson questions her as to why she lived with Felipe and why she doesn't know why she lived with Felipe. Nelson gets because-I-wanted-to answers. Nelson discovers she concealed her whereabouts from her parents, that she never used drugs, and that she never was married.]

[*Mary Ann Lynch Martin*, eighteen, testifies next. She has recently married the man she had lived with in Stonehead Manor. A baby was born three weeks before the wedding. Her parents are divorced and Janet Rivers now lives with Mary Ann and her new husband.]

[On 8 May she, too, thought she heard firecrackers. When she got up and looked across the hall to apartment 9, she saw Wilbur Jackson reload one of his guns and then move out of sight. She heard him say, "Wake up, boy, wake up," and then she heard shots. She also heard Mrs. Jackson shouting, "He shot my baby! He shot my baby!" When confronted by Wilbur Jackson, Mary told him she didn't know where Sally Jo was. Mrs. Jackson's shouts changed to "He's killed my baby!"]

[On cross-examination, Nelson finds that her only job was at the Quickee Donut Shop and that she has been living on income tax refunds.]

Q **I mean, was he [Jackson] composed?**

A He seemed to be.

Q **He did?**

A He did.

Q **Were there any tears in his eyes, for example?**

A I don't believe there were.

Q **Was his face flushed, or was it pale?**

A I couldn't say.

Q **Were his motions and his movements kind of jerky and rapid, or were they slow and deliberate?**

A They were quick and very sure.

Q **Quick and sure?**

A Yes.

Q **And his speech, how did he enunciate when he said what you said he said to you?**

A He more or less—he said it clearly; but it was quickly spoken.

Q **Did he use a conversational tone?**

A No.

Q Did he shout?

A No.

[She tells Nelson she hasn't used narcotics or hallucinogenic drugs. Nelson points out that in the statement she gave the police shortly after the shootings, she didn't mention seeing Jackson reload. Nelson suggests she is lying; Mary Ann Lynch Martin says she just didn't want to go into detail in that statement.]

[*Allison Fletcher*, eighteen, and currently "looking for a job," is the next witness. She had seen Wilbur Jackson on three of the four days preceding the murder. She observed him looking in the building for Sandy, sitting in a car waiting for Sandy, and driving back and forth searching for Sandy. She heard Wilbur Jackson and another man say they wanted their daughters back dead or alive. After hearing the shots, she and four friends hid in her apartment while Wilbur Jackson tried to break down the front door, and Mrs. Jackson tried to enter through the back.]

[On cross-examination, it is brought out that Allison went to a group therapy clinic on Tuesdays, she has had a variety of jobs and residences since quitting school, and she met Sandy scrubbing walls and floors at Open City, a voluntary help center. She was asked about Garfield Powers, who was living there with her, and she allowed that there was sort of a conspiracy-of-silence to keep Wilbur Jackson from hearing of his daughter. She was asked whether Stonehead Manor was a home for runaways and if people were always "sleeping hither and thither and yon."]

Q Have you ever used narcotics or hallucinogenic drugs?

A Yes.

Q What?

A Acid.

Q Acid. What is acid?

A It's a hallucinatory drug.

Q What is it otherwise known as?

A LSD.

Q Pardon me.

A LSD.

Q Were you under the influence of this drug on the night of May 8?

A No, I wasn't.

Q How often have you used it?

A Not very often.

Q Do you still use it?

A No, I don't.

Q When was the last time you used it?

A Last spring.

Q When last spring?

A I don't know.

Q Did you use it fairly frequently last spring?

A No.

Q From whom did you get it.

A Friends.

Q In Stonehead Manor?

A No.

Q If you know, and only if you know as a matter of your own knowledge, did anyone else who in May of 1970 lived in Stonehead Manor use either a narcotic or hallucinogenic drug?

A No one, as far as I know, used a narcotic.

Q Marijuana?

A Yes.

Q And a hallucinogenic drug?

A Yes.

Q Who were they? Name them for us.

A Ricky Walters, Dennis Pemmitt, Mary Lee Von Allstein.

Q What about Carl Richardson?

A Yes.

Q Yes, he used what?

A Used hallucinogenic drugs.

Q LSD?

A Yes.

Q What about Felipe Fernandez?

A As far as I know, no.

Q How about Sandra Jackson?

A No, I don't know.

Q No, she didn't; or, no, you don't know?

A   I don't know.

* * *

Q   **Was Ricky Walters what I suppose you would call 'a real acidhead'?**

A   No.

Q   **Was he on the stuff most of the time?**

A   Once in a while.

Q   **Give me the name and address, if you can, of one friend from whom you have obtained LSD in the last eight months.**

Mr. Gilman: Your Honor, she has indicated she hasn't had any LSD in the last eight months.

Mr. Nelson: All right, ten months; since January 1, 1970.

Mr. Gilman: Your Honor, I have to object to that. I don't think it's relevant or material.

The Court: I will sustain the objection. I don't think it's material.

Friday 20 November

[The next witness is *Georgia Webster*, nineteen, whose parents were divorced when she was three. On 8 May she was visiting with Sally Jo Tucker and two men in the living room of apartment 3. Mr. and Mrs. Eldrin Johnson were in the bedroom. The four in the living room were drinking Boone's Farm wine when Georgia thought she heard firecrackers. She hid in the apartment's bathroom and saw Wilbur Jackson through a crack in the door. Later she fled outside and hid under the porch.]

[Cross-examination reveals that Georgia was in apartment 9 several hours before the murders. She didn't see any drug use, nor did Sandy or the boys there drink any Boone's Farm wine. She describes Wilbur Jackson's movements as poised and his appearance as only a little disheveled.]

[Figure 16 shows a Recorder's Court subpoena used to subpoena several of the witnesses for the Jackson case.]

SALLY JO TUCKER'S TESTIMONY

[*Sally Jo Tucker*, eighteen, testifies next. She was Sandy's childhood friend and had briefly shared an apartment with her.]

Q   **Prior to the early morning of May 8, 1970, did you have occasion to see Mr. Jackson?**

A   Yes.

Q   **Do you remember when it was that you saw Mr. Jackson again?**

A   The Monday before the eighth.

Figure 16 Recorder's Court subpoena

SUBPOENA—RECORDER'S COURT	MURDER	FILE NO.	70 03317
			70 03318
			70 03319
			70 03042

STATE OF PENNSYLVANIA ⎫
CITY OF PITTSBURGH ⎬ S.S.
COUNTY OF ALLEGHENY ⎭

PEOPLE OF THE STATE OF PENNSYLVANIA
vs.

(Seal)

TO: _____

SALLY JO TUCKER	4330 Lincoln	Apt. #3
ALLISON FLETCHER	4330 Lincoln	" #1
SARAH JOHNSON	4330 Lincoln	" #3
ELDRIN JOHNSON	4330 Lincoln	" #3
MARY LEE VON ALLSTEIN	4330 Lincoln	Apt. #1

GREETINGS:

You are hereby commanded that, laying aside all and singular your business and excuses, you be and appear before the RECORD-ER'S COURT OF THE CITY OF PITTSBURGH, in the Court Room of the Hon. JOSEPH A. GILLIS Presiding Judge of said Court, in the Frank Murphy Hall of Justice, corner of St. Antoine and Clinton Streets, in the City of Pitts-burgh on Monday, the 9th day of November, 19 70, at 9:00 o'clock A.M., Standard Time, then and there to give evidence on the part of the People in a case to be tried between the People of the State of Pennsylvania, Plaintiff, and WILBUR CHESTER JACKSON, Defendant.

Hereof, fail not, on pain of the penalty that will fall thereon.

WITNESS, the HON. ROBERT E. DEMASCIO Presiding Judge of the Recorder's Court of the City of Pittsburgh, on the 4th day of November, 19 70.

kb

E. BURKE MONTGOMERY, Clerk

By: *Catherine Rachunok*
Deputy Clerk

Officer in Charge: IRVIN BARANSKI

Precinct or Bureau: HOMICIDE

STATE OF PENNSYLVANIA ⎫
CITY OF PITTSBURGH ⎬ S.S.
COUNTY OF ALLEGHENY ⎭

I HEREBY CERTIFY AND RETURN, That on the 6th day of November, A.D. 19 70, I personally served a copy of the above Subpoena upon _____ by showing the original Subpoena with the Seal of the Court thereon, and upon said *Persons* by leaving a copy of the above Subpoena at his place of residence _____

Robert Wilson
D/Sgt.   METROPOLITAN POLICE

Nov. 9, 1970   Precinct No. Homicide   Badge No. DS646

Q **What time of the day was it that you saw Mr. Jackson?**

A It was about ten o'clock in the morning, at work.

Q **Was that at the Lerner [Dress] Shop where you work?**

A Yes.

Q **Did you see him inside the Lerner Shop, or outside?**

A Inside.

Q Was he by himself, or was he with someone else?

A He was by himself the first time.

Q Did you have a conversation with him at that time?

A Yes.

Q Do you remember what he said to you, and what you said to him?

A Yes.

Q Would you tell the ladies and gentlemen of the jury what that was?

A He said, that he came to get—to find out where his daughter was.

I told him I don't know, that she was probably at school.

He said that he wanted his daughter back, and he wanted her back right away because he worried about her.

And he says that—he told him about my parents worrying about me and my parents wanting me back.

Q Do you want to take a minute? Do you want a glass of water?

A No.

Q All right. So he told you that your parents also were worried about you, and they wanted you back; is that correct?

A Yes.

Q Did he say anything else to you that you can recall?

A He told me that if I didn't tell him where his daughter was, when he found her—(*witness crying*)—when he found her—if I didn't tell him, and he found her—I'd never see her again or talk to her again.

He said he would take her home, he would chain her upstairs in her room to a radiator, and he would keep her there until he got a plane ticket for down south and send her to the House of Rest.

And he said, "Do you know what the House of Rest is?"

And I said, "No, I don't."

He says, "It's a place where you have to wear nylons and heels and a dress, and you can never see anybody ever again or never even talk to anybody ever again."

And he said he was going to get his daughter back one way or the other, dead or alive.

He said he would get her back if it meant taking his own life, that he would rather see her dead than living with the hippies.

Q Did you tell Mr. Jackson where Sandy was?

A No, I didn't.

* * *

[Wilbur Jackson later returned to the Lerner Dress Shop and spoke again with Sally.]

Q   Do you remember what the nature of this conversation was?

A   Mr. Jackson had a piece of paper, and on it it said 4330 Lincoln [the address of Stonehead Manor], big green house on the right or on the left. It had, I think Eldrin's name and then dash and then said nigger boy. It had Anne's name, it had Jonathan's name, Felipe's name, and I don't remember what else it had on it; but he put it in my face and says, "Do you know what this is?"

   I didn't know what to say. He says, "Well, do you know any of these people; I know who you live with, you live with that nigger boy and his wife." [Eldrin and Anna Johnson]

   And I imagine he got the information from Sandy's sister.

Q   Now, did Mr. Jackson say anything else to you at that time besides showing you this piece of paper and indicating what you have already said he said?

A   Yes.

Q   What did he say?

A   He says, "Young lady, you costed me a day's work. I told you to tell me where my daughter was, and you didn't tell me; and you costed me a day's work. I'm going to get Sandy back one way or the other, even if it means I have to go away to prison or take my own life. I'm going to pay five hundred dollars."

   But I didn't know what he meant by that.

Q   He said, "I'm going to pay you five hundred dollars"?

A   No; "I'm going to pay five hundred dollars." I didn't know what he meant by that.

Q   Do you recall anything else that Mr. Jackson said during this conversation?

A   No.

Q   How long did this conversation last, Sally?

A   About fifteen or twenty minutes.

Q   Did Mrs. Jackson speak to you during this conversation?

A   Yes.

Q   Was Mr. Jackson present when Mrs. Jackson spoke to you?

A   Yes.

Q   What did Mrs. Jackson say to you?

A   Mr. Jackson handed the paper to Mrs. Jackson, and she says, "Miss Tucker, all I want is my daughter back."

[Sally Jo's further testimony shows that at about 1:00 A.M. on May 8 she went up to apartment 9 and borrowed some air freshener from Sandy. A short time later she was hiding in her bathroom; she was hearing Wilbur Jackson screaming, "Where's Sally! I want to kill her!" She admitted that she was once arrested for being drunk on wine at a pop festival, and as a result paid a five dollar fine after two nights in jail.]

[Cross-examination was conducted by Mr. Tracy. He brought out that Sally Jo didn't discuss moving away from home with her mother, that she quit school two months before graduation, and that she knew what "stoned" meant but that "Stonehead Manor" had no significance.]

[Sally Jo tells of visiting Sandy in apartment 9 the evening of the murders.]

A   I was up there for about an hour. Then she [Sandy] said her parents had—her mother had come to work and tried to make her go home, and Todd and Ricky had picked her up from work; and Sandy said her mother got on top of their car—Todd's car—and started screaming, "Help! Help!" and one of them went and called the police, and the police came and said, "Ma'am, you will have to get off the car because your daughter is of legal age to leave home because she is able to support herself," and he says that, "You will have to leave them alone."

Q   **Who told you all this?**

A   Sandy. And she says her mother followed her halfway, but they lost her on the expressway.

[Tracy notes that Sally Jo made no mention of Jackson's threat to chain Sandy to a radiator or to send her to a House of Rest in the statement she gave police shortly after the shootings. Sally Jo says that Mrs. Jackson called her mother and blamed Sally Jo for Sandy's death.]

Q   **Now, you went to apartment number 9 at approximately 1:00 A.M. to borrow some air freshener?**

A   Yes.

Q   **And at that time I think you testified that you found Mr. Todd Wilson in bed, is that right?**

A   Yes.

Q   **And you found Mr. Jonathan Carter in bed?**

A   Yes.

Q   **And you found Sandra Jackson in the bathroom?**

A   Yes.

Q   **Did you think that was unusual?**

A No.

Q **Where did you think Sandra Jackson was going to sleep that night?**

A Upstairs.

Q **Upstairs where?**

A In 9.

Q **With either Mr. Wilson or Mr. Carter, is that right?**

A Yes—not with Jonathan, though.

Q **Really, then, you thought she was going to sleep with Mr. Wilson?**

A Yes.

Q **Did you consider that unusual?**

A No.

* * *

Q **Have you ever used narcotics?**

A Yes.

Q **What type?**

A Last summer I used them once.

Q **All right. What type?**

A Mescaline.

Q **Is that an up, or is that a down?**

A I don't know.

Q **Have you ever used marijuana?**

A Yes.

Q **Heroin?**

A No.

Q **LSD or any other kind of hallucinogenic drug?**

A No.

Q **Were you using drugs on this night?**

A No.

Q **Did Sandra Jackson use drugs, to your knowledge, and only if you know?**

A No.

Q **You don't know, to your knowledge?**

A Once last summer.

Q **Well, when last summer?**

A Not the past summer, but the summer before.

Q **'69; but once?**

A Yes.

Q **Do you know a Mr. Tom Ricke?**

A Yes.

Q **What function do you know him?**

A He's with the *Pittsburgh Daily Herald.*

Q **Did you ever have an interview, Sally, conducted by him?**

A I talked to him.

[The jury is excused, and Sally is questioned about information she did or did not give Tom Ricke for an article in the *Pittsburgh Daily Herald* that concerned drug use by the inhabitants of apartment 9. The jury returns.]

Q **You knew Sandra quite well—didn't you Sally?**

A Yes.

Q **You knew her habits quite well?**

A Yes.

Q **She was in college?**

A Yes.

Q **Was Sandra a churchgoer?**

A Yes.

Q **Did you know—to your knowledge, when is the first time that Sandra Jackson used marijuana?**

A Not this summer, but the past summer.

Q **I see. So that would be the summer of 1969.**

    Do you know—and just if you know, to your knowledge—if Sandra Jackson kept marijuana in her home?

A I know one time she had a little bit. Just a little tiny bit.

Q **Okay.**

A She had it in a jar or something; a vase.

Q **All right. Do you know—and I really only—if it is your own particular knowledge—whether Sandra kept hashish in her home?**

A No.

The Court: No you don't know, or no she didn't?

The Witness:	I don't—I don't know if she did.
Mr. Tracy:	**You don't know. Would you have ever made a statement to someone that she did?**

A   I don't remember if I told anyone.

Q   Can you deny you made a statement to someone she did?

A   I can't deny it.

Q   Okay. Do you recall a Sunday in 1969 where you and Sandra visited Tartar Field?

A   Yes.

Q   What was at Tartar Field on this Sunday?

A   It was bands.

Q   Pardon?

A   Group bands.

Q   Well was it like a rock or pop festival?

A   It was a free concert.

Q   It was "a freak"?

A   Free.

Q   Oh, a free. Excuse me.

   Did you ingest some hallucinogenic—

A   Yes.

Q   —drugs on this particular day?

A   Yes.

Q   How much?

A   It was one hit, and then one tablet, and then a half of another one,

Q   And did Sandra ingest some hallucinogenic drugs on this day?

A   One; one tablet.

Q   Okay. And what effect did that have upon you?

A   Well, it made me sick.

Q   It made you sick. Would you say you got high?

A   I got sick.

Q   But before you got sick, did you get high?

A   No.

Q   It was a bad trip?

A Yes.

Q **Okay. How did it affect Sandra?**

A I don't remember.

Q **You don't remember. What effect did it have on you when you got sick?**

A Well, I don't remember; I was just—I was sick; and I was like mad.

Q **Mad. Screaming, yelling?**

A Yes.

Q **Clawing, grabbing?**

A Yes.

Q **All right. Okay. Did you go to Sandra Jackson's home after that?**

A Yes; she took me home.

Q **She took you home?**

A To her house.

Q **All right. And what happened?**

A I went to the hospital.

Q **Right. And when you were delivered to the hospital, were you delivered in a straitjacket?**

A Yes.

Q **Okay. And how long were you in the hospital?**

A Two days.

Q **And what did—what happened to Sandra Jackson; did she get sick?**

A No.

Saturday 21 November

[*Mary Lee Von Allstein*, twenty-two, parents divorced, high-school dropout, lived with Allison Fletcher. In describing Mary Lee, Sergeant Baranski, marvels, "What a brain!" She describes hearing shots on 8 May, then hearing Mrs. Jackson scream, "He shot my baby! He killed my baby!" She heard Wilbur Jackson knocking on her door, hollering, "Show me where Sally is!" Later she went up to apartment 9 and saw Ricky Walters's body. She had stayed on at Stonehead Manor until October, but is now living with her mother due to a "bad financial situation." She had once been convicted of heroin possession, had a $75–$150-a-day habit, and had resorted to prostitution to pay for it. However, after moving to Stonehead Manor, she didn't use heroin.]

[Cross-examination was conducted by Mr. Carney. He brought out that she also had had six accosting and soliciting convictions. She had lived with various boy friends and had gotten pregnant. She admitted using marijuana at Stonehead Manor, but denied telling Tom Ricke of the *Daily Herald* that Ricky Walters had procured drugs. She said she had recently "babysat" for one Frank Laperriere after his wife had gone to prison. Carney attempted to show that she was paid in drugs for her services, but the court would not allow this line of questioning.]

[*Eldrin Johnson*, twenty-one, spent one year at nearby Andrew Carnegie Community College, where he met his wife. Jackson had described him as "nigger boy" on the piece of paper he had shown to Sally Jo Tucker. He enlisted in the United States Army two months after the killings. On 8 May he was sleeping with his wife in the bedroom of apartment 3 (with four people in the living room, drinking Boone's Farm). He describes waking up at 2:00 A.M. with a pistol and a flashlight in his face. Wilbur Jackson, panting, asked him where Sally was. He said he didn't know. The Monday before the murders, he discovered in his apartment Mr. and Mrs. Jackson looking for evidence of Sandy's presence. He admits calling the Jacksons three times from pay phones and telling them where Sandy was. Twice he met with Wilbur Jackson several blocks away from Stonehead Manor, and Jackson paid him twenty dollars. Several hours before the killings, he called the Jackson home and discussed the presence of weapons with Mrs. Jackson. He had been on probation for possession of a stolen credit card and for possession of a stolen vehicle.]

[On cross-examination Nelson discovers that, after the deaths, Johnson took some of Sandy's possessions to Mrs. Jackson, but isn't sure whether he received twenty dollars for them.]

[*Sarah Anne Johnson*, twenty-one, was also awaken at 2:00 A.M. She saw Ricky Walters's body and hid in apartment 1 while Wilbur Jackson tried to get in. She knew nothing of her husband's calls and visits to Wilbur Jackson.]

Monday 23 November

[*Stephen Willard*, describes his visiting of friends at Stonehead Manor. He heard shots, and then Wilbur Jackson was pushing against the door of the room he was in. Jackson fired a shot through the door and came in looking for Sally. On cross-examination, Willard reveals that the last school he attended was Mellon Junior High, and that he doesn't know his parents' address.]

[*Arthur Bohling*'s wife is Mrs. Jackson's sister. He identified Sandy's body at the morgue. On cross-examination he characterizes Wilbur and Sandy Jackson's relationship "as a loving parent to a loving child." He describes Wilbur Jackson as known to have a high reputation for truth and veracity as well as being known as a law-abiding citizen.]

[*Caroline Van Deerlin* is Mrs. Jackson's niece. She, too, identified Sandy's body at the morgue. She says that Sandy got along well with her father, and that Wilbur Jackson is very truthful and a very fine person, and that everyone likes him very well.]

POLICE WITNESSES

[*Richard Weiler*, police officer, got a radio call at 2:28 A.M. on 8 May. His was the first car on the scene.]

[Figure 17 shows Patrolman Weiler's official report.]

[*Thomas Donnelly*, Weiler's partner, describes the scene.]

A   As I recall, we didn't speak to anybody; but we were directed to an apartment in the upstairs.

Q   **Would you tell the ladies and gentlemen of the jury what you observed when you entered apartment 9.**

A   As we entered the apartment, we walked into the kitchen area—it was the immediate room you entered—and I walked through the kitchen to the right into the living room, where I observed a white male, approximately twenty-four years old, lying face up on the davenport. He was covered partially with a blanket, and there was blood gushing from his mouth.

Q   **Did he appeared to you to be deceased?**

A   Yes, he did.

Q   **How was he dressed, if you can remember, Patrolman?**

A   We pulled back the blanket. He was not clothed, although he had a pair of underwear that were pulled down approximately around his ankles; other than that, he was not clothed.

[*Michael Kessler*, another police officer, testifies.]

Q   **Were you the first officer in the bedroom, as far as you know?**

A   I don't recall.

Q   **When you arrived at the bedroom, did you observe where this young Negro male was.**

A   I did.

Q   **Where was he?**

A   He was in a bed, lying face up.

Q   **Did he appear to be deceased to you?**

A   Yes.

Q   **How could you tell that?**

Figure 17 Patrolman Weiler's report

PITTSBURGH POLICE DEPARTMENT
Detective Division
HOMICIDE BUREAU

Date ___5-8-70___

TO:

SUBJECT: REQUEST FOR INFORMATION

    Please forward to the Homicide Bureau, at the earliest possible date, a resume listing events in the order of their occurrence, of the individual action taken by you at the scene of:

___FATAL SHOOTING   UNK 66, 67, & 32.___

which occurred at: ___4330 LINCOLN APT. #9___

on: ___5-8-70___ , at ___2:20___ (A.M.) P.M.

    Also please include a complete summary of your conversation with the defendant and/or witnesses. The return shall be written in the first person, i.e. "I saw", "I talked to", etc. The signature must be in your own handwriting. This information is necessary for the proper preparation and presentation of the case in Court.

Attention: _____
    (Officers in Charge of the Case)

Homicide File # _____

DELORE RICARD
Detective Inspector
Homicide Bureau

DETAILS: *Assisted Sct 2-11 & 2-13 who received R.R. approx 2²⁵ AM 5-8-70 "4330 Lincoln A Shooting." Partner Thomas Donnelly #858 and myself were the first car to arrive at scene. We were met at front door of residence by unk WF who opened up same. As we entered Bldg Georgia Webster 18/NF 10418 Mack #1 & Allison Fletcher 18/WF 4332 Lincoln #1 were sitting on stairway and directed us to upstairs Apt #9 where a shooting had occurred. Grls stated man was lying on couch & was dead. I entered Apt #9, Partner behind, front door opened & thru kitchen. I then saw the feet of a WM UNK #66 on couch in living Rm. Saw WM UNK #66 lying face up with blood gushing from his mouth. All UNK #66 had on was pr. of*

Richard Weiler
Signature

If Necessary, please use reverse side as indicated.

Figure 17 Patrolman Weiler's report (continued)

Officer's Name: RICHARD WEILER

Partner's Name: THOMAS DONNELLY

Assignment: 2-10

DETAILS: (Continued)

WHITE JOCKEY SHORTS & GREY BLANKET OVER THE BODY WITH FEET, HEAD AND NECK SHOWING. I THEN WENT TO STAIRWAY AND T/T GEORGIA WEBSTER 18 N/F 10418 MACK #1 499-8162. SHE STATED WILBUR JACKSON WM/40-50 5755 HILL WAS THERE WITH A GUN AND WAS LOOKING FOR HIS DAUGHTER SANDRA 17/WF. GEORGIA HAD FURTHER STATED SANDRA, RAN AWAY FROM HOME ON PREVIOUS SUNDAY AND HAD STAYED WITH HER AT HER RESIDENCE FOR 1 DAY. GEORGIA HAD HEARD SEVERAL SHOTS AND SAW MR. JACKSON LEAVE APT. #9 AND START COMING DOWN STAIRS. MRS. JACKSON THE WIFE OF MR. JACKSON WAS STANDING BY FRONT DOOR AND TOLD GEORGIA SHE WOULD STOP HER HUSBAND. GEORGIA SHE WOULD STOP HER HUSBAND. GEORGIA THEN RAN INTO APT. #1 AND LOCKED THE DOOR.

    AFTER TALKING TO GEORGIA I WENT BACK TO LIVING RM. OF APT. #9 AND SGT 2-11, 2-13 & 2-70 ARRIVED. AT THIS TIME UNK# 67-32 & JOHN DOE #243 WERE FOUND IN BEDROOM OF APT #9.

    I WENT BACK DOWNSTAIRS AND GOTTEN NAMES OF DETAINED POLICE WITNESSES AND MADE A PCR.

                    Richard Weiler 3466
                      Signature

A   There was no—he wasn't breathing. We felt his pulse. He didn't move at all.

Q   How was he dressed, if you can remember, Patrolman Kessler?

A   He was covered with a blanket.

Q   Do you remember how he was dressed? Was he wearing any clothes, or did you see that?

A   No, I believe he was wearing underwear.

Q   With respect to the white young man, where was he when you first observed him?

A   He was lying next to a white female.

Q   Were they in the same bed as the Negro youth or in a different bed?

A   They were in a different bed.

The body of Ricky Walters. (Position one on the map on page 146.) [Official police photo]

Q **You say he was lying next to the female, is that correct?**

A That's correct.

Q **Who was closer to the door that you entered, the young man or the young lady?**

A The young man.

Q **And the female was lying next to him, is that correct?**

A That's correct.

Q **What was his condition at the time you first observed him?**

A He was gasping for breath, appeared to be choking.

Q **Did he appear to you to have been shot?**

A Yes.

Q **How could you tell that?**

A Blood all over his face, neck.

Q **When you saw him gasping for air, what did you do with respect to him?**

A   Well, at the time we were followed up by—well, I don't know what the time lapse was; but another crew put him on their stretcher and took him to the hospital.

Q   **With respect to the young lady lying next to the young man, what was her condition at the time you observed her?**

A   She was lying face up with her feet in like a crouched position.

Q   **Was she on her back or on her stomach?**

A   She was on her back.

Q   **Did she also appear to have been shot?**

A   Yes, sir.

Q   **Did you disturb any of the property or the bodies in apartment 9?**

A   No.

Q   **How was the young white man dressed?**

A   I don't recall.

Q   **How was the young lady dressed?**

A   She was naked.

Q   **Was she covered by any blanket or anything at the time you observed her?**

A   I believe there was a blanket partially on her.

Q   **What about the young man lying next to her, was he covered at all by that same blanket or a different blanket?**

A   I don't recall.

[On cross-examination Todd Wilson's and Sandy Jackson's nudity is emphasized. Patrolman Kessler also testifies that Jonathan Carter was wearing a white glove with the fingers cut out.]

[See Figure 18 for Patrolman Kessler's report.]

[*Geren Waters*, nineteen, currently an exercise girl at Toledo Raceway, testifies next. Sergeant Baranski describes Geren as "beautiful." She describes watching television in apartment 9 the evening preceding the murders. She left at 11:30 P.M. and wasn't offered either dope or drink.]

[*Lester Scottie*, police officer, also describes the death scene.]

[*Lyle Thayer*, detective-sergeant at homicide, relates finding slugs and shell casings in apartment 9. He repeats that Sandra Jackson was nude and says that although he has investigated hundreds of murders, Jonathan Carter is the first victim he has seen wearing a white dress glove with the fingers cut off. (Nelson had been hoping that the fingerless white glove might be some sort of a cult-recognition symbol. However, Carter had had a skin problem on the back of his hand.

Figure 18 Patrolman Kessler's report

REPORT ON		ASSIGNED TO		M.O. FORM PREPARED?	COMPLAINT NO.

REPORT ON: FaTal ShooTing(s)   ASSIGNED TO: M.O. FORM PREPARED? ☐ YES ☐ NO   COMPLAINT NO.

PLACE OF OCCURRENCE ☐ CHECK IF ON STREET   4330 Lincoln   CENSUS TRACT 06 027   SCOUT CAR AREA 2-10

TYPE OF BUSINESS   APT. Blg.   TIME APP. 2:20 AM   DAY ☐ NIGHT ☒ UNKNOWN ☐

TYPE OF BUILDING   2-STORY   DATE 5-8-70   DAY OF WEEK Friday

PERSON REPORTING OFFENSE AGE SEX COLOR   MARINA Fernandez   TITLE Res.   ADDRESS 4330 Lincoln APT O   TELEPHONE 8319468

COMPLAINANT'S NAME Unk man unk man unk woman   ADDRESS John Doe 243   PHONE BUS. / RES.   AGE SEX COLOR
Unk man NO 66   NO 67   32

RECEIVED BY OFFICER MiKE KESSLER   TIME 3:30AM   DATE 5-8-70   VICTIM AND PERPETRATOR ARE ☐ RELATED ☐ ACQUAINTED ☐ STRANGERS ☐ UNKNOWN   RELATIONSHIP

METHOD OF ENTRY   METHOD OF ESCAPE   DESCRIBE WEAPON ☐ UNKNOWN

STATE NUMBER OF PERPETRATORS HERE OR ☐ CHECK BOX IF NUMBER IS UNKNOWN 1   IF ONLY ONE PERPETRATOR, DESCRIBE HERE ☒   ☒ MALE ☐ FEMALE   ☐ JUVENILE ☒ ADULT   ☒ WHITE ☐ NEGRO   ☐ UNKNOWN ☐ OTHER ☐ UNKNOWN   TOTAL VALUE $

☐ COMPLAINANT AVAILABLE ANYTIME ☐ OR AT   OTHER UNIT NOTIFIED   NAME OF PERSON NOTIFIED   TIME / DATE

IMPORTANT   PRIOR TO BODY OF REPORT BELOW, GIVE NAME, AGE, COLOR, ADDRESS, AND CHARGE OF EACH PERSON ARRESTED. (IF NONE, CHECK BELOW.) GIVE ADDITIONAL DETAILS OF OCCURRENCE, PERSONS, AND PROPERTY NOT INCLUDED ABOVE. IF MORE THAN ONE PERPETRATOR, DESCRIBE BELOW.

☐ NO ARREST   Received RIR[1] To above loc[2] at 2:25AM "A shooting"

Upon arrival writters found unk[3] man "66" lying on couch in the living room of APT No 9 with a bullet wound to the head. Writters also found in the bedroom of same apt 9 — unk man No. 67 was lying on the bed directly in front of The bedroom entrance — to the right in the corner on another bed was John Doe No 243 and unk woman No 32 (No 67 had a bullet wound to the head — John Doe 243 had a bullet wound to the head — unk woman No 32 had bullet wound(s) To the chesT). P.R.O.[4] stated To writters that she was downsTairs in her apartment when she heard an unk No of shots. PRO stated she then ran up the sTairway — reaching the top of the stairs she saw a wlm 45-50 sht. heavy bld no other desc[5] He stated To PRO "wheres Sally wheres Sally" (daughter friend)

SIGNATURE OF OFFICER RECEIVING REPORT Mike Kessler   BADGE NO 3738   PRECINCT 2   ASSIGNMENT 2-13

NAMES OF OTHER OFFICERS INVOLVED Jon Hall   BADGE NO 2637   PRECINCT 2   NAMES   BADGE NO   PRECINCT

SIGNATURE OF RANKING OFFICER CHECKING REPORT   RANK

PRELIMINARY COMPLAINT RECORD
P.P.D. 108 C of D. 783 RE Rev 6 67   FOUR COPIES TO BE MADE ON EACH REPORT PLUS EXTRAS AS NEEDED   PITTSBURGH POLICE DEPARTMENT

Figure 18   Patrolman Kessler's report (continued)

"If I don'T Find Sally you all are going To die"
P. R.O. then ran down sTairs ouT of the blg on To
Trumbull Ave where she sTopped a PSR[6] bus who
noT[7] Police.

Writter arrived aT scene and found above
des person (s) in above des. place(s) All were
lying face up.

A spend cartridge 9mm on evid. Tag
92 39 40 was found along side of the loft
arm of unk man No 66.

John Doe No 243 conveyed To Pitt Gen by 2-7.[8]
CenTrol PhoTo, Homicide, 2-70 & Dr. Hindmem
aT scene.

Unk man No 66 w/m 23-24 - 160 sandy brn hair
Thin bld & was nude — unk woman No 32 w/F 18 long brn
hair 5-5 110 also Nude — unk man No 63, N/M 19 (had jockey shorts on)
5-10 170 dk comp. shoT noT hair — John Doe 243 w/m
20 Thin bld no FurTher des. — also Nude.

1.   radio-response.
2.   location.
3.   unknown.
4.   person reporting offense.
5.   white male, 45-50, short heavy build, no other description.
6.   Pittsburgh Street Railways.
7.   notified.
8.   Pittsburgh General Hospital by patrol car 2-7.

Before going to bed, he treated it with medicine and used the glove to protect the medicine.)]

[Detective-Sergeant Thayer's report and map are shown in Figure 19.]

[*Earl Monroe*, police officer, describes taking Todd Wilson to a hospital, where he was pronounced dead. On cross-examination, Wilson's nudity is emphasized, as is the fact that the apartment was dimly lit.]

[*Joseph Zisler*, homicide sergeant, introduces the bullets that the doctors gave him at the time of the autopsies.]

[Sergeant Zisler's report is shown in Figure 20.]

Tuesday 24 November

[A discussion is held outside of the jury's presence. Sgt. Irvin Baranski, police officer in charge of the case, reports that Felipe Fernandez

Figure 19 Detective-Sergeant Thayer's report and map

May 8, 1970 4330 Lincoln (Stonehead Manor) #)
Activities D/S Lyle Thayer at scene of fatal shootings of
Unknown Woman #32
Unknown Man #66
Unknown Man #67
John Doe #243

The building is a two story, multiple dwelling. It is divided into
nine apartments, with a community bathroom on each floor.

Entering thru the front door you ar immediately confronted by a flight
of stairs leading to the second floor. At the top of the stairs there
are two hallways leading to the rear of the building. Apartment #9
is immediately to your right or the south side of the building as you
reach the top of the stairs.

Entering Apartment #9, you enter the kitchen, to the right or west of
this room is what should be a livingroom. To the left of the entrance
into the kitchen is a doorway leading into a bedroom. Behind the
bedroom or continuing east is a doorway to a small hall area and a door
leading into a bathroom.

Unknown Man #66 was lying on his back on a couch which was placed against
the west or front wall of the livingroom. He was naked but covered with
a blanket. He was suffering (1) thru and thru GSW to the head, the slug
entered his left cheek exited thru the right rear of his head and
continued thru a pillow the couch and lodged in the wall aproximately
10 inches above the floor. Slug recovered and held on evidence tag
#923941. There was a cartridge case (empty) lying on the floor at the
north end of the couch. W/M-22-5-9-160- brown hair.

Unknown Woman #32 was lying on her back on a bed that was placed on
the south wall of the bedroom, she was naked but covered with a blanket.
She was lying next to the wall. She was suffering what appeared to be
(5) GSW (2)-to the middle of the chest and one in the left breast
and a contact wound of the right side. There was also a bullet wound in
the middle of the back. (It appeared that the wound in the left breast
was a wound of exit, two in chest wounds of entry and the one in the back
a wound of exit. W/F-18-20-5-4-110 brown hair.

Unknown Man #67 was lying on a bed which was placed on the east wall of
of the bedroom, he wa clothed only in a pair of white jockey shorts.
he had on his left hand a white dress glove with the fingers and thumb
cut out. He was suffering (1) GSW to the right frontal temporal area.
He was also covered with a blanket. N/M-20-22-5-11-160.

66hn Doe #243, had been conveyed from the scene, a pool of blood on the
pillow next to Unknown Woman #32 and the information received from the
responding officers indicates that he was lying on the bed with Unknown
Woman #32 on the side next to the center of the room.

EVIDENCE PROPERTY:

ET-923941-(1) spent slug found in west wall aproximately 10" above the
floor and in direct line with the thru & thru GSW to Unk. Man #66.

ET-923942-(1) spent cartridge found on the floor just below the head of
unknown man #66.
ET-923943-a list of names found on dresser bedroom.

D/S Lyle Thayer
Homicide Bureau

Building (Apt #9) left in the custody of Patrolmen Wayne Lemonds and
Kenneth Wallace of the Second Precinct, to be held until members of
the Homicide Bureau arrive at the scene. Per Sgt. Jerome Jasinski #2.

Figure 19 *Detective-Sergeant Thayer's report and map* *(continued)*

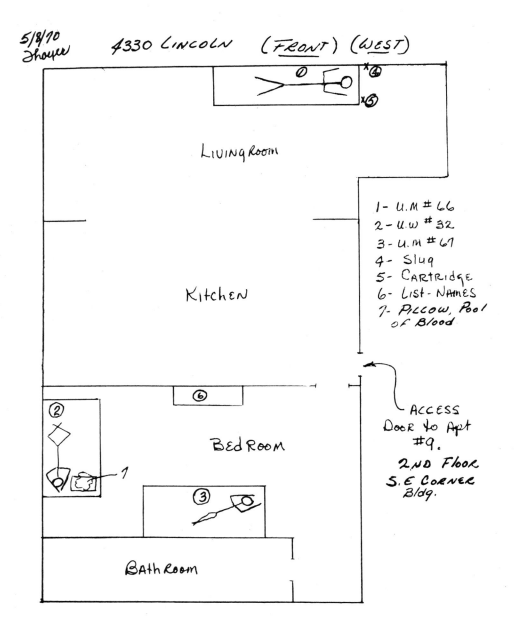

5/8/70
Thayer

4330 LINCOLN (FRONT) (WEST)

LIVING ROOM

1 - U.M #66
2 - U.W #32
3 - U.M #67
4 - SLUG
5 - CARTRIDGE
6 - LIST - NAMES
7 - PILLOW, Pool
     of Blood

Kitchen

BED ROOM

ACCESS
DOOR to Apt
#9.
2ND FLOOR
S. E CORNER
Bldg.

BATH ROOM

Figure 20   Sergeant Zisler's report

PITTSBURGH POLICE DEPARTMENT — Detective Division — Homicide Bureau

DATE 5-8-70

FROM: D/Sgt Joseph Zisler

TO: Insp Delore Ricard

SUBJECT: POST-MORTEM REPORT ON BODY OF PERSON LISTED BELOW.

NAME OF DECEASED JD #243 TODD WILSON   AGE 18   COLOR W   SEX M

ADDRESS 4330 LINCOLN   CITY   ZONE

REMOVED FROM 4330 Lincoln APT 9   DATE REMOVED 5-8-70

MORGUE FILE NO. 3400   MONTH MAY   WRITE UP NO. 86

PROSECTOR DR. TWOREK

PERSONS IDENTIFYING BODY

NAME CARL RICHARDSON   TELEPHONE NO.

ADDRESS   CITY   ZONE

NAME FELIPE FERNANDEZ   TELEPHONE NO.

ADDRESS   CITY   ZONE

LOCATION AND DESCRIPTION OF WOUNDS GSW FOREHEAD BETWEEN EYES
GSW UPPER RIGHT FOREHEAD
GRAZING WOUND UPPER CENTER FORHEAD
(POSSIBLY LACERATION)

CAUSE OF DEATH Gunshot wounds to the head

☐ Natural   ☐ Accidental   ☒ Homicide
☐ Suicide   ☐ Pending   ☐ Other

EVIDENCE RETURNED TO HOMICIDE BUREAU BY: One bullet & 2 particles   OFFICER

PPD 389   Form C of D—845-RE (Rev. 12-62)

Figure 20 Sergeant Zisler's report (continued)

is in a suburban VA hospital suffering from hepatitis. The unresolved question is whether to read his preliminary hearing testimony, take the court to the hospital, or furnish an ambulance to bring Fernandez in if he is physically able.]

[Nelson suggests taking the court to Stonehead Manor, his stated reason being to demonstrate how difficult it would be for Mary Ann Lynch (Martin) to have seen Wilbur Jackson reload. The court suggests a photographer.]

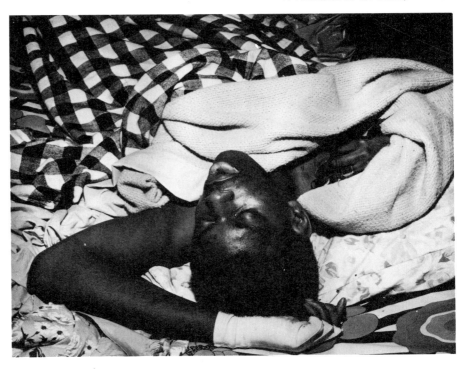

The body of Jonathan Carter. (Position three on the map shown in Figure 19.)
[Official police photo]

[*Virginia Wendell Gordon*, eighteen, married less than a month, relates hearing firecrackers, seeing Wilbur Jackson with a pistol, and calling the police. Cross-examination reveals she used drugs at age fourteen and doesn't want to reveal her present address because she has left her old life and doesn't want any part of the people in it.]

[*Georgia Webster* is recalled for further cross-examination, and it is discovered her name had been Georgia France, but, "My mother had my name changed so my sister could keep me while she went into the army."]

[*Jerome Jasinski* was Second-Precinct Desk Sergeant when Wilbur Jackson entered the police station.]

Q Now, when you saw Mr. Jackson come up to the desk, did you speak to him, or did he speak to you?

A He spoke to me.

Q What did he say to you, Sergeant?

A He said, "I want to turn myself in."

  I asked him what for.

The bodies of Jonathan Carter and Sandra Jackson.   [Official police photo]

And he said, "For murder; I just murdered my daughter and her hippie friends."

Q   When he said that, would you describe how Mr. Jackson appeared at that time?

A   He was crying.

Q   When you say he was crying, was he sobbing crying, or was he just simply crying?

A   He was simply crying; tears were flowing.

[Sergeant Jasinski describes Wilbur Jackson removing his weapons and ammunition.]

Q   What did Mr. Jackson say to you at that time?

A   He said he saw his daughter having intercourse in bed with a man, and he struck the man on the head with a gun, and the gun went off, killing his daughter.

Q   Is that all he said to you at that point?

A   Yes.

Q   Then what did you do, Sergeant?

A   I went, and I telephoned the homicide bureau and told them Mr. Jackson was in the station, and I was going to send him straight down.

[*Joseph Becker* of the Second Precinct tells of taking Wilbur Jackson's pistols, ammunition, and spent shell casings. All are introduced into evidence. He then drove Jackson downtown.]

[*Robert Jones* was a police officer at the Second Precinct.]

Q   Would you tell the jury what Mr. Jackson said at that time?

A   Well, Mr. Jackson stated that he saw a man in bed with his daughter, naked, and that he struck the man on the head with his pistol, and it discharged, killing his daughter.

Q   Did he say anything else to you at that time?

A   He said his wife started screaming, and he said that he had killed his daughter, and his wife was going to hate him for it.

Q   Was he crying at this point when he was telling you this?

A   Yes, sir, he was crying.

Q   Did he say anything else to you?

A   He stated that he worked for the railroad and thought about taking a train to Canada, but decided not to. He also said that he could have gone down south and lost himself, but he didn't want to.

Q   Was that the extent of Mr. Jackson's words to you?

A   His words, yes. This is what I have.

[*Leonard Fashoway*, Becker's partner, rode downtown with Wilbur Jackson in the back seat.]

Q   After you had begun the trip downtown from the Second Precinct, did there come a time when Mr. Jackson said something to you in the back seat of the car?

A   Yes, sir.

Q   Prior to Mr. Jackson saying something to you, did you ask him any questions or say anything to him?

A   No, sir.

Q   What did Mr. Jackson say to you that you can recall in the car—the first thing—do you remember, sir?

A   Yes, sir. He was talking about the shooting incident.

Q   Do you remember what he said regarding that in the car?

A   He stated that he had just killed two or three people, and that his daughter was one of them. He stated that he had taken guns with

The pistols Wilbur Jackson took with him to Stonehead Manor. The .38-caliber Colt revolver is in the foreground, the 9mm Luger in the background. Both are accompanied by spare ammunition that Jackson surrendered.

him, and that he did not intend to hurt anyone, but that he wanted to get his daughter back home with him.

Q Did he say anything else regarding that—wanting to get his daughter back home with him?

A Yes, sir.

Q What did he say? I am speaking of in the car.

A He stated that he had made preparations to hold her against her will, if necessary, in the event he would be able to get her back home.

Q Did you attempt at any time to advise him that he had a right to remain silent during this period of time?

A Yes, sir.

Q Do you remember what Patrolman Becker said to Mr. Jackson?

A Yes, sir. He turned around and said, "You don't have to tell us anything, you can remain silent."

Q Did Mr. Jackson say anything at that time?

A Yes, sir.

Q What did he say?

A I can't quote him, but it was to the effect that either he would rather talk or he preferred to talk or eventually insisted on continuing his statement.

Q And he did continue to speak, is that right?

A Yes, sir.

Q What else did he say?

A He stated that his daughter had been raised by the family, and that she was a good girl, and that apparently she had fallen into bad company, and that he wanted to get her away from this company and to regain her standing in the family group.

Q Tell me the gist of what he told you.

A Apparently, Sally was at the basis of his daughter's having left home.

Q That is what Mr. Jackson said?

A Yes.

Q But you don't recall what he said about Todd?

A No.

Q Do you remember anything else that Mr. Jackson said in this ride down to police headquarters, other than what you have told us already?

A Well, he stated that he was a member of the P.P.R. at our precinct.

Q What does the P.P.R. mean to you?

A Pittsburgh Police Reserves.

Q What else?

A He asked that we not divulge that.

Q He told you not to divulge that information?

A Well, he asked us not to bring it up unless I would expect it was necessary.

Q What else did he say?

A He did not want the image or reputation of the P.P.R. to be tainted by his experience. I think this was the essence of it.

[The jury is excused. Felipe Fernandez is reported to be in bad shape. His doctor says he must remain horizontal. Judge Gillis says he's not important enough for the court to go out to the hospital. Nelson says he wants him, either vertical or horizontal, since he can testify as to the communal life at Stonehead Manor. Since the preliminary hearing, Fernandez has been found guilty of breaking and entering, and Nelson feels the jury should know that the manager is a burglar. Nelson would also like to note where the hepatitis came from— possibly a dirty needle. Judge Gillis decides to read his preliminary-hearing testimony.]

Wednesday 25 November

[*Sergeant Irvin Baranski* of homicide, in charge of the case, testifies.* He introduces pictures of Stonehead Manor and says that he is amazed that apartment 9 was so clean. Baranski testifies that the door lock from apartment 9 had been torn from the door and that he found it behind the stove. In apartment 9 he found clay pipes, cigarette papers, a small residue of marijuana, and twenty-five purple LSD pills.]

[The court and jury are then bused out to see Stonehead Manor, after being told that none of the people living there on 8 May still lived there.]

[The court reconvenes.]

[Again, outside of the jury's presence, Nelson wants Felipe Fernandez in person. Gillis refuses. The jury returns and Sergeant Baranski testifies that Felipe Fernandez is sick. His preliminary hearing testimony is read.]

[*Felipe Fernandez* said that he heard Wilbur Jackson say he would go to any length to get his daughter back, dead or alive, and that he would sell his house, quit his job, and move out of state, as long as he got her back. On cross-examination, he admitted keeping a handgun in his apartment, but denied that sixty people lived in the building, as Nelson suggested.]

[*Detective James Caufield* of homicide testifies that when Wilbur Jackson arrived at police headquarters, he was given his rights, voluntarily waived them, and gave Detective Caufield a verbal statement which he later signed. Detective Caufield interviewed Jackson from approximately 2:50 A.M. until 4:15 A.M.]

---

* At the time of the trial, Sergeant Baranski had been a Pittsburgh police officer for over twenty years. A native of Pittsburgh, he had worked as a cruiser patrolman, a precinct detective, and had been assigned to homicide since 1967.

As the homicide detective in charge of the case, he worked extensively with the witnesses from Stonehead Manor. He says that after the trial he related to kids better than he had before, and that the ones in this case "kind of educated me."

He started the trial with favorable feelings toward Wilbur Jackson but "reevaluated his opinion" as the trial progressed. He now simply states that, "you can't justify the taking of four lives—no way," and that Jackson "stalked that girl like an animal."

He feels Len Gilman did "one hell of a job," the "jurors showed remarkable interest," and, as for himself, the trial took up so much time, that he missed deer hunting for the first time in twenty years.

Sgt. Irvin Baranski

Q   What did Mr. Jackson tell you that he didn't want written down?

A   One thing he told me was that he was a member of the police reserves.

Q   But he didn't want that written down?

A   No.

Q   What else?

A   He told me that he had gone out and purchased fifteen foot of chain and two padlocks, and when he did get his daughter home he was going to padlock her to a radiator and never let her out of the house again.

Q   He didn't want that down either?

A   No.

* * *

[On cross-examination Caufield testifies.]

Q   You took this statement down from him?

A   Yes, sir.

Q   Did you have a chance to study in detail his demeanor when he read this statement and signed it?

A   Yes, sir.

Q   Did Mr. Jackson cry during the taking of this statement?

A   Yes, sir.

Q   Did he cry often?

A   No, sir; just when the fact of his daughter's death was mentioned.

Q   Were these sobs; did he throb when he cried?

A   He just cried; not heavy sobbing, just tears.

Q   Would you consider the clothes to be in disarray or not orderly?

A   Not orderly, disarray.

Q   How was his facial expression?

A   Well, that changed off and on throughout the entire statement. At times he was angry, and at times he was sad, at times he looked very natural.

Q   Did you look into his eyes?

A   Yes, sir.

Q   How did his eyes look to you?

A   His eyes were red and bloodshot.

Q   At times during this interview did he become excited?

A   Not overly excited, no, sir.

Q   I said, did he become excited.

A   Yes, sir.

Q   Did he appear nervous—

A   No, sir.

Q   —at any time?

A   No, sir.

Q   Did he appear agitated?

A   Yes, sir, at times.

Q   Would he become more agitated?

A   At times.

Q **Did he state to you why he wanted to make a statement?**

A Yes; he stated he wanted to tell me why the events had happened, and he wanted to tell me the truth about what had happened.

Q **Did you consider him to have been distraught?**

A He appeared distraught, yes, sir.

Q **Did you ask him at any time whether he wanted to go on?**

A When he cried there when his daughter's death was mentioned, I said, "Are you all right, sir?" He said, "Yes, I am."

Q **At that time didn't you feel that—**

A I just wanted to make sure, you know, that he was all right.

Q **What do you know about the police reserves?**

A That is a group of civilian men who make application to the department where in times of a national emergency or emergency in the city where these men could be put out in the street to assist the police officers in crowd control or the control of traffic.

These gentlemen—I don't know how many meetings they make—they make meetings with patrolmen or members of the department.

They are trained in the use of guns.

They use the police firing ranges.

They are taught traffic control.

Q **Did Mr. Jackson say to you why he did not want his membership in the police reserves mentioned?**

A No, he didn't.

Q **Did you ask him?**

A No, sir.

Q **Did he mention at any time why he did not want the chain and locks mentioned?**

A No, sir.

Q **Did you ask him?**

A No, sir.

[*Lt. Bobby Taylor,* police ballistics expert, gives testimony that Wilbur Jackson's guns fired the bullets found inside the bodies.]

[For Lieutenant Taylor's report, see Figure 21.]

Figure 21 Lieutenant Taylor's ballistics report

PITTSBURGH POLICE DEPARTMENT
SCIENTIFIC BUREAU
REPORT OF ANALYSIS OR EXAMINATION

RECEIVED BY _Pate Modra_ DATE _5-8-70_ TIME _1:15 Pm_

DELIVERED BY _Wilson_ PRECINCT BUREAU _Hom_

DESCRIPTION OF PROPERTY _38 spl Colt off Pol Rev # 941355_
12 - 38 spl Reload Wadcutter clip Tag 923939 5-38 spl R-P Cartrg.

FROM WHOM TAKEN _Wilbur Jackson_ ADDRESS LOCATION

OFFICERS IN CHARGE OF CASE _Baronski + Wilson_ PRECINCT BUREAU _Hom_

DETAILS

1- 38 spl R-P Jcc - w/opn
1- 38 spl Western Jcc } Tag #923939
5- 38 spl R-P Jcc }
1- 38 spl 6L - Lead Bullet (2 frag of lead) Tag # 923948 Zielen Hom 5-8-70 1:45p Bi
1- 38 spl 6L Lead Bullet Tag 923947 Zielen Hom 5-8-70 1:45p BT
1- 38 spl 6L lead Bullet Tag 923950 Zielen Hom 5-8-70 V:?pm JH
Shooting of Anthony Sherman et al

RESULTS

Microscopic Comparison of test Shot from above gun with
1. Fired Cart Case (7) - Pos Ident 5-14-70 JH BT
2. Bullet Tag 923948 - Pos Ident 5-14-70 JH BT
3. Bullet Tag 923950 - Pos Ident 5-14-70 JH BT
4. Bullet Tag 923947 - Pos Ident 5-22-70 JH BT
5. Outstanding Case - Negative

LABORATORY NO. _3116-70_ EVIDENCE TAG NO. _923938_

SIGNATURE _D/Sgt James T Hurt_ (LAB. TECHNICIAN) _5-22-70_

APPROVED _H. Bobby Taylor_ (DETECTIVE INSPECTOR)

RECEIPT

PROPERTY RECEIVED BY: _____ DATE _____ BUREAU OR PRECINCT _P.O._

P.P.D. 382
Form C of D-769-RE (9-65)

[Figure 22 reprints a *Pittsburgh News* article that describes the jury's bus trip to Stonehead Manor.]

Thursday 26 November

Friday 27 November

[Thanksgiving recess.]

Monday 30 November

[*Robert Wilson*, detective-sergeant from homicide, testifies that Wilbur Jackson was always cooperative, and that on 9 May, he was distraught, emotional, weeping, but coherent.]

[The People rest.]

Figure 22 Pittsburgh News **article**

Jackson Returns to Stonehead Manor

By Adrian Crystal and Pat Williams
News Staff Writers

The trial of Wilbur Jackson, accused of murdering his daughter and three young men she was staying with, adjourned today so that the court might visit the scene of the alleged crimes.

Judge Joseph Gillis, prosecutor Leonard Gilman, and the 14-man jury rode in a chartered bus to 4330 Lincoln, the dingy apartment home where Sandra Jackson and her friends met their deaths. Jackson rode in a car with his lawyers.

"I wish we didn't have to go back—I already miss my little girl so much" said Jackson as he prepared to visit the fatal scene for the first time since the shootings. He explained that his wife Mary "didn't want to come along. She doesn't ever want to see the place again. She can't forget it."

Jackson was visibly shaken during the trip. He broke into a torrent of tears on entering "Stonehead Manor" and had to wait in a vacant apartment while the jury toured the building. The jurors saw the apartment where Sandra Jackson, 17, Jonathan Carter, 17, Ricky Walters, 16, and Todd Wilson, 18, died on the morning of May 8th. Blood stains still splattered the unoccupied apartment and bullet holes could be seen in the mattresses on which the young people died.

The building has been painted a bright green and the "Stonehead Manor" sign has been taken down. Several of the current tenants appeared unaware of the tragedy that had occurred there six months ago.

After the court returned to the Frank Murphy Hall of Justice, the jury heard Detective James Caufield describe Jackson's confession shortly after the murders.

From Pittsburgh News. Thursday, November 26, 1970
Section A, Page 4.

THE DEFENSE CASE

[At this point the defense presents its case and, as with the prosecution, testimony is preceded by an opening statement. The defense strategy in this trial is really twofold. During the prosecution's case, the defense concentrated on attacking the morals and life-styles of those who lived at Stonehead Manor. Now, during its case, the defense will attempt to portray Wilbur Jackson in as sympathetic a light as possible. Note that Jackson will never deny the killings, but rather will suggest that the very sight of his once virtuous naked daughter in bed with a boy was the final straw that drove him over the edge into insanity.]

OPENING STATEMENT

The Court:

Ladies and gentlemen of the jury.

We will now have the opening statement by Mr. Nelson.

As I told you when Mr. Gilman made his opening statement, what the lawyers say is not evidence and should not be considered by you as evidence. The only evidence you are to consider is that which you hear from the witness stand and that which you believe from the witness stand.

The purpose of the opening statement is for each side to give you their theory of the case so you will be in a better position to understand the evidence as it unfolds from the lips of the witnesses.

You may proceed, Mr. Nelson.

Mr. Nelson:

Thank you, Your Honor.*

Ladies and gentlemen of the jury, good morning.

A little anecdotal footnote to history—the history of the American Scene—tells us that one of our favorite authors, Samuel Clemens, about a hundred and ten years ago, together with his wife, attended church one nice, bright, sunny May morning at the church of the Reverend Henry Ward Beecher in New York City.

And when the Reverend Beecher assumed the pulpit to deliver his sermon, Mr. Clemens was moved to make a mental note that on this memorable occasion he was going to do something he had never done before:

When they passed the collection basket, he was going to put a hundred dollar bill that he had in his wallet in there.

---

* Defense attorney Oliver Nelson was born in Chicago, but has lived most of his life in Pittsburgh. He graduated from Dartmouth College and the University of Pittsburgh Law School. He has been in private practice for all of his legal life (twenty two years) and specializes in criminal defense work.

Oliver Nelson

Well, after the Reverend Beecher had spoke for about twenty minutes, Mr. Clemens was moved to revise his thinking and decided probably a fifty dollar bill would be enough.

Then, after the Reverend Beecher had spoken for about forty minutes, he again revised his thinking, and he decided that probably a twenty dollar bill would be sufficient.

In an hour and ten minutes after the Reverend Beecher had begun to talk, the story goes, Mr. Clemens got up and walked out of the church, without putting anything in the basket at all.

* * *

Brevity is a very great virtue, not only in the spiritual, but in the temporal field as well, one that isn't ordinarily possessed particularly—and I am sure you have experienced this—by politicians and by lawyers as well.

Nonetheless, it is a virtue, and one that I would very much like to be able to adopt in opening this case for Mr. Jackson in emulation of the example set for me by Mr. Gilman who, you will recall, in opening his case for the People spoke to you very eloquently, very impassionately, but for something less than fifteen minutes.

Now, I don't think I can do this. I don't think that I can portray for you as briefly, as succinctly, and certainly as completely, as he did, what this case is all about; because, and mainly because, this case involves considerably more—considerably more than simply the events that occurred during the early morning hours of May 8 between the time Wilbur Jackson left his work at about 1:35 A.M. and surrendered himself at the Second Precinct Station about ninety minutes later.

Every human event, of course, has dimensions—a beginning and an end—but they don't necessarily begin at the end; in fact, rarely do.

And what you have heard from that witness stand until now concerns itself with the end, with the termination of a whole series, a complex of events and circumstances and nonevents that climaxed in apartment 9 of the Stonehead Manor about 2:00 A.M. on the morning of May 8, 1970, but climaxed only; climaxed tragically, but climaxed only.

The events and the circumstances, the nonevents, the other factors that went into the warp and woof of this situation and led to its happening began about forty-six years prior to this in a very small town in southeastern Tennessee.

And perhaps if Wilbur Jackson had been born into a different environment from the one which he was, in the mountain country of Tennessee, raised in a rigid, fundamentalist manner by strict and rigid parents, perhaps—perhaps, not necessarily so, but perhaps—if he had not been born with a speech impediment whereby he was endowed as a child, as a child and as a mature adult, with a debilitating inferiority complex, very great and overweening sense of personal inadequacy, perhaps he would have gone on to fulfillment in life in the career or in the career opportunity for which he undertook during his early manhood training.

He would have became a teacher, and he would thereby have been enabled to do two things: to develop more fully in himself, thus not to have to live vicariously and achieve vicariously through his oldest daughter, a brilliant student, a girl in whom he focused his dreams; perhaps, too, he would have been somewhat less rigid in his outlook toward life and toward life in this girl and as it applied to this girl.

And perhaps then he would have been more malleable of a person, more capable of withstanding life's buffets.

And perhaps as a result of this, he wouldn't have gone on the night of May 8 or the morning of May 8 to the Stonehead Manor.

The fact of the matter is, however, that he is what he is, and on May 8 was what he was; and testimony will go into this record to show you what he was and why he was and why he is as he is.

He did go down there. He did go down there after spending the better part of a week—from the preceding Sunday—virtually without sleep, on the Sunday preceding May 8 having worked back to back a double shift, having worked overtime every afternoon that week except one that he took off, and having spent the rest of his time, for the most part, with or without his wife, looking for his daughter to get her home, to get her back; to get her back, you will learn, authoritatively this time, to where he could keep her and in a manner in which he could keep her until he could get her to put her feet once again, in his estimation, on the paths of righteousness.

This man, whom you will learn has never even so much as gotten a traffic-violation ticket up until this date, went down there armed.

Why did he do this?

Because, you will learn, he was forewarned and fully expected to meet resistance.

You will hear—you will hear him use this curious expression during the course of the presentation of this evidence—you will hear him say, "And, much to my surprise, the door was unlocked, and I got in," by which he means to indicate that in his mind he not only expected a locked door, he expected a custodian on that door.

He expected to meet resistance and very possibly armed resistance when he went into the Stonehead Manor.

So he went, as he did, armed.

And, much to his surprise, not only found no resistance, he found the door unlocked.

And you will learn that he knew where his daughter was, having been told so, having been told so by a gentleman who sold him that information.

And, accompanied by his wife, he immediately went up to apartment 9, burst open the door, burst into the apartment, flashed a flashlight around, saw one boy sleeping in one room, two boys in another, one of them—one of them—

And this is where Wilbur Chester Jackson, ladies and gentlemen of the jury, began to be driven over the edge of sanity.

He saw the light of his life, the scholar, this vessel whereby he intended to undertake, to realize everything that he himself had not been able to realize in life, naked in bed with a boy also naked, embracing.

This is where he began to go over the edge of sanity.

He took the light that he had had in his right hand, put it in his left hand; and by that light looked at this situation, looked at it, thereby being deprived ever again of the opportunity of telling himself or telling anyone else that his daughter was a virtuous woman, something that means and has always meant much to those who come from where he comes.

And he wanted to vent his wrath on this thief, on this sneak thief, this sneak thief who had stolen the one most valuable and cherished thing he and his daughter had, her virtue.

And he pulled this pistol and delivered a blow to this boy's head, accidentally discharging the pistol into his daughter—into his daughter—and he looked with his own eyes, and he could see the life's blood pouring from this girl, and he could hear and see his wife beside him screaming, "You killed my baby."

And that is when he toppled over the edge of sanity; that is when he went mad and ran amok.

Firing from two guns a total of eight more rounds, seven of them into four young, vital, breathing human beings, and another into a door in an effort to get at that one person who in his mind he conceived to be the agency whereby his daughter was led away from home and led into this environment of sloth, this debilitating atmosphere of antiestablishmentarianism.

Fortunately for her, he didn't find her; and he ultimately left, whereupon immediately beginning to recover, beginning to recover from the impulses, from the mental turmoil that he had been experiencing, and surrendered himself at the Second Precinct Station to a sergeant to whom he said, "I want to surrender myself; I have just killed my daughter and her hippie friends."

But even at that point, you will recall the testimony of these officers, he didn't know what he had done or to whom he had done it; he didn't even have the count right.

So I say to you, ladies and gentlemen of the jury, the defense in this case is that of temporary insanity.

And at this juncture we ask of you only that which we have a right to ask and which you have a duty to accord and which I have noted, my colleagues have noted, you have noted in full measure up to this point.

We ask that you give the testimony that you are about to hear, that measure of attentiveness and careful scrutiny that you have given all the testimony that has been presented in this matter up until now.

And that, then, having heard all the testimony and being told the law that you are to apply to this factual contention by Judge Gillis, you then go into that juryroom; and on the basis of the testimony, and on the basis of the law as it's given to you from the bench, and on those bases only, fairly, according to your own consciences, and bringing to your deliberations your own experience and knowledge as members of humanity, as members of the common social world, deliver a verdict in this case that to you seems fair and just and equitable.

And we thank you.

[During a recess, a spectator approaches Nelson, calls him a "fascist honky" and spits on him.]

[The defense's first witness is *Walter Kenworth*, assistant principal at the school Janet Rivers said she was attending. Mr. Kenworth says he has no records of her. On cross-examination Gilman asks if she might be going to night school. Kenworth makes a telephone call and discovers she enrolled two weeks before the trial.]

[*Thomas Ricke* of the *Pittsburgh Daily Herald* testifies, Mary Lee Von Allstein told him "Ricky turned us on to some good weed" the night he was killed.]

(Proceedings held outside the presence and hearing of the jury.)

Mr. Carney: Your Honor, we discussed briefly last week the use of diagnostic reports and recommendations as evidence in this trial; but I would like now to direct the court to the statute which refers to commitments to diagnostic facilities.* The last sentences contained therein state:

"Within that period the center or other facilities shall prepare diagnostic reports and other recommendations which are to be transmitted to the committing court."

"Diagnostic report and recommendation shall be admissible as evidence in the [competency] hearing, but not for any other purpose in the pending criminal proceeding."

*   *   *

Mr. Carney: The whole point of this is:

If Dr. Roby and Dr. Blunt are going to testify, they being the resident psychiatrists, one being the head of the Forensic Center at McKeesport State Hospital, they will not be able, according to the statute I have just read, to use any of the reports or records at the Forensic Center and so testify.

The Court: They can't use the report; and by the word *report*, we mean a piece of paper.

Mr. Carney: That report, Your Honor, if the court please, is based on some sixty days of Wilbur Jackson's residence up there. I don't believe you can do indirectly what you can't do directly.

Mr. Tracy: And I believe the attorney general has instructed them so.

The Court: Well, let's have one person at a time on the motion.

---

* Wilbur Jackson was committed to the Forensic Center to determine if he was competent to stand trial.

Mr. Carney: I have talked to Arthur Young, assistant attorney general in charge, so to speak, of matters concerning Forensic Center, and he has instructed them, and his office has instructed them, that the reports, material, recommendations are not to be used in any hearing but the sanity hearing or the competency hearing, as the case may be.

The Court: Well, all right, continue.

Mr. Carney: I think we should bar all of the testimony based on the reports, the tests, psychological tests, and even the brevital tests that are out there at the psychiatric center.

* * *

Mr. Gilman: I think the court will find when Dr. Robey gets here that Dr. Robey didn't do any of the work on Mr. Jackson during the sixty days that Mr. Jackson was at the Forensic Center. He didn't do any of the work as to whether Mr. Jackson was competent to stand trial.

Since the defense of insanity has been raised by defense counsel, Dr. Robey has studied the reports that were made while Mr. Jackson was at the Forensic Center and has interviewed Mr. Jackson at Mercywood Hospital.

Now, it is our contention, Your Honor, that the People's witnesses possibly cannot go into any of the reports concerning Mr. Jackson's competency to stand trial; but, as far as the ultimate issue of criminal responsibility is concerned, I think they have a right, just as any psychiatrist would have a right, to give an opinion to the jury as to whether Mr. Jackson was responsible or irresponsible at the time of the commission of the acts.

I don't think that the mere fact Dr. Blunt or Dr. Robey works at the Forensic Center should at all interfere with their being called as witnesses in this case.

* * *

The Court: I am giving the ruling now that we are going to let it in.

Mr. Gilman: I don't disagree with the court's ruling; but the statute indicates that the diagnostic report and recommendations—by *recommendations*, I think the statute means recommendations on competency to stand trial—shall be evidenced in the hearing, but not for any other purpose.

We don't intend to introduce that report on Mr. Jackson's competency to stand trial, or the recommendations.

I think it's a separate issue.

I think they should be permitted to testify, just as Dr. Tanay and Dr. Miller [witnesses for the defense] are permitted to testify.

The Court: I am going to permit them to testify.

I will refer you to Wharton's Criminal Evidence 818, volume 3, page 171.

The doctor-patient privilege does not exist here. These doctors were not treating him when they were examining him.

Mr. Carney: If I can make the point, for the record, there is no doctor-patient privilege; there is a statutory prohibition.

It is our position that Dr. Blunt and Dr. Robey should not be allowed to testify from the reports and information gleaned from Mr. Jackson while he was in residence at the psychiatric center.

The Court: I have made the ruling.

I think we might as well adjourn now.

I might call the attention then of the spectators to the fact that we are going to have a flag-raising ceremony outside of this building.

We have one flag pole with the American flag on it—due to the generosity of Kaufman Company—we are going to have a ceremony at which we are going to raise the State of Pennsylvania flag and the Pittsburgh flag.

It's at high noon on the front steps where we dedicated the statue yesterday.

[And court adjourns for the noon recess.]

MARY JACKSON

[After the noon recess, Mary Jackson testifies. She is able to testify only because her husband waived spousal immunity. Most jurisdictions prohibit a spouse from testifying unless the other spouse on trial permits it. This is similar to the attorney-client, doctor-patient, or priest-penitent privilege. These privileges exist so that one may freely confide in, for example, a priest without fear that what he says to the priest could be used against him. Likewise, married couples should be free to communicate with each other without reservation. Hence Mary Jackson is able to testify only because her husband allows her to.]

[*Mary Jackson,* Wilbur's wife, was born in Union City, Tennessee, in 1928 and lived on a farm with her parents. She is one-eighth Cherokee Indian. She met Wilbur in 1947 while riding on a bus and married him eleven months later. They moved to Pittsburgh in 1951. She is currently attending Allegheny County Community College. Surviving children include Debbie, seventeen; Paul Chester, thirteen; and Roger David, one and one-half.]

[She discusses how Sandra had good grades, graduated from high school at sixteen, and was pre-med at Allegheny State. She tells how Wilbur worked odd shifts at the railroad yards, often receiving only two hours' notice. As a result, she had more contact with the children.]

[She relates making clothes for herself and her daughters, mentioning bell-bottoms in particular. She says she would firmly correct

Sandy when her daughter called the police "pigs," and she thought Sandy's waist-length hair was beautiful and not too long. She says she worried when she heard that Sally Jo Tucker stayed overnight with a boyfriend. She remembers the time Sally Jo came back from a concert stoned and used profane and obscene words which Mrs. Jackson would not care to repeat.]

[She tells that in April Sandy moved out with Sally Jo, but was persuaded to return home the next day. On Sunday, 3 May, the Jacksons were visiting relatives. When they came home, they found Sandy gone and a letter she had left. The letter is introduced and read by Mr. Tracy after Mary indicates she does not wish to read it.]

[The letter is reproduced in Figure 1 at the beginning of this volume.]

[On Monday, Mary and Wilbur went looking for Sandy around the Allegheny State area. They saw Todd Wilson, but he left before Mary could talk to him. Wilbur saw him later but Todd ran. Then Ricky Walters gave them the 4330 Lincoln address of Stonehead Manor. They went there, persuaded Felipe Fernandez to open up apartment 3, and there they found some of Sandy's clothes.]

Tuesday 1 December

[The testimony of Mary Jackson continues as she describes the events on the Monday before the murder. She tells of Wilbur visiting Sally Jo Tucker at the dress shop and says her husband didn't use the expression "nigger boy" on the paper Sally saw. Later they went back to Stonehead Manor and waited outside for Sandy. That afternoon Wilbur went to work, returning home at midnight.]

[On Tuesday, Eldrin Johnson called. They went to meet him and Wilbur gave him twenty dollars. Johnson later called Wilbur at work. Wilbur returned home at 1:30 A.M.]

[Wednesday, Johnson called again. Another meeting was arranged and Johnson was paid another twenty dollars. The Jacksons spent several hours looking for an address Johnson gave them—it turned out to be a school playground. Johnson called once more and described Stonehead Manor. He said the people there had guns. Wilbur came home at 1:00 A.M.]

[On Thursday, Wilbur and Mary drove around Allegheny State unsuccessfully looking for Sandy. After Wilbur left for work, Mary went to the dentist's office where Sandy worked part-time. There she found Sandy, who agreed to come home; but Todd Wilson and Ricky Walters grabbed her and locked her in their car. When they tried to leave, Mary jumped on the hood, yelling and screaming. Todd tried to shake her off by stopping and starting quickly. During these antics, Mary observed her daughter crying and asking Todd not to do that. the police arrived, discovered that Sandy was over sixteen, and said she didn't have to go home with her mother.]

[For about ninety minutes, Sandy went back and forth from her mother to the two boys, apparently trying to make peace. Mary and Sandy talked in a restaurant while Todd and Ricky stood menacingly nearby. Sandy again agreed to come home, but again Todd and Ricky dragged her into their car and drove off. Mary Jackson chased them down the Lodge Freeway at high and reckless speeds, apparently at 80 MPH. She caught them at a traffic light where Sandy screamed she'd be home in two hours. Mary returned home and later took a call from Eldrin Johnson, who said Sandy and the boys were in apartment 9 and would be leaving for Washington, D.C., the next morning. Wilbur, still at work, called home and was told what had happened. He returned at 1:30 A.M. He said he was going over to Stonehead Manor and was taking guns for protection.]

[*Max Roder,* police officer, testifies that he found Mary Jackson on the hood of Todd Wilson's car. He says Sandy proved she was old enough to leave home and thus there was nothing he could do.]

[Mary continues. She describes going to apartment 9 with her husband and seeing him hit Todd with his pistol. She saw the flash and realized Sandy was hit. (*At this point, Mary is so shaken she cannot continue. Judge Gillis gives her time to recover. Mary weeps silently.*) She ran out before any more shooting and during the following minutes ran in and out of both apartment 9 and the building several times. She doesn't remember hearing any more shots. She and Wilbur drove to the police station where her husband told her to go home and take care of the kids.]

[Later that morning Mary Jackson was taken to police headquarters where she made the statement shown in Figure 23.]

[Mary remembers that on the way to the police station Wilbur talked about suicide. She then describes her daughter.]

Q Did you ever consider your daughter what is known as a hippie?

A Yes.

Q You did?

A Yes.

Q What justification or basis did you have for considering her a hippie?

A Well, I guess the way she—generally, the people she wanted to associate with, the way she dressed a lot of times, things of this nature.

Q Was that something that you resented?

A No, not really; because I figured that she would grow out of it.

Q Do you feel in the last several years in this country and in this state there has been a change of attitude?

A Yes, there is.

Figure 23 Mary Jackson's statement

5:10 A.M. May 8, 1970

Det. James Canfield

Homicide Bureau

Statement from Mary Jackson ⁴⁴/NF 3-29-26

5755 Hill 826-2734 — Housewife. Re:

Fatal Shooting —

My daughter Sandra left home and left us a note saying she was leaving. Monday morning My husband Wilbur went up to Alleghney State campus to look for Sandy. I Saw Sandy's Boyfriend Todd and he ran off when he saw us. Then we saw Todd's friend Ricky and he told us Sandy was staying at 4330 Lincoln Apt #9. My husband and I drove to 4330 Lincoln and talked to the Caretaker and he told us he hadn't seen Sandy. That evening we returned to 4330 Lincoln with our friends Mr and Mrs Tucker whose daughter Sally had left home and was living at that address. We

Figure 23   Mary Jackson's statement (continued)

talked to the caretaker again. He still
said he hadn't seen Sandy. My
husband and I then went up to Apt #9
And Sally's parents went up to Apt #3.
When we got to Apt #9 Adelle and her
husband were there with two colored
fellows. We asked if Sandy was there
And they said "No" We then left
the building with Mr & Mrs Tucker and
went home.

On May 7, 1970 I went with my
13 year old son Chester to the
Dentists office at 7 mile and
Greenfield where Sandy works to get
her to come home. We waited in the
waiting room for Sandy, She came out
And we left the building with her.
And Sandy ran to a car with Todd
And Ricky in it and they let her in the
Car and locked the door and I ran up

Mary Jackson

Figure 23   Mary Jackson's statement   (continued)

And jumped on the hood of their
car and started screaming and
yelled for someone to call the Police.
A colored couple pulled his car
up and blocked Todd's car and my
son stood behind it. The Police
came and let them leave. I then
went home. Around 10:00 PM in the
evening my husband called me and I
Told him what had happened at
the Dentists office.
      Today May 8, 1970 my husband
came home between 1:00 AM and
1:30 AM. We both talked about going
to go up to get Sandra. My husband
went and got his guns and put them
in his belt because we had heard
the people over in two of the
apartments at 4330 Lincoln had guns.
My husband also got a flashlight lantern.

Mary Jackson

Figure 23 Mary Jackson's statement (continued)

We got into the Volkswagen and my
husband drove over to 4330 Lincoln
The front door was ajar and we went
in and walked upstairs to Apt #9.
I don't remember if my husband
knocked on the door or not but he broke
the door open. My husband went in first
and went directly into the bedroom.
Todd and Sandra were in the bed on
the right in the nude. Todd started to
raise up. My husband hit him in the
head with the gun and the gun went
off and hit Sandra. I started to
scream you killed my baby. I started
running around screaming and I ran
out the door and down the stairs
and then back up. My husband was
shooting his gun and I ran downstairs and outside. I didn't know
what to do. My husband finally came

Mary Jackson

Figure 23   Mary Jackson's statement   (continued)

up to me and told me we were
leaving I said No I've got to
stay with Sandra and get some
clothes on her. We got in the
Car and my husband drove to the
Police Station and my husband said
he was going in and turn himself
in. He told me to go home and
take care of the children.

                              X Mary Jackson

Mary Jackson

[*Jessie Ruiz,* chief time-keeper for the Penn Central, is called. His records, introduced as evidence, show the following working hours of Wilbur Jackson: Friday 1 May—4 P.M.–12 P.M., Saturday 2 May—4 P.M.–12:45 A.M., Sunday 3 May—8 A.M.–12 P.M., Monday 4 May—3 P.M.–2 A.M., Tuesday 5 May—3 P.M.–1:30 A.M., Wednesday 6 May—2:45 P.M.–2:50 A.M., Thursday 7 May—2:45 P.M.–1:40 A.M. (During the five days preceding the murders, Wilbur Jackson worked 60.5 out of 112 hours.) On cross-examination Ruiz says many others worked overtime too and Jackson was ordered to work overtime—he had no choice. (During this week he usually worked without a fireman, thus qualifying for both extra work and higher pay.)]

[Mary Jackson is recalled for cross-examination, but cross-examination is quickly curtailed.]

[There follows a discussion on obtaining a videotape machine and operator in order to show the jury a film.]

Wednesday 2 December

[Before the jury enters, defense attorney Nelson asks Judge Gillis to tell a man in a white shirt and green sweater to stop saying the case is fixed because Wilbur Jackson is out on bail. The judge tells the spectator to be quiet.]

[Cross-examination of Mary Jackson continues. At the time she and Wilbur entered apartment 9, Mary recalls seeing Todd Wilson on top of Sandy. She also remembers Wilbur Jackson saying, "I've killed all these people" and "I've done a horrible thing." She denies that she told the police Sandy's boyfriend did the shootings. On redirect she tells of Eldrin Johnson giving her two of her daughter's rings for twenty dollars after Sandy had been killed. The lantern Wilbur Jackson used on 8 May is introduced. Mary Jackson says that Wilbur Jackson put great emphasis on the virtue of his daughter.]

WILBUR JACKSON

[*Wilbur Jackson,* the defendant herein, was thereupon called as a witness in his own behalf, and after having been first duly sworn by the court, testified upon his oath as follows:]

DIRECT EXAMINATION

Mr. Nelson: **Q   Mr. Jackson, state your full name, for the record.**

A   Wilbur Chester Jackson.

Q   On the twenty-first day of September of this year you were forty-six years old, is that not correct?

A   Yes, sir.

Q   Where were you born?

A   A small town in Tennessee: Erwin, (*spelling*) E–R–W–I–N.

Q   **What county in Tennessee is that town located in?**

A   Unicoi County, (*spelling*) U–N–I–C–O–I.

Q   **Your father's name?**

A   Roger Donald.

Q   **And your mother's?**

A   Rebecca Kay.

Q   **Your mother's maiden name, Mr. Jackson?**

A   Caine, (spelling) C–A–I–N–E.

Q   **Are both your mother and your father still alive?**

A   Yes, sir, they are.

Q   **Are they both natives of the state of Tennessee?**

A   No.   My father was born in North Carolina; my mother in Tennessee.

Q   **Well, they live today in Tennessee; do they not?**

A   Yes, they are residents; my father is here.

Q   **Your father is here for purposes of this trial, is he not?**

A   Yes, sir; he's here in the courtroom now.

Q   **You live and have lived with your family for some years at 5755 Hill in this city; have you not?**

A   Yes, sir; since July of 1955.

Q   **Is that when you undertook to acquire this house?**

A   Yes, sir.

Q   **What part of town is that house located in?**

A   It's on the west side, near the U.S. Steel factory.

Q   **As a matter of fact, it isn't very far from the inbound and outbound Penn Central marshaling yards, is it?**

A   No, sir; it's just a few blocks away.

Q   **And you and your family have lived there since '55?**

A   Yes, sir. I wanted to get within walking distance of my job.

Q   **You are employed—or until the eighth of May this year were employed—as a locomotive engineer by the Penn Central Railroad, were you not?**

A   Yes, sir.

Wilbur Jackson's home

Q   How long have you worked for the Penn Central?

A   I hired out April 6, 1951; for nineteen years.

Q   How long have you been a locomotive engineer?

A   I was a fireman for five years, and then I was promoted.

Q   Promoted to locomotive engineer?

A   Yes, sir.

Q   Now, your work has always been of a local nature, has it not?

A   Mainly, sir.

Q   You have never engineered, let's say, passenger trains or freight trains destined for remote cities, have you?

A   No, sir; I worked as a helper on those jobs only.

Q **Did you acquire your formal education in the state of Tennessee, Mr. Jackson?**

A Yes, sir.

Q **You attended grade school, I assume, in your home town of Erwin?**

A Yes, sir.

Q **After you completed high school, did you go on to college?**

A No, sir. World War II was going on at the time, and I worked in a defense plant for a few months and then went into the navy.

Q **How long were you in the navy, Mr. Jackson?**

A Two years and nine months.

Q **Thirty-three months?**

A Yes, sir.

Q **Were you honorably discharged from the navy?**

A Yes, sir; I was.

Q **Can you tell me when?**

A Yes; on March 3, 1946.

Q **What rank did you hold when you were discharged?**

A I was only a seaman, first class.

Q **Seaman, first?**

A Yes, sir; that is equivalent to corporal in the other services.

Q **Did you have a specialty?**

A I was in radar, range finding.

Q **Did you do any sea duty while you were in the navy?**

A Yes, sir; approximately half the time was sea duty.

Q **On what vessel or vessels did you serve at sea?**

A I was aboard two cruisers; the USS *Houston,* and the USS *Wichita* for a couple of weeks.

Q **What occasions your being transferred from the one cruiser to the other?**

A We were damaged somewhat on the *Houston,* and we were picked up by the *Wichita.*

Q **What kind of damage was it that was inflicted on the *Houston*?**

A We were under attack by Japanese suicide planes, and we took a torpedo midship, and then the next day we got one in the stern or the rear of the ship.

Q **Upon being discharged from the navy, did you enter college, Mr. Jackson?**

A Yes, sir. I waited a few weeks before I did and just relaxed, I guess, during that time.

Q **What college?**

A A small college in eastern Tennessee, Milligan, (*spelling*) M–I–L–L–I–G–A–N.

Q **What was your class year at Milligan?**

A '49.

Q **What particular course of study did you adopt and major in at Milligan?**

A My degree was in business administration, but I wanted to become a teacher.

Q **When did you receive your degree?**

A In the summer term, July of '49.

Q **By that time had you married?**

A Yes; I married while I was in school.

Q **When were you married?**

A We were married on Christmas Eve in 1947.

Q **In Erwin, Tennessee?**

A Yes, sir; a small wedding in the home of my parents.

Q **After receiving a degree in business administration at Milligan, did you further pursue your formal education?**

A Yes. For a few months I attended the University of Tennessee in Knoxville.

Q **Did you receive any advanced degree from the University of Tennessee?**

A No, sir, I didn't; my grades weren't up to a B average that was required.

Q **Meanwhile, had you become certified to teach in the state of Tennessee?**

A Yes, sir, I was certified at the time I graduated from the first school—Milligan.

Q **Did you, in fact, ever undertake to earn a living as a teacher?**

A No, sir; all I did was some practice teaching.

Q **In Tennessee?**

A   Yes, at the time to get the degree or the certification.

Q   **When you were a young lad going to grade school and high school in Erwin, Mr. Jackson, were you capable of speaking as you speak now?**

A   Well, I still can't speak very well. I had a speech impediment until I was about twelve years old, I guess.

Q   **Did you ever receive any medical assistance in an effort to cure this impediment?**

A   No, sir; I guess we didn't have any specialists at that time.

Q   **Did you ever have any special therapy in or out of school?**

A   No sir.

Q   **So whatever cure has been effected from this impediment has been one that you effected yourself and through your own efforts only, is that right?**

A   Yes, sir.

Q   **Now, there came a time, did there not, Mr. Jackson, when you came to Pittsburgh?**

A   Yes, sir; January of '51.

Q   **When you came up here, were you accompanied by your wife?**

A   No; I came alone by bus.

Q   **By bus?**

A   Yes, sir.

Q   **Did you look for work?**

A   Yes.

Q   **Did you find work?**

A   Yes. I hired out on the assembly line at the Bethlehem Steel Company.

Q   **How long did you work there?**

A   Just until April of '51 when I found an ad in the newspaper for locomotive fireman, and I thought that would be a better job; so I applied.

Q   **As a matter of fact, your father was a railroad man, was he not?**

A   Yes. He is retired now; but he was a railroad man.

Q   **And at various times in your younger life you had worked for the same railroad he had worked for, is that right?**

A   Yes, sir; I had worked on the labor gang during my school vacations.

Q On track maintenance and that sort of thing?

A Yes.

Q What was the name of that railroad?

A Clinchfield, (*spelling*) C–L–I–N–C–H–F–I–E–L–D, Railroad.

Q Your father, as a matter of fact, was a locomotive engineer, just as you later became, is that correct?

A No, sir; my father was a shop employee, repairman.

Q Where was the repair shop of the Clinchfield Railroad?

A They were located within the city limits of the town where we lived.

Q So it was in 1951—April of 1951—that you became a Penn Central employee, is that correct?

A Yes, sir. The company was called the New York Central at the time.

Q But it later merged with the Pennsylvania and became Penn Central, is that right?

A Yes, sir.

Q And they have virtually gone into bankruptcy since then, have they not?

A Unfortunately, yes.

Q Have you worked at all since May 8, 1970?

A No, sir; I haven't worked since the seventh day of May.

[Wilbur Jackson describes coming home after his last evening of work. His wife tells him again that she was unable to get Sandy back and that Eldrin Johnson called and had said Sandy and the others were going to Washington, D.C. He says he bought the murder weapons in Tennessee—the revolver was kept loaded under the mattress; the World War II Luger he has never fired. He talks of joining the Pittsburgh Police Reserves, of buying Sandy a Volkswagen, and of working many overtime hours. He describes getting Sandy's final letter and the time thereafter he spent looking for her. He then discusses his first meeting with Sally Jo Tucker in the dress shop.]

Q Did you then have a conversation with Sally Jo Tucker?

A Yes, I did.

Q Tell us, if you will, as best you can recall, what you said to her and what she said to you in the course of that conversation.

A Well, I wasn't sure that she was with Sally; so I acted as if I knew she was, and I told her that I had come to get my daughter back.

   And she said, "I'm not sure that she wants to go back, Mr. Jackson."

Sally was very polite, but she was uncooperative.

Q Did you tell her what you proposed to do with your daughter when you got her back?

A I told her that if she didn't cooperate, that they wouldn't be friends any longer, and I would take the daughter out of the state to my home town to go to school.

Q Your home town of Erwin?

A Yes, sir.

Q Did you plan, perhaps, to send her to Milligan College where you yourself had been in attendance?

A Either that or the other school there, East Tennessee State Teachers College.

Q Did you tell Sally of a plan to keep your daughter chained at home until you could transport her to Tennessee?

A No, sir, I did not.

Q Did you mention to Sally some place called the House of Rest?

A No. I might have mentioned that she might be placed under house arrest, or we intended to keep her at home for a while.

[And the second meeting a short time later.]

Q On this occasion did you again indicate to Miss Tucker what your intentions were with respect to your daughter Sandra when you got her back in the family fold?

A Yes, sir; I told her we wanted our daughter back.

Q Did you tell her anything about sending her down south somewhere where she was going to have to go about attired all the time in nylons and high heels?

A No, sir.

Q How long did this interview with Miss Tucker take?

A Oh, just a few minutes.

Q And then you left, is that right?

A Yes, sir.

Q Accompanied by Mrs. Jackson?

A Yes, sir.

[Jackson goes step-by-step over the events of the week preceding the murder, closely paralleling his wife's testimony. He denies that he said he'd bring Sandy back dead or alive.]

Q Do you recall when you actually signed yourself out from work on Friday morning the eighth?

A Yes, sir; at 1:40 A.M.

Q And you then went home by the most direct route, did you not?

A Yes, sir.

Q Mr. Jackson, why did you choose a career in railroading? Why didn't you go on to achieve what apparently had once been your ambition, to be a teacher?

A Well, I didn't feel I was fully qualified to be a teacher.

Q Why?

A I couldn't talk very well.

Q Pardon me?

A I didn't figure I could speak very well.

Q Were you proud of your daughter Sandra—

A Oh, yes, very much so.

Q —and her academic achievements?

A Yes, sir.

Q She was moved up a grade when she was going to Chadsey High School, was she not—

A Yes, sir.

Q —one full year—

A Yes, sir.

Q —and thereby got out of high school a year earlier than she would have otherwise; is that correct?

A Yes, sir.

Q Were you elated by that success?

A I think we were pleased.

Q Well, I am not talking about you in the plural, Mr. Jackson; I am talking about you yourself.

A Yes, sir, I was.

Q You loved your daughter, did you not?

A Very much so.

Q On the early morning of May 8, you shot and killed your daughter, didn't you?

A Yes, sir; I can never forget that.

Q **Did you intend to do that?**

A No, sir, I didn't.

Q **And you shot and killed three other young people, didn't you?**

A Unfortunately, yes.

Q **Did you intend to do that?**

A No, sir.

Q **On the early morning of May 8, you went down to the Stonehead Manor armed like a road agent, didn't you?**

A Yes, sir.

Q **Why?**

A I guess as—well, for my protection and the family's protection; I guess I was afraid of Mr. Richardson and Mr. Fernandez, mainly.

Q **When you walked into the bedroom of apartment 9, did you have your flashlight in your hand?**

A Yes, sir, I did.

Q **Which hand did you have it in?**

A In my right hand.

Q **Was it on?**

A I don't recall whether I had it on outside the door; I had it on inside the door.

Q **You had to go through a beaded curtain to get into that bedroom, did you not?**

A Yes, sir, I believe that's right.

Q **Was Mrs. Jackson with you when you went in there?**

A Yes, sir, she was just a few steps behind.

Q **So that you were the first of the two of you that went in?**

A Yes, sir.

Q **Do you recall thrusting aside this beaded curtain?**

A I guess so.

Q **You guess you do?**

A Well, I went through the door; I must have pushed it aside.

Q **Now, can you tell us what lights in that apartment unit were on, if any, when you went in?**

A I believe the apartment was in total darkness.

Q When you got into the bedroom, was your flashlight on or was it not on?

A I'm not sure. When I first entered the apartment, when I found everything was dark, I turned the light on—my flashlight on.

Q When you entered the apartment, did you immediately go into the bedroom?

A I believe so.

Q And was the light on when you got into the bedroom—the flashlight?

A Yes, sir; I turned it on when I entered the room; I don't recall which.

Q What did you see in that room?

A I saw two people in bed.

Q Did you recognize them?

A Yes, sir.

Q What else, if anything, did you see in that room?

A That's all I saw.

Q Did you keep the beam of the flashlight on these two people?

A Yes, I believe I did.

Q What were they doing?

A They were lying in bed.

Q What did you do?

A I walked rapidly across the room, and I struck the young man over the head with the barrel of the gun.

Q What gun?

A The one I carried in my waistband.

Q Well, you had two in there, did you not?

A Yes, sir.

Q Which one of the two?

A The revolver was next to my right hand.

Q I thought you had the flashlight in your right hand.

A I changed the light from the right hand to the left hand and drew the revolver with the right hand.

Q When you hit that boy over the head, were his eyes open?

A Yes, sir, they were.

Q Did he say anything to you?

A   No, sir.

Q   **Did you want to hit him again?**

A   No, sir; God help me.

Q   **When you hit him, what happened?**

A   The gun accidentally discharged and struck my daughter in the chest. That is something I can't forget.

Q   **What did you do then, Mr. Jackson?**

A   I don't know.

Q   **Did you reload that gun?**

A   No, sir.

Q   **Pardon me?**

A   I don't think so.

Q   **Did you go looking for Sally?**

A   Yes, sir, I did.

Q   **Did you shout going through that apartment house for Sally?**

A   I remember yelling on at least one occasion or more.

Q   **And then you left?**

A   Yes, sir.

Q   **And you drove to the Second Precinct Station?**

A   Yes, sir.

Q   **And you went in, and you told the desk sergeant that you had just murdered your daughter and her hippie friends; is that right?**

A   Yes, sir, that's right.

Q   **What did you, before all this, Mr. Jackson, foresee for your daughter Sandra in the way of a career?**

A   Well, she had always wanted to be a doctor—a missionary doctor.

Mr. Nelson: You may examine.

[On cross-examination Wilbur Jackson says he thinks a sixteen-year-old boy could make it on his own but a seventeen-year-old girl couldn't. He allows that he might have told Sally Jo Tucker he would chain Sandy to a radiator, but he didn't mean it. He thinks Carl Richardson (assistant Stonehead Manor manager) is a pretty tough customer, as he had been in Vietnam. He once saw Richardson with a bulge which he thought might be a concealed weapon. He denies saying he'd bring Sandy home dead or alive but did say he'd go to New Castle (prison) in order to get her back. He says Eldrin Johnson told him Felipe Fernandez was a gun collector and had five guns.]

Q And you believed in your mind that your daughter was staying with Mr. Wilson, is that correct?

A   Yes, sir.

Q How did you feel about that, Mr. Jackson?

A   Well, I didn't like it.

Q Were you angry about that?

A   Well, I don't know whether I was angry or not.

Q Were you disappointed about that, Mr. Jackson?

A   Yes, I was disappointed.

Q Why didn't you knock on the door?

A   I wish I could say I did; but I didn't.

Q Why didn't you? That is what I want to know.

A   I believe it was because of the fact that she might hide in there, and they wouldn't admit us.

Q So you felt that you had to break your way in to get your daughter out, is that correct?

A   I guess that is the way I felt.

Q Did you see the light on there in the hall when you went up the stairs?

A   Yes, I believe the hallway was lighted.

Q After you broke into apartment number 9, you had the flashlight in your hand at this point; is that correct?

A   Yes, sir.

Q You hadn't drawn either one of those two guns, is that correct?

A   I believe that's correct.

Q You immediately went to the bedroom, is that correct?

A   Yes, sir.

Q Did you know that the bedroom was to the left, Mr. Jackson?

A   Yes. I had been there once before—just inside the door.

Q Could you see at that time that the bedroom was on your left as you entered the apartment?

A   Yes, sir.

Q And you remember definitely that all the lights in apartment number 9 were out, is that correct?

A   To the best of my knowledge, they were out.

Q You remember that?

A Yes, sir.

Q Now, when you entered into the bedroom, you observed two people in bed; is that correct?

A Yes, sir.

Q And you identified these two people as Todd Wilson and your daughter, is that correct?

A Yes, sir.

Q Could you see Sandra's face at that time?

A Perhaps I didn't see her face at first; but I soon did.

Q When was it that you saw her face?

A Well, when I walked toward the bed, I guess.

Q As you got closer, you made out that it was your daughter in bed; is that correct?

A Yes, sir.

Q Now, at the time you entered the bedroom, did you see another bed in the bedroom?

A No, sir.

Q Your attention was drawn to the bed in which the two forms were lying is that correct?

A Yes, sir.

Q When you observed these two individuals, were they lying side by side, Mr. Jackson?

A Yes, sir, they were.

Q Now, you approached the bed and decided at that point to strike Todd with the gun, is that correct?

A Yes, sir.

Q You put the flashlight from your right hand to your left hand and produced a gun, is that correct?

A Yes, sir, I believe that's correct.

Q Now, why did you want to hit Todd in the head with the gun, Mr. Jackson?

A I don't know exactly. I just wanted to strike out, I guess.

Q Did you feel he had taken advantage of your daughter Sandy?

A I think I did.

Q Did you talk to him before you struck him with the gun?

A   No, sir.

Q   You didn't ask him one question, did you?

A   No, sir.

Q   Now, when you struck him with the gun, Mr. Jackson, did you have your finger on the trigger of the gun?

A   I don't think I did.

Q   You don't think you did. All right. Who was lying closest to you, Mr. Jackson, was it Todd or was it Sandra?

A   It was Todd.

Q   Did you deliver a hard blow to Todd's head with the gun?

A   Yes.

Q   Did you hit him as hard as you could?

A   Well, I hit him pretty hard.

Q   This would be with that .38 with the white or silver handle, is that correct?

A   Yes, sir, I believe that's correct.

Q   And it's your testimony that when you hit Todd in the head hard with the gun, the gun went off and hit your daughter in the chest?

A   Yes, sir.

Q   Now, after you had observed that your daughter was shot, what did you do then, Mr. Jackson?

A   I don't know for sure. I think I went berserk.

Q   Do you remember shooting your daughter a second time in the chest?

A   Oh, no, I don't.

Q   Do you remember shooting your daughter a third time in the side?

A   Golly, no.

Q   Do you remember shooting Todd Wilson twice in the head?

A   No, sir.

Q   Are you sure about that, Mr. Jackson?

A   I believe I'm sure.

Q   Do you remember shooting Jonathan Carter?

A   No, sir, I don't.

Q   Do you remember seeing Jonathan Carter?

A   I think I remember seeing him.

Q   When did you see him, Mr. Jackson?

A   Well, after the first shot, I believe I saw him afterward.

Q   Do you remember what you thought when you saw Jonathan Carter?

A   *(No response.)*

Q   Would you like me to rephrase the question?

A   If you will, please.

Q   Did you think Jonathan Carter had taken advantage of your daughter also?

A   I think I did.

Q   But you don't remember shooting him in the head, is that correct?

A   That's correct.

Q   Do you remember leaving the bedroom, Mr. Jackson?

A   No, sir, I don't believe I remember leaving. I remember certain things, and some things I can't.

Q   What is the next thing you remember?

A   I remember being out in the hallway, and I was yelling for Sally Tucker.

Q   Is that the next thing you remember, Mr. Jackson?

A   I'm not sure. This entire thing has been like a nightmare.

Q   I understand that, Mr. Jackson. Is that the next thing that you remember: being in the hall, shouting for Sally?

A   I believe that's correct.

Q   You don't remember reloading your gun, is that correct?

A   No, sir, I don't remember reloading.

Q   You don't remember putting two bullets into Ricky Walters's head?

A   No, sir.

Q   Do you remember seeing Ricky Walters?

A   I believe I remember seeing him on the couch.

Q   Now, did anything go through your head or go through your mind when you saw Ricky Walters on the couch?

A   I don't believe so. Ricky Walters had been very friendly toward me.

Q   You didn't think that Ricky Walters was taking advantage of your daughter?

A   I don't believe so.

Q **Do you remember telling Ricky Walters, "Wake up, boy; wake up, boy," and then firing two bullets into his head?**

A No, sir, I don't remember saying anything.

Q **Now, the next thing you remember is being out in the hall shouting for Sally; is that correct?**

A Yes, sir; and I remember I shot into a door lock mechanism.

Q **Do you remember if this shouting for Sally occurred on the second floor or on the first floor?**

A No, I don't, but it might have happened on both floors.

Q **Why were you shouting for Sally, Mr. Jackson?**

A Well, I guess I blamed Sally for most of the trouble.

Q **Did you intend to kill Sally if you found her?**

A I guess I would have, and I'm very grateful that I didn't find her.

Q **Now, you do indicate that you remember firing a bullet into a door downstairs; is that correct?**

A I remember a door lock mechanism; I don't remember what door it was.

Q **Do you remember, after firing that bullet through that door, going into the door?**

A I don't remember entering the room; but, evidently, I did.

Q **I am just asking you what you remember. You don't remember entering the room, is that correct?**

A That's correct.

Q **You don't remember looking under the couch or behind the couch?**

A No, sir. I remember talking to someone, though.

Q **Was it a young man that you talked to?**

A I believe so.

Q **Do you remember what you did after you left that doorway that you had entered?**

A I remember looking for Sally Tucker, and I remember asking one or two people if they knew where Sally was.

Q **Have you recognized any of these people when they testified here during the course of this trial?**

A No, sir, I haven't recognized any of them.

Q **Do you remember pounding on doors, asking for Sally?**

A Yes, sir I believe I remember that.

Q   **Did there come a time, Mr. Jackson, that you left 4330 Lincoln?**

A   Yes, sir.

Q   **How long would you say you were in that building?**

A   Judging from the time I left work until the time I went to the police station, I'd say about twenty or thirty minutes.

Q   **Do you remember drawing that 9-mm Luger while you were in apartment number 9?**

A   Seems like I do.

Q   **When did you do that, Mr. Jackson?**

A   Seems like I remember snapping the revolver on empty cartridges, and I believe I put it back in my waistband and drew the other gun.

Q   **So after you saw you were out of bullets from the .38, you drew the 9-mm Luger. What did you do with it?**

A   Well, I don't recall; but, evidently, I shot Mr. Walters.

Q   **Well, I am not asking you what you think you did. I am asking do you recall what you did with the 9-mm Luger?**

A   No, sir, I don't recall.

Q   **Did you take the flashlight from 4330 Lincoln?**

A   I don't remember taking it; but it was back in the car.

Q   **But you don't remember taking it with your hands and carrying it back to the car, is that correct?**

A   No sir, I don't remember it. I must have had it in my left hand all the time.

Q   **Do you remember putting spent .38 cartridge casings back into your pocket?**

A   No, sir, I don't.

Q   **Now, you got into the car and drove to the Second Precinct; is that correct?**

A   Yes, sir.

Q   **During the course of the ride from 4330 Lincoln to the Second Precinct, did you indicate to your wife that you had shot others in apartment number 9 besides your daughter and Todd Wilson?**

A   I think I did.

Q   **Did you indicate that you were sorry for the horrible thing you had done?**

A   Yes, sir, I guess I did.

Q   **And you are, in fact, sorry for doing that; aren't you, Mr. Jackson?**

A Yes, indeed.

Q **Now, when you had arrived at Second Precinct, do you remember speaking to your wife?**

A Yes, I remember that.

Q **What did you say to her?**

A I told her to go home and look after the other children.

Q **And it was at that point that you went up to the desk and surrendered yourself to Sergeant Jasinski; is that correct?**

A Yes, sir.

Thursday 3 December

[The court allows a prosecution psychiatrist to sit in court and observe Wilbur Jackson's testimony as well as that of the defense psychiatrists.]

[Cross-examination of Wilbur Jackson continues as he admits he gave a statement to the police after the shootings.]

Q **Now, do you remember signing your name to the first page and the remaining pages of this statement, Mr. Jackson?**

A No, sir I don't remember; but it looks like my signature.

Q **But you don't remember signing it, is that correct?**

A No, sir.

Q **Do you remember shooting Todd Wilson, Mr. Jackson?**

A No, sir.

Q **Did you tell Sergeant Caufield:**

     'After I knew my daughter was dead, I shot Todd in the head two or three times.'

A I read that in the statement.

Q **Did you tell Detective Caufield that?**

A I must have.

Q **Now, do you remember shooting Ricky Walters, Mr. Jackson?**

A No, sir.

Q **Do you remember telling Detective Caufield that you shone the flashlight at Ricky on the couch, and you shot him, you believe, through the forehead?**

A I read that statement; I must have said it.

Q **But you don't remember doing that?**

A My mind was not very clear; but I can remember sketches of it.

Q Now, you indicated yesterday that you really didn't have the same feeling about Ricky Walters that you had about Todd and Jonathan in relation to having taken advantage of your daughter, is that correct?

A Yes, sir, I believe that's correct. Ricky Walters had been very cooperative with me. He gave me the address.

Q As a matter of fact, he told you that your daughter was staying at 4330 Lincoln?

A He gave me the address of the building.

Q Did you tell Sergeant Caufield, on page three of your statement, after you had told him that you shot Ricky through the head, that you believed he was having intercourse with your daughter also, that they all ruined your daughter? Did you tell him that, Mr. Jackson?

A On reflecting back on the case, I must have at the time.

Q Do you remember telling him that?

A No, sir, I don't.

Q Do you remember seeing Eldrin Johnson in the apartment that you entered after firing your gun through the door?

A No, sir, I don't remember seeing him. I saw somebody there.

Q But you don't remember whether it was Eldrin or not?

A No, sir.

Q And you didn't shoot this male, as you indicated earlier?

A No, sir.

Q Do you remember telling Detective Caufield that you were a member of the Pittsburgh Police Reserves?

A Yes, sir, I remember that; and I asked him not to say anything about it.

Q You remember that. Let me ask you a question. You really weren't a member of the Pittsburgh Police Reserves at that time?

A No, sir; I was in the process of joining them.

Q And you told him not to mention anything about that, is that correct?

A Yes, sir.

Q You didn't want your activities or what you had done to reflect on the Pittsburgh Police Reserves, is that correct?

A That's correct.

Q **Did you also tell Detective Caufield that you had planned on chaining your daughter to the radiator?**

A I don't remember that statement. I may have made it; but if I did, I think it was just a figure of speech. We had a dog that we kept chained; and I'm sure I wouldn't have chained my daughter like the dog.

[Gilman concludes his cross-examination, and Nelson asks a few questions on redirect.]

Q **Can you honestly say now, Mr. Jackson, that what you have related from this witness stand is the product of your own independent recollection of the events of the early morning of May 8, as distinguished from things that have become muddled into your mind and into your thinking as a result of all this testimony you have heard and all these interrogations you have undergone relating to this matter and following May 8?**

A It's very difficult for me from what I can remember and what I don't remember, due to the testimony of various people. I have been confused, I know. I have made conflicting statements, I guess, too. I can remember portions of things, and some I can't remember.

For example, on the ride down to the station, I can remember parts of the trip, and parts I cannot remember.

I can remember headlights coming toward me, and I was on the wrong side of the road, and I almost hit a big truck. I only remember a portion of the journey.

It's not clear in my mind what I remember and what I don't sometimes.

[*Donald Carty* is the next witness. He is a career Air Force officer and Wilbur Jackson's first cousin. He remembers the moral support Wilbur gave him when he attended Annapolis and says that Wilbur himself had wanted to attend Annapolis and fly airplanes, but believed himself too old.]

Q **Are you familiar in the context and in the community in which you know Wilbur Jackson—that would be his family, would it not—what his reputation for truth and probity and veracity is?**

A Sir, he has the reputation in our family as being a gentleman, very nice, very likable, easy-going, very serious-minded, loved his family, and just a number-one friend to my parents and to my family anyway.

Mr. Nelson: Thank you, Captain.

You may examine.

Mr. Gilman: **Q** **How long prior to May 8 was the last time, Captain, that you saw Mr. Jackson, do you remember?**

A Yes, sir; it was in 1967.

Q **So prior to May 8, 1970, the last time you had seen him was 1967?**

A Yes, sir.

Q **You don't know anything of your own knowledge about what happened, if anything happened, between Mr. Jackson and Mrs. Jackson and their daughter Sandra between 1967 and May 8, 1970?**

A No, I don't.

Mr. Gilman: I have no further questions.

(Witness excused.)

[*Gerald Patry* follows. He is a Penn Central engine dispatcher.]

Q **What kind of notice do you give [the employees]?**

A I'd say Wilbur was one of the best employees we had, as far as working goes.

* * *

Q **What about Mr. Jackson, how much time would you generally have to give him?**

A If you were in a jam and needed somebody there right away, Wilbur could be there in ten, fifteen minutes.

Q **You are familiar with Mr. Jackson in the community which you know him, that is, at work. What is his reputation for truth and veracity among fellow employees?**

A If the man told you something, you could believe it; he would always stand by his word.

Mr. Carney: Thank you, sir.

[*Richard Picknik* is an engine crew dispatcher.]

Q **Was Mr. Jackson considered a dependable person?**

A Yes.

Q **Do you know what Mr. Jackson's reputation for truth and veracity is among his fellow employees?**

A Very honest employee, as far as I'm concerned.

Q **How would you term his employment—him as an employee?**

A Very reliable.

Mr. Carney: Nothing further.

[*Camille Paquette* is the supervisor of the train-and-engine crew dispatchers.]

Q **Does Mr. Jackson work for you?**

A Yes, sir, directly under me.

Q How long has he so worked for you?

A Well, since the last six years, I mean, as an engine man.

Q Now, you are familiar with Mr. Jackson's reputation for truth and veracity among his fellow employees, are you not?

A Yes.

Q What is his reputation?

A Very good.

Q How would you term him as an employee?

A Very good employee.

Mr. Carney: I have nothing further.

CROSS–EXAMINATION

Mr. Gilman: **Q** When was the last time you worked directly with Mr. Jackson, Mr. Paquette?

A Oh, seven, eight years ago; I wouldn't have the exact date.

Q Did you ever visit with Mr. and Mrs. Jackson and their family at home?

A No, sir.

Q You never socialized with the Jacksons?

A No, sir.

Mr. Gilman: No further questions.

[*Leonard Tucker*, divorced father of Sally Jo, testifies that on the day he and his ex-wife accompanied the Jacksons to Stonehead Manor, Wilbur never said he would bring his daughter back, dead or alive.]

[*Louise Tucker* saw her daughter Sally Jo at Stonehead Manor. She picked up her dog that was sick; a veterinarian said it was from dirt.]

CROSS–EXAMINATION

Mr. Gilman: **Q** Why didn't you want your daughter to see Sandra Jackson, Mrs. Tucker?

A Well, I thought maybe she would quit dressing like she did—the both of them would.

Q Did you think Sandra Jackson was a bad influence on Sally Tucker?

A No, sir, I didn't.

Q Did you think Sally Tucker was a bad influence on Sandra Jackson?

A   No, I didn't.

Q   **Explain why you didn't want them to see each other again.**

A   I just told you, I didn't like the way they dressed; and I thought maybe if we kept them apart, they would stop dressing this hippie way.

Q   **You thought by separating them, they would change; is that correct?**

A   I hoped it would.

Q   **You didn't particularly care for the hippie way that Sally was dressing herself?**

A   That's right, I didn't.

[*Ronald Smigelski* is a police officer in suburban Ingram. Until two and one-half years ago he had been a neighbor of the Jacksons and has seen them frequently since moving away.]

Q   **Are you familiar with Mr. Jackson's reputation for truth and probity and veracity in the community in which you know him—the neighborhood?**

A   Yes, I am very familiar with that.

Q   **What is his reputation for truth and probity and veracity?**

A   He is respected by everybody in the neighborhood as being a truthful man. He had been very pleasant to talk to everybody there, as far as I know.

One thing that impressed me about him is his mild-mannered techniques, and so forth, when he talked to you; he was very pleasant.

Another thing, he never used any profane language; and I was very impressed by this in a man of his age.

Q   **Now, are you familiar with the reputation that he had in the community in which you knew him—the neighborhood—for his relationships with his family, and particularly with his children?**

A   Yes.

Q   **What is his reputation in that respect?**

A   He was always a family man. He was talking of his family constantly.

One thing he used to tell me was about his daughter Sandra, how proud he was of her that she got double-promoted and went on to college and was going to pre-med school.

Q   **You are not related to Mr. Jackson in any way, are you?**

A   No, I am not.

Mr. Nelson: Thank you.

DR. LYNN BLUNT

[*Dr. Lynn Blunt* is the acting clinical director of the Center for Forensic Psychiatry, Pennsylvania Department of Mental Health. He examined Wilbur Jackson to determine if he was competent to stand trial.

[He discusses a videotaped "truth serum" test he administered to Wilbur Jackson.]

Q You conducted, except for a few questions asked by myself, the interrogation of Mr. Jackson, and you also administered this drug to him; did you not?

A That's correct.

Q Describe for these ladies and gentlemen of the jury the process of administration of this drug.

A The drug is sodium brevital, which is a barbiturate, which is medication which is similar to that found in some sleeping medications; and this is given in the vein over a period of time—continuously, in other words—in amounts that I feel are clinically indicated as the evaluation is conducted.

This is the medication which will put the patient to sleep; but the aim is not to put him to sleep, but to put him in a state near sleep, in a semisleep state, much like the state someone is in just before they go to sleep.

In addition to the sodium brevital, I might mention, I did initially administer another drug into the vein called Ritalin, *(spelling)* R–I–T–A–L–I–N, which is a stimulant.

This technique is used in addition to the sodium brevital itself in order to make the patient not quite so susceptible to the sleeping effects which might make him go to sleep during the administration of the sodium brevital itself.

The sodium brevital puts him into this state which is somewhat similar to that which might be induced by alcohol.

Q Sodium brevital, colloquially and rather parochially and imprecisely is referred to by some lay people such as myself upon occasion as truth serum; is that not right?

A That's correct.

Q The purpose for administering the drug is to lower the resistance of the person to whom the drug is administered, is that not right?

A That's correct.

Q You say it's administered intravenously—

A That's correct.

Q —with a syringe?

A   That's correct.

Q   **When this task was conducted on Mr. Jackson, how much of the drug was actually administered to him?**

A   Over the total time of the interview, which I believe was just about an hour and five or ten minutes from the time he began receiving the drug until he stopped receiving it, he received a total of three hundred milligrams [about 2 ounces].

Q   **This is administered with a syringe, is it not?**

A   That's correct; it is a very large syringe, 50 cc syringe.

Q   **You yourself administered this drug, such as it was administered—**

A   That's correct.

Q   **—and also questioned Mr. Jackson?**

A   That's correct.

Q   **You first began the injection of this drug into his bloodstream; and when it became manifested to you as a physician that the drug was beginning to take effect, you initiated your questions, did you not?**

A   That's correct.

Q   **Now, you, in addition to starring in this film, have seen it; have you not?**

A   Yes, I have.

Q   **Upon how many occasions have you seen it, doctor?**

A   I saw it, I believe, on three occasions.

Q   **Now, as a participant in the film, does it fairly and truly and accurately depict the events that went forward before the camera?**

A   Yes, I would say it does. I must apologize for the sound quality, which was rather poor.

CROSS–EXAMINATION

Mr. Gilman: Q   **Dr. Blunt, as I understand your testimony, Mr. Nelson and co-counsel Mr. Carney and Mr. Tracy requested that you perform this test and also asked they be allowed to be present while you were doing the test?**

A   That is not quite correct. I asked them if they would agree to my performance of the test and if they would like to be present, and they answered in the affirmative; and, of course, it also took the patient's permission as a special medical procedure.

Q   **Mr. Jackson agreed to the test?**

A   After much hesitancy, he did.

Q **Now, you indicated also that sodium brevital, the drug you administered Mr. Jackson, is in no sense of the word truth serum; is that correct?**

A That's correct. It could be compared in any way with a controlled drug. Many persons who drink quantities of alcohol, it becomes easier for them to talk.

[Before the videotape is shown, Judge Gillis gives some preliminary insanity instructions.]

But you do have the problem of deciding the sanity of the defendant as it existed on May 8, 1970.

The rule on that is as follows. I am quoting from an old case that is nearly a hundred years old, and this is the rule in Pennsylvania today. It actually was decided in 1886. So it's nearly a hundred years ago.

Now, here is the rule in Pennsylvania:

"It must appear in this case that the defendant is a man of sound mind."

Now, by sound mind is not meant a mind which is the equal of any mind possessed by any mortal in the world.

We all know that there is a difference in the minds of our acquaintances. Some men are very bright, others are very dull; but they are held accountable.

McNAGHTEN→ Perhaps it would be enough to say, and leave it right here, that if by reason of disease the defendant was not capable of knowing he was doing wrong in the particular act, or if he had not the power to resist IRRESITABLE→ the impulse to do the act by reason of disease or insanity, that would be an unsound mind.

But it must be an unsoundness which affected the act in question and not one which did not affect it.

There is a simple question for you.

You have heard the evidence in the case—and you are about to hear more evidence from the psychiatrists—and you can judge from all the evidence in the case and all the expert testimony, including the transaction itself and his conduct at the time, whether or not he exhibited evidences which leave a reasonable doubt in your minds of the soundness of his mind in that transaction.

Did he know what he was doing, whether it was right or wrong?

And if he did, then did he know or did he have the power—the willpower—to resist the impulse occasioned?

You are not to draw the inference because a man acts frantically mad and angry, very angry, that he does not resist the impulse, that that is unsoundness of mind.

This unsoundness must be the result of a disease and not the result of his having allowed his passions to run until they have become uncontrollable.

We frequently meet men in courts of justice who claim that they have committed a crime because they were drunk. The law holds them responsible because they should not have got drunk, they should not have formed the habit.

So the law requires a man that he will curb his passions and restrain himself, and if he does not do it, holds him accountable, unless it is by reason of disease which renders him unable to do it.

Now, these words were spoken by a judge some eighty-four years ago, and they are still the law in the state of Pennsylvania, and they are basically instructions I will give you.

I may rephrase them in a little different language later on.

That is the law, and that is what you are looking for.

VIDEOTAPE OF TRUTH SERUM TEST

*(The following is a transcript of the videotape shown within the presence and hearing of the jury.)**

[Wilbur Jackson waived his right to be present during this part of the trial.]

Dr. Blunt:

Q You will be able to see people here in the camera; Mr. Nelson and myself and yourself, mainly. Probably won't be able to see—

A This is a new experience.

Q I understand that. I want you to relax now, just relax.

A Should I keep my eyes open or closed?

Q You can keep them open. Tell me when you feel a little tired, okay?

A I have a slight feeling of—(*inaudible*).

Q Okay, you can talk.

A I'm getting groggy, groggy.

* * *

Wake up, and look at me.
Mr. Jackson.

(Doctor touching patient's face.)
Wake up and look at me.
Wake up.

---

* This was the first time a videotape of a sodium brevital test had been used in a major criminal trial in Pennsylvania.

Wake up.

Wake up.

Come on.

Take a big, deep breath, and look at me.

That's it.

Take a big, deep breath, now, Mr. Jackson.

Come on, a big, deep breath.

Come on, that's it, another one.

Take another big, deep breath.

Okay.

Now, just relax.

Tell me your full name, Mr. Jackson.

What is your full name?

A   Wilbur Jackson.

Q   What is your middle name?

A   Chester,

Q   Where were you born, Mr. Jackson?

A   Erwin, Tennessee.

Q   How long did you live there?

A   *(Inaudible.)*

*   *   *

[There follow some questions about Wilbur Jackson's early life and his relationship with Sandy.]

Mr. Nelson: Did you ever find any paraphernalia of drug use in her room or in your home?

The Defendant: No. We looked for some; but we were unable to find some; but we had a suspicion that she was on drugs.

Dr. Blunt: **Q   How were you going to discipline her? How did you plan to discipline her?**

A   I thought first I would punish her—

Q   How would you do that? How would you punish her?

A   I thought I would whip her first with a yardstick.

Q   Whip her with a yardstick?

A   I hate to have to. Yes. Because she's too old. But I thought it was the thing to do.

Q   Did you do that? Had you done that before? Had you punished her that way?

A   A few times; not very often.

Q   When was the last time you punished her?

A   She was getting too big for that.

Q   When was the last time you whipped her?

A   I don't know exactly. It must have been weeks before that. We wanted her to grow up to be a decent girl.

Q   And you were going to whip her to make her be a decent girl?

A   I considered doing it when she came home. I was going to take my belt and whip her. I hated to.

* * *

We didn't want her to work; but she wanted to, and we wanted her to have independence.

Q   Did you whip her when she came home in April?

A   I had planned to; but I didn't. I was angry at her for what she had done, but—

Q   What did she do that you were so angry about?

A   Well, she left home without any warning whatsover.

Q   Is that all she did? Was there anything else she did?

A   That evening, I think it was around nine o'clock, two cars parked in the alley, and the people came in; her boy friend—I mean her girl friend Sally and two boys whom I had met—

Q   Uh-huh.

A   —and they helped her pack her clothes.

Q   How did you feel about that, Mr. Jackson?

A   I thought she was making a terrible mistake, and I thought at the time that they were going out to spend the night together, and it hurt me very much.

I wanted my daughter to be—I wanted my daughter to be a virgin when she married so when she—her husband—

She was a virgin when I married her, and she was a very good girl.

Q   You mean a virgin like your wife?

A   Yes, uh-huh.

Q   You wanted her to be one, too?

A   Yes, I did, very much so.

Q   Tell us about the night of May 8. What happened? Your wife was upset.

A It's too hard to me to talk about it.

Q Come on, you can talk about it now, Mr. Jackson. You can tell us all about it. Just relax, and tell us all about it.

A It was such a tragedy. We had found out the building she was living in two or three days prior to this, and we didn't know for sure which apartment she lived in. I believe there were eighteen apartments in the building.

And there were long-haired boys in the building. I don't mind long hair. I think a man should wear his hair any way he wants to.

But I personally prefer a short haircut. I think it looks more manly—more masculine.

These long-haired boys, sometimes you can't tell whether they are male or female.

And she had taken up with a red-haired boy, and I thought he was awfully homely looking.

I guess she loved him, and she had a right to choose her own boy friends.

I didn't know that boy at the time; but later I learned his name was Todd Wilson, and later I learned he was a Jewish boy, and he lived with a colored boy.

Q How did you feel about that?

A Well, I found out that; and I don't want my daughter mixed up with that.

Q How do you feel about the Jewish boy?

A Well, I respect Jewish people.

Q Did you like her dating the Jewish boy?

A They can take advantage of—of—of (inaudible). They are very smart people, and I think they would—(inaudible).

Q What happened this night that you went home, and your wife was upset, and you went over there?

A I got home, and my wife had arrived home before I did. She had went to the Allegheny Community College—the wife had.

(Inaudible, something about finishing high school and going on to college.)

I wanted to be very proud of her. I am proud of her. She is going to—

I have never found a woman I liked any better than my wife.

Q Have you found some other women that you liked?

A   Well, I like a swayback derriere. I think that's very attractive.

* * *

Q   **Let's talk about the shooting incident in May, okay?**

A   All right.

Q   **Let's talk about the shooting incident. You came home, and your wife was hysterical, and you talked to her, and she told you what happened, and you decided to go over to where your daughter was; is that right?**

A   Yes, sir.

Q   **Did you wife want to go or you want to go or both or what?**

A   I suggested going.

Q   **You suggested going?**

A   I told her, "We have got to get our daughter back home."

Q   **Did you take any guns with you?**

A   Yes, I took two guns; I took a .38 Special Police gun that I had bought from a policeman down—*(inaudible)*—and he bought a new one.

Q   **Did you have any other guns with you?**

A   Yes; I had a reserve gun. Police always carry reserve. In case my gun got empty, I could pull out the other one; because I wouldn't have to stop and reload.

Q   **Did you plan to do some shooting over there?**

A   No, we hadn't sir—hadn't planned to shoot anyone. We took the guns along for protection.

Q   **What was the third gun you had—what kind of gun you had? What was this reserve gun?**

A   I took the riot gun, sir, shotgun; put it in the trunk of the Volkswagen.

Q   **I see.**

A   It's illegal to carry one in the car.

Q   **But you had the two guns in the car with you, didn't you?**

A   Yes.

Q   **Isn't it illegal to carry those, too?**

A   Yes.

Q   **Didn't you know that?**

A   Yes; but I thought I could get by with it. I had been taking reserve police training at Vernor Highway Station, and I know most of the guys there, and—

Q **I see.**

A —although we weren't supposed to carry guns, they said that unofficially we could, not to let anybody know we were; and if we got stopped with a gun, all we would have to do was show our ID badge, and they would generally let us go.

Q **So you thought you were safe then in that?**

A I thought I was sir, as long as I kept them concealed.

Q **Why did you think you were going to need the guns that night?**

A I took the guns for protection for the wife and I.

Q **Protection from who?**

A From the man who lived in the apartment. We had been there several times before—or three times—and I heard from an informer—I paid him fifty dollars to give me information.

I asked him—this was a colored boy—I asked the white boy—

Q **What was the colored boy's name? Was this one of the boys in the apartment?**

A I didn't know his name at the time; but later on I found out his name was Bob Hope, famous Bob Hope, the comedian Bob Hope—Bob Hope is supposed to have five hundred bananas—entertainer.

Q **What happened? You said you thought you would need protection from the man that owned the apartment?**

A Yes.

Q **Why was that?**

A Because this informer, who wanted to keep his identity secret, told us that—gun collection—he owned about half a dozen guns—gun fancier.

Q **Did you plan to shoot this man if you had to?**

A No, sir, I hadn't planned to hurt him.

Q **What were you going to do?**

A I was going to ring the doorbell; and when he came to the door, I was going to ask to get in.

And if he hadn't wanted to let us in, I guess I would have rapped on the door with the gun barrel and forced him to let me in.

Q **You would have forced your way in then?**

A Yes; but I wouldn't have shot him, just slugged him.

Q **But you didn't need to force your way in, is that right?**

A The door was unlocked. Always before we found it locked. Then later the caretaker assisted us.

Q   What did your wife say about taking the guns with you, about your plan?   Was she in agreement with this?

A   She didn't want to take the guns because she thought they were too dangerous.   She thought we might get in trouble by taking the guns.

Q   She didn't want you to take the guns?

A   No.   She insisted I didn't take them.

Q   But you did anyway?

A   I did anyway; but I thought that was my ace in the hole in case I got stuck up and fired on.

*   *   *

Q   How did you get into the door of the apartment where your daughter was?

A   To begin with, we got in the outside door—

Q   Yes.

A   —without any trouble—

Q   What about the inside door?

A   —didn't disturb anybody—*(inaudible).*

Q   Tell me about the inside door.   How did you get in that?

A   Yes, sir, I'm getting to that.

I tried the door; the door was locked.

I hesitated about breaking the door down because I know it's illegal; but I desperately wanted to get my daughter—*(inaudible, something about running out the window).*

I put my shoulder against the door, with all my force on the door; it fell off.

I learned later that the lock had loose screws in it, and they found that on the floor.   There were four screws.   The door was not broken, just forced the lock on it.

I did realize that I did wrong because breaking and entering—

Q   What did you do when you got in?   What did you see?

A   I had a light in my right hand.   My left hand was empty.

And I shined the light in around the room.

And, much to my horror, my light picked up my daugther's nude body and her boy friend's nude body, and they were embracing.

My daughter was facing the—I mean she had her back to the wall facing me, and he had his back toward me; and they were very surprised.

I don't know whether they even recognized us or not because strong light was in their eyes.

I wanted to call out to my daughter, but I didn't.

It was so horrible. I thought she was—I thought she was a virgin.

Q How did you feel? How did you feel right then?

A I felt terrible. I guess I went into shock.

Q What did you do?

A I wanted to hurt the boy but I knew the girl was guilty, too.

But because she was my daughter, I didn't want to hurt her.

So I sprang across the room, my wife was behind me; and then as I walked, I took out the revolver from the right side of my trousers.

I had put a pair of imitation pearl handles on the gun, and I had a Luger on the other side of my belt.

Q Which gun did you take out, the .38?

A I took out the revolver, sir; it's a six-shot.

Q What did you do with it?

A I grabbed it by the handle and struck the boy over the head—his left forehead. His back was turned toward me.

He had a look of surprise on his face. I felt sorry for him. He was such a small man. I didn't want to hit him, but—I just wanted to frighten him, I guess.

But when I struck at him, the gun barrel came down on his left forehead. I don't think it hurt him very much. I don't think it knocked him out.

And—so upset—

Much to my surprise, the gun discharged.

How stupid of me. I should have realized it and hit him with the butt of the gun. I thought I knew how to handle guns.

I was in the police reserves, Vernor Station; I enjoyed going to it.

Q The gun went off and struck your daughter?

A It struck the daughter. I don't know where it hit her. She let out a moan. I knew she was dead or dying.

Q How did you feel? How did you feel, Mr. Jackson? How did you feel right then? How did you feel?

A I felt like taking her to the hospital; but she laid so still with her eyes closed.

And I put my head on her chest to see if she was breathing; and I felt of her pulse, and she didn't have any, and—or it was very faint, I wasn't sure.

Q   What did you do?   How did you feel?

A   I felt like my world had ended.

Q   What happened?   What happened next?

A   I thought—(*inaudible*).

Q   What happened?   What happened next?

A   I shot her again.

Q   Why did you do that?   Why did you do that?

A   I thought she was suffering; and it hurt me to shoot her when I shot her.   I felt like I shot myself, too.

Q   You shot her again on purpose then to help her out, to relieve her suffering?

A   Yes, I shot her, I shot her.   It was in the breast.

   I didn't think it was fatal, though.

   I think it went through the breast, and it went out the other side.

Q   You shot her in the heart almost?

A   I didn't know it was the heart.   I thought the heart was more in the center of the body.   I just couldn't control myself.

Q   Couldn't control yourself.   What did you do then?

A   (*Inaudible.*)   Oh, my daughter, my daughter.   I wanted to grab her in my arms and take her out of there; wrap a sheet around her and take her to the hospital, possibly Mercy Hospital was the closest one.

Q   What did you do then?   You relieved her suffering.   Then what did you do?

A   (*Inaudible, something about without saying anything.*)

   She wasn't saying anything.   I realized she was dead.

Q   What did you do when you realized she was dead?   What did you do then, Mr. Jackson?

A   I didn't know what to do.

Q   What did you do?   What did you do when you found she was dead?

A   I looked around the room, and I saw these other poor boys laying there; and I felt sorry for them because I told them they were just out for a good time.   I thought they had taken advantage of my daughter and had talked her into going up there.

   Then, I guess, I shot Todd.

Q   You shot Todd then?

A   Yes, I think I shot him—

Q   You shot him because you felt sorry for him?

A   Well, I felt sorry for him—

Q   **Why else? Did you have some other feelings about him? What were your feelings?**

A   It was a mixed feeling. I felt sorry—

Q   **What was the other feeling?**

A   I felt disgusted that he would take advantage of my girl like that.

    I'm sure the girl loved him; but I didn't think he loved her. I thought he was just taking advantage of her.

Q   **Then what did you do after you shot Todd?**

A   I guess I just went all to pieces.

    I realized what I had done.

    And I shot two people.

    I didn't have any control over shooting Todd.

    If I could only have gone, I wouldn't have shot him. If I could only have thought, I could take my daughter to the hospital for medical treatment. They do wonders nowadays and are able to save people.

Q   **But you didn't do that. You relieved her suffering. Then you shot Todd. Then what did you do?**

A   I shot her to relieve her pain.

Q   **Did you shoot the other boy in the room?**

A   Yes.

Q   **Why did you shoot him?**

A   I don't know exactly. I didn't want to. I didn't blame them much.

    I got a suspicion maybe they were all taking turns with my daughter.

Q   **You thought they were all taking turns with her?**

A   Yes. I felt they were all ganging up on her. She was so innocent. I think she had sex desire at seventeen years old. I wanted her to try to overcome the desire.

Q   **Why should she overcome it?**

A   Because it's immoral to have sex outside of marriage. We wanted her to be pure and—(*inaudible*)—when she got married. So many people get married, and they don't seem to care whether the girl has had any experience or not.

Q   **Did you shoot the boy in the other room then?**

A   Yes.

Q **Why did you shoot him? Did you think he was taking turns, too, or was there another reason?**

A I thought he was taking turns, yes.

Q **How about Sally, did you want to—**

A The boy was colored, too; and I tried to get along with colored people.
   But I don't believe in intermating.

Q **Did you shoot him because he was colored?**

A Not especially. I respected him. I thought he was a nice boy.
   But I thought he had probably—(*inaudible*)—at my daughter around, too.
   I don't believe in sex between the races.
   I respect colored people.
   But I think they should—should respect white, and white should respect colored.
   And I don't think they should intermarry.

Q **How about Sally, where was she?**

A I didn't know where she was; but I assumed she was down in her apartment. We thought about going to her apartment—

Q **What for?**

A —and seeing if the daughter was there. We hoped she was there.

Q **What about after the shooting? After the shooting, did you go to Sally's apartment? Did you try to find Sally?**

A Yes.

Q **Why did you try to find Sally?**

A Before that I looked around the apartment to see if anyone else was in there, and I remembered a couch over near the window—over near the front of the window—and I looked all through the apartment because we had been there before, and some of the people had hid. We didn't know they had hid until we found it out later. And we thought somebody else might be hiding in there.

Q **You say 'we.' Was your wife with you during this time?**

A Yes, my dear wife was with me.

Q **Was she with you all this time?**

A Yes; and she was heartbroken. She went hysterical and screamed after the gun went off; and I wanted my daughter, I wasn't sure where she was hit. It must have been fatal. She let out a moan and—

Q **How about Sally, did you go to look for Sally?**

A Yes.

Q **Why were you looking for Sally?**

A Later I looked for her.

Q **Why? Tell me why.**

A I wanted to—I wanted to—

Q **What did you want?**

A I either wanted to frighten her, or I wanted to maybe shoot her. I wasn't sure whether I was going to shoot her or not.

I was getting over this by this time, and I realized something of what I've done.

I was so in shock; I hated myself for my lack of self-control and thought, "Oh, God, what have I done."

I accidentally shot and either killed or fatally wounded my daughter, and then I shot her companions; and I shouldn't have shot them because they were just having a good time, but I thought they were using my girl.

I'm sure she had never had intercourse before, and I wanted her to be pure.

Her mother was a virgin when I married her. She was the first virgin I had ever found.

Q **Did you ever find Sally that night?**

A No. No, I looked for her. I spoke to some of the people in the hall. These poor people were frightened. I held my gun down.

Q **How did that make you feel to have these people frightened around you?**

A I was awfully ashamed. I didn't want to hurt them.

I told one or two of them that I wouldn't hurt them, not to fear, that my quarrel wasn't with them, that I wanted to see a girl that I thought had led my girl astray.

* * *

[The videotape runs out before the examination is finished.]

[The *Pittsburgh News* reported that two women jurors "were noticed to have tears in their eyes during the showing" of the videotape.]

[*Jessie Burke* is a New York Central track operator.]

Q **And you have known him for eighteen years, is that right?**

A Right, sir.

Q **Are you familiar with his reputation for truth and veracity in the community where you know him, that is, among your and his fellow employees at Penn Central?**

A   Yes, sir.

Q   **What is his reputation in that respect?**

A   Every day when I see him—when he came on the job—he would speak; he's nice and a gentleman.

Q   **Would you believe him under oath?**

A   Yes, sir.

Q   **Are you familiar with his reputation for being a law-abiding member of the community?**

A   Yes, sir.

Q   **What is his reputation in that respect?**

A   His reputation—he was an engineer at that particular time.

Q   **What is his reputation for being a law-abiding person, if you know?**

A   I don't know, sir.

Q   **Do you consider yourself to be a friend of Mr. Jackson—**

A   Yes, sir.

Q   **—and he a friend of yours?**

A   Yes, sir.

Mr. Nelson: All right, you may examine.

Mr. Gilman: Q   **Mr. Burke, how long has it been since you worked directly with Mr. Jackson?**

A   How long?

Q   **Yes. How many years?**

A   I'd say five years, sir.

Q   **Have you ever known Mr. Jackson other than on the job—other than at Penn Central railroad?**

A   No, sir.

Q   **You have never had occasion to socialize with him?**

A   No, sir.

Q   **You have never had occasion to visit his home?**

A   No, sir.

Q   **You know nothing about his relationship with his family?**

A   No, sir.

Mr. Gilman: Thank you. No further questions.

Friday 4 December

[*Mrs. Learner Naomi Bennine* is called. She says Wilbur Jackson is always polite and well mannered. On cross-examination she discloses that Wilbur Jackson took her home from work and that she thinks he is honest because he is polite.]

[*Irene Smigelski,* mother of the Ingram police officer, also gives Wilbur Jackson high marks for truthfulness and honesty.]

[*Mary Jackson* is recalled and says that Wilbur Jackson called her from the police station to discuss care of the children. On cross-examination she once again denies telling the police that Todd Wilson did the killings.]

DEBBIE JACKSON

[*Debbie Jackson,* seventeen, testifies.]

Q   **Ever in your presence did Sally Tucker encourage your sister to move out of the house?**

A   Yes.

Q   **Was that one time or many times?**

A   Many times.

Q   **Where would those conversations take place, Debbie?**

A   At the apartment and at church, you know, on the way to church and at my house.

Q   **Did discussions like that take place at 4330 Lincoln—**

A   Yes.

Q   **—in the period of time between the time Sandy moved away the first time and she moved away the second time?**

A   Yes.

Q   **Did she, in fact, encourage Sandy to move out of your home in defiance of your parents' wishes?**

A   Yes.

Q   **You have known Sally Tucker, as you say, for a long while; haven't you?**

A   Yes.

Q   **Have you known her well enough that you have been able to form an impression as to her reputation for truth and veracity in the community?**

A   Yes.

Q   **And what is that reputation?**

A Well, she lied a lot, I thought.

Q **Now, there came a time one Sunday in May that Sandy moved out again, didn't she?**

A Yes.

Q **Was this again a surprise to you?**

A Yes, it was.

Q **And did you have an opportunity to read a letter that Sandy left at home?**

A Yes.

Q **During the week that followed, Debbie, of your knowledge, did your parents look for their daughter Sandy?**

A Yes.

Q **Did you participate or were you with them at any time when they were looking for her?**

A Yes.

Q **Your father, throughout your life as you remember, has been a hard-working man?**

A Yes.

Q **Do you feel that he is working hard, in your mind, to provide for his family?**

A Yes.

Q **Now, all that week that went by before the tragic events of May 8, did you ever once hear your father threaten any harm to your sister Sandy?**

A No.

Q **Did your father love your sister Sandy?**

A Yes.

Q **Are you afraid of your father today?**

A No.

Q **Do you love your father today?**

A Yes.

Mr. Tracy: I have no further questions.

[On cross-examination Debbie says she thinks Sally Jo Tucker controlled Sandy's mind.]

[*Robert Herbertson,* court clerk, testifies that on 25 September Wilbur Jackson took one and one-half to two hours to sign a personal bond form.]

[With psychiatric testimony coming up, Mr. Nelson asks that Wilbur Jackson be excused in his medical interests. The request is granted, but the court refuses to remove the prosecution psychiatrists from the court.]

[Figure 24 is an example of a *subpoena duces tecum,* a process by which the court commands a witness to produce documents or papers at a trial.]

DR. HUBERT MILLER

[*Dr. Hubert Miller,* forty-three, has been a psychiatrist since 1954. He is a Pittsburgh native and served as City Physician in which capacity he made over two thousand house calls. He currently works at Mercywood Psychiatric Hospital in Fox Chapel and has never before testified in a criminal case.]

[He first saw Wilbur at Mr. Nelson's request and found him depressed and suicidal. On Dr. Miller's recommendation, Jackson entered Mercywood, 6 October and stayed until 14 November. The doctor prescribed Thorazine (tranquilizer), Tofranil (antidepressant), and sodium amytal (sedative). When Wilbur remained depressed and uncommunicative, he was given, with his consent, electroconvulsive treatments. After Wilbur was anesthetized and given a muscle relaxant to prevent jerking, electrodes were placed on his temples to pass an electric current through his skull, causing an epileptic seizure. This was done six times; Dr. Miller saw Wilbur about fifteen times in the hospital. During the trial, Wilbur was still taking Triavil (mixture of antidepressant and tranquilizer) in moderately heavy dosage and an average dose of Placidyl (sleeping drug).]

Q You said he behaviorally was—there were some incidents while he was in the hospital that could be characterized as somewhat antisocial; is that right?

A There were episodes of bizarre behavior, as we describe it; some were antisocial.

Q Describe those episodes for us.

A He became very upset with another patient; I think frightened by another patient. The other patient was kind of an overbearing, arrogant kind of man. They almost got in a fight on several occasions.

Mr. Jackson, in the state he was in—the other man was in a seclusion room—he would go in and flick the lights on and off in a manner to irritate him and, I guess, succeeded.

Figure 24 Subpoena duces tecum

SUBPOENA - DUCES TECUM - RECORDER'S COURT

STATE OF PENNSYLVANIA
CITY OF PITTSBURGH
COUNTY OF ALLEGHENY

70-03042

PEOPLE OF THE STATE OF PENNSYLVANIA
     vs.

WILBUR CHESTER JACKSON

         TO: Mrs. Ardell Roeske
            Medical Records Librarian
            Mercywood Hospital
            4038 Jackson Road
            Fox Chapel, Pennsylvania

GREETINGS:

You are hereby commanded that, laying aside all and singular your
business and excuses, you be and appear before the Recorder's Court
of the City of Pittsburgh, in the Courtroom of the Honorable Joseph A.
Gillis, presiding Judge of said Court in the Pittsburgh, Hall of
Justice, corner of St. Antoine and Clinton Streets, in the City of
Pittsburgh, on Tuesday, the 1st day of December, 1970 at 9:00 o'clock
A.M. standard time, then and there to give evidence on the part of
the People in a case to be tried between the People of the State of
Pennsylvania, Plaintiff, and Wilbur Chester Jackson, Defendant; You
are further commanded to bring with you all medical and/or psychiatric
records, charts, reports, examinations, nursing records, out-patient
and in-patient records, consultations reports and any other records
pertaining to the above named person up to and including the current
date.

   Hereof, fail not, on pain of the penalty that will follow
thereon.

WITNESS, the Honorable Joseph A. Gillis, Judge of the Recorder's Court
of the City of Pittsburgh, on the 30th day of November, 1970.

Joseph A Gillis
JOSEPH A. GILLIS

        E. BURKE MONTGOMERY, Clerk

Seal Judge of Recorder's
      Court

        By: *Catherine Bachanek*
           DEPUTY CLERK

This was inappropriate behavior, specially because this man was of an assaultive nature.

I had to warn him several times on this.

Another time he secreted, without the knowledge of the attendants, twenty three apples in his room in a drawer. He would sneak them and put them in his drawer. He became uprighteously indignant when they discovered he had the apples.

* * *

The story he gave me at that time was that of growing up in terms of a rigid, as I describe it, background.

Q What do you mean by the use of that particular term?

A Rigid means when you are confronted with a set of circumstances, you always have the same kind of a response; and that contrasts with flexible, which means you might have various responses to the same situation.

* * *

Q In specific address to his activities with reference to his daughter Sandra following her leaving home in early April 1970, returning home, and then leaving home again in early May 1970, what history did you obtain from this man?

A Well, he told me several times about her leaving and about he and his wife getting her to return home at that time.

He told me he loved her and that he cared about her and that he had hopes for her—he indicated that in other ways—that he had hopes for her that she would become a doctor. This was something that meant a great deal to him. He hoped that she would marry.

It was important to him, as he reported it to me, that she would be virginal at the time of her marriage; something that he put a great deal of stress on.

Q Do you have any ability to discern why he put stress on that?

A Well, I believe that this was in terms of his own value system as he grew up as he was trying to live his life.

You can oversimplify it and call it the value system of a man coming from the mountains.

His cultural background, this kind of thing, is extremely poor; more so, I think, than in other people.

Q What else did he tell you with reference to his efforts concerning his daughter?

A Now, he had gotten—or I believe bought her a car—or bought a car for her use in his own name as a kind of inducement and reward in terms of her wanting to go to college, and he was encouraging that.

I believe in his own mind that he thought of her as an extension of his own being, that her being in school was her doing the things that he had wished to do and was unable to do for the various reasons.

Q   What were his various reasons as he related them to you?

A   Well, he has an attitude about himself. I think you could oversimplify it and call it an inferiority complex.

He did not feel he was specially articulate, that he could speak well, that he was very intelligent.

He was not a very assertive person in terms of searching for work.

For example, he has a college degree and was qualified as a teacher in his home state and never, apparently, sought out such work.

The work he did seek out, by my standards, is not quite the achievement of being a teacher; but, by his, I think they are.

I feel that he is underachieved; and I feel he had the intelligence and ability to do something a little more white-collar in nature.

Q   His inability to achieve—

A   In terms of his training.

Q   —was as a result of some inner feeling of personal inadequacy?

A   I believe so.

Q   Do you attribute certain specific—well, certain specifics to his sense of inadequacy, what you say can be imprecisely referred to as an inferiority complex?

A   Yes.

Q   What would they be?

A   It's hard to give you specific examples.

This is the man's demeanor, the way he carried himself, his obsequiousness with other people.

With me, for example, he always refers to me as sir.

Other people who he feels are more educated or more intelligent or more powerful than he is, he is very obsequious, deferring.

* * *

Q   In what way and to what extent did that circumstance [working sixty hours in five days] affect his state of mind as of 2:00 A.M., May 8, 1970?

A   From what he has told me—his description of it—I believe that he was exhausted.

Q   You mean physically exhausted?

A   Physically and mentally. I don't think that his judgment was operating in any normal way.

Q Now, what effect, Doctor, would this state of physical and mental exhaustion have upon Mr. Jackson's ability to formulate logical judgments consistent with problems of a very moving nature that he felt he was then and there compelled to deal with?

A It would interfere with his being able to be logical, I think, substantially, materially, that he would not be able necessarily to put on the usual brakes, inhibitions, and behavior that characterized him in the years before this time, as I know of him.

* * *

Q You are aware, though, of the fact that he was unable to physically locate his daughter Sandra during that four-day period?

A That's right.

Q Now, what effect upon this man, in the state of physical and mental exhaustion, would the frustration of an unavailing four-day search for that girl have, in your judgment?

A It would make his feeling of frustration and his desire to find her all the more intense, all the more urgent.

Q Would it be fair to characterize it as being all-consuming?

A I think so.

Q Based upon your professional and academic knowledge, Doctor, and your experience as a thirteen-year veteran in the field of psychiatry, and the evaluative and diagnostic work that you did during the course of your exposure—your professional exposure—to Mr. Jackson, having seen him *in toto* upon sixteen different occasions for the specific purpose of evaluation and psycho evaluation, not including six occasions when you saw him for the purpose and the specific purpose of administering to him electroconvulsive therapy, do you have an opinion as to his mental and his personality state; and, if so, what is that opinion?

A At the moment—and I'm talking about now.

Q Yes.

A —I see him as a man who is convalescing from a severe depression and controlled, in part, by medication.

That is right now.

Q You are telling us right now that this man is under medical controls right now—

A This moment.

Q —and not what he might otherwise be if he were not, is that right?

A I don't know what he would be otherwise.

Q All right.

A   The depression might return. That is my opinion of him at this moment.

Q   **What, in your judgment, Doctor, based upon these same factors, was this man mentally and personalitywise at 2:00 A.M., on May 8, 1970?**

A   At that point when he walked into the building there—

First of all, the most obvious thing is that he was in a state of exhaustion; regardless of what else he might have been, he was that. It affected his control of himself and his ability to appreciate the reality around him.

This is as he walked in.

Now, when he got up there, it's my opinion that the last thing that—the last shred, I should say, of control of his own behavior and his own reasonableness was lost at the moment that he walked in that room and saw the girl and the boy in bed together; and I believe at that moment—

I would have to call that an acute psychotic episode, which means that he was divorced from reality; and the behavior that he went through, I would say, was acute and not something that he could control.

Q   **Incapable, Doctor?**

A   I don't believe he could have controlled himself after that time.

Q   **Incapable of control?**

A   Incapable.

Q   **Now, did he tell you, Doctor, in relation to his history to you, that he initially went forward and with a drawn pistol, with the barrel of a drawn pistol, struck the boy who was in bed with his daughter over the head?**

A   Many times he told me about that.

Q   **What was he endeavoring to do in doing that?**

A   He, as he told me about it, in my opinion about what he was telling me, was that he wanted to punish this young man for having taken his daughter's virginity or being a party to it; because he believed they were all involved.

Now, up until that time, no matter what anyone had told him, he could still in his own heart and in his own mind deny it; because that's what he did, because he had evidence prior to that time, from what I gathered from him, that she might have been doing something of this nature; but at that moment he could no longer deny it.

Q   **Because there it was for his own naked eyes to see, is that right?**

A   That's right. I believe that was quite a shock to him. That's putting it mildly. Whatever self-control he had, whatever ability he had to maintain behavior, which he has most of the time, was lost.

Q   What happened to this man, Doctor, at the terminal end of that blow, pistol discharged, and the bullet hit his daughter, dealt her a mortal wound?

A   At that moment, I believe that he was already in a state that he was no longer behaving realistically. I don't believe that he—

I have to put it the other way around.

I believe he was psychotic at that moment, and from that point on—from that moment that he saw them there—is not explainable in any reasonable manner. He was out of control. All his hurt, disappointment, rage, were not things he could control anymore at that point.

Q   He was beyond the point where he had any control over his actions at all, is that right?

A   I believe so.

The Court: I think at this point we will adjourn for the weekend.

Monday 7 December

[Juror number five, Mrs. Wiley, calls up and reports that she has the flu. She is excused. Judge Gillis suggests the jury send her a get-well card. Nelson announces he too has the flu and will try to give it to Mr. Gilman.]

[Dr. Miller is cross-examined.]

Q   How did you first come to be involved in this case; who approached you, Dr. Miller?

A   Mr. Nelson.

Q   Did you know Mr. Nelson previous to that?

A   Yes.

Q   How long have you known Mr. Nelson?

A   On, since early in the year; sometime in the spring, late winter of last year.

Q   How did you happen to meet him?

A   At lunch; the same way I met you.

Q   At Carl's?

A   Carl's. [Carl's Chop House—a judicial favorite]

Mr. Nelson: If that's relevant—the length of time he's known me—I don't know if that has anything to do with this.

The Court:	Well, we would like to find out where you are getting around.
Mr. Nelson:	I'd just as soon nobody knew that.
The Court:	Maybe he met you professionally—his profession.

[Dr. Miller testifies he did not give Wilbur Jackson an electroencephalogram (measuring the brain's electrical activity) or a Rorschach (inkblot) test, or a thematic apperception, or a Bender gestalt, or a Wechsler Adult Intelligence Test because they would have indicated only that Wilbur Jackson was receiving electroconvulsive treatments.]

Q Well, tell me, once again, what that conclusion was, Dr. Miller, regarding the illness or the problem that Mr. Jackson had on May 7 and the early morning of May 8.

A Well, I feel—it is my opinion—that he was functioning as an obsessive-compulsive person on the surface with a paranoid kind of underpinning, that is, beneath that was the potential for a mental illness.

That when he got there; and with the various factors involved: the fatigue, exhaustion, his great apprehension for his daughter, his concern for her; and then walking in and seeing this one thing in terms that was something that was extremely important to him, the idea of her virginity, he could no longer deny to himself that she was not a virgin; that the underlying illness broke out.

Q You say it broke out. Was it at that point, you testified, Mr. Jackson could no longer control his conduct?

A Yes.

Q Was it before the gun fired, before he struck the young man on the head with the gun, that he couldn't control his conduct, or after that?

A My testimony was that when he saw his daughter in this position with this young man; at that point.

Q At that point he could no longer control his conduct?

A That's right.

Q You indicated that one of the factors that went into that opinion was the fact that Mr. Jackson had worked a great deal of time during the last week before that incident, is that correct?

A Yes.

Q Are you aware that Mr. Jackson, during his service with the New York Central and Penn Central Railroad, worked overtime a great many times during his nineteen years?

A He so informed me, yes; he sought it out.

Q As a matter of fact—well, you recall being a young intern, don't you, Dr. Miller?

A Yes, I do.

Q They work pretty hard, don't they?

A Yes.

Q Do you remember how many hours straight you worked during the course of your internship at any one time?

A Well, one time comes to my mind, yes.

Q How many hours straight did you work?

A I worked thirty-six hours in all.

Q And that's without any rest at all?

A Without any rest.

Q I take it you didn't commit any crimes during that period.

A Well, that's the reason I recall it. On my way home I lost control of my automobile because I was partly asleep and because the pavement was slippery, and I collided with the rear end of a truck.

Q You remember doing that, though, don't you?

A I remember. There was a little lapse in my awareness as to where I was on the road, yes.

Q You are not saying, are you, that working a great deal causes mental illness?

A It causes exhaustion.

Q It causes one to be tired?

A Right.

Q Now, do you feel that Mr. Jackson had control of himself when he went to the building 4330 Lincoln on Monday and on Tuesday?

A From what I'm able to reconstruct, yes.

Q He knew what he was doing when he went there on Monday and Tuesday?

A Yes.

Q And he knew what he was saying, is that correct?

A As far as I am able to determine.

Q Now, on Thursday night–Friday morning when he came home from work and had his normal glass of milk, he at that point had not lost control of his activities or of his conduct; is that correct?

A As far as I can tell, he was in control of himself.

Q When he took the three guns with him and loaded them, he was in control of himself?

A   I would have to say so.

Q   **And when he drove over there, he was in control of himself; is that correct?**

A   That summary of time I'm not sure about.

Q   **So you are saying it's possible that he might have lost control earlier?**

A   It's possible; I don't know.

Q   **So even possibly driving over there is when he could no longer control himself, is that correct?**

A   It's possible.

Q   **Would you say that at that time Mr. Jackson didn't know the difference between right and wrong?**

A   I think he knew the difference between right and wrong.

Q   **Would you say when he drove over there he couldn't help driving over there; was he acting under an irresistible impulse when he drove his car over to 4330 Lincoln?**

A   He was acting under a very compelling need; now, whether that fits the idea of irresistible impulse, I don't think I am competent to say. That's a rather foggy term.

Q   **Well, that is the law, however.**

A   It's still a foggy term.

Q   **So you are not sure whether or not he was acting under an irresistible impulse at the time he drove over to 4330 Lincoln?**

A   He had a compelling need to go and get his daughter.

Q   **All right, so he wanted to go and get his daughter back at that point. Could he have stopped himself from going?**

A   I don't think he could have; I think he had to go.

Q   **You think he had to go?**

A   Right.

Q   **When he arrived and locked his car and went up the stairs and broke the door in, is it also your opinion that he couldn't stop what he was doing at that point?**

A   I don't think he could.

Q   **He couldn't turn around and go back to the car and go home at that point?**

A   I don't think so.

Q Now, when he broke in the door and walked into the bedroom, would that hypothesis continue, that he could no longer control what he was doing?

A He had to get his daughter.

Q Now, did he change any when he saw his daughter in bed with this young man?

A I believe so.

Q What happened then?

A I believe that his entire world collapsed at that point. Everything that he felt, everything he had wished for this girl, the ideas that he had about her career and about her marrying, was all immediately, instantaneously washed out.

Q What happened to his mind at that point; what happened to his thinking process?

A I believe that there was a change in the state of his organization of his thinking.

Q What was that change?

A It was what I call a regressive change. He became suddenly much more primitive, unrealistic, and much more subject to wish, and he was no longer behaving in regard to the reality of the situation.

Q Could he control what he was doing?

A I don't believe he could.

* * *

Q Do you believe that all criminals are mentally ill, Doctor?

A No, I don't.

Q Now, at what point in the Vernor Station was it that Mr. Jackson regained control?

A I don't know.

Q All right.

A I say at sometime after. I can't give you an exact time.

Q Why do you say it occurred at sometime after?

A Because of the nature of his behavior. Going there. He was compelled to go and confess. He was compelled to give a confession. He was compelled to give great detail in his confession. This was his usual conscientious obsessive personality operating with a vengeance. Vengeance was on himself at this point. He had to do that.

* * *

Q Dr. Miller, if a police officer had been standing next to Mr. Jackson at the time he saw his daughter in bed with this young man, would Mr. Jackson have stopped at that point?

A Contrary to what he himself said, I think he could not have stopped himself.

Q So, even though Mr. Jackson told Dr. Robey and Dr. Blunt that he would have stopped if a police officer had been present, it's your opinion that he could not have stopped?

A That's correct.

* * *

Q Are you aware that on the twenty-sixth day of October while at Mercywood Hospital, Mr. Jackson threatened to kill a patient there?

A I don't remember the exact date; there was quite a bit of—

Q I want you to attempt to refresh your recollection by reading this entry from the twenty-sixth day of October *(producing instrument).**

A *(Examining instrument)* Yes.

Q And on that date did he threaten to kill a patient?

A According to this note. I wasn't there.

* * *

Q I will show you an entry that was made on Wednesday, October 28, Doctor, by a registered nurse at the hospital.

I will ask you, on that day did Mr. Jackson tell an attendant that he would squash him like a bug for giving him orders?

A *(Examining instrument)* This is a registered nurse's description of behavior on ward during that shift.

Q Do you rely on the nurse?

A This one I think is a reliable nurse, yes, sir.

Q Did she indicate that Mr. Jackson indicated to an attendant that he would squash him like a bug?

A It says that here.

Q Is it a fact that during his stay there Mr. Jackson made what I would call passes at several of the nurses that work at the hospital?

---

* Leonard Gilman later stated, "We got an anonymous phone call from Mercywood Hospital. We don't know to this day who called, who told us what was in those records. It was because of that phone call that I subpoenaed the records from Mercywood Hospital and found all these strange things that were happening between Jackson and people at Mercywood."

A   Yes.

Q   **Is that unusual or not unusual?**

A   Very unusual.

* * *

Q   **Did this nurse report that Mr. Jackson told her that he is a revengeful person, "people I hate in 1949, I still hate; people I then loved, I still do."**

He then told the nurse, according to this record, that he had killed three people, "three of the killings I'm proud of; the other one I'm not. I would have two daughters; one would be a little over seventeen. I have one quirk, and that is that I believe in virginity. I have set rules for morality for those girls. Anything they do outside of that, I always stood up for. My sons could do anything they want; murder each other if they want, that's their business."

This nurse also reported that Mr. Jackson said he did not agree with his doctor's disappointment in his behavior.

He also stated, the only reason he goes to RT—

Is that recreational therapy?

A   That's correct.

Q   **—is for a little flirtatious enjoyment.**

Did he also tell the nurse—does the record indicate he told the nurse, he is an aggressive man. "I have always threatened, forced, or bribed my way through life. I can't do that here, and I don't like it."

Does the record also reflect that Mr. Jackson told the attendant that he had told his daughter that because of his high regard for virginity that when she married he would sign a contract with the bridegroom to the effect that he could bring the bride back after the wedding night if he weren't satisfied.

Did he also tell the attendant that he had had an unhappy childhood because of his speech impediment and his light weight.

Does the record reflect that he told the nurse that he had bought a strait jacket at an auction and dog chain; that these were for the purpose of restraining his daughter. This was after she had left home. This was for the purpose, quote, "to break her in like you would a new horse."

Does the record also reflect that Mr. Jackson described the murder scene, that he stated that he hit the daughter's companion on the head with the gun which discharged and hit his daughter; that he referred to a female companion of his daughter that he felt led the daughter astray.

Then he added to the nurse, "I would have killed her, too."

He stated that he has always been a social misfit.

Did he also state that he attended P.M. recreational therapy and spent the entire evening at a table of teenagers who were laughing a lot, and Mr. Jackson stated the girls were telling dirty jokes, and that he didn't know girls that age knew such jokes, and he seemed to enjoy the evening program, which was a sing-along.

Now, is that what the records reflect as to what Mr. Jackson told the nurse on November 2?

A   That's what she wrote there.

* * *

DR. EMANUEL TANAY

[*Dr. Emanuel Tanay* is a native Pole and a former concentration camp inmate. He holds many psychiatric titles and organization memberships. He authored a psychiatric study of homicide, which he presented to the American Psychiatric Association and was printed in the *American Journal of Psychiatry*. He also presented a paper on Jack Ruby (the killer of Lee Harvey Oswald) to the World Congress of Psychiatry. He has examined eighty homicide defendants and testified that fifty were insane. He has examined Wilbur Jackson twice, for three hours each time, in addition to reviewing his history.]

A   I also was particularly interested in what kind of a person Mr. Jackson is. What kind of a person he was prior to this act.

And, again, just to summarize it very, very briefly, I received a picture that he has been a very rigid person, an individual who was raised in an environment of adherence to religious—strict religious principles. He was a very submissive person throughout his life, self-abasing. He impressed me as someone who would not be able to express anger or feelings, in fact, of any kind of an overt basis, it would have to always be indirect. And there are many examples of that in my contact with him.

For example, he was extremely polite, excessively so, I would say, and this is characteristic of him.

He also makes himself out to be habitually—not consciously, but habitually—kind of a country bumpkin. Although, I think he is much more; he is intelligent, and, in fact, well educated, yet his usage of the language and the way he relates generally, conveys that he has great many feelings of inferiority about himself, and has always had.

So that's one important feature, and I think we could elaborate upon this quite a bit. But the fact is that throughout his life he has been a very law-abiding, strict, rigid individual.

Then the other facet—and I might elaborate on this later—was the fact that he was very identified with his family, particularly his deceased daughter, Sandra. She was his favorite. And both Mrs. Jackson and Mr. Jackson were quite open about this.

* * *

A   Mr. Jackson is the product of a very rigid environment; his parents are Southern Baptists who, for example, do not want to have a television. In the area where he grew up, to have a television was a sin.

    Mr. Jackson recalled that when—not so long ago, I don't remember now when it was—when he purchased a television for his father there was considerable discussion about it.

    This was an environment where one was very repressed. He does say that he worships his father, who was, in fact, an extremely strict individual.

    So this is the reason, the foundation, for his own rigidity.

* * *

A   So that essentially dissociative reaction is a condition where the ego of the individual has been overwhelmed by a stress situation.

Q   **I see. Dissociative reaction, however, is a mental or personality manifestation on the neurosis level, is that right?**

A   That is right. It is a mental disorder that falls in the general category of neurosis.

Q   **All right. Now how does it—how does it manifest itself upon an individual that succumbs to it?**

A   Primarily by the breakdown of the customary defenses of an individual. The habitual way of behaving is broken down.

* * *

A   On page 469 of *Psychiatric Textbook on Modern Clinical Psychiatry*, dissociative reaction is described as, quote:

    "At times an anxiety may so overwhelm and disorganize the personality that certain aspects or functions have become dissociated from each other. In some instances the personality may be so disorganized that defense mechanisms govern consciousness, memory and temporarily even the total individual with little or no participation on the part of the conscious personality."

    Which essentially describes the features that I have referred to, and, in my opinion, also refers to the case at hand.

Q   **All right. Now, Doctor, based upon your knowledge and experience in the field of psychiatry, extending over a period of time embracing now the better part of two decades, and your academic background in this field, you have rather an intimate exposure to the field of psychiatry as it particularly applies to the legal ramifications of psychosis and neurosis, and so forth, do you have an opinion—and**

if so what is your opinion—as to what happened to Wilbur Jackson at about 2:00 A.M. on May 8, 1970, when he burst into apartment 9 on 4330 Lincoln, and thereupon found his daughter naked in bed with another boy, embraced with that boy who was also naked in that bed?

A   Now, psychiatrically, I would say that this—when he entered that particular apartment, and keeping in mind that he has been exposed to stress over all this particular—this whole week practically, hasn't slept, was in constant search for his daughter, has been frustrated in that respect, suffered a recent humiliation in terms of his wife and son having been roughed up; that at that point he was really on the brink of some kind of a breakdown, and this additional stress of seeing his daughter, whom he believed to be a virgin, to whom it was very important to him that she should be highly moral, and in his mind she always was, he described it to me repeatedly as dainty, innocent, to see his daughter in bed in what could have been construed as the act of intercourse, with other persons present, I think this was such an overwhelming stress to him that his conscious ego was overwhelmed and he entered a state of dissociative reaction. And at that point he had no conscious control over his behavior. Simply reacted; his whole pent-up anger exploded.

Q   **Doctor, would it be inconsistent with your finding that he did become overcome by this state; that he thereafter was unable to recall all the details of his actions while he was in apartment 9 and while he was in 4330 Lincoln, or Stonehead Manor, on the early morning of the eighth of May?**

A   It would not be inconsistent. In fact, it would be supportive of this particular opinion that there was faulty recollection as to what transpired.

Q   **As a matter of fact, while he was at the Vernor Station, within a matter of twenty minutes or twenty-five minutes of the occurrence of the events that have led him here to trial, he found it necessary to call his wife and ask her how many people he had shot, or if he had shot a colored boy, would that be inconsistent with your findings?**

A   No it would not be inconsistent. In fact, it would be supportive of it. It would indicate that when these activities were taking place he was not fully conscious of what was going on. Certainly, killing a human being is an event that no one, if he did consciously participate in it, could forget. Or, at least, not willingly could forget.

*   *   *

[Dr. Tanay explains why Wilbur took his guns with him on 8 May.]

A   My impression is that he might have had the intention to possibly threaten someone, you know, to say—or to scare someone if he encountered any opposition.

I believe that might have been one of the reasons.

Q   To possibly overawe any potential opposition?

A   I believe sometimes people refer to a gun as a persuader.

Q   Yes.

A   And although I consider it to be a rather poor judgment to use it in this fashion, but many people who have guns view guns as such, or refer to guns as equalizers or whatever.

I believe that something like that might have been in back of Mr. Jackson's mind.

Q   Well, do you believe, Doctor, that he intended to kill four people when he armed himself with those two revolvers when he left his home?

A   No, he did not. It would be so inconsistent with the whole history of this individual. With his whole makeup. He could not, in my opinion, formulate the conscious notion, the wish, or the intent, to kill anyone, and certainly not killing his daughter.

So I would say that at the time when he took the guns with him, he did not have the intention to kill anyone.

Tuesday 8 December

[On cross-examination Dr. Tanay reveals that in various court appearances he has testified twice for the prosecution and twenty times for the defense. In seventeen out of twenty times he said the defendant was suffering from dissociative reaction. He saw Wilbur Jackson only twice before the trial began; Mary Jackson was the only other person he interviewed.]

Q   All right. When he entered into the bedroom and saw his daughter in bed, that's when the dissociative reaction began, is that correct?

A   That is my opinion, yes.

Q   All right. Now at that moment did Mr. Jackson know the difference between right and wrong?

A   Oh, I think that would not even be relevant, since he had from that point on acted in a kind of automatic fashion so that there would be no time for reflection, for certainly he is an individual when consciously in control knows the difference between right and wrong. But that particular time it was just like a reflex response so that there would be no reflection upon it.

Q   So he couldn't stop what he was doing at that point?

A   That is my view of it.

Q   Incidentally, Doctor Tanay, in your experience have you talked with people who, after doing something that they feel is wrong or un-

pleasant, tend to want to forget what they did. Doesn't that happen, as a matter of fact?

A Oh, yes. That happens, and it happens particularly if what the individual did is inconsistent with their own self-image.

Q So is it possible then, Dr. Tanay, that Mr. Jackson is trying to forget what he remembers as a terrible, horrible experience to him?

A I am sure he is trying to forget various aspects of it, but I am also sure that in that particular status he was at the time, things transpired which he did not remember immediately.

You see, I think what you are referring to is the process of repression. Something unpleasant happens, and then an individual does utilize this defense mechanism of repression. I think that happens too.

But I think in this instance the hazy recollection that Mr. Jackson has for the event has to do with the fact that he was not functioning; was disrupted.

[Dr. Tanay says that when Wilbur Jackson was at Mercywood he was sick, psychotic, and paranoid and should not have received shock treatments. Dr. Tanay is cross-examined closely concerning his seemingly frequent diagnosis of dissociative reaction. Dr. Miller, in his testimony, had said Wilbur suffered an acute psychotic episode, not dissociative reaction.]

[Outside the presence of the jury there is a discussion about a mysterious "Jay" who originally rented apartment 9 with Todd Wilson.]

THE PROSECUTION'S REBUTTAL

[The defense rests, and Gilman calls his first rebuttal witness.]

[*Henry Crawford* is a Pittsburgh police officer. He arrived at the Jackson home ninety minutes after the shootings. He found the front door barricaded with a sofa and dresser. He took Mrs. Jackson to police headquarters, and, on the ride downtown, she said Sandy had been killed by her boy friend.]

[*Dr. Ames Robey* is called. He is the director of the Forensic Center where Dr. Blunt worked. Dr. Robey, born in Boston and educated at Harvard and Boston University Medical School, had been director of Bridgewater (Mass.) State Hospital for the criminally insane. There he had had contact with some two thousand patients. He estimates he testifies for the defense in 50 percent of his court appearances. He said the Forensic Center had been established as a result of a professional article he wrote. He is the first and only director of the center.]

[Dr. Robey states that he did not treat Wilbur Jackson during his sixty-day stay at the center, but saw him at Mercywood Hospital in Fox Chapel. He says that Wilbur Jackson believed that Stonehead Manor "catered to addicts and blacks and whites and addicts and pushers" and that "they made stag movies there." He testifies that Wilbur Jackson believes Sandy and Todd had just finished intercourse when they were rudely interrupted. Dr. Robey says Wilbur Jackson feels the police did not use the proper toxicological tests, as they (the police) should have found evidence of drugs in the bodies. Wilbur also told Dr. Robey how much he loved the train crew.]

[Dr. Robey continues:]

I asked him how old he was; and he said he was forty-six now, had been married since the age of twenty-three, having been married on Christmas Eve 1947; his wife was twenty-one at the time, and she was a virgin when he first slept with her before marriage; and he had said to himself since the age of twelve if he ever found a virgin, he would marry her.

Then he said:

"I'm not strict; but this thing is very important to me. I'm certainly no saint myself; but I place a high price on virginity.

"I like to say about my daughters, if their husband wasn't satisfied, they could return them after the first night.

"But this doesn't apply to myself. I might step out on my wife; but I might destroy my wife if she ever stepped out on me."

I asked him about:

"Isn't this an interesting sort of double standard, where you can step out, but she can't?"

And he returned to this very high price on virginity, that this meant everything.

[Dr. Robey also states that Wilbur believed the occupants of Stonehead Manor to be rough Vietnam veterans who knew karate. Wilbur had once found a cartridge in an ashtray there, leading him to believe guns were stored there.]

Wednesday 9 December

[Dr. Ames Robey continues to relate Wilbur Jackson's thoughts. Apparently, Wilbur believed Stonehead Manor harbored deserters from the service. Wilbur was very disappointed when Sandy was allowed to leave with the boys following the Mary-on-the-car-hood incident— "the police just sat there with their fingers up their ass. I have little respect for the law." He was horrified at the thought of his wife chasing after Sandy at 80 MPH and yelling, "We will take you to Disneyland," and Sandy yelling back, "Later, mother, later."]

[Wilbur told Dr. Robey that he'd chain Sandy up if necessary and that he even had a straitjacket. He said he didn't like integrated schools or racial mixing. He felt that if Sandy had had a nightgown on, or there hadn't been a "colored boy" sleeping in the room, the whole thing probably wouldn't have happened. Wilbur also said he would dedicate his life to fighting drugs.]

Q   What was your diagnosis of Mr. Jackson, Dr. Robey?

A   It was my diagnosis that as of the moment I saw him Mr. Jackson was showing a reactive neurotic depression that I considered to be in response to his entire situation of being charged with murder, and that there was a basic personality disorder, long-term, all his life, that I felt was most accurately described as a mixed personality.

Because he showed three major elements.

The obsessive-compulsive personality disorder, in which this careful detail in everything is done just exactly so.

The passive-aggressive aspect, which is a funny psychiatric term I can explain later.

And a relatively new term in the new *Diagnostic Manual,* called explosive personality.

I saw no evidence of psychosis and no evidence that any had existed.

I saw no evidence of any neurotic pattern above and beyond the depression that I felt was reactive to his present setting.

Q   Then you indicated that at the time you saw him you felt Mr. Jackson was suffering from a personality disorder; is that correct?

A   Well, "suffering from" might not be the word; but certainly he had a personality disorder.

Q   Is a personality disorder a mental illness?

A   No, sir, they are not generally considered so.

They are a life-style. There are a good many types of them. They are certainly not seen as sick. They are not hospitalized.

Q   I see. And this personality disorder you indicated was made up of three parts or three separate characteristics?

A   Yes, sir.

Q   The first you term as what?

A   Obsessive-compulsive.

Q   The second you indicated was passive-aggressive?

A   Yes, sir.

Q   What does that mean?

A   It's an interesting term. It sounds as though it's a misnomer.

How can you be passive and aggressive simultaneously?

It's a person who is going to do as little work as possible; and, by God, they are aggressive about it.

With all due respect to your office, Mr. Gilman, you have a secretary upstairs who when you go up she scowls at you and just sits there; and you really have to push her to get her to do anything.

Now, this is a good example of passive-aggressive.

She is certainly not psychotic.

Q   Go ahead, doctor.

A   This picture, I think, is well brought out.

His attitude toward the railroad; the delight in which he expressed so many times over and over again through the interview of having a job in which he was being paid, but he could sit and read his newspaper, or that he could, if there was a five-man crew, get off and go do something else or take another job; that he could take his radio and put his feet up on the cab window; and that it was high pay for no work, is the implication.

I think this kind of thing is very typical of the passive-aggressive.

They will be there at their job; but when it comes down to actually producing work, they are often less happy about it.

Q   Now, you indicated that the third part of this personality disorder was the explosive ingredient.   What does that mean?

A   Well, very much just as it implies; that this is an individual that tends to have a great deal of underlying anger.

Now, most of the time he hides it.

In fact, quite typically, at least outside the home, they are very polite, almost as though they are going way over the other direction; they are tying to hide the fact that they are angry.

But we see it at home, mostly.   They are rather angry people. They will explode suddenly.   They will very often strike out physically, hitting a wife or a daughter or a family member.

Outside the home this is rarely seen.   That they have to be pushed relatively far, again, outside the home.

But when they are pushed, finally they get furious, and they explode.

*   *   *

Q   Did you find any evidence of dissociative reaction when you examined and spoke with Mr. Jackson?

A   No, sir; and, of course, because of the possibility that this diagnosis might arise, I went over him extremely carefully, looking for possible evidence of a dissociative reaction, and could find no indication from either the history of the events or from his whole past history any previous signs of any kind of neurotic reaction and the like. Just no evidence.

I can't say there wasn't sexual conflicts.

I think the whole very strong concern and this whole double standard where the male may run around, but the female must remain absolutely pure, certainly implies that he has some very strong underlying sexual feelings.

But whether these are based in any kind of emotional problems, or whether they are based just on very rigid upbringing, it is difficult to sort out.

[Dr. Robey also testifies that Wilbur Jackson had no amnesia, but that events occurred so rapidly he couldn't retain them all.]

Q What is your opinion, Dr. Robey?

A It is my opinion, from review of all the material, that he was indeed legally sane as I understand the law concerning sanity.

Q Did Mr. Jackson suffer from any mental illness or mental defect at the time he was in apartment number 9 and committed the acts with which he is charged?

A No, sir. Personality disorder, being extremely angry, losing his temper, yes. But, at least diagnostically, these cannot be seen as mental illnesses. So I see no indication that there was even a mental illness.

Q Did he know the difference between right and wrong at the time he was in apartment number 9, Dr. Robey?

A Yes, sir.

Q Was he acting under an irresistible impulse at the time he shot and killed those four young people in apartment number 9?

A Well, irresistible, no.

[Dr. Robey is not shaken on cross-examination.]

[Dr. Lynn Blunt, who conducted the videotaped sodium brevital interview, returns to the stand as a prosecution witness. He is questioned extensively on his qualifications, his background, and his duties. He was in charge of determining whether Wilbur Jackson was competent to stand trial.]

Q Based upon your evaluation of Mr. Jackson, and on your experience, do you have an opinion as to what has caused Mr. Jackson to forget certain aspects of what happened on the early morning of May 8th?

A Yes. I feel—and this was brought out in psychological testing also—that Mr. Jackson is a rather primitive type of personality who tends to use a considerable amount of denial, and this accompanying some repression of the events which I think would be kind of natural in terms of wanting to forget this kind of thing, took place after the fact.

Q So any memory loss Mr. Jackson claims to have suffered, in your opinion, took place after the events of May 8th?

A From my evaluation of all the facts involved, I would say that this would be the case.

* * *

Q Dr. Blunt, do you have a diagnosis of Mr. Jackson as of the time that you saw him, November 4, 1970? At the time you saw him last.

A Yes, I do.

Q And what is that diagnosis?

A Personality disorder of the obsessive-compulsive type with passive-dependent and explosive features.

Q And does that diagnosis concur with the diagnosis made by Dr. Robey?

A Well, not exactly, but roughly. It's a question of which personality characteristics you feel are most important.

Q I see. In your opinion was Wilbur Jackson suffering from a dissociative reaction on the early morning of May 8, 1970?

A I see no evidence of that whatsoever.

Q What leads you to believe he was not suffering from a dissociative reaction?

A Well, I think the fact that, first of all, I don't see that there was any real amnesia for what happened. I think this is borne out by the confession that was made. I think that on the second part, in a dissociative reaction, the action that results from the person having a dissociative reaction is something that is not connected directly with what is going on at the time.

Thirdly, Mr. Jackson himself referred to, he said, quote: "I don't know why I lost my temper." We said in the interview at Mercywood that he blew his stack, and it was very obvious, I think, that he simply became extremely angry and had an unresisted impulse rather than an irresistible impulse.

Q All right. And would you define an unresisted impulse?

A An unresisted impulse is an impulse to do something which somebody can keep from doing if they want to, or if the conditions are right, or if there were some conditions, such as a policeman being present, if this would deter it, then I say it is unresisted impulse.

Q I see. In your opinion was Mr. Jackson legally responsible on the early morning of May 8, 1970, when he shot and killed four people in apartment number 9?

A   Although he was under a lot of pressure, I feel that he was criminally responsible at that time.

Q   **All right. Do you feel that he knew the difference between right and wrong at that time?**

A   I feel that he did. I think that, in fact, in terms of his going to the police department to turn himself in indicated that he knew that he had done something wrong.

Q   **Do you feel that Mr. Wilbur Jackson acted under an irresistible impulse at the time he killed those four young people?**

A   No, I don't.

Thursday 10 December *

[Dr. Blunt is cross-examined. Although the court has previously ruled that he may testify, defense counsel Tracy attempts to show that since Wilbur Jackson went to the Forensic Center only to have his competency determined, Dr. Blunt should not be able to judge his sanity. The doctor is questioned at some length concerning his procedure, and he displays his color-coded file system. He says that his diagnosis is independent of Dr. Robey's, and vice versa.]

[The People rest.]

[There is a discussion outside of the jury. The defense wants a chance to rebut Drs. Robey and Blunt. Gilman says rebuttal could go on forever. The defense promises to keep it short. Dr. Tanay will be allowed to return. There is a discussion concerning the propriety of calling one Clark Shanahan as a witness and further talk of the mysterious "Jay."]

[Defense counsel Tracy and an assistant prosecutor discussed the case in a crowded elevator. Upon unloading, they discovered juror number ten, Mrs. Smith, had overheard them. When called into the judge's chambers, Mrs. Smith says she wasn't influenced by their conversation.]

THE DEFENSE'S REBUTTAL

[The defense begins its rebuttal.]

[*Dr. Emanuel Tanay* is recalled. He declares Wilbur Jackson not to be a racist or a bigot. Although Wilbur may not believe in racial intermarriage, Dr. Tanay feels he has no ill will toward blacks. Dr. Tanay repeats that dissociative reaction is common and that the prosecution's psychiatrists are wrong when they say it is uncommon.]

---

* Upon a motion by Mr. Gilman, the court grants Dr. Miller thirty-five dollars a day for three days as an expert witness fee. Drs. Blunt and Robey are allowed sixty-six and forty-four dollars, respectively, to cover travel costs at ten cents per mile.

[Dr. Tanay is cross-examined about the alleged alacrity with which he discovers dissociative reaction. Gilman finds thirty-seven dissociative reactions in fifty-three cases a very high average. Dr. Tanay is questioned further about race, at which point Nelson suggests that the prosecution's psychiatrists have introduced a racial red herring.*

[Attorney *Clark Shanahan* is the last witness. After a hearing, he is allowed to testify for purposes of impeachment only. He served as counsel of the Pennsylvania House Committee on Mental Health and says Dr. Ames Robey had nothing to do with the establishment of the Forensic Center.]

[The Defense rests.]

PROSECUTION'S CLOSING ARGUMENT, PART I

Friday 11 December **

[Court opens at 10:35 A.M. without the jury. There is a discussion concerning the proposed judge's instructions to the jury that each side is submitting. Thereafter the jury is brought back in to hear the closing arguments. A closing argument, unlike an opening statement, is meant to be persuasive. The prosecution, since it has the burden of proving its case beyond a reasonable doubt, speaks twice. The prosecutor proceeds first, the defense responds, and then the prosecution is given a final opportunity to rebut. After argument the judge gives instructions to the jury, and the jury then leaves the courtroom to deliberate. Jury deliberations are held in a closed room with no one present but the twelve jurors.]

[Leonard Gilman now makes his initial closing argument, lasting some seventy-five minutes.]

Mr. Gilman: May it please the court.

Ladies and gentlemen of the jury, good morning.

As Judge Gillis indicated—we are almost at the end—this portion of the proceedings is known as the closing argument.

This is an opportunity for the People, the triers of the fact, to present to you our theories and any reasonable inferences we feel you can draw from the evidence that was heard in this case.

What I tell you now is not evidence. What I tell you is our theory and what we feel you can draw from the evidence.

---

* During the trial, a man believed to be Jonathan Carter's cousin sat in the front row of the spectator section, staring at the jury.

** The *Pittsburgh News* reported that on 11 December, as during most of the preceding four weeks, Roger Jackson, age seventy-two, watched the trial of his son.

I told you at the outset of this case, some four or five weeks ago, that the People in this case have a burden of proof.

We must prove a defendant guilty beyond a reasonable doubt, beyond a doubt based upon reason, beyond a doubt based upon common sense.

And I told you if at the conclusion of this case, I felt we had met that burden, I would come back and ask you to do your duty as jurors and find the defendant guilty.

And that is exactly what I am about to do.

We have established beyond a reasonable doubt, beyond a doubt based upon reason, beyond a moral certainty, beyond a doubt based upon common sense—and Judge Gillis will define that definition to you—that on the early morning of May 8, 1970, Wilbur Chester Jackson committed four murders, and at the time he committed these murders he was legally responsible for his conduct, he did know the difference between right and wrong, he was not acting under an irresistible impulse from which he could not stop.

And I am not going to ask you ladies and gentlemen of the jury to bring in a verdict based upon sympathy for anyone—and I am sure if Mr. Nelson were up here, he wouldn't ask you for a verdict based upon sympathy in any way—I ask you for a verdict based upon the evidence, the cold hard facts that you have heard for one month.

* * *

The courtroom where Wilbur Jackson was tried

Not only do we have the opinion of four psychiatrists to consider in this case; but, I think, more important than that, we have the words of Mr. Jackson himself and Mr. Jackson's conduct on the days preceding and the early morning of the time that he killed four people.

And I think all of those factors, ladies and gentlemen of the jury, are clear evidence that Mr. Wilbur Jackson knew exactly what he was doing when he fired his two guns into apartment number 9, he knew exactly what he was doing at the time he broke down the door to apartment number 9 and entered.

Let's look at some of the evidence.

Wilbur Jackson lived at 5755 Hill in the city of Pittsburgh with his wife Mary with four children, one of whom was a young lady named Sandra Jackson, a young lady who at the time of her death was seventeen years old, and a young lady that on two occasions—one in April and one in May—decided to leave home, decided to leave 5755 Hill.

Why, we don't know; Sandra Jackson isn't here to tell you that.

But Wilbur Jackson told you on the stand that everything was wonderful in the Jackson household, no arguments, no major disagreements, no real problems with their daughter Sandra.

Mary Jackson told you the same thing, they had no major arguments or disagreements with Sandra, everything was fine, it was a beautiful family.

Well, I will leave that for you to determine, ladies and gentlemen of the jury, from the testimony we have heard during the course of this trial, if the Jackson family was the beautiful family that Mr. and Mrs. Jackson claim it was.

The fact of the matter is that Sandra Jackson left home in April and in May; on both occasions she left suddenly, and on the second occasion that she left she never returned.

* * *

Sandra Jackson—and I will tell you, I never knew Sandra Jackson but from that letter; Sally Tucker didn't lead Sandra Jackson around by her nose; you can tell that from reading that letter.

Sally Tucker didn't make Sandra Jackson leave 5755 Hill on the third; she left on her own free will, and she left for reasons that we will probably never really know.

But, believe me, everything wasn't beautiful and wonderful and great in the Jackson household.

But something made her pick up and leave that house; but , once again, we will never know what that was. Something made her go down and move in at 4330 Lincoln, and something made her move in with Georgia Webster on Mack and spend the better part of that week, instead of living at 5755 Hill where she had grown up.

Everything wasn't really that tremendous at 5755 Hill.

* * *

The fact that Mr. Jackson worked sixty hours during that period of time:

Does that cause a man to commit murder?

Does that cause a man to take the lives of four people?

The fact that he was tired, perhaps?

Sure, he was tired.

But does that cause him to take the lives of four people?

We have all worked long periods of time.

We don't all commit murder.

So don't blame four murders on the fact that Mr. Jackson was tired; that is no excuse at all, believe me.

On Monday afternoon and on Monday morning, Mr. Wilbur Jackson showed just a little of how he truly felt about the fact that his daughter left home.

And I asked him—and Sally Tucker testified—"Mr. Jackson, did you tell Sally Tucker that if you got your daughter home, you would chain her to a radiator?"

And this concerned, loving parent told you from the witness stand:

"Well, I might have said that; but, you know, I was joking."

* * *

Mr. Jackson would have you believe that because he came from Tennessee, everything is all right.

That is the problem with Mr. Jackson, he came from Tennessee; therefore, we excuse his conduct.

Believe me, ladies and gentlemen of the jury, that conduct isn't excused in Tennessee, in Mississippi, in California, or anywhere in these fifty states; we don't excuse people's conduct because they came from another part of the country.

Mr. Jackson wanted to keep his daughter home.

Mr. Jackson wouldn't let her leave for any reason.

And Mr. Jackson would do anything, go to any extreme, to keep his daughter at 5755 Hill.

That is not a loving parent.

That is a selfish parent, that is an angry parent, that is a disturbed parent.

That is Wilbur Jackson.

* * *

And I ask you to recall the testimony of these witnesses, and I also ask you to remember who is on trial in this case.

These kids aren't on trial.

Wilbur Jackson is on trial.

Don't let Mr. Nelson put these young kids on trial.

Remember, it's Wilbur Jackson that is charged with four murders, not any of those kids that lived in that place.

They are telling you the truth as they remember it.

They have no interest in the outcome of this case, none whatsoever. They are witnesses that were called in here to tell it to you like they remember it, and that is exactly what they have done.

And they told you that on the evening of Monday, May 4, Mr. Jackson came to 4330 Lincoln with his wife, with another couple—that, in fact, is the case—Mr. and Mrs. Tucker.

They didn't like where she was living, they were concerned parents; but they asked her:

"Sally, come home with us."

Sally said, "No mother; no father. I want to stay here. I would rather stay here."

So they let her stay.

Sally Tucker got the chance to come home.

Sandra Jackson didn't get the chance.

Sure enough, Sally Tucker came home last week; and you heard Sally Tucker's mother testify to that.

Sally Tucker's father, he is no less concerned about his daughter than Wilbur Jackson was; and he is from the South, and Mrs. Tucker is from the South.

But they didn't go over there and try to drag their daughter out of 4330 Lincoln; they didn't go over there with three guns and break down doors in an effort to get their daughter away from what they felt was the wrong life for her.

They allowed her to find out for herself; they allowed her a chance.

Sandra Jackson never had that chance.

Todd Wilson never had that chance.

Jonathan Carter never had that chance.

Ricky Walters never had that chance.

They never had the chance to come home.

* * *

Now, ladies and gentlemen of the jury, we come to Thursday; and during this time Mr. Jackson, in his efforts to get his daughter home, had even offered to pay a young man fifty dollars.

And you heard that young man testify, a young man who has a criminal record. He laid it out to you. He told you that he had been convicted, and he told you that he has paid his debt; and now he is in the armed forces stationed in Georgia.

And he came here to give testimony, and he told you that he called the Jackson home on two or three occasions because he needed the money.

Well, some people would call Mr. Johnson a fink, a stoolie.

I don't think he was that at all.

I think he needed the money. I think he really needed the money at that point. He needed the money for his wife, he had just gotten married, and he would go to any lengths to get that money.

Do you really think Eldrin Johnson knew what would happen on the early morning of May 8, 1970, when he accepted the money from Mr. Jackson?

Do you think he really would have accepted it if he had known what would have happened?

I don't think he is that kind of young man; I don't think he is a bad young man. He made a mistake; but don't call him a fink or a Judas or anything like that.

Georgia Webster testified that Sandra Jackson wasn't living in sin, in Sodom and Gomorrah, in hell; on Monday night and Tuesday night and Wednesday night and on Thursday, she was staying with her, because she didn't want to go home, even though, according to Mr. and Mrs. Jackson, home was a great place to be.

* * *

And then he came home at 1:40 A.M. [Friday, 8 May]

And what does he do?

Just like always, Mr. Jackson has a glass of milk.

Is this insanity, legal insanity?

Doing just as he had always done, he had his glass of milk.

Is this the concerned parent grabbing his wife and saying:

"Honey, let's go get our girl, we know she is over there in apartment number 9."

I don't think so.

He has his glass of milk, and then he proceeds to arm himself to the teeth.

He takes a 9-mm automatic which he had never used in his life, according to his testimony, and loads it.

He takes a .38-caliber police revolver and loads it.   It was loaded, he said.   He kept it under his mattress.

And then he takes a shotgun, which he called a riot shotgun, and loads that.

That isn't enough, though, for Mr. Jackson, this poor, loving parent who only took these guns for protection.

He also took ammunition, plenty of extra ammunition.

Did he really need all this, all this that he took over there for protection?

Do you really believe that, that he took three guns over there with extra ammunition for protection?

Or is it more possible that, as he told Dr. Robey, he always carries extra ammunition when he goes hunting?

This is the state of mind of this man.

This man knew exactly what he was going to do when he got there.

* * *

So, as far as the positions of Todd and Sandra, all we really know is that they were lying in the same bed; that is all we really know.

And then Mr. Jackson claims in his testimony that he dashed or sped across the room and delivered a blow to the head of Todd Wilson.

And I asked him:

"Mr. Jackson, did you hit him hard?"

And he said, "Yes, I hit him hard," or "Yes, I hit him hard," or, "Yes, sir, I hit him hard," as Mr. Jackson does.

And he hit him, he says, with the barrel of the gun like that *(demonstrating)* as hard as he could.

And yet, ladies and gentlemen of the jury, you heard the testimony of the doctor who performed the autopsy on the body of Todd Wilson—Dr. Tworek, I believe.

Dr. Tworek testified that Mr. Wilson did have a laceration on his head; but, if you recall the testimony—and it's been a month—she testified that the laceration was only three-quarters of an inch long, and it was only superficial.

And I ask you, if you hit a man on the top of his head with a gun as hard as you can, as Mr. Jackson claims he did, would that cause a three-quarter inch superficial wound?

So the physical evidence, I think, conflicts with Mr. Jackson's testimony.

But Mr. Jackson testified that he hit him, and the gun went off.

This gun, a .38-caliber revolver.   And you can take that back there and examine it.   It takes six shots, and it also takes eleven pounds of pressure—eleven pounds of pressure—to fire the trigger of that gun when the hammer is not cocked.

And I asked him:

"Mr. Jackson, did you have your finger on the trigger when you hit Todd?"

Mr. Jackson said:

"No, I didn't; I was just holding it, and I hit him; and, yet, the gun went off—"

Well, that's Mr. Jackson's testimony.

"—and the gun went off and struck my daughter in the chest." *

Consider that Sandra Jackson had two bullet wounds in her chest side by side, neither one of these wounds went into her body on an angle, a downward angle; both of them went in straight, passed through into her back—one was recovered, one went straight through—neither one of these two shots went in on a downward angle.

But Mr. Jackson says this is the way it happened; he struck Todd, accidentally the gun discharged and hit his daughter.

Then on direct examination Mr. Jackson said:

"I don't remember anything after that until I was outside yelling for Sally."

But on cross-examination Mr. Jackson did remember some other things.

"Do you remember seeing Todd? Do you remember seeing Jonathan?"

And he remembered on cross-examination seeing Jonathan, and he remembered seeing Ricky on cross-examination.

All Mr. Jackson forgets is shooting each one of these two young men in the head; and he forgets it, ladies and gentlemen of the jury, because he wants to forget it and because he wants to repress the scene, the activity in apartment number 9, out of his mind forever.

And because if he is insane—if he was insane at the time—he has to forget it; he couldn't possibly remember it.

But, ladies and gentlemen of the jury, once again, examine the physical evidence—examine the physical evidence.

Mr. Jackson didn't miss with one shot, every shot that he fired in apartment number 9 inflicted a fatal wound, every shot out of each one of those two guns that he had.

---

* Detective-Sergeant Irvin Baranski of the Pittsburgh Homicide Bureau was the police officer in charge of this case. In an interview he stated that it was doubtful whether such a gun would discharge in the fashion Jackson claimed it did. During jury deliberations, strange knockings were heard from the jury-room. It was the jury striking Jackson's revolver against the wall to see if it would discharge.

His own daughter was shot twice in the chest side by side; each one of those wounds was fatal. Then she was shot in the right side.

And the doctor testified that that wound was a contact wound. The gun that fired that wound was no more than six inches from her body. There was tattooing or powder burns, which indicate that it was a contact wound.

Mr. Jackson put that gun to his daughter's side and fired.

But he doesn't remember doing that; he doesn't remember because he doesn't want to remember.

* * *

Now, according to Mr. Jackson's statement, and according to the tape of the sodium brevital interview, Mr. Jackson felt at the time he saw his daughter in bed that she had been taken advantage of by the little boy with red hair and he felt that the young black youth in the same bedroom had also taken advantage of his daughter, and he also felt that Ricky Walters lying on the couch in the living room had also taken advantage of his daughter.

And that, ladies and gentlemen of the jury, is why this tragedy took place; this stupid, senseless tragedy.

Four lives were lost because this loving parent felt his poor daughter—who, believe me, ladies and gentlemen of the jury, could take care of herself; and you read that letter, and you tell me if I am wrong—he felt his daughter had been taken advantage of by the people that were in apartment number 9.

* * *

And he had a chance to shoot Mary, and he had a chance to shoot Janet Rivers.

He didn't shoot either one of those two young ladies, thank God.

And he went into apartment number 9—still he is insane, according to the defense—and he looked for Sally Tucker in there.

And in apartment number 3 he comes into contact once again with people.

With Mr. Willard, who testified. Does he shoot Mr. Willard?

No. He's got his gun drawn, but he doesn't shoot Mr. Willard.

Is this a man that's out of control?

Is this a man that can't control his conduct?

* * *

But Detective Caufield has a five-page statement from Mr. Jackson.

And he says Mr. Jackson cried a couple of times during the interview, but he has seen worse.

And he, as a police officer, is trained; and if Mr. Jackson would have been insane at the time, if he had acted like a lunatic at the time, Detective Caufield wouldn't have taken that statement.

I ask you to examine the handwriting of Mr. Jackson; the clear, concise way Mr. Jackson has written his name on that statement.

* * *

He was angry, and he was frustrated, and he was bent on destruction when he took those three guns to apartment number 9, and he knew exactly what he was going to find when he entered.

Sure, it bothered him; it would bother any parent to see their daughter in bed with a young man.

But he knew, he knew that his daughter was with Todd; he knew she was in apartment number 9.

And he took three guns with him to defend himself, this 260-pound man, against a little boy with red hair.

Are you kidding me?

He took those guns to kill, and he did kill; and he walked into the Second Precinct, and he said he had.

Don't let him get away with it, ladies and gentlemen of the jury.

Mr. Jackson's conduct at Mercywood Hospital is the way Mr. Jackson is; and all those shock treatments did was to bring it out a little clearer.

Mr. Jackson threatened people at the hospital.

Mr. Jackson said at the hospital he was proud of killing three of those people, but was only sorry about the fourth, because that's the way Mr. Jackson is.

He is an explosive individual, an individual who feels that he hasn't gotten anywhere in the world; and, therefore, everybody should excuse him for his conduct, because he came from the South, because he had certain ideas, that is enough to let him get away with it.

Well, I ask, you, ladies and gentlemen, not to let him do that.

I ask you to examine his conduct, the way he acted and what he did and the physical evidence; and after examining all this conduct and using your good common sense, I ask you to hold Wilbur Jackson responsible to the state of Pennsylvania for his conduct.

I ask you to find him guilty of first-degree murder on three of those cases and guilty of second-degree murder as to Ricky Walters.

I ask you to do your duty.

[Court adjourns for lunch at 12:05.]

DEFENSE'S CLOSING ARGUMENT

[Court reconvenes at 1:40 P.M. and Mr. Nelson makes a fifty-minute final argument.]

The Court: You may proceed, Mr. Nelson.

Mr. Nelson: Thank you, Your Honor.

Ladies and gentlemen of the jury, good afternoon. I hope you all enjoyed your lunch.

You had quite a bit to digest over the noon hour together with that sandwich or whatever it was you had for lunch.

First, and lest I neglect to do so, my client and his wife and my colleagues and I all wish to thank you for the attentiveness with which you have followed the testimony here throughout, by my count, twenty-three rather tedious days of testimony during the course of which you heard from some fifty-seven witnesses.

It's gratifying, gratifying indeed, to know that people can and do treat the affairs of their fellow man with the conscientiousness that you have during the course of these proceedings.

Therefore, this afternoon, with your indulgence, I will endeavor to respond—to respond to and comment upon, not only what Mr. Gilman did say to you in the course of his remarks in the morning, but I will endeavor to address myself as well to some significant areas that I find he neglected to bring to your attention.

And I ask you to revisit his argument with me for the moment and to review what he did say.

Well, he said—he said the People's witnesses, all of them, deserve your belief—deserve your belief, ladies and gentlemen, because they have no interest—no interest in the outcome of these proceedings and, therefore, no bias.

Is that indeed the case?

Let us see.

He says that the defendant's witnesses do not deserve your belief; obviously, he says, in the case of the defendant and his wife, they do have—they do have a real and a very intimate interest in the outcome of these proceedings.

So what they say is not worthy of your credence; and, as for the rest of them, he rather slyly suggests, neither are they worthy of your belief because they are really nothing more than hessians, hired mercenaries whose testimony has been bought and paid for.

And let us, at a little later point, examine that little salient point.

He says to you that the young people who testified here during the past twenty-three some-odd days of trial—the Allison Fletchers and the

Sally Jo Tuckers and the Felipe Fernandezes and the Carl Richardsons and the Mary Lee Von Allsteins and the rest—are not on trial and should not and can not be put on trial; nor, he says, should their life-style be tried here in this court and in these proceedings.

And I agree; I agree.

Except—except, of course, to the extent that they—they share, at least in equal measure, with the man who is on trial here, culpability for the frightful bloodletting that occurred in apartment 9 of the Stonehead Manor during the predawn hours of the eighth of May last.

Not, members of the jury, because they—the most of them—have opted out and chosen to escape from life and from reality rather than to undertake to live life, not for that reason.

Not because by keeping and maintaining what cannot be characterized as anything other than a hippie commune, a place of refuge for a girl who thought that she too might like to escape from rather than live life; an escape, escape into an ethic and a mystic of pot and mescaline and LSD and sex, not for that reason.

But for the reason that they—they share in the responsibility for the carnage to which I have already alluded, at least in equal measure with Wilbur Jackson, because they brought about and put into effect and motion some of the elements that coalesced into that awful event by building and maintaining, in a very careful and a very pernicious way, the wall, the screen of silence, and obfuscation and deceit and ultimately of absolutely uncontainable frustration that led to this man's act on that morning, by aiding and abetting this little girl in her efforts to remain away from home.

* * *

I see this entire situation as almost a parallel to one we are told in the books of Samuel occurred about eight thousand years ago among the Bronze Age Israelites involving their Golden King, the Lion of Judah, the one and only David, and occurring in the latter days of his life—and, in fact, in his seventy-sixth year—when, by reason of his own life-style, that of a hedonist, surrounded by all the means and apparatus of the invocation of pleasure and his concubines, he broke the laws and the covenants of his people's God, brought all sorts of calamity upon his people by doing so for the reason that their God turned his face away from them and ultimately brought that most desperate of all calamities upon them, a civil war; which, when it emerged into the light of day—from the covert into the overt—was being led by his own son Absalom; and as a result of which David, the King of the Israelites, the Lion of Judah, was harried right out of his own capital, stoned out of his own capital of Jerusalem, and had to put together an army of mercenaries to defend himself and regain that which had been his.

But on the day these forces met, those of the Israelites, in the Wood of Ephraim, you will recall, he enjoined his captains:

"Watch out for Absalom; don't let anything happen to Absalom."

But something did; he was killed.

And when word was sent back of a victory to David by his captains, it was necessary for them to send back as well word of the fact that his son had died.

And when he got this word—I ask you to remember, ladies and gentlemen—it was in this context:

"And the king said unto Cushi, 'Is the young man Absalom safe?'

"And Cushi answered, 'The enemies of my lord the king, and all that rise against thee to do thee hurt, be as that young man is.'

"And the king was much moved, and went up to the chamber over the gate, and wept: and as he went, thus he said, 'O my son Absalom, my son, my son Absalom! Would God I had died for thee, O Absalom, my son, my son!' "

And did we not hear that from that stand from the lips of this man here on trial now concerning his daughter?

And did not, ladies and gentlemen, David ultimately and successfully expiate himself and his sins in the eyes of his God and in the eyes of his people and go on to become the greatest of all the kings of the Israelites; and did not from that it become manifest that the Israelites, these primitives, and their God, this granite-faced disciplinarian, took David as he was and forgave him.

And must we not do the same thing here with Wilbur Jackson.

And that is why I said when I addressed you—it seems like a thousand years ago—in an opening statement that the genesis of this case goes back forty-six years to southern Tennessee when this man was born.

In his childhood he went through the grades in the little town of Erwin, Tennessee—Erwin, Tennessee—sixty miles from Dayton, Tennessee, sixty miles from the scene of the most famous case that has been tried in this country in this century: the *Scopes* case.

* * *

A man who, because of his own urgently felt inadequacies, undertook to achieve what he had failed to achieve vicariously through a bright and dearly beloved child.

And can there be any doubt in the mind of any among you ladies and gentlemen that he did not dearly love this child and all his children?

* * *

And I submit to you that he drove himself to the edge of madness in the process of doing so [searching for his daughter], drove himself to a point where he was susceptible of having what did come over him, come over him when ultimately—ultimately at or about 2:00 A.M. on the eighth of May he burst into this dingy, dinky, little apartment, there to discover the light of his life through whom he, the under-achiever, was going to achieve, locked in the embrace in a state of nakedness with a boy—with a boy.

And that, ladies and gentlemen, is when this man went mad.

Even Dr. Blunt, finally, grudgingly, had wrung from him the concession that the man had no intention of killing anyone when he went forth to 4330 Lincoln.

He armed himself—and he armed himself like a veritable road agent; even I don't think he armed himself because he thought he needed to protect himself—he armed himself in a manner as he did to appear to be so imposing as to be able to overcome all and any opposition that he might encounter.

And I submit to you and suggest to you that he had every reason in the world to believe that he was going to encounter opposition.

And it was only by the grace of God that he did not.

The man, simply stated as I can, went mad when he saw his daughter in bed with this boy and didn't recover—and didn't recover until some time—some time during the course of his ride to the Second Precinct Station or after his arrival there.

* * *

Now, we did indeed—all of us—go out to the Stonehead Manor; and I am almost sorry we did, when we found there what I found there.

I ask you, though, only as touching upon the probity of this young lady Mary Martin or Lynch or whatever her name is—

How in the name of God is she going to see something going on at that kitchen table? [When she testified, she said she saw Jackson reloading on the kitchen table.]

I don't know, and I don't think it's very important, except as it touches upon the believability of these young people.

Now, ladies and gentlemen, two—in fact, three—of Pennsylvania's most reputable and well-known psychiatrists have come before you; and in four long, tedious days of testimony have dissected and picked apart and examined and reexamined, as I said before, employing for that purpose the most sophisticated means available to modern man to get inside the mind of his fellow man and see what is going on there.

And three of them—three of them—at least share the view that the man had no intention of killing anyone when he went down to that apartment house; and two of them—two of them—have told you the man went mad when he saw his daughter in bed with the boy she was in bed with doing what she was doing.

And what, in the demeanor, the manner, the testimony, the manner of their giving their testimony, would lead you to believe that either Dr. Hubert Miller, who is not a forensic psychiatrist, who did treat Wilbur Jackson over an extended period of time, and who did do the remarkable job of rehabilitating this broken man to the point where, sedated, we could bring him down here and prop him up and keep him in front of you long enough to get this trial over and done with—

And that was a remarkable job because on the twenty-fifth of September when he stood where I stand now, he was nothing but a hulk, a speechless, mindless hulk.

—but who, nonetheless, did formulate the opinion that this man underwent what he called a psychotic block at that moment in time and went out of control, out of control like a runaway locomotive charging down the side of a mountain.

And what is there—what is there in what Dr. Tanay, Emanuel Tanay, one of the state's leading forensic psychiatrists—that would lead you to the belief that he would come in here and deliberately disassemble?

And did he not tell you, using a term somewhat different than that used by Dr. Miller to describe what overcame Wilbur Jackson at that moment and time when he saw his daughter, he called it dissociative reaction.

But he, too, said that this psychotic phenomena rendered—rendered this man absolutely incapable of controlling his actions.

He said that the best way he could describe what happened to Wilbur Jackson at that moment in time was the very term that Wilbur Jackson himself used; the man had run amok.

Then we have the eminent Dr. Robey.

This vainglorious, pompous, arrogant, pragmatic, dangerous man.

This man would have you accept him, as he had Wilbur Jackson accept him, as being something very different from that which he was.

What was remarkable about his testimony and his manner of delivering himself up there?

Why, he even acted out the roles.

You will be told, ladies and gentlemen, and I say this to you in specific address to the testimony of this evil and dangerous man, that if you find demonstrated on the record that a witness—any witness, even a professional witness—has lied on any material point, you can, if you so choose to do, disregard all of his testimony except that which is corroborated independently.

He [Dr. Robey] would have you believe that a man shot and killed his daughter and three other young human beings in cold blood, like so many dogs, because he lost his temper.

I am not going to read those definitions. Remember them, though, as they came from that stand from a temperate, literate, cognizant, decent man: Emanuel Tanay.

Ladies and gentlemen.

Leonard Gilman, in effect, has said to you:

"Bring in a verdict of guilty of murder against Wilbur Jackson because he has broken the fifth commandment; these young people deserved life, and Wilbur Jackson has offended our law and God's law, and they are unoffending."

[Nelson has an open Bible in front of him.]

Now, God alone knows—God alone knows; Wilbur Jackson knows, as well, to whom ultimately he is going to have to answer, to whom he is now answering, undertaking to wash the blood of this carnage from his hands in the expiating water of remorse and contrition; and there is no way that I or anyone else can come before you and undertake to justify what he did.

But let us keep in mind, ladies and gentlemen, that there were not one, but ten commandments, another of which is:

"Thou shalt not commit adultery."

And, yet, another of which is:

"Honor thy father and thy mother: that thy days may be long upon the land which the Lord thy God giveth thee."

Keep that in mind in that juryroom when reviewing what you have heard from that witness stand.

I ask you, members of the jury, if you cannot—if you cannot—acquit Wilbur Jackson in these cases, give him that measure of consideration which the law accords him, and find him not guilty by reason of insanity.

I thank you.

PROSECUTION'S CLOSING ARGUMENT, PART II

[After a short recess, Mr. Gilman proceeds with his final argument, lasting twenty minutes.]

Mr. Gilman: May it please the court, ladies and gentlemen of the jury.

We are almost there. All you have to do is listen to me, and I promise I won't take as long as I did this morning; although I told you that this morning, too.

As Judge Gillis told you, I get two chances to talk to you; and that is because we have the burden of proof, we must prove guilt beyond a reasonable doubt.

Now, Mr. Nelson, at the outset of his argument, told you that he would show you in his argument that our witnesses—the young people that lived at 4330 Lincoln—had an interest in the outcome of this case, had some reason to alter their testimony.

He didn't do that; he said it, but he didn't do it.

They came here to tell the truth; they came here to tell the way they recall Mr. Jackson's behavior on May 3, May 4—and most important of all—on May 7 and the early morning of May 8.

Their testimony is important; I ask you to remember their testimony.

They were there. They saw the way Mr. Jackson acted. They heard what Mr. Jackson said.

Dr. Blunt wasn't there, Dr. Robey wasn't there, Dr. Tanay wasn't there, and Dr. Miller wasn't there, on May 8.

You remember, the witnesses that were there, remember what they testified to regarding Mr. Jackson's behavior; and then judge for yourselves whether Mr. Jackson was quote, "out of control," at the time or whether he could, in fact, have stopped at any time, could have, in fact, considered what he was doing.

And he did consider what he was doing when he went around that apartment building looking for Sally Tucker, when he came into contact with a number of other people and didn't kill any of them, when he only killed the three people and his daughter—the three people that he felt had abused his daughter.

Now, Mr. Nelson tells you that—I believe that these are exact words—the kids that lived at 4330 Lincoln should share equally in the guilt, should share equally in the culpability, in the responsibility, for the deaths of those four young people because, Mr. Nelson says, they didn't tell Mr. Jackson where his daughter was.

Ladies and gentlemen of the jury, I want you to remember the testimony of Debbie Jackson, Mr. Wilbur Jackson's daughter.

Debbie Jackson didn't tell her own father and mother where her sister was, didn't tell her own parents, even though she knew her sister was at 4330 Lincoln.

These kids, including Debbie Jackson, shouldn't share any responsibility for the deaths of those four young people; don't try to shift the burden of responsibility.

That responsibility is squarely on his shoulders and squarely should be faced by him, and he should squarely be held responsible.

Mr. Nelson tells you that he is not going to put on trial the kids that lived at 4330 Lincoln; he says they shouldn't be put on trial.

Then he talks about the hippie commune that they lived at, the pot smoking, the mescaline eating.

He is putting them on trial, even though he says he is not going to.

But they are not on trial, and their style of life isn't on trial at all in this case.

These kids all came from homes that there were problems in; all of them had parents that were either separated or divorced or some family problem that led them to leave their home and try to make it on their own.

Just like Sandy Jackson said that she was trying to do in her letter.

These kids were not criminals; they weren't bad kids.

They deserved a chance, all of them that lived there; and all of them except for four will get that chance.

Four of those kids won't get any chance at all.

Mr. Nelson says that poor Mr. Jackson suffered so much since the incident.

Well, I feel sorry for Mr. Jackson.

But I feel sorrier for four kids that won't even get the chance to do anything.

They are dead; they are gone.

So Mr. Jackson is suffering; and I am sure he has suffered.

That doesn't mean he shouldn't be held responsible to society for his conduct.

That is what we have laws for. Men are here to judge men—their conduct—and that is your function. You are here to judge Mr. Wilbur Jackson's conduct.

And if his conduct violated the laws of the state of Pennsylvania—and I tell you, from the evidence, that it did—you are here only to do your duty as jurors and to hold him responsible for his conduct.

Mr. Nelson tells you that I called—I didn't call—I referred to Mr. Jackson as a despicable tyrant.

I did no such thing; I didn't do that at all.

I simply told you that it was never brought out in this case the real reason why Sandy Jackson wanted to leave home, that's all.

And I refer you to statements of Mr. Jackson like—

"I will break her like a horse.

"I will chain her to a radiator.

"I would rather have her home with her arms and legs cut off, and dead."

I don't think Wilbur Jackson bears any resemblance to David, King of the Israelites, in his concern over his daughter.

Otherwise, why would he make statements like he has?

Why would he make statements like he would shackle her to a radiator, that he had purchased a straitjacket to keep her at home?

Is that David, King of the Israelites; or is that the man who sits charged before you, just a man, not anything above that?

Mr. Nelson, once again, as he told you in his opening statement, tells us that Mr. Jackson couldn't help being what he is, that he was from Tennessee, that he grew up there, that he came from a rigid environment.

Well, I am sure thousands of other people were born, grew up, and came from rigid upbringings in Tennessee; but who don't go around killing their children and killing other people's children just because they are angry and just because they are mad and just because they are frustrated because they can't bring their children home, and they are frustrated in wanting their children to remain with them.

That is precisely what Wilbur Jackson did.

Don't blame it on Tennessee; blame it on the man who is responsible for it.

Mr. Jackson has lived in the city of Pittsburgh for nineteen years.

First of all, I don't think Tennessee is the end of the world. I think they have laws in Tennessee just like they have laws in Pennsylvania.

But, besides that, Mr. Jackson has lived in the city of Pittsburgh for nineteen years.

Mr. Jackson is acquainted with the laws in this city.

Mr. Jackson should be held responsible under those laws for his conduct.

Now, one thing Mr. Nelson brought up that I want to discuss with you:

Mr. Nelson somehow didn't really try the young people at 4330 Lincoln that much; but he did start to try or indict Dr. Ames Robey, he is blaming Dr. Ames Robey.

He says Dr. Ames Robey is an Olympian, pompous, egotistical, not worthy of belief, is a liar—Dr. Ames Robey is a liar.

Well, I would never—I would never refer to Dr. Miller or Dr. Tanay or Dr. Blunt or any professional who comes in here as an expert as an egotistical Olympian who has altered the truth to suit his own ends.

Dr. Robey has come in here to tell the product of his fifteen or twenty years of experience with people.

And then he proceeded to give you his evaluation and his opinion on the responsibility or irresponsibility of Wilbur Jackson.

And, lo and behold, Dr. Robey gets put on trial.*

* * *

---

* After the trial a reliable source stated that Dr. Robey read of the case in the newspapers, then contacted the prosecutor's office to volunteer his opinion that Jackson

Ladies and gentlemen of the jury, that is about all I have to say.

I simply want you, once again, to do your responsibility as jurors.

If all parents acted the way Wilbur Jackson did on the early morning of May 8, 1970, there wouldn't be very many kids left to inhabit this earth.

You don't act that way.

You act reasonably; you act logically.

You don't let your anger and let your frustrations overcome logic.

And that is what Wilbur Jackson did on the early morning of May 8.

He was angry, and he was frustrated; and he went over there to take care of all the anger and all the frustration that had accumulated in his forty-six years of life.

And I ask you to hold him responsible to this state for his conduct and find him guilty; find him guilty of murder in the first degree on three cases, and murder in the second degree on one case, because there can be no doubt that Mr. Wilbur Jackson is guilty as charged.

Thank you.

JUDGE'S INSTRUCTIONS TO THE JURY

The Court:

Ladies and gentlemen of the jury.

It is my duty to instruct you in the law that applies to this case, and you must follow the law as I state it to you.

As jurors it is your exclusive duty to decide all questions of fact submitted to you and for that purpose to determine the effect and value of the evidence.

In performing this duty, you must not be influenced by pity for a defendant or by passion or prejudice against him.

You must not be biased against a defendant because he has been arrested for this offense, or because a charge has been filed against him, or because he has been brought to trial.

None of these facts is evidence of his guilt, and you must not infer or speculate from any or all of them that he is more likely to be guilty than innocent.

* * *

It has been said that a juror is satisfied beyond a reasonable doubt as to a matter in controversy when, after a full and fair consideration

---

was sane. At this time Dr. Robey's sister worked at Mercywood Hospital where Wilbur Jackson was confined and treated by Dr. Miller.

of all the testimony given in the case, he can say that he has an abiding conviction to a moral certainty that the charge made has been established as having been committed by the accused.

In that connection, you should bear in mind that it is essential that each element of the offense charged must be proved by that measure of proof beyond a reasonable doubt.

A *reasonable* doubt is what the word implies: a doubt founded in reason, a doubt for which you can give a reason for entertaining; a doubt growing out of the evidence or lack of evidence in the case; a doubt which would cause you to hesitate in the ordinary affairs of life.

Murder, at common law and as charged in these informations, may be defined as where a person of sound memory and discretion wilfully and unlawfully kills any human being against the peace of this state with malice aforethought, express or implied; and this common-law definition is still retained in our statute.

If you come to the conclusion that the respondent is guilty of murder, as I have defined it, it will be your duty to determine whether it's murder of the first degree or murder in the second degree.

The difference between murder in the first degree and murder in the second degree is this:

Murder in the first degree is a killing done wilfully and with premeditation.

While in murder in the second degree the element of premeditation is absent.

To convict the respondent of murder in the first degree, it must appear that the killing was wilful and premeditated.

It is not necessary that any definite period of time should have elapsed between the forming of such intention and the firing of the shot which killed the deceased, provided the shot was premeditated and the respondent acted wilfully.

On the other hand, if the killing was done under a sudden impulse, without premeditation or previously formed intention, the offense would be murder in the second degree.

Now, the statutes of this state, so far as they are applicable to the crime of murder, read as follows:

"All murder which shall be perpetrated by means of poison or lying in wait or any other kind of wilful, deliberate, and premeditated killing, shall be murder of the first degree." *

---

* An individual convicted of first-degree murder "shall be punished by solitary confinement at hard labor in the state prison for life."

Second-degree murder is defined by statute as follows:

"All other kinds of murder shall be deemed murder of the second degree." **

Then the statutes go on to read:

"The jury before whom any person indicted for murder shall be tried shall, if they find such person guilty thereof, ascertain in their verdict whether it be murder of the first or second degree."

The crime of manslaughter is not defined in the statutes. We use the common-law definition.

Embraced also in the information is a third offense known as manslaughter.

Manslaughter is defined as the unlawful and felonious killing of another, without malice, express or implied.†

The term malice as used in these definitions, signifies a wrongful act done intentionally, without legal justification or excuse.

The real test of malice is to be found in the presence or absence of adequate cause or provocation to account for the homicide.

The law implies from an unprovoked, unjustifiable, or inexcusable killing, the existence of that wicked disposition which the law terms malice aforethought.

If a man kills another suddenly and without provocation, the law implies malice, and the offense is murder.

If the provocation is such as must have greatly provoked him so that he acted from sudden passion, caused by some great provocation, the killing would be manslaughter.

The instrument with which the killing was done may be taken into consideration; because the intention to kill, in the absence of evidence showing a contrary intent, may be inferred from the use of a deadly weapon in such a manner that the death of the person assaulted would be the inevitable consequence.

In this case you are aware of the fact that the defendant has raised the defense of insanity.

In other words, although the defendant has pleaded not guilty, he has also pleaded not guilty by reason of insanity.

The fact that he has interposed the defense of insanity does not mean that he admits that he has committed the crime.

It is perfectly consistent under the law of this state for a person to plead not guilty and also to plead not guilty by reason of insanity.

** Second-degree murder is punished by "imprisonment in the state prison for life, or any term of years."

† Manslaughter is punished by "imprisonment in the state prison not more than 15 years or by fine not more than $7,500, or both."

The defense of insanity is a legal defense available to any defendant under the criminal law.

We must first start with this basic proposition:

It is a rule of law that a defendant coming into a court of justice in a criminal case is presumed to be sane.

However, when the defendant introduces any evidence of insanity, then it is incumbent upon the People to prove the defendant sane beyond a reasonable doubt.

This is not to say that this burden is any different, any greater or any less, than the burden required of the People in proving every other element of the offense.

This is just to say that once the insanity defense was interposed by the defendant, it became the burden of the People to prove his sanity, like every other element of the offense, beyond a reasonable doubt.

I have previously defined a reasonable doubt for you.

MCGNATEN

Now, in determining the sanity of the defendant in this case, and considering each of the acts or homicides with which he is charged separately, if you find that the defendant was at the time of each of these acts, of such unsound mind that he was unable to know whether his acts were right or wrong, then you must find him not guilty by reason of insanity.

You are not to draw the inference that because a man acts frantically mad and angry so that he does not resist an impulse, that this is necessarily unsoundness of mind.

The unsoundness of mind must be the result of a disease, and not the result of his having allowed his passions to run until they have become uncontrollable.

If, however, you do find that by reason of insanity the defendant was not capable of knowing he was doing wrong in each particular act or homicide, or that if he had not the power to resist the impulse to do each particular act by reason of his insanity, that would be such an unsoundness of mind which would require you to bring in a verdict of not guilty by reason of insanity.

Another way of looking at it is that if you find from the evidence that the defendant was afflicted with insanity, and that there was a causal connection between such insanity and each of the criminal acts; that is, that such affliction of insanity was the efficient cause of each of the acts with which he is charged, then similarly you should bring in a verdict of not guilty by reason of insanity in each case.

Now, if you find the defendant not guilty by reason of insanity, I further instruct you, if you reach such a verdict, the defendant shall be committed immediately by order of this court to the Department of Mental Health for treatment in an appropriate State Hospital, and that the defendant would then be eligible for release—would not be eligible for release either on convalescent care or for final discharge until he is evaluated and recommended for release by the Center for Forensic Psychiatry.*

Now, the defendant has been a witness before you, as he had a right to be; and you have a right to weigh his testimony and give it such credit as you think it fairly entitled to.

His interest is to be considered only so far as it affects his credibility.

His testimony is to be scanned and treated the same as that of other witnesses.

If rational, natural, and consistent, it may outweigh the testimony of other witnesses.

If inconsistent with established facts or his prior statements, you may treat it the same as you would that of any other witness whose testimony is thus defective.

There has been evidence of the criminal record of some of the witnesses involved in this case.

You may consider those criminal records in evaluating the credit and weight to be given their testimony.

A word, ladies and gentlemen of the jury, in regard to the opinions of medical experts.

In that connection, I charge you that the opinions of medical experts are to be considered by you in connection with all the other evidence in the case, but you are not bound to act upon them to the entire exclusion of all other testimony; taking into consideration these opinions, and giving them just weight, you are to determine for yourselves, from the whole evidence, whether the defendant is guilty of the crime charged.

You are not to take for granted that the statements contained in the hypothetical questions which have been read to the several witnesses are true.

You are to determine from the evidence what the real facts are, and whether they are correctly stated or not in the hypothetical question or questions.

For, in law, ladies and gentlemen of the jury, an opinion based upon a hypothetical question, based upon a hypothesis wholly incorrectly assumed or incorrect in the material facts to such an extent as to impair the value of the opinion, has little or no weight upon the matters stated in such hypothetical questions and which are involved in the case.

---

* In interviews both Nelson and Gilman indicated that they felt the psychiatric testimony was above the jury's head, and that the psychiatrists themselves balanced each other out. Both, however, agreed that the insanity defense and this charge in particular gave the jury an easy out.

You are also instructed that if you find that a witness has testified falsely, and deliberately so, on a material point in this case, you may disregard the entire testimony of that witness.

However, you may believe that testimony that is worthy of belief or that is corroborated by other reliable witnesses.

You, ladies and gentlemen of the jury, are the sole judges of the credibility of all the witnesses—both expert and *res gestae*—sworn here in open court before you, and of the weight to be given to their testimony.

A credible witness is one who gives competent testimony, worthy of belief.

In determining the credibility of a witness, you may consider his conduct, manner, and bearing on the witness stand; his interest in the outcome of the case; his opportunity to know and remember the events about which he testifies; his willingness to speak the truth, and all the surrounding circumstances that show his willingness to testify to the truth.

His reliability or unreliability; his apparent fairness or want of fairness; the fact of whether the witness has been corroborated or contradicted by other witnesses; the probability or improbability of the truth of the statements in view of all the other evidence and other facts and circumstances apparent in the trial.

Now, there are nineteen possible verdicts.

I will give you a copy of the possible verdicts.

In File No. 70–03042, Death of Ricky Walters:

You may find the defendant guilty of second degree murder, guilty of manslaughter, not guilty by reason of insanity, or not guilty.

In Files 70–03317, 70–03318, 70–03319, Death of Sandra Jackson, Death of Todd Wilson, Death of Jonathan Carter, there are five possible verdicts in each of those cases.

You may find the defendant guilty of first-degree murder, guilty of second-degree murder, or guilty of manslaughter; you may find him not guilty by reason of insanity or not guilty.

Your verdict must be unanimous; all twelve of you must agree.

Now, the procedure will be for you to retire to the juryroom, elect one of your members as foreman or chairman, and begin your deliberations.

If you want any of the evidence—exhibits here—knock on the door, and we will attempt to assist you.

If you want any further instructions from the court, knock on the door, and we will attempt to assist you.

After you have reached a verdict, knock on the door, and we will bring you out to receive the verdict.

Now I want you to retire to the juryroom. Do not begin your deliberations until so instructed by the court, as there may be further instructions.

The clerk will now draw out one of the names.

The Clerk: Vincent West.

(Whereupon juror number eleven, Vincent West, left the jury-box.)

The Court: The twelve jurors will retire to the juryroom. Do not begin your deliberations until you are instructed to do so by the court.

(Whereupon the jury left the courtroom.)

[After the jury is excused, both sides say they are satisfied with the charge. The jury returns and is given special instructions concerning "Jay." The courtroom is cleared of spectators, reporters, parties, and witnesses. The court explains that apartment 9 was originally rented by Todd Wilson and "Jay." "Jay" is an undercover agent for the Pittsburgh Police Department. He was living at Stonehead Manor in order to observe certain subversive activities there. He was not present at the time of the shootings and cannot be called into court or forced to reveal his identity in public.]*

[The jury begins its deliberations at 4:05. An hour later, court is adjourned until the following morning.]

THE VERDICT

Saturday 12 December

[Deliberations resume at 9:45. At 1:00 P.M. the jurors get their lunch instructions: they are allotted $2.50 for lunch and are told they have to pay their own tips. Upon Mr. Nelson's suggestion, the court raises the limit to $3.00, then "within reason."]

[At 2:30, deliberations continue. An hour later the jury asks for the definitions of first-degree murder, second-degree murder, and manslaughter. At 4:30 the jury announces it has reached a verdict.]

(Proceedings held within the presence and hearing of the jury.)

(Roll call by the court clerk; all jurors present.)

---

* In an interview Leonard Gilman explained what he knew about "Jay." "I found out about the police informant during the trial. To this day I don't know who Jay was or what he was doing in the house. During that time there was a lot of political activity in Pittsburgh with respect to the Black Panthers and the SDS. There was a group in the Pittsburgh Police Department who was assigned to infiltrate these groups and to keep an eye on them. I think, however, that Jay was involved with drugs—he was looking to make some buys in the place. I don't think there was any great SDS or Panther involvement at the Stonehead Manor." According to Sergeant Baranski, "Jay" was present during a preliminary examination, but made obscene gestures and was accordingly thrown out of court.

The Clerk:	Members of the jury, have you arrived at a verdict; and, if so, who will speak for you?
The Foreman:	*(Indicating.)*
The Clerk:	Would you all rise, please.
	What is your verdict in the case of the *People v. Ricky Walters*, File 3042—
The Court:	It's not *People v. Ricky Walters*.
The Clerk:	—*People v. Wilbur Jackson*, in the death of Ricky Walters.
The Foreman:	Second-degree murder.
	(Whereupon the jury was duly sworn by the court clerk.)
The Clerk:	What is your verdict in the case of the death of Sandra Jackson:
The Foreman:	Guilty of manslaughter.
	(Whereupon the jury was duly sworn by the court clerk.)
The Clerk:	What is your verdict in the case of the death of Todd Wilson?
The Foreman:	Second-degree murder.
	(Whereupon the jury was duly sworn by the court clerk.)
The Clerk:	What is your verdict in the case of the death of Jonathan Carter?
The Foreman:	Second-degree murder.
	(Whereupon the jury was duly sworn by the court clerk.)
The Court:	All right, I will remand the defendant to the County Jail for a pre-sentence report.
	We already have a clinic report.
	Sentence will be next Friday, December 18.
	The jury will retire to the juryroom. We will take you up later to get your coats.
	(Whereupon at 4:35 P.M. the court was adjourned until Friday, December 18, 1970.)

Figure 25 "Lou Gordon Program" transcript

December 13, 1970 10:00 PM Channel 56   Pittsburgh, Pennsylvania

From THE LOU GORDON PROGRAM

Jackie Gordon:

What do you think of the conviction of Wilbur Jackson for murder of
his daughter and the three young men in a hippie pad last May?

Lou Gordon:

Well, I'm glad they convicted him quite frankly and I would have been
very upset had they found him not guilty. I don't think that it was
proper to attempt to try the style of life of those youngsters who were
murdered. I don't approve of that style of life and Mr. Jackson
killed four people including his own daughter. Nobody has the right
to take the lives of other people. He committed murder; he should pay
the penalty.

I'm quite concerned, however, about the penalty. Judge Joseph Gillis,
before whom he has been tried, has a strange record of passing sentences
in his courtroom. For example, Gus Kolakosidis, who was convicted of
bribing a police officer in the Grecian Gardens was given probation
by the same Judge Joseph Gillis. The man whose name escapes me who
was involved in the abortion ring, Dr. Spalter, was brought back from
Florida surreptitiously and brought before Judge Gillis and given a
suspended sentence or a sentence which amounted to no time in prison,
and I hope when Judge Gillis sentences Mr. Jackson Friday it will not
be that kind of sentence, which is probation. Now Judge Gillis,
in my view indicated some sentiments toward Mr. Jackson when he let
him out without bail before this trial began.

I think that another question I'd like to have answered for me is why
three lawyers for Mr. Jackson — who paid these three lawyers, Mr.
Carney, Mr. Nelson and Mr. Tracey? Did the taxpayers pay for this and
if so, why did we have to pay three lawyers for a man who's charged
with murder? What about all the psychiatric tests — did the taxpayers
pay for that? And what about the families of the kids who were
murdered — we get back to the same old point. I suppose the Jackson
family, if Mr. Jackson goes to jail, will be put on Welfare, supported
by the taxpayers. What about the parents of the kids that were
murdered — does anything go to them? And this is the old story I've
raised many times of the victims of crimes and criminals: we do
nothing for them, but we take care of the criminal.

THE SENTENCE

The Court:

Case of the *People v. Wilbur Chester Jackson*.

Mr. Jackson, you were found guilty by a jury of three counts of second-degree murder and one count of manslaughter.

Are there any circumstances that you wish to bring to the attention of the court prior to the imposition of sentence?

[Figure 25 shows a transcript from "The Lou Gordon Program" of WKBG–TV in Pittsburgh, wherein an opinion is given of Judge Gillis's sentencing record.]

The Defendant:

(No response.)

The Court:

Is there anything the attorneys wish to say?

I have a pre-sentence report.

Mr. Gilman?

Mr. Gilman:

Yes, Your Honor. Thank you for the opportunity to speak.

As the court well knows, Mr. Jackson no longer stands before the court as an innocent man.

A jury of twelve has found Mr. Jackson guilty on three cases of feloniously, wilfully, and maliciously taking three lives, and in a fourth case unlawfully killing his own daughter.

A total of four lives were taken by Mr. Jackson on May 8, 1970.

We only ask that the court use its wisdom and take that fact into consideration in imposing sentence on this man.

I would point out that since the date of this incident Mr. Jackson has engaged in conduct which we feel makes him a danger to society.

At Mercywood Hospital he threatened the lives of at least two individuals.

At McKeesport—Forensic Center—he attempted to escape and struck an attendant with handcuffs and inflicted wounds.

He has demonstrated by his statements that he has no remorse whatsoever for taking three of those lives.

Of course, he is sorry for taking the life of his daughter.

But he was indicated that he is proud of taking three of the lives.

We simply ask the court to exercise its discretion wisely in this case and impose a large sentence, a sentence commensurate with the large crimes that have been committed by Mr. Jackson.

The Court:

Mr. Nelson?

Mr. Nelson: I would like an opportunity, if Your Honor please, to respond to Mr. Gilman's remarks.

First of all, I would like to be heard to observe that in sixteen years of practice in this tribunal, so far as I am aware, the Prosecutor's Office being heard from in relation to the matter in affixation of a sentence or fixing of a sentence is absolutely unprecedented.

Secondly, I don't think I need invite Your Honor's attention to the fact that every one of the statements which Mr. Gilman has attributed to Mr. Jackson is a hearsay statement; and, in the case of most of them, double hearsay.

Thirdly, I would urge Your Honor to take into consideration—

I know that you have to be intimately familiar with Mr. Jackson from a psychiatric point of view.

I know that you have a full and complete probation report.

I am fully confident that you are going to use that measure of wisdom that you have been accorded and that you have acquired as a result of years on this bench.

And I think in doing so you are going to deal somewhat more realistically and intelligently with Mr. Jackson than you have been requested to do by Mr. Gilman.

The Court: Of course, there is no sentence that would restore four lives.

The sentence of the court in the second-degree murder cases will be ten to forty years.

The sentence of the court in the manslaughter case will be ten to fifteen years.*

You will be given credit for 146 days served in the Allegheny County Jail awaiting trial.

Now, it is my duty to inform you that you have a constitutional right to appellate review of your conviction.

If you are financially unable to provide counsel to perfect such appeal, the court will appoint counsel for you and will furnish counsel with such portions of the trial transcript as counsel requires to prepare post-conviction motions and to perfect an appeal.

I further advise you that if you claim financial inability and request the court to appoint counsel, such request must be made within sixty days from this date.

For that purpose, use the form which is now handed to you, which form you must execute under oath. That request must be

---

* In an interview Judge Gillis explained his reasons for the sentences. Under Pennsylvania law Wilbur Jackson could be released on parole after six years, four months of his concurrent sentences. Judge Gillis wanted to insure that even if Jackson served the minimal possible time in prison, his remaining daughter would have time to grow up and move away from him. Judge Gillis also felt that at the same time the baby son would be beginning to need a father.

accompanied by detailed answer to the questionnaire form which is also now handed to you. This, too, must be sworn to. It is for the purpose of assisting the court to determine whether or not you are indigent.

At this point, sign the receipt for the questionnaire form and also for the form requesting appointment of counsel.

(Whereupon the case was concluded.)

[See Figure 26 for the court reporter's statement.]

[See Figure 27 for the order of conviction and sentence for Wilbur Jackson.]

Figure 26 Official court reporter's statement

I, Glenn, W. Rose,

Official Court Reporter, do hereby certify that I have recorded

stenographically the proceedings had in the foregoing cause, before

HON. JOSEPH A. GILLIS,

one of the Judges of a Recorder's Court of the City of Pittsburgh,

and a Jury, on date and at the time and place hereinbefore set

forth, and that the foregoing transcript is a full, true, and

correct transcript of my said Stenotype notes.

Glenn W. Rose, Official Reporter

DATED: March 17, 1971

Figure 27 Order of conviction and sentence

THE RECORDER'S COURT OF THE CITY OF PITTSBURGH

ORDER OF CONVICTION AND SENTENCE

STATE OF PENNSYLVANIA ⎫
COUNTY OF ALLEGHENY ⎬ ss.
CITY OF PITTSBURGH ⎭

THE PEOPLE OF THE STATE OF PENNSYLVANIA

vs.

Wilbur Jackson

File No. *7003317*

At a Session of the Recorder's Court of the City of Pittsburgh, held in and for said City, in the Court Room
of the Honorable _*J A Gillis*_, a Judge of said Court, on the _*12*_ day of _*Dec.*_,
A.D. 19_*76*_, the defendant in the above entitled cause, was convicted by (Jury) (Court) (Plea), of having
committed the crime of _*Manslaughter*_ in the City of Pittsburgh, County of Allegheny, Pennsylvania.

And upon said conviction, the said Court, at a Session thereof, held as aforesaid, and the defendant
*Wilbur Jackson*, present in open Court for Sentence on the _*18*_
day of _*Dec*_, A.D. 19_*76*_, is heard in response to the statutory questions propounded
to him, (he) (she) being the age of _*46*_ years, and is sentenced by the Court to be committed
to _State Prison So. PENNA., place designated by PENNA Corrections Commission_ and therein confined for a term of not less than
_*10*_ nor more than _*15*_ years. Recommendation _*Concurrent*_.
The maximum statutory penalty for the crime of which said defendant stands convicted is _*15*_
years.

Attorney for defendant, _*O C Nelson*_, was present at the
time of sentence.

The defendant to be given credit for _*146*_ days served in the Allegheny County Jail. Said credit
to be applied to minimum and maximum sentence.

Warrant and Commitment papers to issue.

*Joseph A Gillis*
Judge of the Recorder's Court

C of D—5-OR (Rev. 12-67)

[B138]

Figure 27 Order of conviction and sentence (continued)

CERTIFIED COPY OF JUDGMENT AND SENTENCE — Pennsylvania Corrections Commission-State Prison, Southern Pennsylvania the place
designated by the Commission

STATE OF PENNSYLVANIA ⎫
County of Allegheny ⎬ ss.   tg
CITY OF PITTSBURGH ⎭   THE RECORDER'S COURT OF THE CITY OF PITTSBURGH

THE PEOPLE OF THE STATE OF PENNSYLVANIA ⎫

WILBUR CHESTER JACKSON ⎬

⎭

File No. _____70 03317_____

Information for _____
Murder 1st Degree

Before Judge JOSEPH A. GILLIS

At a session of the Recorder's Court of said City, held in and for said City, at the Court Room of said
Court, on the _____12th_____ day of _____December_____, A.D. 19 70,
the above named defendant, in the above entitled cause, and, by a jury duly empaneled and sworn, after a
full hearing in his presence, and on his former plea of NOT GUILTY, was convicted of having (on the
_____8th_____ day of _____May_____, A.D. 19 70), committed
the crime of _____MANSLAUGHTER_____

Statute Section: _____750.321 C.L. 1948_____

at the City of Pittsburgh, County of Allegheny, Pennsylvania.

And upon the said conviction, the said Court, did, on the _____18th_____ day of
_____December_____, A.D. 19 70, adjudge and determine that the said defendant,
who is now the age of _____46_____ years should be committed to the Pennsylvania Corrections Commission by delivery to the State Prison of Southern Pennsylvania, in the County of New Castle, the place designated by the Commission, and therein safely kept and employed according to the laws thereof, for the period
of not less than _____Ten_____ years and _____no_____ months, from and including this date, to _____Fifteen_____
years, _____no_____ months. Maximum Statutory Penalty _____Fifteen (15) Years_____
Recommend Concurrently with files 70 03318, 70 03319 & 70 03042

Attorney for defendant, _____Oliver Nelson_____ was present
at the time of sentence.

The defendant to be given credit for _____146_____ days time served in the Allegheny County Jail. Said
credit to be applied to both the minimum and maximum sentence.

STATE OF PENNSYLVANIA ⎫
County of Allegheny ⎬ ss.
CITY OF PITTSBURGH ⎭

I, E. BURKE MONTGOMERY, Clerk of the Recorder's
Court of the City of Pittsburgh, do hereby certify that the foregoing is a correct abstract from the minutes
of said Court in the above entitled cause, of the conviction and sentence of _____
WILBUR CHESTER JACKSON

IN TESTIMONY WHEREOF, I have hereunto set my hand and affixed the seal of said Court, at Pittsburgh
this _____18th_____ day of _____December_____, in the
year of our Lord one thousand nine hundred and _____70_____.

E. BURKE MONTGOMERY
Clerk

C of D—2-MI (1-68)

THE VIEWS OF TRIAL COUNSEL

[The authors interviewed both Leonard Gilman and Oliver Nelson during the course of separate visits each made to Harvard Law School. Although these interviews were several months apart, the answers of Gilman and Nelson are presented together for the sake of contrast.]

THE DEFENSE ATTORNEY

Question: Mr. Nelson, could you explain just why you took this case?

Nelson: I took the case, first of all, because I was asked to take it by a good friend of mine on the Recorder's bench. But essentially and primarily I defended him because I sympathized with him. I felt sorry for him. I thought he was in a terrible predicament and I thought he was there through no fault of his own.

Question: Would you take anyone's case simply because you felt sorry for them?

Nelson: I was thinking that I probably only gave you part of the answer when I said that I took it because I felt sorry for Jackson. I think you'll find that everybody who does the kind of work that I do has kind of an aggressive personality and they just like to get into court and mix it up; and I can't say that that isn't a part of my personality; and I can't say that that isn't a part of the reason why I wanted this particular case. I felt that it was the proper vehicle to become somewhat better known in the Pittsburgh area than I would have otherwise. I didn't have any racial motives or political motives.

Question: But didn't the case have strong political overtones?

Nelson: I don't think the case had any particular political overtones. I don't think hippieism or the hippie element is a political element; it's a lifestyle in my judgment; it's apolitical. I believe that there are an awful lot of people in Pittsburgh who regard running around with beads and pot and funny pants and so forth as an absolute anathema. They regard it as a course of conduct that is calculated to give offense, and they are offended by it. You'd be surprised at the number of people who made it a point to come up to me and say: "too bad about Jackson; I would have done the same thing myself."

[Authors' Note: During the trial the Jacksons received various pieces of "fan mail" from people who had read of the trial in the newspapers. This "fan mail" generally indicated support or sympathy for Wilbur Jackson. Figure 28 shows a letter and a poem received by the Jacksons, examples of "fan mail."]

Figure 28 "Fan mail"

[Mrs. Wilbur Jackson,
       C/O Pittsburgh Police Headquarters,
           Pittsburgh, U.S.A.

Dear Mrs. Jackson:

   I have just read the most recent issue of "TIME" magazine, and
I must beg you to forgive me for writing to you at all in this time
of sorrow and trouble. I am a Canadian citizen of 70, and so this
is no idle letter of curiosity or mockery etc. and perhaps you will
get many from the present Hippie and panther type, who are so intent
on their dope and pleasures and freedom from any responsibility to
either parents, country or society. They are certainly not the
builders of any nation, rather the destroyers of all that others
have built at great cost, and most are educated and know exactly
what they are doing. Every day on the radio there are appeals for
boys and girls to return home to their anxious parents, you can
just imagine the response they make to this, and it is not the slum
type alone any more, it is in every walk of society, and mainly the
educated.
   My deepest sympathy and admiration go to your husband, who is
truly a father in every way, a rare thing today, and who was deeply
anxious and worried over your daughter Sandra. Do you find many
fathers who truly want to protect the morals of their offspring
until such time as they make a satisfactory and happy marriage.
Mostly it is the mother who is upset over a straying daughter or
son, especially in these days of perversion, pornography, sex
movies, casting aside all morals and decency, and spreading V.D.
and ruining their own health of both body and mind by being available to any verminous long haired filth that comes along. Except
perhaps for the size of their feet and sexes today cannot even be
distinguished, and by being induced to take dope it follows that
they are easy victims for anyone who hasnt a scruple or moral. You
will recognize this as a fact, and they cannot be excused as they
know exactly what dope, drink, indiscriminate sex and immorality
can do to their lives.
                        *   *   *
   I admire President Nixon and Mr. Agnew for their fight against
the filth and sewerage and killing and crime and Hippieism and four
letter filth, obscenity and immorality of these days. . . .
   If your husband accidently shot his daughter can this be held
against him? Dont accidents happen every day, and some pass as
such and are really intended. What can one say about Senator
Kennedy, who left a girl to drown after a party where his friends
and some woman, NOT wives, were having a party. What do you call
this? This type and the panthers who kill innocent and bystanders
are truly murderers, but a father who knew his daughter was violated
and led astray, and likely by a few dirty immoral Hippies, he had
every moral right to Kill them and one could compare it to a member
of a family being threatened by some rapist, for what else are they,
but also by some rattler or cobra, or mad dog. Any father would
instinctively act so. I admire your husband, I admire the
courage and the desire to put out of existence the dirt threatening
his family, and for myself, you may say this is bloodthirsty, but
as his wife I would have handed him a machine gun and let him
destroy more of these scum who are certainly not human, and are
definitely sub normal, it would stop them from reproducing their
sewer type.

Figure 28 "*Fan mail*" (*continued*)

*   *   *

Anyway, your husband was prompted by a deep love and a desire to protect, is-this a crime? Definitely NOT. And if his girl died at least it was over an attempt to save her. And if she had lived and continued to service every dirty Hippie, is this not a worse death? Surely you as her mother must know what the ultimate end would have been.

*   *   *

. . . I am sure your other children will appreciate the anguish you have, and will also appreciate the deep love and thought their father held for his own. No court or anyone can condemn this, and at no time should he feel he is a murderer, even in hunting people kill their loved ones by mistake. What about the countless household accidents? Can one call these murders? And many who have had their girls and boys ruined by contact with these filthy Hippies, who also shoot so many fathers who are police and deprive the families of support and care, will applaud your husband for his action, whether done in rage and confusion and loss or in cold blood. These depraved vermin are no asset to any nation, and they make addicts of many to whom they peddle their mind killing dope. Isn't this wholesale murder, and in cold blood?

*   *   *

I truly wish your husband a speedy return to normal life, to many he will actually be a hero, to others the emblem of a true father.]

PRAISES

Let others chant the praises of the Moderns of our time
The Homos and the Lesbians who crawl from out the slime
The Hippies and the Yippies, the queers and sewer rats
The Dopeheads and the Beatles, who yowl like alley cats.
Should one applaud a cult of crime, V.D. and hairy Apes
Who only know obscenities, and flaunt their naked shapes.

*   *   *

My voice is raised in honest praise of all our may Squares
The decent class of every land, who still believe in prayers.
The ones who pay their taxes, work hard, and do their best
Who help to heal a world of ills, the Bible calls them blest.
These are the shining candles in the darkness of today
Who spread their glow of sunshine to all along life's way.

Question:	Do you believe that punishment makes any sense in the case of someone like Wilbur Jackson who's not likely to commit future crimes?
Nelson:	I suppose that the question is most easily answered by simply saying that when someone transgresses, he is expected to pay for the transgression. That is the way in which we have operated ever since we entered the Christian Era, and presumably will operate in the future. Perhaps some day we'll arrive at a method of dealing with people who have violated the law that won't require someone like Wilbur Jackson going to prison. But right now I think that everybody who is involved in the enforcement of law or in the administration of justice feels that, if for no other reason, Jackson had to go to jail because of the deterrent effect upon other people who might very well do the same thing.
Question:	More generally, what is it that makes a defense attorney? Why does somebody want to be a defense attorney?
Nelson:	I think maybe because of the same peculiar mixture or chemistry that led me to have wanted to play guard for Dartmouth during the 1940s. A certain pugnacious nature or something like that. It's a constant challenge. It's reasonably rewarding. I don't do badly financially. It's something that I certainly like to do, and I certainly would not want to be delivering milk now and spending the rest of my life wondering if I perhaps could have done something that I liked doing as much as I like doing this.
Question:	What's the biggest single kick you get as a defense attorney?
Nelson:	I suppose I should say when you win one.
Question:	When you win one where the defendant was plainly innocent or where you win one when the defendant might have been guilty?
Nelson:	I don't think things are usually that clear-cut, to be quite frank with you. I think maybe the biggest kick you get these days after you become jaded is when you get paid.
Question:	When you get into a trial, do you feel yourself pursuing justice, or simply trying to win a contest?
Nelson:	I look upon my function as being a man who, by reason of special skills acquired in law school and otherwise endowed by the law with the responsibility of representing a defendant, attempts to produce the most favorable result that can be obtained. And I believe that in doing so I am, first of all, properly representing him and, secondly, going about what the law is designed to do, which is to see to it that justice is done to each individual. Quite frankly, as often as not that leads me to a judgment that the person whom I represent should very well go in and avail himself or herself of the opportunity to plead guilty to a lesser included offense. And quite frequently the matter is disposed of in that way.

I believe there is a tendency on the part of those who sit in the Prosecutor's Office to overcharge whenever they can because they know that somewhere along the line there is going to be plea bargaining, and they want to give whomever is going to have to bargain something to work with so they can come out with what the man should have been charged with and found guilty of in the first place. So I think it all works out in the end.

Question: Are you friendly with the prosecutors? Do you feel bitter toward them after a case?

Nelson: Not as a general rule. I think that we as often as not find ourselves seated in the Athens Bar having a beer or two with them when we get done with a day's session in court.

I kind of feel this way: that I would like to operate under a system—such as they use in England—whereby someone could be called upon to either go in and prosecute a case or might be called upon to go in and defend the very same case. I'd like to see things work in that manner. And I believe that would much more closely approximate the true advocate rule. But I don't think we will ever get around to doing that.

Leonard Gilman was one of the two or three most capable staff assistants in the Allegheny County Prosecutor's Office. He has since left; he's gone to Westmoreland County where he performs a similar function at considerably more money and I was sorry to see him go. I believe that he did an outstanding job in the Jackson case, and I think he beat me fair and square. I can't put it more differently than that. I just can't say enough good about Len Gilman and the way in which he handled this particular case.

Question: I'd like to run you through a series of things that will look like ethical dilemmas. One question comes right out of *Anatomy of a Murder* by Judge Robert Traver. There, the defense counsel is very careful not to elicit the full facts from his client and in fact tells the client enough of the law to give the client a good opportunity to tell the defense counsel such facts as might prepare an adequate defense, or to at least make an adequate defense possible. Do you regard that as proper, and have you ever done it?

Nelson: I'd have to say that I have done that. I'd also have to qualify that by saying that I haven't done it very often. But I didn't do it with Jackson, and there are several reasons why. First of all, I didn't think it was necessary, and most importantly, I just didn't think that Jackson would have been able to understand what it was I was trying to do.

Question: If you came across a piece of evidence while you were investigating a case that indicated that your man was guilty or just a piece of evidence that the prosecution would very much like to know as part of their case, would you feel any obligation to turn that piece of evidence from your investigation over to the prosecution?

Nelson:	No.
Question:	Would you feel free to cross-examine a witness that you believed was telling the truth?
Nelson:	Yes, I would. I think there's a good example of that in this Jackson case. We had [Ames Robey] come down to Pittsburgh from whatever mountain he came down off of with absolutely damning testimony to the psychiatric issues involved. I went ahead in a purely ancillary manner; went after him on his qualifications and on his testimony that emanated from nothing more than sheer ego on his part that he had drafted the law establishing the Forensic Center, which was not true at all. We brought in somebody who had served as counsel for the legislative committee that had drafted that law, and he testified that he had never even heard of him [Robey] before he'd been hired to run the Forensic Center.
Question:	What if your client told you he had committed a certain act. Would you allow him to take the stand and deny it?
Nelson:	No, I don't think I'd be able to do that.
Question:	If it were one step short of that, and he didn't tell you but your own conclusion from talking with him, meeting with him, seeing him, talking to his alibi witnesses, was that he had almost certainly committed the act. Would you then allow him to take the stand and deny it?
Nelson:	Yes, that's more often the case.
Question:	Is that very frequently the case?
Nelson:	Yes, it is.
Question:	If you had someone whom you thought would be a good witness, believable, but whom you also knew was going to commit perjury and whose testimony you considered fairly essential to your case, would you put him on the stand?
Nelson:	Not if he was going to commit perjury. You just can't do that.

THE PROSECUTING ATTORNEY

Question:	Mr. Gilman, I think an argument can be made that Wilbur Jackson killed once, killed in a fit of rage, and will never kill again. If this is true, then what can be gained by sending him to prison?
Gilman:	How do you know that Wilbur's not going to kill again? What if his younger daughter, Debbie Jackson, leaves home and goes down to Allegheny State University and moves in with Joe Jones? Who knows. Who's to say he's not going to kill again?
	I really think Wilbur Jackson felt sorry that he killed his daughter. I don't think he felt sorry that he killed the other three because I think

he really felt that they had turned his daughter on to a horrible type of life. I think he really, sincerely felt sorry, and I think he suffered greatly because he killed Sandra. But big deal. I'll give him one free murder because he felt sorry? This guy took four lives. Four kids aren't here today because of Wilbur Jackson. So I thought Judge Gillis was very light in giving him a sentence of ten to forty, and I'm sorry that he's in New Castle Prison, but I think that's where he belongs.

Question: Do you plan to stay on working as a prosecutor?

Gilman: I'm going to stay on for a while. I made a commitment to the prosecutor in Westmoreland County to stay at least a couple of years. I like it. It's a lot of fun. I enjoy trying cases. I think I'm on the better side of the fence, so to speak. I don't think I'd enjoy representing defendants in criminal cases. I'd enjoy doing defense work, but not representing defendants charged with crime. I'd have a very difficult time doing that.

I like the job I do, and I like to be with my family. Defense attorneys in private practice work till eleven or twelve o'clock at night. I'm not like that. I just don't want to work that hard. Normally, prosecuting is an eight-thirty to five job, a nine till five job, and I really don't have to take my problems home with me. I don't have to worry about clients calling me at three in the morning and telling me their husband just threw them out of the house again and to please do something for them or saying, "I've just been arrested; get a writ for me and get me out." I like what I do. I really enjoy being a prosecutor.

Question: How difficult are most of your cases to try?

Gilman: I have tried so many cases that all a murder is is an assault and battery that's gone a little too far. The facts are a little bit more complex, and there are a few more witnesses, but there's not that much difference between offenses unless you're involved in an embezzlement case or an extortion case. Those can be really complicated, but murders usually aren't that complicated.

Question: Aren't there crimes that you just wouldn't want to prosecute? What do you do with marijuana cases, for example?

Gilman: We have a rule of thumb in our office that if it's one or two or three or four cigarettes, we don't recommend a warrant. We just confiscate it and the person isn't charged with a crime. Because, you know, charging a person with a crime is a pretty serious thing. This is where a prosecutor can be just as effective for civil liberties as a defense attorney because we come in right at the outset when a person's arrested. We have the responsibility to decide whether a person is going to be charged with a crime. What's more important than that? When you charge somebody with a crime, you have got to make damn sure you've got something because you can ruin their life by just charging them with a crime, so we've got an important function to perform, too. We don't get that many young kids into the Prosecutor's Office. That's a little pitch for the Prosecutor's Office.

Question: How do you feel about really stiff jail sentences?

Gilman: I think they're fair. I think punishment is one purpose of sentencing. I think rehabilitation is the most important purpose. And by keeping someone in jail for thirty years—obviously you're not going to rehabilitate him—you're going to keep him off the street. That sometimes is a good thing.

I think if judges would sentence people to stiffer prison terms for crimes like robberies and planned murders, that's as great a deterrent as turning on a gas chamber and wiping them out.

RELATIONS WITH THE POLICE

Question: How did you get along with the police in the Jackson case? Do you think they did a good job?

Nelson: I think they did a first-class job. I happen to have a great deal of respect for the officers in the Pittsburgh Homicide Bureau; I think they're very professional, much more so than people holding similar jobs in other communities or with the state police, and I think they're even more professional than the FBI. I think they are really fine officers, and I believe the two in the Jackson case were both first-class.

Gilman: At the time of the Jackson trial, I was assigned to major felonies and homicides in the Allegheny County Prosecutor's Office. All I handled were murders, and I worked with the Pittsburgh Police Department's Homicide Bureau, and they were the most cooperative bunch of guys in the world until this case. All of a sudden they weren't very cooperative. And Sergeant Baranski, who is really a great guy, had some typical family problems with his daughter at the time of this trial.

During the course of the trial, the police saw what kind of a guy Wilbur Jackson was, particularly Baranski. Baranski was rooting as much as I was for a murder-one conviction. I wanted to convict the guy on the nose. We didn't, and I can understand why we didn't. There were mitigating circumstances that went against premeditation, and I could understand the jury coming back with murder two.

Question: To what extent does the DA's office guide in police investigations?

Gilman: It depends on where you're working. The Allegheny County Prosecutor's Office only gets the case upon completion of the investigation by the Police Department, unless it's a police shooting. If it's a shooting by a police officer of a citizen, the Allegheny County Prosecutor's Office will conduct an independent investigation and interview all the witnesses, because the police are killing a lot of people in Pittsburgh and a lot of people are getting killed. But in the Jackson case, the police conducted their investigation.

Out in Westmoreland County, where I work now, if it's a major felony, you're assigned to the case from the moment it happens or from the moment the police are notified. I'm in trial right now in a case in which a police officer was killed last May. I was at the scene of the crime forty-five minutes after the officer was killed. That's really a good thing because a lawyer is there to coordinate the investigation. A lawyer is there to recommend whether a search warrant is needed; to recommend whether hair samples should be taken; to recommend whether blood samples should be taken. And all the things that would have to be done if I wasn't there or if another prosecutor wasn't there would have to be done within a few days' time.

Question: Have you lost cases simply because you weren't there to direct the activities of the police?

Gilman: I don't say that it's because I or another prosecutor wasn't there, but it's because sometimes they overreact. They make mistakes. We lose cases because of that. We lose cases because of lots of reasons. That really is a minor reason.

Question: How hard is it to prosecute a policeman who's charged with felonious assault or something like that?

Gilman: There was a police wives' dance at a building in downtown Pittsburgh and seven or eight policemen got bombed out of their minds and chased a group of black kids that were at another dance at the same building. One guy took a shot at them, and there was a lot of stuff that happened. There was some publicity, very little, but some, and the defense attorney, representing the policeman, made a motion for a change of venue in front of a very police-minded judge. So I had to try the policeman up in Farmersville, which is really out in the woods. And I didn't have a snowball's chance. I was picking a jury and this guy was wearing a gas station attendant's outfit. He says, "Hey, those police have taken enough; they got a right to crack some skulls." I said thank you very much for your honesty. But if you're trying a policeman in Pittsburgh today, you've got a good chance to convict him. There's a really antipolice viewpoint.

Question: Do you ever have a problem with police officers falsifying their testimony?

Gilman: There's this doctrine called plain view. The plain view doctrine says that anything the officer sees with his own two eyes, if he's in a place where he has a right to be, is admissible in evidence and doesn't constitute a search and seizure. So some officers feel justified in altering their testimony, though not all officers will do this. But some officers will. When an officer stops a suspicious-looking guy and pats him down and finds a half-ounce of heroin in his pocket, he had no right to search the guy. But he comes to court and says, "I was following this guy because he had white lights to the rear of his car (and that's a traffic ordinance in the city of Pittsburgh), and I saw him pitch this thing out of his car, and I drove by and saw it was what I believed to be heroin, and I picked it up and then I arrested him." A guy that has heroin in his possession should be punished for having heroin in his possession. And some police feel justified in taking that position. On the other hand, there's a lot of straight ones that will come in and say: "Hey, listen, I got a half-ounce of heroin in here, but I made a bad bust and let's just confiscate the heroin and release the guy."

Sometimes you have to say that. If you really believe that it's a phony case, you just say: "I'm sorry that's insufficient evidence. We're not going to recommend a warrant." But most of the time it's very difficult to say: "Hey, listen officer, you're a liar. I just don't believe you. I believe this guy here who's got a four-page record." It puts me in the position of being a fact finder, and that really is the jury's job.

Question: When Jackson came to trial, did you have trouble finding the kids who had lived in Stonehead Manor?

Gilman: A week before the trial, we went out looking for these witnesses, and naturally they're all transients—they move from place to place to avoid going back home—and we found Carl Richardson, who located every witness in the case for us. He was the most cooperative guy in the world. Here's a guy who said he had been convicted of conspiracy to overthrow the government. He went out and found every witness in the case and brought them to court on his own time and drove maybe five hundred miles to find some of these people. We got a lot of help from the kids.

PLEA BARGAINING

Question: Was plea bargaining ever seriously considered in the Jackson case?

Gilman: Jackson wouldn't plead guilty to anything from the outset. And we didn't offer him anything, which is really a very unusual situation in Recorder's Court. More than 90 percent of the cases are disposed of in Recorder's Court through plea bargaining; 10 percent of the cases are tried. So it's an unusual case that goes to trial without any plea bargaining at all.

Nelson: I don't think Jackson—I think it's entirely fair to say that at no point in time did Jackson ever even consider pleading to a lesser included offense, nor did I. That's not why I took this case. I took this case to try it, and I enjoyed trying it very much.

Question:	How well does the plea bargaining process work in your area? Are you forced to give up good cases against really serious criminals?
Gilman:	In Westmoreland County, no; in Recorder's Court, yes. There's a tremendous volume of cases that go through the city of Pittsburgh. We really don't give up anything in offering a plea if the judge still has the discretion to sentence a man hard. In other words, if a man charged with robbery armed, who has no prior record, goes to trial, he might get two to fifteen. If I let him plead to robbery not armed, that carries a fifteen-year maximum. So the judge still has the discretion to give him that same two to fifteen. So we really aren't losing that much in offering a lesser plea.
	In New York they negotiate sentence in plea bargaining. We don't; the judge will not participate in pre-trial plea bargaining negotiations.
Question:	Would you accept a plea if you think that there's a good chance the defendant is innocent?
Gilman:	If the defendant wants to plead guilty, and he says he's guilty, who am I to second-guess him? In Pennsylvania the defendant has to say not only I'm guilty but I shot John Smith on a certain day with a gun. You have to put the facts in the record. So I'm not going to second-guess a person who wants to plead guilty.
Question:	How frequently do prosecutors jack up the number of counts brought against a defendant?
Gilman:	Sometimes that happens and then you're talking about overcharging. Sometimes that will happen in order to get a plea. It doesn't happen that often. Say a man is driving a car and somebody shoots directly at him with a gun and shatters the windshield. The gun is aimed right at the driver but it doesn't hit him, and he isn't injured at all. Well, you could charge the shooter with assault with intent to commit murder because a jury may find that by shooting at the driver at point blank range he intended to kill him, which carries life imprisonment. You could charge him with assault with intent to do great bodily harm less than murder, which carries ten years. What's probably going to happen is that it's going to wind up felonious assault. But what a prosecutor might do is charge him with great bodily harm or intent to commit murder and let him plea to felonious assault, which carries four years.
	If we recommend probation, the judge will follow it almost every time. It's unfortunate that prosecutors don't participate in the sentencing process as much as they should. We should be at every sentencing and make a recommendation, but most prosecutors don't do that. When we're there, I think the judge gives a lot of weight to what we say.
	Some judges will, believe it or not, punish a guy for going to trial. They really don't like that too much if a guy goes to trial just to have a

trial when he really knows he's guilty and there's a strong case against him. He's entitled to a trial; the Constitution says he's entitled to a trial; but there are certain judges that will raise the sentence a bit. Of course the higher sentence may be justified under the theory that confession to crime is the first step toward rehabilitation.

[The Recorder's Court in which Wilbur Jackson was tried has released statistics on the disposition of cases in that court. Some interesting figures from the most recent annual report include:]

FELONY ARRAIGNMENTS

Crimes against people:

Murder	355
Armed robbery	763
Robbery	150
Rape	226
Other sex offenses	189
Armed assault	418
Assault with intent to murder	162
Assault with intent to rob	81
Assault with intent to rape	24
Other assaults	287

Crimes against property:

Breaking and Entering—building	693
Breaking and Entering—auto	144
Auto theft	243
Larceny over $100	485
Receiving stolen property	691
Checks and forgeries	342
Credit card offenses	63
Arson	112
Destruction of property over $100	48
Commercialized vice	3

Miscellaneous crimes:

Narcotics	1,725
Carrying concealed weapon	788
Fugitive	95
Resisting police officer	23
Gambling	15
Other	2,679
	10,804

[There were also 6,350 misdemeanor arraignments. The most commonly charged misdemeanors were the following: larceny under $100 (2,768), assault and battery (1,653), destruction of property under $100 (459), and loitering (211).]

[Of some 10,543 felony defendants 4,614 (44%) were released on personal bond. Surety or cash bonds were set for another 5,685 and of those 2,877 were able to post bond. The remainder were not released on any kind of bond. Of those released on personal bond, 12% failed to appear for trial, sentencing, etc., while the figure was 11% for those on surety or cash bond.]

[The disposition of felony cases during that year was as follows:]

Entered guilty plea	5,833
Found guilty by jury	409
Acquitted by jury	286
Found guilty by judge	401
Acquitted by judge	258
Dismissed	3,331
	10,518

[Interestingly, the chance of being acquitted by a jury (41%) was not significantly better than the chance of being acquitted by a judge (39%).]

[Of 6,917 defendants actually sentenced during the year: 3,225 received probation or a suspended sentence; 1,113 were sent to the local jail for varying terms; and 2,579 were sentenced to the state prison.]

JURY SELECTION

Question: Let's talk about jury selection in the Jackson case. Was it different from most cases?

Gilman: Jury selection in this case was completely different from the way it is in other cases. I wanted to get the most intelligent jury I could find, which is not the way I would normally approach it. Normally, I want followers. I want people who will follow the lead of one strong, middle-aged factory worker type who dislikes crime and whom the other jurors will follow. In this case I wanted really a bright, intelligent jury who would disregard the clothes and the beards and all that.

Nelson: Ordinarily, if you defend a homicide case in Pittsburgh, it would be fair to say that you're defending someone between seventeen and twenty-six who is charged with the commission of a felony murder, a murder which was committed in the course of the perpetration of a robbery, burglary, an arson or a rape. About 90 percent of the time, but perhaps even more often than that, you're defending a black who is between eighteen and twenty-six and you want one particular kind of a jury to try that kind of a case, but you want a very different kind of a jury to try Wilbur Jackson.

Frankly, I was hoping that we could get that case moved out of Pittsburgh—even to Greensburg—but certainly moved away from the city somewhere so that we would have less exposure to those kinds of individuals whom I felt would not be—could not be—basically sympathetic to Jackson's positions or attitudes or anything else. They don't fill up a baseball stadium with fifty thousand to sixty thousand people and permit defense counsel to wander about and say this looks like the kind of a person I like. You get a very mixed bag of jurors. It's not a matter of getting what you want; it's having to settle for the best that you can get.

Question: What was the average age of your jury?

Nelson: A little over forty.

Question: And what was the racial and sexual division?

Nelson: We tried to get as many men on there as we could. We tried to get as many whites as we could. We had two blacks and ten whites on the final jury.

Question: Did you in addition to excluding blacks, try to exclude Jews from the jury?

Nelson: Yes. What I was trying to do, to be quite frank with you, was to get as many people on that jury who came from the northeast part of Pittsburgh and who had Polish or Italian surnames.

Question: Do you have any idea how the jury reached its verdict?

Nelson: I believe that the jury didn't really arrive at a verdict in this case at all. I believe that they compromised. I believe there were some people who were committed to acquitting Jackson in all four cases. And I believe there were some other people, for reasons that are really extraneous to the case itself and the issues of the case, that were equally committed to having Jackson found guilty of first-degree murder. They finally compromised.

Question: Could you expand on that a bit?

Nelson: I believe that it was the two blacks that held out for first degree in that case, and they finally made their point by getting second degree.

Question: Do you think the pre-trial publicity affected the jury?

Nelson: Not really, no. First of all it wasn't all that bad. Most of the articles that were written about the whole affair were essentially sympathetic to Jackson and were pretty objective and pretty straightforward and factual. They didn't get into too much of the rhetoric that you usually find in the more sensational tabloid-type reports of those things—that came later. Up until the trial's end, I believe there was a conscious effort on the part of the reportorial staff of both papers to be a little bit careful about that.

I think there was a very concerted effort on the part of the Police Department—that most professional bureau of the Police Department—the homicide officers—to keep that kind of stuff out of the papers just so that it wouldn't have an effect. I think Jackson initially had the sympathy of most of the wearers-of-blue in Pittsburgh and certainly of the homicide officers that were responsible for putting this case together—not to the extent that they didn't do their duty in the case, which they did in all respects. They were essentially sympathetic.

I think that there was a feeling in the editorial rooms of both papers that this thing could trigger some kind of a "civil disturbance," which is a euphemism that everybody uses now to characterize a riot. I think there were many, many people going around telling other people to cool it. But I believe their objectivity and their lack of sensationalism to the extent that they forebore sensationalism with reference to this case was the result of that.

THE INSANITY DEFENSE

Question: Mr. Nelson, do you really feel your client was insane, or was it merely the only defense you had open to you?

Nelson: I believed and still believe that Jackson should have been acquitted. He should have been acquitted and he should have been sent, instead of being sent to New Castle Prison, to the Templeton Reformatory for the Criminally Insane, where he should have been kept until in the judgment of the Pennsylvania Department of Mental Health it was reasonably safe to free him, and then he should have been freed.

Question: How long do you think that might have been?

Nelson: I believe that he would have been out in about thirty days on a writ because the psychiatric staff of the Forensic Center where he was submitted prior to trial had already promulgated a judgment that he was within the meaning of the Pennsylvania rule sane and wasn't in need of hospitalization. They had already committed themselves to that diagnostically; they couldn't very well change their minds once he had been sent in there under sentence.

Question: There seems to be a conflict there. On the one hand you're saying that he should have been acquitted on the defense of insanity; but on the other, that he probably would have done only about thirty days because he really wasn't insane.

Nelson: Our defense was that he temporarily went berserk, he just literally ran amok, and that he succumbed to an irresistible impulse and was temporarily insane at the moment he committed these homicides and thereafter recovered his sanity. There wasn't any real reason to keep him under psychiatric restraint. Therefore, I say thirty days, because I assume that's about what it takes to process someone when they go in there.

Question: The way you're describing insanity is that it is something which just suddenly falls upon you.

Nelson: The issue is one of criminal responsibility. In Pennsylvania there's this one case in which the Supreme Court of Pennsylvania, years and years ago, used the term irresistible impulse. If someone, through defects of his character or whatever, succumbed to an irresistible impulse and did something that's completely irrational, he can be within the purview of this rule acquitted. And several people have been. Now I don't mean to quibble psychiatrically; I'm simply saying that we endeavored to avail ourselves of what you might say is a defensive tool. We tried to utilize that in behalf of Jackson, and not too successfully.

Question: Given any kind of a combination of irresistible impulses and temporary insanity, how can you explain to a jury that the man was so selective about his killings?

Nelson: He wasn't; he killed everybody in the place.

Question: But then didn't he go downstairs to another unit where there were people and not shoot them? Did his insanity last just five minutes?

Nelson: It was temporary insanity.

Question: Did you ever give Jackson any sort of advice as to what it would be helpful to remember, and what it would be helpful to forget?

Nelson: The fact that he testified at the trial that he couldn't remember certain details of the events that occurred in that place didn't surprise me at all, and I didn't think it was particularly important because he had been in a rather prolonged state of very, very intense mental depression. He had to be given electrotherapy to get him out of it, to rehabilitate him to the point where we could even get the case tried.

I didn't discuss the legal ramifications of his testimony at all with Mr. Jackson. I discussed many times the events and got rather conflicting statements from him upon occasion. Statements also that conflicted in some respects with what his wife said and what other people said.

Question: Did you ever seriously consider making the defense that he was not temporarily insane, but was, in fact, insane and had always been insane?

Nelson: No, I never even considered that. There were several reasons for it. I don't think Jackson or his wife would have permitted me to defend the case on that theory, nor do I believe that the jury would have bought it. I don't believe it was saleable. I don't think that Jackson's family life and his background were indicative of facts that would have justified anybody seriously trying to sell that kind of defense. If you will recall, he was a graduate of a normal school in Tennessee; he worked and had a responsible position for two decades with the New York Central Railroad; he had what many of his neighbors and acquaintances characterized as being an idyllic home life; this was of course all upon the surface. But we just wouldn't have been able to put that one across at all.

Question:

How much effect do you think the psychiatric testimony had on the jury? Do you think they listened to it; do you think they understood it?

Nelson:

I don't believe the psychiatric testimony had all that much effect upon that jury, and the reason I don't is because Jackson had been exposed to that jury for about twenty or twenty-five days of trial. They sat there and followed him; they had an opportunity to observe him in court. They saw him come and go. Incidentally, I believe that it was a tactical mistake to have Jackson out on personal bond when we were trying the case. I think it would have been better if he was brought into court every day shackled and sat down in front of that jury. The point I'm trying to make is that I believe that the defense of insanity is a defense that a jury will buy if they can empathize or sympathize with the person who is on trial, and not otherwise. And I don't believe Jackson had the sympathy of that jury when they decided that case.

Gilman:

The insanity defense is a defense that is often tried and is very rarely successful. But that doesn't mean it can't succeed. I think it will succeed when a person has a prior history of mental difficulties and where for no apparent reason he kills somebody. And where he had no recollection of killing somebody—where he just doesn't recall doing it.

The most important thing, from my point of view, is to bring out the facts, because you can march in ten psychiatrists on each side who will have the opposite point of view. You can get ten on one side to say that he was suffering from a dissociative reaction, and I can get ten others who will say the guy just got angry and blew his top and shot four people. The most important thing is to go to the conduct of the person and to bring out from each witness how the person acted during the course of the crime. I tried to do that with the witnesses to show that he killed four people, that he tried to kill Sally Tucker, and that he ignored everybody else in the building; that he drove a car there; that he drove a car away from there; that he went to the police station. And I don't think the jury regarded the psychiatric testimony on either side as of much importance.

Nelson:

Of the four psychiatrists who testified, I think the one who came across with the greatest degree of believability was the one that I least relied upon—Hubert Miller. And I think that only because of his lack of any previous experience or skills. I believe that he came across well because he had a kind of folksy way about him that the other three did not have. They were very professional and weren't just psychiatrists, but forensic psychiatrists.

Of the three professional forensic psychiatrists who testified (Lynn Blunt, Ames Robey, and Emanuel Tanay), I think the one who certainly impressed me the most was Emanuel Tanay. It's perfectly true that in virtually every case he's testified for the defense. He has used dissociative reaction, but that's just another way of saying the same thing so far as I'm concerned. He makes these nice little distinctions between dissociative reaction and irresistible impulse that I think are distinctions without a difference. They mean something to him; they don't mean anything to me.

Ames Robey, on the other hand, just said there wasn't any such thing; that there is no such diagnostic entity known to the field of psychiatry, which is a crock because it's recognized as such in every psychiatric journal that I ever looked at. I think that Ames Robey was pretty well discredited when we tried this case.

I think, finally, that the jury said, "Oh well, the hell with all these guys; we're not going to pay any attention to that stuff because it doesn't mean anything." I think they got to where they finally regarded all four of them as just four hired guns in there to do a job; and so they didn't really pay much attention to them.

Question:

Wilbur Jackson claimed at the trial that he struck Todd Wilson over the head and that as a result his pistol accidentally discharged, killing his daughter. Do you believe this story?

Gilman:

He just went in there and saw them in bed, saw them nude, took out the guns, and started shooting. He might have hit Todd, too. But not with the gun. Or it might have happened to Todd earlier in the day. If he hit Todd Wilson as hard as he said he did, he would have fractured his skull.

Nelson:

Well, I believe that it happened more or less as Jackson said it did. I think that he hit the kid over the head; well I know he hit the kid on the head because the kid had a hole in his head.

It was reasonably obvious that Jackson had struck the young man probably with his pistol or with his flashlight, and it's not clear to me yet which instrument he used. I believe it was at that point in time, if not when he came through that beaded curtain into that bedroom, that he blew his mind. I do believe that Jackson's first act of violence was to strike either with the flashlight or with the pistol, and more likely his pistol than his flashlight.

TRIAL TACTICS

Question:

Mr. Gilman, I remember that Mr. Nelson quoted from the Bible during his closing argument. Would you do the same?

Gilman:

The Bible went out with Clarence Darrow as far as I'm concerned. You're just getting away from the facts, and it shows. If you don't have the facts on your side, and you don't have the law on your side, you argue the Bible.

Question: Is it generally good practice to try to discredit the opposition witnesses?

Gilman: We got Jackson's records from Mercywood Hospital, and one of the defense attorneys tried to imply to the jury that Dr. Blunt had obtained those records in some sort of illegal fashion because his sister worked at Mercywood Hospital as a nurse. It turned the jury off completely because Dr. Blunt was the best of the four psychiatrists in my opinion.

Question: Do you believe character witnesses serve any purpose?

Gilman: Character witnesses don't carry much weight in a criminal case. In this case they had no social contact at all with Wilbur Jackson. The defense put a bunch of guys on that he worked with, and I wasn't contending that he was a bad engineer; I was contending he was a murderer. Nelson couldn't find anybody that socialized with Wilbur Jackson. He found the best he could find—guys that worked with Wilbur Jackson.

I tried a policeman for felonious assault two years ago. We had a really weak case. The defense attorney said, "Your Honor, may I call my next witness?" And into the courtroom comes _____, you know, the quarterback for the Miami Dolphins. The jury didn't even have to go out and deliberate.

Nelson: I don't think they had any appreciable effect upon the building of Jackson's image to the jury. I think they already had his image pretty well stereotyped by the time the character witnesses got on there. Maybe if the character witnesses had got on out of order and testified at the very beginning of the case, they might have had a little more effect than they did have. Jackson had been there for some twenty-odd days; he'd testified; they'd heard him and seen him in that videotape. They knew him as well as they were going to know him, and I don't think they paid any great amount of attention to those character witnesses at all.

Question: Mr. Gilman, the Pennsylvania statute says that the diagnostic report and recommendation from the competency examination shall not be admissible as evidence. Now did you know that there was a calculated risk in having a psychiatrist who was at the competency examination testify?

Gilman: The only doctors that generally testify for the People are the same doctors that perform the competency examination. That's because you can get them for nothing. If we go out and hire a doctor, it costs $150 an hour and so why not use the same doctor?

Dr. Robey hadn't participated in the competency examination, so I felt he could testify. And I felt the defense had opened the door to Dr. Blunt by calling him as a witness in their case for the purpose of introducing the sodium brevital film. When they called him—had him testify to his portion of the competency examination with respect to the sodium brevital test—I felt that that had opened the door and that we could call on him in rebuttal to their testimony.

In addition, I argued—and this is probably the weakest argument—that the statute in question should be interpreted narrowly to the competency report itself, and we never used the competency report in our case. We used the psychiatrists that did the examination, and the defense psychiatrists as well had access to the competency report. So I argued that because the report wasn't used, the statute wasn't applicable.

Question: Mr. Nelson, I've been wondering why you wanted the jury to see that film of Jackson during the sodium brevital test.

Nelson: That's a judgment that you have to make when you're a man's trial counsel. Jackson was dead opposed to our using the videotape of that sodium brevital examination, but I disagreed with him and so we used it. And the reason we used it is simply because I finally decided that it was more exculpatory than it was inculpatory. Now he said some things during the course of that sodium brevital or psychoanalytical session that were terribly damaging. But nonetheless the bulk of what he said—the substance and the thrust of what he said—was that he just absolutely blew his mind when he went in there and found his daughter in bed with this chap whom he didn't like because of racial reasons and found somebody else that he liked even less waiting in the bed next door. I believe that that's exactly what did happen. That's what he said when he was examined on the videotape and that's what he said to the jury.

Question: Mr. Gilman, what were your feelings about the tape?

Gilman: The defense made a motion to have that videotape admitted; and before Judge Gillis ruled on it, he wanted an opportunity to look at the tape because no videotape up to that point had been admitted into evidence. I wanted to reserve any position I would take on the motion till I saw the tape.

So I went up to the Forensic Center one evening and they ran this tape. And I looked at this and I'm trying to figure out what the hell the defense is trying to show by putting this tape in because the tape is good for me. The guy's crying a lot. Maybe that's what they wanted to show. But in addition, he looks like a racist; he admits remembering every killing. It went to negate the defense of insanity, and it went to show just what kind of person Wilbur Jackson was.

So after the tape was shown I said I concur with the motion to admit the tape; let's show the tape. One round of appeal in this case, which was denied by the Court of Appeals, was that the three defense attorneys were incompetent for wanting to admit that tape into evidence. The Court of Appeals said that that was just a tactical trial decision and not incompetency.

THE FUTURE OF
THE CITY

Question: Is there any hope for a large city like Pittsburgh, Chicago, New York, or Detroit? I mean, is there really any way crime can be controlled?

Gilman: The only thing that can do any good is an effort to try to get the guns out. You've got to control the manufacture of guns. There were two policemen killed in Pittsburgh within the last two days. You've got to get the guns out.

Homicides . . . how can a policeman control the homicides? You can't control a homicide. Homicides in Pittsburgh occur because somebody won't give somebody else an extra swig out of their bottle of wine or somebody won't give somebody else an extra potato chip out of their bag of potato chips. You know, people kill each other. You're not going to control it by getting more police out in the streets.

[The jurisdiction where Jackson was tried has been the scene of several other notable murder/insanity trials that generated much the same sort of sympathy for the defendants as Wilbur Jackson received.]

[In 1964 the Pierre Paulin murder case was tried with Robert Colombo as defense counsel. Colombo is now Judge Robert Colombo, Judge Gillis' next-door neighbor on the fifth floor of the Pittsburgh courthouse.]

[Pierre Paulin was a radio station disc jockey who had fallen on hard times. At the time of the crime he was running a disc jockey school. Paulin attended Alcoholics Anonymous meetings where he met Mrs. John Fraser and a used car salesman.]

[Paulin invited Mr. Fraser over to his disc jockey school. When Fraser arrived he discovered his wife and the used car salesman in bed making pornographic movies. Fraser killed them both. He turned around and found Paulin laughing at him. Fraser reloaded and killed him as well.]

[Fraser, whom Colombo describes as "a real gentleman," eventually plead guilty to three counts of manslaughter. He was placed on five years probation by Judge Vincent Brennan, who now sits on the Pennsylvania Court of Appeals. Brennan wrote the appellate decision in the Jackson case. Two years to the date of the murders, Fraser suffered an apparent heart attack and drove into a tree. He was instantly killed.]

[By 1971 Colombo had ascended to the bench and presided over James Johnson's murder trial. Johnson worked at a U.S. Steel foundry, and one day he chased two foremen around the plant with a carbine. He killed them both and another worker as well. He was tried before Colombo and presented a defense of "industrial insanity" based on the plant's poor working conditions. Johnson was acquitted by a jury and committed to a mental institution. In February, 1974, another worker beat and killed a foreman at the same U.S. Steel foundry.]

Nelson: If I knew, I'd be a wiser man than I am. Let me answer this question [Is there hope of controlling crime in a large city?] by first saying that I don't believe that there is any need for further legislation with specific reference to the possession of guns or the carrying of guns. There are all kinds of laws that make that illegal. And if those laws were vigorously enforced, as they are now beginning to be, I would see no need for further legislation in that area. I think about two-thirds or perhaps even more of homicides are drug-related. Therefore, the shutting off of available drugs is the first step to be taken in that direction.

Among other things, the police should try to impart more visibility to the constabulary. The Detective Bureau ought to be taken out of the anonymity of the station house and put out on the street. Basically, the uniformed force should be out on the street doing what they're supposed to be doing.

My family and I live in the northwest side of Pittsburgh in what's called the Sixteenth Police Precinct. The Sixteenth Precinct is bigger in area than some cities of about 150,000 people, and there are certain hours when the Sixteenth Precinct and the Fourteenth Precinct—which adjoins and is about as big as the Sixteenth—are covered by one cruiser that's got three non-uniformed officers in it and one scout car with two uniformed officers; that's for everything: traffic, vice, just plain street patrols, everything.

To give you an idea of the enormity of the problem, take Detroit. Detroit has lately—not so lately—become known throughout the United States as the murder capital of the world. Take note of the fact that last weekend, Easter weekend, was commemorated by the population by the fact that they succeeded in blowing away about twenty-two of their fellow members of the populace, which I think is some kind of a record.

[Crime statistics for the jurisdiction in which Jackson was tried show a record 751 murders in 1973, up from the previous record 693 murders in 1972. According to FBI figures, this averaged out to 44.5 murders per 100,000 people. By way of comparison, the rate of homicides per 100,000 people in New York City was 25.0.]

[Some 44% of these murders were committed during arguments between friends or relatives in situations similar to Len Gilman's "when somebody doesn't give somebody else a swig of wine or another potato chip" example. In fact, in over 70% of those 751 murders the killer and his victim knew each other.]

[More specific figures for the first half of the year show over 50% of the victims murdered with handguns. About 60% of the killings occurred in private homes, slightly over 20% on the street, and 5% in bars.]

[The first 282 murder suspects of 1973 were charged as follows:

Murder	204
Homicide in self-defense	26
Manslaughter	17
Justifiable homicide by a policeman	13
Justifiable homicide by a private citizen	13
Negligent manslaughter	8
Justifiable homicide by a private policeman	1

[Most of the 751 homicides in 1973 were intraracial. Blacks accounted for 80% of the victims and 85% of the suspects. Underworld drug wars were blamed for 84 of the deaths. A mind-boggling 500,000 handguns are estimated to be kept by private citizens in the jurisdiction—that averages out to about one for every three people.]

[April, 1974, established a new one-month record of 89 killings during 30 days, or one every eight hours. Those 89 deaths broke the prior record of 76 set in the previous September. Blacks killed blacks in 75% of those murders; whites killed whites in 16%; while interracial murders accounted for 9%. Average age of the victims was 31; the suspects averaged 32.]

[Of the 89 homicides, 34 occurred from midnight to 6:00 A.M., 2 from 6:00 A.M. to 6:00 P.M., and 28 from 6:00 P.M. to midnight. Monday was the most popular day for killing, followed closely by Saturday and Sunday. Men accounted for 80% of the victims and nearly 90% of the killers. A breakdown of murder methods shows guns: 63; knives: 15; beatings: 7; and assorted (strangulation, forcible drowning, etc.): 4.]

APPELLATE PROCEEDINGS

[Figure 29 shows Wilbur Jackson's affidavit of indigency, and Figure 30 shows a letter from Jackson to Mr. Glenn Rose, who was the court reporter from Jackson's trial.]

While Wilbur Jackson was confined in prison, appellate proceedings were initiated on his behalf by Jack and Sidney Kraizman,* his court-appointed appellate attorneys. In August of 1971 the Kraizmans moved for a new trial. They claimed:

1   Wilbur Jackson was charged with four murders and so should have been allowed twenty peremptory challenges for each murder, especially as the "jurors all had been brainwashed by the news media and been exposed to the Pittsburgh ghetto subculture of narcotics and debauchery."

2   A change of venue should have been granted to assure Jackson an impartial jury, as provided by the Fourteenth Amendment.

    "Only [through] a change of venue to a community in the State of Pennsylvania not exposed to the inflammatory screaming lines of the news media, and where morality, decency, and justice is a way of life, could the Defendant have gotten a fair and impartial trial in accordance with the Federal and State Constitutions."

3   The trial court should not have allowed doctors Robey and Blunt to testify as to Jackson's sanity, as they had previously examined him for competency.

4   The trial court erred in allowing defense counsel to introduce the videotape of Jackson during his "truth serum" test.

5   The jury should have been sequestered due to news media sensationalism. The jurors "would not be human if they refrained during a period of six weeks not to pick up a newspaper, not to turn on a radio, and not to turn on a television."

6   The prosecution "failed to present sufficient evidence to the jury to prove the defendant guilty . . . beyond a reasonable

---

* Jack and Sidney Kraizman are a father-son, two-man law firm. They have done a substantial amount of court-appointed work and have been notably successful in several appeals to the Pennsylvania Supreme Court.

Sidney Kraizman attended Allegheny State Law School where he was a classmate of Michael Mueller. Mueller took over the case when Len Gilman left the Prosecutor's Office, and has done both trial and appellate work during his four-year legal career, all of it spent in the Prosecutor's Office.

Figure 29 Affidavit of indigency

RECORDER'S COURT
AFFIDAVIT OF INDIGENCY SUPPORTING PETITION FOR
COUNSEL FOR APPELLATE REVIEW

7003042
7003312
7003318
7003319

Sentenced by Judge _Honorable Joseph A. Gillis_ File No. _7003319_

Name _WILBUR CHESTER JACKSON_ Offense _Manslaughter 3 2nd degree murder_

Last Address _5755 HILL ST. PITTSBURGH, PENNSYLVANIA_ Age _46_

Rent_____ Own Home _Yes_ Equity $ _All_ Balance Owing $ _None_

Marital Status: Single_____ Married _Yes_ Divorced_____ Widower_____

Name of Nearest Relative _MARY JACKSON_ Relationship _WIFE_

Address of Nearest Relative _5755 HILL ST.   PITTSBURGH, PENNSYLVANIA_

Number of Dependents _4_ Resident of _ALLEGHENY_ County _20 Years in early Jan. 71_ Years

Former Employer _PENN. Central Trans. Co._ Address _2975 Livernois Ave._
Last day worked May 7, 1970. I worked Average of 12 hours per day last 5 days. Pittsburgh Pennsylvania
Last Weekly Earnings $ _Around 350.00_ Savings $ _None_ Prison Account $ _None_
Basic hourly wage 4.30 - basic daily wage 34.45 - Varied greatly due to unpredicated
List Source of Present Income to Yourself or Dependents: _overtime, sometimes worked double shift._
I haven't worked since May 7 1970. Wife is Job hunting. she sells AMWay
Products & some household items I purchased at weekly Auctions at Ferris Bros.
6667 Vernor Highway, we have received help from All Relatives & some neighbors Amount $ _200.00 per month_
Amount Dependents Receive from A.D.C. and Welfare $ _None at Present Time_
14 year old son has Morning Daily Herald Route since 12th birthday.
Real Property $ _5755 Hill St._ Other Assets $ _Toyo Volkswagen, 67 Ford 68._ List all debts _Sears motorcycle_
our debts are monthly utility bills, Taxes, perhaps some medical bills and
Dr. Tanny. This information to the best of my knowledge & belief. We are in debt
to everyone for their many kind deeds. My parents & Two sisters are willing to mortgage
Does anyone owe you any money, or have in their possession any property which you claim belongs to you. Give
details in full: _NO   Their homes if I could make Reasonable bond while Trying to_
Win an Appeal.

I would Never Run away And I Present No
Threat To Anyone. I wouldN'T defend my
STATE OF PENNSYLVANIA } ss.
COUNTY OF _ALLEGHENY_ } _Self if Attacked. I'm Sick of Violence._
I Plea in the Spirit of Christmas And in
the memory of A dear girl.
I, _WILBUR CHESTER JACKSON_, being duly sworn, depose and say that all of the above
statements made by me are true and that I have no money, property, assets or income not mentioned in this ap-
plication for the appointment of counsel, and that I make this statement for the purpose of securing appointment
of counsel to perfect appellate review.

Signed _Wilbur Chester Jackson_

Institution Number _ARM band. NO. 70-12-22751_

Address _Allegheny County Jail_
525 Clinton Street
PITTSBURGH PENNSYLVANIA

Subscribed and sworn to before me
this _19th_ day of _December_, 19_70_

Notary Public, _ALLEGHENY_ County, Pennsylvania

My commission expires_____

Appointment of Counsel:

Approved:_____ Denied:_____

Figure 30   Letter from Wilbur Jackson to Glenn Rose

Name	
MR. GLENN W. ROSE	

No. and Street or R. R.
1441 ST. ANTOINE STREET

City	State	Zip Code
PITTSBURGH, PENNSYLVANIA		

Name	
WILBUR C. JACKSON	

Institution
SOUTHERN PENN. PRISON

No.	Date	WED.,
127775	AUGUST 18, '71	

Relation
COURT REPORTER & FRIEND

CSO - 110

Dear Mr. Rose,

I was delighted to receive your notification today of the completion of the long transcript in my tragic case. I know that you have put forth a lot of effort and have used a lot of your valuable time over the past weeks and months of expeditious preparation of this lengthy and valuable transcript.

It's been time spent that you could have used for more pleasureable purposes. Entertainment and hours in the sun you have foregone and no doubt many times you worked when you were tired and sleepy and not feeling up to par. I'm so grateful to you.

You have a reputation of being one of the best Recorder's Court Reporters, Mr. Rose. I think you are the very best.

We are so indebted to so many people for their help and their kindness. You have a pretty wonderful man to work for. A bit strait-laced, perhaps, but he has a streak of compassion and mercy. I did something over which I had absolutely no control and I've been bewildered and confused ever since. I'd agree with anything the Interviewer would suggest. We, as parents have paid a terrible price but I think the joys of parenthood have been worth the suffering and heartache.

I still cry every night and I pray daily. When I go to bed at night and when I get up in the morning I kneel by my bedside and say a simple prayer that this is the day that the Lord has made. Let us rejoice. I work hard and I study and try to learn all I can. I would like to be the humblest and kindest man in this prison. I'm deeply grateful to you, Mr. Rose,

Sincerely,
Wilbur Jackson
127775

Jack And Sidney Kraizman, appellate defense attorneys

doubt" with respect to Jackson's insanity. "Both Doctor Robey and Doctor Blunt were playing with words, were calling an 'apple' a 'banana', and were clearly dishonest."

On 26 November 1971, Judge Gillis denied the motion for a new trial.

In December 1971 the Pennsylvania Court of Appeals decided *People v. Martin.* That case specifically addressed the question of whether a psychiatrist conducting a forensic examination could also testify concerning the issue of sanity. It was just such testimony, that of Dr. Blunt, that Jackson's trial attorneys had objected to. The Court of Appeals held in the *Martin* case that:

"We conclude that a psychiatrist who conducts a forensic examination may not be called to testify in the criminal trial if there is an objection to the admission of such testimony by the defendant."

Thus encouraged, the Kraizmans pushed ahead with Wilbur Jackson's appeal.

An appeal involves a procedure very much different from that of a trial. There are no witnesses, no testimony, and no jury present in an appeal. Instead, the appeal is "on the record." The losing party will argue that the trial judge made errors during the trial and that those errors denied the defendant a fair trial. The appellate court will

Michael Mueller, appellate prosecutor

review the record (the trial transcript and any exhibits introduced into evidence) and decided whether the trial judge, as a matter of law, made incorrect rulings. The appeals court will not make an independent decision on the question of guilt or innocence, but will only decide whether the trial judge made a mistake. If a mistake was made of sufficient magnitude to possibly change the ultimate outcome of the trial, the appellate court will order a new trial.

The appellate court system varies from state to state. Most, but not all, states have two appellate courts. Generally a losing party has a guaranteed right to have an appeal heard by the lower appellate court. Usually the party who loses in that court may then petition the higher appellate court to hear the case. However, the higher court does not have to accept the case and generally does not do so unless the issues involved are unusual or significant. Once a party has lost all of his appeals in the state court system he may petition the United States Supreme Court to hear his case. However, since the Supreme Court accepts only a minuscule portion of the appeals directed to it, the chances of having a case heard there are very, very slim.

Note that the names given to courts change from state to state. Many jurisdictions call the lower appellate court the Court of Appeals and the higher court the state Supreme Court. Maryland, for example, terms its appellate courts the Court of Special Appeals and the Court of Appeals while Virginia currently has only one appellate court, which is named the Supreme Court of Appeals. Perhaps even more confusing, the lower appellate court in New York is called the Supreme Court while the highest court is the Court of Appeals.

Appellate procedure also varies from jurisdiction to jurisdiction, but most states require attorneys for each side to file written documents called briefs which contain their arguments as to why the trial judge was or was not in error. After the appellate judges have had an opportunity to study the briefs, oral argument is held. Oral argument affords counsel for each side a time, generally thirty minutes, to verbally stress the points he or she has made in the brief. During this time, the judges will often ask questions, and frequently an appellate argument will be a sparring match between counsel and the court. After the argument, the members of the court hearing the case will decide the case and issue a written opinion explaining their decision. The decision and opinion may be released several weeks or many months after the argument, depending on the speed of the judges and the work load of the court.

CIRCUIT COURT OPINION

The Kraizmans appealed to the lower appellate court in Pennsylvania, the Circuit Court (see Figure 31). In their brief and at oral argument they raised the same arguments they had used in their petition for a new trial. On 7 December 1972, almost two years after the jury verdict, the Circuit Court handed down its decision.

Figure 31   Circuit Court opinion

AT A SESSION OF THE CIRCUIT COURT OF THE STATE OF PENNSYLVANIA, Held at the Circuit Court

in the City of   Pittsburgh   on the   7th   day of

December   in the year of our Lord one thousand nine hundred and seventy-two

People of the State of Pennsylvania,
    Plaintiff-Appellee

vs   **Judges**

Wilbur Chester Jackson Nos. 13105 thru 13108
    Defendant-Appellant

This cause having been brought to this Court by appeal from   Recorder's Court

, and having been argued by counsel, and due deliberation

had thereon, it is now ordered by the Court, that the   judgment   of the

Recorder's Court   be and the same is hereby

reversed and remanded.

STATE OF PENNSYLVANIA—ss.

    I, Ronald L. Brown, Clerk of the Circuit Court of the State of Pennsylvania, do hereby certify that the fore-going is a true and correct copy of an order entered in said court in said cause; that I have compared the same with the original, and that it is a true transcript therefrom, and the whole of said original order.

                IN TESTIMONY WHEREOF, I have hereunto set my hand
                and affixed the seal of said Circuit Court at Harrisburg,

                this   21st   day of   February

                in the year of our Lord one thousand nine hundred and

                seventy-three.

                                        Clerk   [B136]

PEOPLE of the State of Pennsylvania, Plaintiff-Appellee,

v.

Wilbur Chester JACKSON, Defendant-Appellant.

Circuit Court.

Jan. 6, 1973.

Released for Publication April 21, 1973.

Rehearing Denied Feb. 15, 1973.

Defendant was convicted before the Recorder's Court, of three charges of second-degree murder and one charge of manslaughter and he appealed. The Circuit Court held that testimony of psychiatrist based upon observations made by psychiatrist while defendant was committed to Forensic Center to determine his competency to stand trial was not admissible at trial over defendant's objection.

Reversed and remanded.

———

Presiding Judge.

Defendant Wilbur Chester Jackson was charged in the Recorder's Court with the killing of four young people, including his daughter. He was specifically charged with murder in the first degree in the deaths of Sandra Jackson (his seventeen-year-old daughter), Todd Wilson, and Jonathan Carter. He was charged with second-degree murder in the death of Ricky Walters. The four homicides occurred at about 2:00 A.M. on the morning of May 8, 1970, in an apartment located at 4330 Lincoln Street.

These cases were consolidated and tried together before a jury from November 9, 1970, through December 12, 1970. Evidence introduced at trial indicated that the deceased, Sandra Jackson, left home on the Sunday preceding the homicides; she left a note stating her intentions to her parents. Defendant virtually went without sleep during the week, working double shifts, and spending the remainder of his time looking for his daughter. He went to the apartment building twice during that week looking for his daughter and became acquainted with the place. He found out through a paid informer that his daughter was living in apartment number 9. At approximately 2:00 A.M. on May 8,

1970, he went to the apartment house after arming himself with two guns, because, as he testified, he expected resistance.

When he arrived at the apartment house, accompanied by his wife, he immediately went up to apartment 9 on the second floor of the building, burst open the door and went into the apartment. He flashed a flashlight and saw his daughter Sandra with Todd Wilson in one bed in the nude; Jonathan Carter was also lying in the nude on a cot near them, and Ricky Walters, also in the nude, was sleeping in the next room. Defendant testified further that he pulled out one of his pistols from his waist and delivered a blow to Todd Wilson's head, accidentally discharging the pistol into his daughter. His wife Mary screamed, "You killed my baby." Defendant then claims he lost control of himself and proceeded to shoot his daughter several more times and also killed the three young men in the apartment. He then descended to the first-floor apartment of Sally Tucker where he shot once through the door and forced his way into the apartment; he could not find Sally Tucker. Sally Tucker was Sandra Jackson's girl friend who Mr. and Mrs. Jackson believed to be responsible for what they considered their daughter's waywardness. The defendant then left the building, got into his automobile, and drove to the Vernor Police Station in the city of Pittsburgh. He told his wife to drive home; he walked into the station and surrendered himself, informing the police officers that he had just killed his daughter and three "hippie friends."

On December 12, 1970, the jury brought in a verdict of second-degree murder in the three cases involving the deaths of Todd Wilson, Jonathan Carter, and Ricky Walters; the jury returned a verdict of manslaughter in the case involving the death of Sandra Jackson. On December 18, 1970, the court sentenced defendant to prison terms of from ten to forty years on the charges of second-degree murder and ten to fifteen years on the charge of manslaughter. Defendant appeals his conviction.

Defendant's first argument is that the trial court erred by failing to allow a sufficient number of peremptory challenges. The right to challenge members of the jury peremptorily is statutory in origin; the relevant state statute provides:

"Any person who is put on trial for an offense punishable by death or imprisonment for life, shall be allowed to challenge peremptorily 20 of the persons drawn to serve as jurors, and no more; and the prosecuting officers on behalf of the people shall be allowed to challenge peremptorily 15 of such persons, and no more. In cases involving 2 or more defendants, who are being jointly tried for such an offense, each of said defendants shall be allowed to challenge peremptorily 20 persons returned as jurors, and no more; and the prosecuting officers on behalf of the people shall be allowed to challenge peremptorily as many times 15 of the persons returned as jurors as there may be defendants being so jointly tried."

The trial court granted the defendant twenty peremptory challenges. The defendant argues that in this case, since he was charged under four separate informations, he should be entitled to twenty peremptory challenges for each information, a total of eighty challenges.

The defendant correctly observes that the only two state cases which even remotely deal with this subject are not on point. Neither *People v. Sweeney*, nor *People v. Bloom*, deal with cases involving charges under several informations, but rather they deal with different counts within one information.

The purpose of statutes such as the one under consideration is to assure the defendant an impartial jury by permitting him to dismiss jurors with no explanation or justification. The legislature has determined that in certain classes of cases, a certain number of such challenges will suffice to insure the defendant an impartial jury. Merely because the defendant is charged under four separate informations, it does not follow that it will be four times as difficult to empanel an impartial jury. We therefore conclude that the trial court granted the defendant the full number of peremptory challenges to which he was entitled by statute.

Defendant's second argument is that the trial court erred by denying defendant's motion for a change in venue, which motion was made two weeks prior to the trial. The defendant argues that all jurors eventually seated had heard of the case. Defendant contends that the extensive newspaper coverage accorded the case displayed the defendant as a man possessed of an outdated moral code and argues that the community in

general is hostile to individuals with such a moral code.

After examining copies of the newspaper reports and the transcript of the *voir dire* examination, we conclude that defendant's argument is not well taken. The trial court did not rule on the defendant's motion before attempting to empanel a jury. An examination of the *voir dire* transcript indicates that while almost everyone had heard of the case, most individuals possessed only a fleeting recollection of the circumstances. Furthermore, the newspaper coverage accorded the incident involved was not highly inflammatory or prejudicial, but direct and straightforward reporting of incidents with little prejudicial editorialization.

This court's analysis of the venue issue in *People v. Jenkins*, is both concise and thorough. We regard it as dispositive of this issue and set it forth in full:

"The grant of a change of venue is in the discretion of the trial court. This discretion is limited and capable of review where there is an abuse of discretion manifestly subversive of justice. Discretion in the trial court is not a private, arbitrary or personal discretion, but must be exercised according to the established principles of law. The better rule as to the course of action to be taken where there is a motion for change of venue is reservation of a decision by the trial court on the motion until an attempt has been made to obtain a fair and impartial jury.

"Jurors who have heard of or have read of the case, without more, are not disqualified as jurors, and their inclusion does not deny defendant a fair trial. A juror who has formed an opinion may not be challenged for cause, providing the opinion is not positive in character, and he may render an impartial verdict. In this case, all jurors who sat stated that they had no fixed opinion as to the guilt or innocence of the accused and that they could render a fair and impartial verdict.

"Counsel refers us to a decision on due process of law as provided by the 14th Amendment, regarding a fair trial, as binding on our determinations in this matter. It is true that a trial judge may not allow the press to interfere with the course of trial or allow the decision to be based on extraneous publicity. *Sheppard v. Maxwell* (1966), 384 U.S. 333, 86 S.Ct. 1507, 16 L.Ed.2d 600. This situation, however, is not alleged to be present in this case. We deal with the problem of prior information and community feeling as affecting a defendant's right to a fair trial. We are referred to and examine in detail the decision of *Irvin v. Dowd* (1961), 366 U.S. 717, 81 S.Ct. 1639, 6 L.Ed.2d 751, and regard it as controlling. In American and Anglo-Saxon jurisprudence there is the invaluable right to jury. It must be a panel of impartial jurors. There must be a fair tribunal which renders a verdict on evidence presented at trial for a proceeding to meet the minimum standards of due process. It is not necessary that they be without impression or opinion. They must, however, be able to lay aside their impressions and base their verdict on the evidence. Where there is strong community feeling and a pattern of deep and bitter prejudice in the community, the influence of that opinion makes a strong impression, nearly impossible to detach from the mental processes of the average man. Trial under such influence denies due process. The burden of showing the existence of these conditions is on the challenger.

"The defense has shown that there were newspaper articles and that some of the jurors had read or heard of the case. This showing, without more, is not sufficient. Defense presents no evidence of a strong community feeling. The trial judge in the community has his senses and personal knowledge of the community to detect this community feeling. An appellate court has only the cold record upon which to rely. There must be a definite, clear showing of abuse of discretion to overturn the trial judge's decision to commence or to acquiesce in the continuance of a trial. Such a showing has not been made in this case either in the denial of a change of venue or in the denial of a continuance."

Defendant's third argument is that the trial court erred by permitting the reception into evidence, and the viewing by the jury, of a videotape of the defendant while under the influence of a drug. On the tape, Jackson was interviewed

by a psychiatrist while the former was under the influence of sodium brevital. In response to questions by the psychiatrist, and counsel for the defendant who was also present, the defendant gave details of the shootings.

The defendant now argues that the videotape presented to the jury a picture of the defendant so totally different from his insanity defense, that he was prejudiced by the admission of the tape. It must be remembered, in discussing this question, that the tape was accepted into evidence on motion of the defendant's counsel. The question before the court is therefore not the admissibility of a videotape of a criminal defendant while under the influence of a specific drug, but whether, by seeking the admission of this tape into evidence, defendant's counsel committed a mistake so serious that it deprived the defendant of a fair trial. The standard which the courts have used in considering allegations of this nature was set forth by this court in *People v. Degraffenreid*, as follows:

"Ordinarily a new trial will not be granted unless it appears that if a new trial is ordered during the conduct of which the mistake is not repeated the defendant may very well be acquitted."

This writer has had occasion to view the videotape in question, and to review the record in this case. We do not feel that the defendant's allegation of error meets the standard of review set forth in *Degraffenreid*, supra.

The defendant's testimony that he had no recollection of the incident after his daughter had been shot was reconciled with defendant's statements as presented to the jury on the videotape. The psychiatrist who conducted the test testified that the drug which was injected into the defendant tends to lower certain mental barriers, and facilitates discussion of otherwise repressed matters. We feel that defendant's counsel could have sought to admit the tape either to gain sympathy for the defendant, or to demonstrate vividly the defendant's mental condition in support of his insanity defense. We do not decide whether such videotapes are admissible, we only decide that under these circumstances the admission of this tape did not deprive the defendant of a fair trial.

Defendant's fourth argument is that the trial court erred by permitting, over defendant's objection, certain psychiatric testimony regarding the defendant's sanity at the time of the shootings. This testimony was based on tests and observations made while the defendant was committed to a Forensic Center to determine his competency to stand trial. The statute which provides for such commitment also provided the basis for defendant's objection; in pertinent part, it states:

"(3) Upon a showing that the defendant may be incompetent to stand trial, the court shall commit the defendant in the criminal case to the custody of the center for forensic psychiatry or to any other diagnostic facility certified by the department of mental health for the performance of forensic psychiatric evaluation. The commitment shall be for a period not to exceed 60 days. Within that period the center or other facility shall prepare a diagnostic report and recommendations which are to be transmitted to the committing court.

"(4) Upon receipt of the diagnostic report and recommendations the sheriff shall immediately return the defendant to the committing court and the court shall immediately hear and determine the issue of competence to stand trial. *The diagnostic report and recommendations shall be admissible as evidence in the hearing, but not for any other purpose in the pending criminal proceedings.*" (Emphasis Supplied.)

Defendant argues that the emphasized portion of the statute would bar a psychiatrist from testifying if he had participated in the competency proceeding. The court permitted the doctor to testify and he did base his conclusions to a significant extent on observations made while defendant was committed pursuant to the statute. In fact, the majority of his testimony would only be admissible at a competency hearing, not at a trial.

The admission of the doctor's testimony constitutes reversible error. The Court of Appeals recently stated in *People v. Martin*, reported after the trial in this case, that:

"a psychiatrist who conducts such a forensic psychiatric examination may not be called to testify in the criminal trial if there is an objection to the admission of such testimony by defendant."

Such a practice was also condemned by this court in *People v. Schneider*. On this basis, defendant's conviction must be set aside.

Defendant's final argument is that the trial court erred by failing to sequester the jury during the course of the trial although defendant's trial attorneys never requested the court to take such an action. This matter not having been raised before the trial court, it will not be considered here unless a clear injustice has occurred. We have read the newspaper coverage of defendant's trial, and the trial court's repeated admonitions . . . to the jury to avoid the publicity the case was receiving, and we do not believe the trial court erred by failing, *sua sponte*, to sequester the jury.

Reversed and remanded.

Figure 32   State's appellate brief

STATE OF PENNSYLVANIA

IN THE

COURT OF APPEALS*

PEOPLE OF THE STATE OF PENNSYLVANIA, Plaintiff-Appellant v WILBUR CHESTER JACKSON, Defendant-Appellee	Court of Appeals No. 54,677

Recorder's Court Nos. 70–03042
70–03317
70–03318
70–03319
Circuit Court   No. 13105–8

APPELLANT'S BRIEF ON APPEAL

WILLIAM L. CAHALAN
Prosecuting Attorney

DOMINICK R. CARNOVALE
Chief, Appellate Department

MICHAEL R. MUELLER
Assistant Prosecuting Attorney

* This is not in fact a Pennsylvania Court. The case was actually litigated in another state.

The state then filed a motion for rehearing before the Circuit Court. At this point, 28 December 1972 the Kraizmans moved that Jackson be released on bail. In their motion to Judge Gillis they noted:

1   that while in prison Jackson "has been a model prisoner,"

2   that Jackson was released on personal bond during the trial "and subsequently appeared at all proceedings,"

3   that Jackson "had no criminal record prior to the charge in this case, and he has roots in the city of Pittsburgh, and there is no likelihood that he would ever leave the jurisdiction of this court."

"Wherefore, defendant moves this honorable court for an order granting release on personal bond pending his appeal."

On 2 January 1973 Judge Gillis denied the motion. In an interview he explained that he did not want to release Jackson from prison only to have to send him back again if his appeal was ultimately unsuccessful. Several attorneys involved in or interested in the case expressed surprise that the Kraizmans didn't press harder for Jackson's release. These attorneys felt that had the issue been pressed, Jackson would have been released pending review in the Court of Appeals.

On 30 January 1973 the Circuit Court denied the state's motion for a rehearing.

The state then applied for leave to appeal to the Court of Appeals. On 20 June 1973 the court, in a 5–1 decision, granted leave to appeal. The court further directed that the matter be remanded to Recorder's Court for a determination of Jackson's indigency and, if established, that the Kraizmans be reappointed as Jackson's attorneys.

Indigency was established and on 6 November 1973 Judge Gillis appointed the Kraizmans as Jackson's attorneys for the appeal. Gillis further ordered that the Kraizmans "will be furnished with such portions of the record, at public expense, as they may require."

In March 1974 the case was argued before the Court of Appeals. Figure 32 shows a selected portion of the State's appellate brief.

ARGUMENT

Psychiatrists from the Center for Forensic Psychiatry Who Examine a Defendant for Purposes of Determining Competency to Stand Trial Should Be Allowed To Testify at Trial as to Sanity at the Time of the Crime.

* * *

The defendant has contended that the trial court committed reversible error in allowing Dr. Robey and Dr. Blunt to testify on the issue of criminal responsibility at trial, and the Circuit Court, relying primarily on *People v. Martin,* argued:

> ". . . a psychiatrist who conducts such a forensic psychiatric examination may not be called to testify in a criminal trial if there is an objection to the admission of such testimony by defendant." *Martin,* 425.

Appellant submits that this court in *Martin,* despite the language quoted, does not mean to say that Forensic Center psychiatrists who examine pursuant to the statute may not be called to testify at trial *as to sanity at the time of the crime* but means to say rather that they cannot testify *as to guilt or innocence.* Consequently, appellant contends that the Circuit Court in this case should be reversed.

The essential inquiry is whether defendants are harmed if Forensic Center psychiatrists are allowed to testify at trial on the issue of the defendant's sanity at the time of the crime and whether the People of Pennsylvania are harmed if these doctors are not allowed to so testify.

* * *

Because of the statute, a defendant can be compelled to submit to a psychiatric examination for competency to stand trial and because of *Martin* he can be compelled to submit to an examination for sanity at the time of the crime. Because he can be compelled for both examinations, why cannot the Forensic Center psychiatrist do both?

What consequent harm would accrue to the defendant? The defendant's responses during an examination presumably should be true and therefore consistent. To require separate examinations to allow inconsistent responses by the defendant would not be the sort of fair safeguard envisioned by our criminal justice system. Defendants cannot realistically claim that as a practical matter Forensic Center psychiatrists are more prone to testify that a defendant is sane at the time of the crime than is any other psychiatrist who would perform a compelled examination, because, as a practical matter, the Forensic Center psychiatrists have been prepared on numerous occasions to testify that defendants were indeed insane at the time of their acts. In fact Dr. Robey testified that in approximately half of the cases in which he has testified as to criminal responsibility he has testified for the defense. Throughout the proceedings in the case at bar the defense attorneys both at trial and on appeal have failed to do more than merely assert that the statute absolutely bars the testimony in question. They have at no time even mentioned that any conceivable harm, unfairness, or prejudice results from the testimony of the Forensic Center psychiatrist.

* * *

While defendants are not harmed by a rule which would allow the Forensic Center psychiatrist to testify as to sanity at the time of the crime, the rule which prevents them from so testifying does create a tremendous hardship on the people of Pennsylvania. The cost in terms of time, effort, and money where unnecessary duplication of effort is required is obvious. Psychiatrists are the most expensive of all expert witnesses. For the people of Pennsylvania to pay independent psychiatrists to examine a defendant and to testify in court rather than to pay at a greatly reduced rate a state employed Forensic Center psychiatrist, especially when he has already completed a great amount of work necessary for such an examination while he was examining the defendant for competency to stand trial is ludicrous. The defendant asserts relative to this point that the Forensic Center psychiatrists must not be allowed to testify as to sanity at the time of the crime because an examination for competency to stand trial is different from an examination for sanity at the time of the crime. However it should be obvious to any person with even a modicum of understanding of psychiatric medicine that there would be a considerable duplication of effort. A psychiatric diagnosis is made after a thorough examination and evaluation of the patient's personality and history. A determination as to sanity at the time of the crime would be based only in part, even small part, on an examination as to the details of the event constituting the crime. The greater part of the examinations for competency and for criminal responsibility are the same. United States v. Mattson, (C.A.9, 1972) 469 F.2d 1234. With the construction presently placed upon the statute by the Circuit Court of Appeals, this examination and evaluation must be made twice. It must be made by the state employed Forensic Center psychiatrist and by an independent psychiatrist who would be paid by the people of Pennsylvania both for the time used during the examination and for his time in court.

In addition to the duplication of time, effort, and money, there are other problems resulting from the Circuit Court's position in this matter. The fact that a second examination would be required would create an unnecessary delay which the defendant must undergo before he can come to trial. There is room for abuse where an independent psychiatrist is used to perform the examination for sanity because he is directly appointed by and therefore dependent on the court, and especially in counties with smaller populations, is likely to have more direct contact with the prosecutor and is likely to have closer involvement and feeling with the community so that he has a reduced objectivity where a crime against that community is concerned. In some jurisdictions he would come to be the "prosecution's doctor" with the same lack of objectivity which is apparent in certain defense expert witnesses. In the Forensic Center, on the other hand, we have a facility which is entirely independent of the court and law enforcement institutions for its existence and maintenance. The volume of cases with which its doctors deal increases the probability of objectivity by those doctors. Furthermore, if a greater proportion of examinations for criminal responsibility is performed at one facility, there is a consequent increase in the uniformity of medical testimony so that an individual defendant will know that he is being treated fairly relative

Figure 33 Wilbur Jackson's appellate brief

STATE OF PENNSYLVANIA

◆

IN THE

COURT OF APPEALS

◆

Appeal from the Circuit Court

PEOPLE OF THE STATE OF
   PENNSYLVANIA,
         Plaintiff-Appellant,
           v
WILBUR CHESTER JACKSON,
         Defendant-Appellee.   No.

Circuit Court Nos. 13105, 13106,
   13107 & 13108
Recorder's Court Nos. 70–03042,
   70–03317, 70–03318 & 70–03319

DEFENDANT–APPELLEE'S ANSWER TO PEOPLE'S BRIEF

◆

KRAIZMAN & KRAIZMAN

Attorneys for Defendant-Appellee

to all others who claim insanity at the time of the crime, a factor which would also have a positive effect on the defendant's potential for rehabilitation. Moreover, in some jurisdictions it is entirely foreseeable that the prosecution would be unable, through unavailability, to produce competent medical testimony to rebut a claim of insanity, so that the fact finder's accurate assessment of the defendant's mental state would be seriously impeded.

Therefore, allowing the Forensic Center psychiatrist to testify as to sanity at the time of the crime does not harm the defendant, benefits the people, and also benefits the defendant.

RELIEF

WHEREFORE, the People of the State of Pennsylvania by William L. Cahalan, prosecuting attorney for Allegheny County, and by Michael R. Mueller, assistant prosecuting attorney, respectfully request this honorable court to reverse the decision of the Circuit Court and reinstate the decision of the trial court.

Respectfully submitted,

WILLIAM L. CAHALAN
Prosecuting Attorney

DOMINICK R. CARNOVALE
Chief, Appellate Department

MICHAEL R. MUELLER
Assistant Prosecuting Attorney

Dated: October 25, 1973
MRM:er

(Figure 33 shows a section from Wilbur Jackson's appellate brief.)

ARGUMENT

The Trial Court Erred by Permitting, over the Defendant's Objection, Certain Psychiatric Testimony by Two Forensic Psychiatrists Regarding the Defendant's Sanity at the Time of the Shootings, Said Testimony Being Based on Tests and Observations Made While the Defendant Was Committed to the Forensic Center to Determine His Competency to Stand Trial.

The Appellate-Prosecutor for the People seems to be confused as to the issue as well as the facts in this case. Neither defense counsel nor the trial prosecutor, Mr. Leonard Gilman, were confused as to the issue and the facts before the trial court. The argument between them was whether the psychiatrists were barred from testifying if they used the diagnostic reports and recommendations of the Forensic Center in their testimony.

Mr. Gilman admitted that these two psychiatrists were going to use the Forensic Center's diagnostic reports and recommendations in their testimony, but he argued that as long as they were not going to be admitted as exhibits the doctors could use them to testify from. The trial judge ruled: "They can't use the report; and by the word 'report,' we mean a piece of paper." But the court ruled that the doctors could use these reports and recommendations as a basis for their testimony. The basis for the defense counsel's objections was the statute which provides:

"(4) Hearing on issue of incompetence. Upon receipt of the diagnostic report and recommendations the sheriff shall immediately return the defendant to the committing court and the court shall immediately hear and determine the issue of competence to stand trial. *The diagnostic report and recommendations shall be admissible as evidence in the hearing, but not for any other purpose in the pending criminal proceedings.*" (Emphasis added.)

It is nonsense for the People to argue at this time that the two psychiatrists didn't use these diagnostic reports and recommendations. As a matter of fact, here is what Dr. Lynn Blunt said on redirect examination by Mr. Gilman, the trial prosecutor:

"Q. Now, based upon your contacts with Mr. Jackson that began in July of 1970, lasted until August 13 of 1970; based upon your review of the tests that were conducted on Mr. Jackson; based upon your interview with Mr. Jackson on November 4, 1970; and based upon your experience as a psychiatrist, Dr. Blunt, do you have a diagnosis of Mr. Jackson as of the time that you saw him, November 4, 1970? At the time you saw him last.

A. Yes, I do."

Dr. Ames Robey said on cross-examination by Mr. Nelson:

"From his whole reaction to me and to Dr. Miller and Dr. Blunt when we all saw him together, and the way we had responded in terms of his wife, his family; *in terms of the history that I had mentioned, that I had already seen about his prior past history,* as well as that portion of the past history I obtained in my interview." (Emphasis added.)

We also must remember that these two psychiatrists had placed their signatures to the letter and to the Report of Psychiatric Examination on Competency to Stand Trial to the trial court on August 19, 1970. Without a doubt, they knew his case by heart, because the defendant was their most famous patient and they used the diagnostic report and recommendations at the trial.

* * *

The People argue that the defendant relies primarily on *People v. Martin*, for his claim of error, but that is only part of the defendant's claim.   The real issue was raised before the trial court, was raised in the Circuit Court, and is being raised before this honorable court, and that is whether the testimony of Forensic Psychiatrists who participated in such proceedings is admissible when it is based upon the diagnostic reports and recommendations made of defendant while he was admitted there to determine his competency to stand trial?

The Circuit Court recognized the clear issue in this case and further recognized that the forensic psychiatrists based their conclusions to a significant extent on observations made while the defendant was committed pursuant to the statute.   The Circuit Court concluded:

> "In fact, the majority of his testimony would only be admissible at a competency hearing not at a trial."

The People seem to disregard the purpose of the statute which Mr. Justice Adams in *People v. Martin*, supra, dwells on at such great length.   It was to protect an accused, who is committed to the Forensic Center for the purpose of determining whether he is competent to stand trial, from self-incrimination.   The privilege against self-incrimination not only protects an accused from being compelled to testify against himself, but also protects him from being compelled to provide the state with evidence of a testimonial or communicative nature.   Armando Schmerber v. State of California, 86 S.Ct. 1826. Conviction of an accused person who is legally incompetent violates due process.   Bishop v. United States (1956), 350 U.S. 961, (76 S.Ct. 440, 100 L.Ed. 835).   State procedures must be adequate to protect this right.   Pate v. Robinson (1966), 383 U.S. 375 (86 S.Ct. 836, 15 L.Ed.2d 815).

It is for this reason, to determine whether a defendant is competent to stand trial, that the statute was enacted into law.   With the protection given a defendant by this statute that any information that he may divulge of an incriminating nature will not be disclosed in any other proceedings in his case against him, he can freely disclose all facts to the Forensic Center psychiatrists necessary to a determination whether he is competent to stand trial, including any incriminating facts that are ordinarily protected by the Fifth Amendment of the United States Constitution.

The People accuse Justice Adams of not meaning what he says in his well-written opinion, and presumably because the present members of this august Court of Appeals, with the exception of justices Levin and Coleman the newly elected justices, concurred with Justice Adams they too are confused—what chutzpah.

* * *

The People argue that following the provisions of the statute "creates a tremendous hardship on the people of Pennsylvania. The cost in terms of time, effort, and money" in the appointment of psychiatrists to examine a defendant as to responsibility by the prosecution. The appellate prosecutor is not aware that trial courts are notorious for granting low fees to lawyers and psychiatrists—the members of this honorable court undoubtedly remember how little they were paid for handling assigned criminal cases. Counsel for defendant remembers one member of this august body being given a voucher for a mere pittance by Judge Joseph A. Gillis, Sr., now deceased, for trying a murder case that took five days to try—the fact that the defendant was acquitted might have had something to do with it.

*   *   *

In the case at bar, the People would deprive the defendant of all constitutional privileges. Upon reading the total direct examination of Dr. Lynn Blunt and especially of the direct examination of Dr. Ames Robey it is clear that their testimony deals with statements by defendant that violate the defendant's rights against self-incrimination. The admissions and confessions which Dr. Ames Robey quotes as having been made by defendant were such that the very ghosts of the infamous Star Chamber of the seventeenth century must have rubbed their hands in diabolic glee in the shadows of the Frank Murphy Hall of Justice. The testimony of the two psychiatrists and their opinions appear like rubber stamps of the report they filed with the trial court on August 19, 1970.

What is more sensible, trial Judge Gillis's opinion that the prohibition of the diagnostic reports and recommendations deals with "exhibits" or "pieces of paper" and not their substance, or *People v. Martin*'s logic that the statute means that the diagnostic reports and recommendations are not admissible under any form—no matter whether it emanates from the testimony of two forensic psychiatrists who use the diagnostic reports and recommendations in their opinions and testimony before the jury or whether the diagnostic reports and recommendations are to be used as exhibits in themselves.

*   *   *

The People further argue that a second examination would create "abuse where an independent psychiatrist is used to perform the examination for sanity because he is directly appointed by and therefore dependent on the court, and especially in counties with smaller populations, is likely to have more direct contact with the prosecutor and is likely to have closer involvement and feeling with the community so that he has a reduced objectivity where a crime against that community is concerned," while forensic psychiatrists would be impartial. This is indulging in flights of fantasy. The trial court has the duty to appoint competent and impartial psychiatrists, and the fact that he is a prosecution witness would not corrupt his thinking. The fact that he is a member of the community would not affect his thinking either, and we don't even know what the community's thinking might be at any given time anyway.

On cross-examination by defense counsel Nelson, Dr. Ames Robey demonstrated the impartiality that appellate-prosecutor has in mind. Dr. Robey testified that he teaches law at the University of Pittsburgh Law School. He further testified that he was sitting at the prosecutor's table "on several different days for varying periods of time and provided Mr. Gilman, the prosecutor, with suggested questions for him to address to Dr. Tanay in his cross-examination of Dr. Tanay"— may the Lord deliver all accused everywhere from such Robey impartiality!

RELIEF

The defendant-appellee Wilbur Chester Jackson, respectfully submits that the decision of the Circuit Court should be sustained and that the defendant's conviction should be vacated and this case be remanded to the trial court for a new trial.

Respectfully submitted,

KRAIZMAN and KRAIZMAN
By: /s/ JACK J. KRAIZMAN
Attorney for Defendant–Appellee

COURT OF APPEALS OPINION

On December 19, 1974, four years, three months, one week, and four days from the date of the deaths of Sandra Jackson, Todd Wilson, Jonathan Carter, and Ricky Walters, the Court of Appeals handed down the final decision in the case of the *People v. Wilbur Jackson.* The controlling issue, for the majority of the court, had not even been addressed by the parties. Portions of the opinion follow.

PEOPLE of the State of Pennsylvania, Plaintiff-Appellant,

v.

Wilbur Chester JACKSON, Defendant-Appellee.

Court of Appeals
Jan. 6, 1975.

Released for Publication Jan. 17, 1975.

Majority Opinion.

* * *

. . . [It was] stated less than three years ago in *People v. Martin.*

"We conclude that a psychiatrist who conducts such a forensic psychiatric examination may not be called to testify in the criminal trial if there is an objection to the admission of such testimony by defendant."

HOLDING

There is no need to consider whether this is a correct or incorrect interpretation of the relevant state statute inasmuch as in the instant case there is a clear waiver of the statute on the record. Defense counsel made specific reference to the Forensic Center competency diagnosis in the questioning of their own expert witness, Dr. Miller [98a–100a]. The defense introduced a videotape of defendant's sodium brevital examination at the Forensic Center. The defense introduced into evidence the Forensic Center file.

* * *

This finding of statutory waiver resolves this case and obviates the necessity of this court reviewing the above analysis in *Martin*. I agree fully, therefore, with Section V of [the following concurring] opinion on waiver. I would not, however, go further in *obiter dicta* to discuss aspects of this case involving constitutional issues where there is no necessity to do so.

The Circuit Court is reversed; the defendant's conviction is affirmed.

Concurring Opinion.

Wilbur Chester Jackson shot and killed his daughter Sandra, a young man who was in bed with her, and two other young men who were

sleeping in the same apartment. He was convicted of manslaughter for the death of his daughter and of second-degree murder for the deaths of the three young men.

The principal issue at trial was Jackson's sanity at the time of the killings.

The Circuit Court reversed the convictions, on the authority of *People v. Martin,* because psychiatrists associated with the Center for Forensic Psychiatry, one of whom had examined Jackson to determine his competency to stand trial, were permitted to testify on the issue of his sanity.

A statute provides that upon a showing that a defendant may be incompetent to stand trial, the court shall commit him to the Forensic Center for evaluation, diagnostic report and recommendations. The statute further provides: "The diagnostic report and recommendations shall be admissible as evidence in the hearing [to determine competency to stand trial] but not for any other purpose in the pending criminal proceedings."

In *Martin,* supra, this court declared in reference to this statute limiting the use of *diagnostic report* and *recommendations:*

"We conclude that *a psychiatrist who conducts such a forensic psychiatric examination may not be called to testify* in the criminal trial if there is an objection to the admission of such testimony by defendant." (Emphasis supplied.)

The prosecutor appeals claiming "that *Martin* does not hold that psychiatrists from the Forensic Center who have conducted a psychiatric examination on the defendant pursuant to the relevant state statutes are not allowed to testify at trial as to the issue of the defendant's sanity at the time of the crime" and that the statutory language should be read to prohibit examining psychiatrists from testifying as to guilt or innocence, but not as to sanity.

Jackson maintains that, in allowing the Forensic Center psychiatrists to testify on the issue of sanity, the trial judge derogated both the statutory restriction against use of the "diagnostic report and recommendations" and the constitutional right against self-incrimination which, he contends, the statute is designed to protect.

We all agree that the Circuit Court should be reversed and the convictions reinstated, but disagree as to the basis of that disposition.

The majority states that they are in accord with the result of this opinion—reversal of the

Circuit Court and affirmance of defendant's convictions—but do not agree that the discussion in Sections I–III of this opinion "is necessary to reaching the proper result in this case."

In Part I we address the contentions of the parties revolving around the previously quoted words of the *Martin* opinion, and conclude that this statute, limiting the use of diagnostic report and recommendations, does not—contrary to the declaration in *Martin*—prohibit a psychiatrist who conducts a competency examination from testifying at trial. In Part III we state that the purpose of the statutory limitation on the use of diagnostic report and recommendations is simply "to prevent prejudice possibly resulting if the jury were to learn that the defendant recently had been found competent and were to infer erroneously that he was, therefore, sane at the time the offense was committed." In Part II we address Jackson's self-incrimination claim and conclude that the Fifth Amendment privilege does not bar the psychiatrist who examines to determine competency from testifying at trial on the sanity issue.

The majority states that there is no need to consider whether *Martin* "is a correct or incorrect interpretation" of the statute because . . . "there is a clear waiver of the statute on the record."

The waiver of the statute which we find in Part V is a waiver of the purpose of the statute declared in Part III, a purpose with which the majority declines to associate themselves.

If one reads the statutory purpose as we do (Part III), a defendant who himself brings to the attention of the jury that he was examined and found competent to stand trial cannot properly complain of prosecutorial reference to the competency examination.

* * *

However, *if* a purpose of the statute is, as the *Martin* Court declared, the prohibition of testimony on the issue of sanity by the psychiatrist who examined to determine competency, then merely because a defendant waives the right to prevent the jury from learning that he had been found competent would not constitute a waiver of his separate *Martin*-declared statutory right to prevent the examining psychiatrist from testifying concerning sanity. Waiver of one right does not constitute waiver of the other.

Jackson repeatedly objected to the trial court's ruling that the psychiatrist who had conducted the competency examination would be permitted to testify on the issue of sanity. Those objections were voiced both before and during the People's presentation, before the defendant introduced any evidence whatsoever. Those objections cannot properly be construed as a waiver of the statutory purpose declared in *Martin;* the waiver of the Part III-declared purpose occurred during Jackson's presentation.

One cannot waive except knowingly and intelligently. We cannot associate ourselves with the conclusion that Jackson, who did all that he reasonably could have been expected to do to assert his *Martin*-declared right, waived it "on the record."

And, *if*, as Jackson claims, his constitutional right against self-incrimination bars the psychiatrist who examined him to determine competency from testifying on the issue of sanity then, again, merely because he waived his right to complain about the jury learning that he was examined and found competent would not constitute a waiver of his Fifth Amendment right.

. . . To properly resolve this case, it is necessary to decide whether Jackson was deprived of the *Martin*-declared and asserted constitutional rights to bar the psychiatrist from testifying on the issue of sanity.

* * *

. . . In countless trials the people are being put to the expense and inconvenience of calling a second psychiatrist. We believe that this court should address—for the first time—this important question when, as here, it is properly presented.

I

The majority states that there is no need to "go further in *obiter dicta* to discuss aspects of this case involving constitutional issues where there is no necessity to do so." The shoe is really on the other foot. It is the *Martin* Court and the present sitting court, to the extent it gives continuing running room to *Martin*, that indulges in *obiter dicta*. The *Martin* declaration was dictum on an issue *neither raised nor argued by the parties nor pertinent to the decision* —Martin's conviction was affirmed.

* * *

Jackson offered psychiatric testimony in support of his insanity defense. In that context we would accept, contrary to *Martin*, the unanimous view of the United States Courts of Appeals which have considered the question, that there is no absolute bar to the psychiatrist who conducts the competency examination testifying also on the issue of sanity.[2] The federal statute reads much like the state statute.[3] The federal courts have reasoned that, since a defendant raising an insanity defense can be compelled to submit to a psychiatric examination, no useful purpose would be served by requiring the government to have different psychiatrists examine the defendant separately on the issues of competency and sanity. In reaching that conclusion, the federal courts have considered the cost of duplicative psychiatric examinations, the problems of trial delay, and the apparent absence of prejudice to defendants.

II

Most courts agree that there is no constitutional bar to compelling a defendant who raises an insanity defense to submit to a psychiatric examination.[4] Some courts have simply asserted, without explanation, that the privilege against self-incrimination does not apply to psychiatric examinations.[5] Others have reasoned that the privilege does not apply because evidence of a defendant's mental state is "real" not "testimonial"; like fingerprinting or handwriting, it is nothing more than an exhibition of part of the body.[6]

In *Martin*, this court ruled that a defendant who raises an insanity defense "must submit himself to examination by the People's experts as ordered by the trial court 'to obtain knowledge not about facts concerning defendant's participation in the criminal acts charged, but about facts concerning a defendant which are themselves material to the case.'"[7] We agree with the *Martin* court that a defendant who raises an insanity defense can be required to submit to an examination by the people's experts, but disassociate ourselves from the court's analysis.

The Fifth Amendment, which protects an accused person in a criminal case from being compelled to be a witness against himself, precludes the state from compelling production of evidence of a testimonial or communicative nature.[8]

The scope of the psychiatric examinations in this case, both the examination to determine competency and the sanity examination, demonstrate that communications to a psychiatrist are within the ambit of the Fifth Amendment privilege. During both examinations, Jackson was asked to relate the details of the events giving rise to the offenses charged against him—"facts concerning defendant's participation in the criminal acts charged," not just "facts concerning a

---

2. Ruud v. United States, 347 F.2d 321 (C.A.9, 1965), cert. den., 382 U.S. 1014, 86 S.Ct. 624, 15 L.Ed.2d 528 (1966); Birdsell v. United States, 346 F.2d 775 (C.A.5, 1965), cert. den., 382 U.S. 963, 86 S.Ct. 449, 15 L.Ed.2d 366 (1965), reh. den., 383 U.S. 923, 86 S.Ct. 900, 15 L.Ed.2d 680 (1966), and 384 U.S. 914, 86 S.Ct. 1347, 16 L.Ed.2d 368 (1966); Edmonds v. United States, 106 U.S.App.D.C. 373, 273 F.2d 108 (1959), cert. den., 362 U.S. 977, 80 S.Ct. 1062, 4 L.Ed. 2d 1012 (1960); United States v. Mattson, 469 F.2d 1234 (C.A.9, 1972).

3. "No statement made by the accused in the course of any examination into his sanity or mental competency provided for by this section, whether the examination shall be with or without the consent of the accused, shall be admitted in evidence against the accused on the issue of guilt in any criminal proceeding. A finding by the judge that the accused is mentally competent to stand trial shall in no way prejudice the accused in a plea of insanity as a defense to the crime charged; such finding shall not be introduced in evidence on that issue nor otherwise be brought to the notice of the jury."   63 Stat. 686 (1949), 18 U.S.C.A. § 4244.

4. 21 Am.Jur.2d, Criminal Law, § 365; Anno.: Validity and Construction of Statutes Providing for Psychiatric Examination of Accused to Determine Mental Condition, 32 A.L.R.2d 434, 444–447. Contra, see Shepard v. Bowe, 250 Or. 288, 442 P.2d 238 (1968), citing other cases.

5. State v. Coleman, 96 W.Va. 544, 549, 123 S.E. 580, 582 (1924).

6. See State v. Grayson, 239 N.C. 453, 458, 80 S.E.2d 387, 390 (1954). See, also, 8 Wigmore on Evidence (McNaughton Rev.), § 2265, pp. 395–399.

7. This distinction, based on United States v. Albright, 388 F.2d 719, 723 (C.A.4, 1968), has been criticized. See Thornton v. Corcoran, 132 U.S.App.D.C. 232, 237, 407 F.2d 695, 700 (1969); Lewin, Criminal Procedure, 23 Syracuse L.Rev. 465, 468 (1972); Note, Requiring a Criminal Defendant to Submit to a Government Psychiatric Examination: An Invasion of the Privilege Against Self-Incrimination, 83 Harv.L.Rev. 648, 661, fn. 89 (1970).

8. Schmerber v. California, 384 U.S. 757, 760–761, 86 S.Ct. 1826, 1830–1831, 16 L.Ed.2d 908, 914 (1966).

defendant which are themselves material to the case."

Information so imparted often reaches the prosecutorial authorities; there is no way to assure that it will not. The privilege against self-incrimination, if it means nothing else, most assuredly protects a man against being required to discuss with employees of the state the details of events which form the basis of the charged offense. We conclude that answers and other communications solicited by a psychiatrist from a defendant in a criminal case are testimonial and protected by the Fifth Amendment privilege.

Although the Fifth Amendment privilege applies to psychiatric examinations, a competent defendant manifestly can waive the privilege.[9] On the same principle that a plaintiff in a personal injury case can be compelled to submit to an examination by the defendant's doctors, a number of courts have ruled that a defendant in a criminal case who gives notice of his intention to call a psychiatric witness in support of a sanity defense can be compelled to submit to an examination by the people's psychiatrists as a precondition to proffering psychiatric testimony at trial.[10]

The Fifth Amendment privilege has never been thought to be absolute. A defendant who chooses to testify in his own behalf subjects himself to cross-examination. A defendant who offers psychiatric testimony in support of an insanity defense must, similarly, be deemed to have waived his Fifth Amendment privilege to the extent of subjecting himself to examination by the people's psychiatrists. Any other rule would preclude effective cross-examination of the defendant's psychiatrists, impede the prosecutor in offering effective rebuttal psychiatric testimony and would, accordingly, constitute an abuse of the constitutional privilege.

There is no constitutional requirement that a psychiatrist, who has learned in the course of an examination to determine competency what he thinks necessary to enable him to testify on sanity, conduct yet another examination or that the state provide yet another doctor to examine the defendant on the sanity issue.

III

The apparent purpose of the statutory prohibition against use of the diagnostic report and recommendations is to prevent prejudice possibly resulting if the jury were to learn that the defendant recently had been found competent and were to infer erroneously that he was, therefore, sane at the time the offense was committed.

There is no inconsistency between that purpose and conducting only one examination to acquire information on both the issue of competency and the issue of sanity, or between that purpose and allowing the same doctor to testify on both issues.

That purpose could be frustrated, whether one doctor testifies for the people on both issues or different doctors testify on the two separate issues, if a doctor or the prosecutor were to advert to the competency examination before the jury.

Whether one or two doctors appear for the People, the essential point is that the prosecutor and the People's witnesses should avoid any reference to the competency examination or the results of the examination in the jury's presence.

IV

The short of it is that in this case the prosecutor did not offer as evidence or seek otherwise to bring to the attention of the jurors either the diagnostic report or the recommendations. Nor were the report or recommendations the basis of the opinions expressed by the state's psychiatrists concerning Jackson's sanity.

* * *

V

While the prosecutor neither offered in evidence nor otherwise sought to apprise the jury of the diagnostic report and recommendations, the jury did learn that Jackson had been examined to determine his competency and had been found competent. The defense introduced a videotape of Jackson's sodium brevital examination at the Forensic Center. The jury's attention was again

---

9. Lee v. County Court of Erie County, supra, p. 441, 318 N.Y.S.2d 705, 267 N.E.2d 452.

10. See Lee v. County Court of Erie County, supra, p. 442, 318 N.Y.S.2d 705, 267 N.E.2d 452; State v. Whitlow, 45 N.J. 3, 24, 210 A.2d 763, 774 (1965); Pope v. United States, 372 F.2d 710, 721 (C.A.8, 1967), vacated and remanded on other grounds, 392 U.S. 651, 88 S.Ct. 2145, 20 L.Ed.2d 1317 (1968); State v. Myers, 220 S.C. 309, 313, 67 S.E.2d 506, 508 (1951).

focused on the competency examination when one of Jackson's lawyers asked the judge to explain to the jury his objections to the testimony of the psychiatrists associated with the Forensic Center. Also, a lawyer for Jackson had Jackson's psychiatrist on redirect examination read the diagnosis contained in the forensic report. The defense introduced as an exhibit the forensic file, specifically the notes taken by Blunt.

The statutory bar against admission of the diagnostic report and recommendations, designed for the defendant's protection, is not absolute. This protection may be waived by the defendant if he thinks it advantageous to present evidence from the competency examination to the jury.

Jackson was represented by three experienced criminal defense lawyers. They purposely chose to focus the jury's attention on details of the competency examination. They, no doubt, saw advantages to Jackson in that course. We could not properly predicate reversal on the clear and purposeful waiver of the statutory protection.

The Circuit Court is reversed. The defendant's convictions are reinstated.

EPILOGUE I

One of the authors, Bill Kenety, revisited the scene of the crime and talked to some of the people involved. His report follows:

The house at 4330 Lincoln still stands in a decaying neighborhood near the Allegheny State campus. Most of the nearby buildings boast official city of Pittsburgh signs warning "Danger—Keep Out. Condemned as Dangerous and Unsafe." Like many of its neighbors, 4330 is deserted. The sign proclaiming it "Stonehead Manor" is gone; only trash, discarded clothes, and unwanted furniture remain. Apartment 9 remains much as it was on the morning of 8 May. The beds on which Sandra Jackson, Todd Wilson, Jonathan Carter, and Ricky Walters met their deaths remain as mute reminders of the tragedy.

Judge Gillis still renders decisions from the bench in the modern Pittsburgh Hall of Justice in downtown Pittsburgh. He was recently reelected. He is justifiably proud of the shortness of his trial backlog—currently defendants in his court are tried thirty to forty days after their arrest.

Among the hundreds of lawyers who daily pass through the Hall is Oliver Nelson, one of the most respected trial attorneys in the city. Leonard Gilman has moved to suburban Greensburg where he works as a Westmoreland County prosecuting attorney. He was recently involved in a major case where he obtained first-degree murder convictions of three young men who brutally murdered a fifteen-year-

Stonehead Manor Today

old Greensburg newsboy. Mrs. Gilman is currently taking law courses.

Sergeant Baranski recently retired after twenty-five years with the police department. Before retiring he made news when he chased and caught a fleeing suspect while pursuing in an electric golf cart. He is now working with the Criminal Justice Institute in helping to integrate small town police departments into a statewide system wherein the local police use uniform filing systems, radio calls, etc. Of his retirement, Baranski writes, "I am enjoying my present position in private life, but miss the blood-and-guts of homicide investigation. It was one hell of an education." (See Figure 34 for a *Pittsburgh Herald* article concerning Sergeant Baranski's retirement.)

Baranski's partner, Sgt. Robert Wilson, retired in January of 1971. Wilson is now living in Seattle and working construction for his brother-in-law. When Wilbur Jackson's appeals are exhausted, his .38 revolver and his Luger will be taken by the State Police and melted down into scrap metal.

Sergeant Baranski still hears from some of the witnesses: Carl Richardson occasionally calls collect from Miami where he is managing a motel. Baranski says that he "wasn't a bad kid" and that he only "needed a break" which he got in Miami. Janet Rivers went away to college while Georgia Webster is going to Allegheny State. Allison Fletcher is living in Castle Shannon and, when last heard from, was looking for a job. Mary Lee Von Allstein is living with her mother in a trailer park outside Pittsburgh. She has gone back to high school and apparently has changed her ways.

Sally Jo Tucker still works at Lerner's Dress Shop in downtown Pittsburgh. She recently married and now lives with her husband in a small house on the edge of the city. Sally Jo was the subject of a sensational article in *Man's World* magazine wherein she was depicted as the organizer of a secret sin-and-sex society at Stonehead Manor. Sally Jo successfully sued for a retraction of the story.

I talked to Sally Jo in February of 1974. She's a small, bright, even bouncy girl whose energy seems endless. She is an extremely animated person, full of cheer, yet at times she seems almost flighty. She is not strong-minded and definitely more of a follower than a leader. It seems inconceivable to me that she could have led or even pushed Sandra Jackson in the direction of Stonehead Manor. Sally Jo is pleasant but not pushy.

The Jacksons have rented the house on Hill Street and moved to suburban Whitehall. Mary Jackson found work as a hostess and waitress at a Holiday Inn several blocks from the baseball stadium. Connie Jackson works for a hospital food service; her eldest brother attends high school and has a paper route.

I visited Wilbur Jackson several times at New Castle Prison. When he first entered prison he was involved in several racial incidents and at one point his cell was firebombed. Since then he has for the most part avoided black prisoners. Most days he works for the prison food service.

Figure 34 Pittsburgh Herald **article**

Homicide Expert
Baranski Retires

By Betty Paul

After 25 years on the city police force, Sgt. Irvin Baranski hung up his badge for the last time last week. Baranski, the city's foremost homicide detective, called it quits after a career that involved him in most of the city's prominent murder cases.

Reviewing his years on the force, Baranski judged those years "a hell of a good time. I always tried to treat people decently and compassionately" the hom- icide ace recalled.

Baranski's compassion was perhaps best evidenced in the widely publicized Flynn murder case. After an elderly couple was brutally beaten to death, Baranski was assigned to the case. After studying footprints at the crime scene, he arrested two teenage brothers who had been neighbors of the Flynns. Baranski separated the youths until one broke down and confessed. After he cracked the case he was the toast of the force, but most people never knew of Baranski's other side. Each day, after work he stopped by to see the brothers' mother, just to see if she was all right.

Among Baranski's other triumphs was the Wilbur Jackson case where a distraught father killed four teen- agers, one of them his daughter. Baranski also solved the famous "Mr. Bones" case where a cremated corpse was found in a furnace.

The sergeant was also involved in the "Rochester Avenue Shoot Out" when city policemen and off-duty county sheriffs shot it out on a city street. Then there was the "Hazelwood Massacre," where eight suspected drug dealers were gunned down in one of America's biggest gangland executions.

Two months ago Baranski cracked the sickening murder of school teacher Beverly Jacquit which ended fears of a possible sex maniac on the loose.

Along with the triumphs came disappointments, most notably the 1970 murder of Burton Gordon, executive director of the state Civil Rights Commis- sion. Gordon's bullet-riddled body was discovered in a downtown garage one winter evening.

"That's still a whodunit and I really wish we'd cleared that one up before I left," said Baranski. "I've always said that you can solve most murders if you have enough time, manpower, and dedication. Not all, but most, and that one I wanted bad." Baranski, now 44, plans to take it easy for a while and then begin work with the Criminal Justice Institute.

from the Pittsburgh Herald
Monday, March 18, 1974

Wilbur Jackson has now totally embraced religion.   When I first saw him in the summer of 1973, he wore a large white plastic cross and a "God Saves" button. When I last saw him in February of 1974, the plastic cross had been replaced by a sterling silver one.

Jackson has had problems with the prison authorities concerning church attendance. Prisoners are allowed to attend services of the religion of their choice, but Jackson's choice was all the services of all religions. A compromise was worked out whereby Jackson could "crosscut" and attend some but not all services. He told me he has given up liquor, cigarettes, and even soft drinks; one of his major disappointments is the failure of the prison store to stock enough fresh fruit juices.

Wilbur Jackson is a quiet, almost unassuming man, yet he has a certain earnestness about him that is appealing. He talks freely about the tragedy and his plans for the future. The events of May 8 seem to have faded somewhat from Wilbur's mind; perhaps from repression, perhaps merely from the passage of time. Somewhat ironically, he told me that three years in prison have convinced him love and kindness bring far better results than discipline.

In some ways Jackson seems bitter. He appears ready to take his punishment, yet angry that others are being let off or let out. He still says he did nothing wrong—he did it but it wasn't wrong. He seems genuinely sorry about his daughter, but apparently feels little regret over the deaths of Todd Wilson, Jonathan Carter, and Ricky Walters. It is almost as if he feels they deserved to die.

Jackson is still angry with the Pittsburgh Police Department. He believes that they should have been on his side—i.e., the side of morality, decency, etc. He feels that there were traces of drugs in the dead bodies and can't understand why the police wouldn't admit it.

Jackson keeps daily track of the prison population. He was able to give me up-to-the-minute statistics showing that the number of inmates is decreasing. Jackson is naturally disappointed that he isn't among the departing. He further keeps remote control track of trials in Pittsburgh and listed several defendants who were acquitted or received light sentences for crimes he believes were far more repulsive than his. All of the defendants were black.

Wilbur Jackson's hair is grayer and thinner now than it was in pictures of him taken before May 8. Sometimes he seems bitter, other times mellow and unemotionally marking time. He speaks longingly of the Tennessee he once knew and seems to hope and believe that it hasn't changed. He talks of returning there when he completes his prison sentence and of raising his remaining children the right way. For Wilbur Jackson, a return to the simple life may help erase the memories of a long, deadly night in Stonehead Manor.

EPILOGUE II

In September 1983 Oliver Nelson died after a long illness. At the time of his death, he was a Juvenile Court Referee. His antagonist during the trial, Len Gilman, has left the local prosecutor's office to work for the State Attorney General. Of the appellate attorneys, Jack and Sidney Kraizman are still in active practice while I was unable to locate Michael Mueller. Judge Joseph Gillis still presides on the Recorder's Court and is considered a wise and respected jurist.

On 23 October 1978 Wilbur Chester Jackson, inmate number 127775, was paroled from New Castle Prison. Under the terms of Jackson's parole the Pennsylvania Department of Parole and Probation transferred supervision to the state of Tennessee, and Jackson returned home to his native town.

I spoke to Mike McPeak, Jackson's parole supervisor, several times during 1979 and again in 1983. Interestingly, McPeak's view of Jackson changed markedly during those four years.

During the year following his release, Jackson settled back to life in a small, rural town. He lived with his elderly parents and spent much of his time caring for them. His family did not accompany him, but one of his children did attend East Tennessee State University. Jackson did not drink, swear or smoke. The crosses that once hung from his neck gave way to a large brass belt buckle emblazoned with the word "LOVE."

In late December 1979, McPeak described Jackson as "very much community-oriented" and related that Jackson was active in what might be termed a "lay ministry" while preaching the need for strong family ties. McPeak spent considerable time with Jackson and termed him "the only guy on my case load I could totally trust". McPeak had originally required Jackson to work and had found him a job but ultimately concluded that Jackson was better off staying close to home and community.

Jackson's hometown has no black residents and hasn't had any since the thirties. In another way time has finally caught up with Jackson: drugs have arrived in town. McPeak says that although the situation "is not like 'the city' and dope is not dripping off the street," there is still a serious problem, at least by his standards.

One day in 1979 Jackson emerged from the local jail and saw a deputy sheriff on the steps of that institution. The deputy was selling a gun, a potent .357 Magnum. Jackson took the gun from the deputy, the deputy clearly having no knowledge of Jackson's background. As McPeak watched wordlessly, Jackson fondled and caressed the pistol, as if fascinated by its very presence. After some time Jackson returned the gun and silently walked away, a strange smile on his face. McPeak wondered for a long time what to make of the incident.

Wilbur Jackson successfully completed parole on 23 October 1980 and was released from any further supervision. One of the special conditions of his parole had been that he not own or possess any weapons or be in the company of those who did.

Perhaps it was because the pressure of being a parolee was off or perhaps it was because he had little to look forward to in life; in any event, Wilbur Jackson, in the eyes of one person who knew him well, "went to the dogs."

He apparently began associating with what was termed a "rough" crowd, took up with a "shabby" woman, and, unfortunately, became involved with weapons.

By 1983 Mike McPeak felt that Jackson's life was going down the drain. Jackson's father had died, and McPeak related that during Jackson's unsuccessful stint in a job-training program those involved became downright scared of him. McPeak considered that Jackson's good behavior during his parole might simply have been a show to get him through his parole period.

During 1982 federal agents investigated and ultimately arrested Wilbur Jackson on firearms possession charges. On 31 January 1983 he was sentenced in United States District Court in Knoxville, Tennessee, to five years of probation and five hundred hours of community service. To escape a jail sentence, he apparently made an eloquent plea to the presiding judge. Since that time he has been quiet.

Is Wilbur Jackson still bitter about what he calls "the tragedy"? Yes, in a strange sort of mellow way. He still feels that the incident would not have happened if he had received backing from the Pittsburgh Police when he and his wife were trying to bring Sandy home. He is also displeased with his trial because he feels one important point was not emphasized: Jackson believes that it was obvious from the positions of the bodies that none of the boys had moved or attempted to run after being awakened by the first shot; Jackson's belief is that they were so drugged that they couldn't wake up, let alone run.

However, he also believes that, given the changing social standards, he might not have committed the crimes today. He says that since many people now actually live together before marriage, it might have been acceptable for his daughter to do that too. Since things are different today, he says, he might not have done it.

Like many convicted criminals, Jackson expresses his guilt in the passive: "They say I killed four people," as if denying that knowledge himself. In any event, he isn't prone to talk about the events in Stonehead Manor.

Mike McPeak told me another story, a story that is perhaps fitting to remember Jackson by. McPeak is acquainted with Lamar Alexander, the current governor of Tennessee, and Mr. and Mrs. McPeak attended the festivities when Alexander was inaugurated. At a public reception for the new governor, the McPeaks spotted Wilbur Jackson in the receiving line wearing an ill-fitting blue suit. Jackson was quietly holding a balloon in one hand and a small card in the other.

He waited patiently in line until the governor autographed the card. McPeak then watched him leave. Amidst the bustle and hoopla of the reception, he saw Jackson slowly walk away, still holding his balloon, still clutching his card. Eventually Jackson faded away into the bleachers and was seen no more. That may be the way to remember Wilbur Jackson. He waited for eight years in prison, sometimes patiently, sometimes bitterly. When he was released he deliberately sought a certain kind of oblivion in the small town he knew. For Wilbur Jackson, fading away is what he has most sought and perhaps most deserves.

William H. Kenety
November 1983

GLOSSARY OF LEGAL TERMS

Bail Bail is the process by which a person charged with a crime or crimes is released from custody pending trial. Bail may be made by pledging property or money as a promise that the defendant will appear for trial. If the defendant does not appear, that money or property is forfeited. In minor cases a mere promise to appear will often suffice.

This practice developed from medieval England. In that age a person was released pending trial only when a third party made bail for the defendant by personally promising that the defendant would return for trial. If the defendant failed to appear, the third party was tried in his or her place!

The system has developed over the years so that now either the defendant or a third party merely pledges property or money as a condition for release. The defendant may not even know the third party, such as a bail bondsman. It is thus not surprising that the number of defendants failing to appear for trial is somewhat higher than it was five hundred years ago.

Note that failure to appear for trial while released on bail is in and of itself a crime in many jurisdictions.

Beyond a Reasonable Doubt Plaintiffs in civil lawsuits must prove their cases by a "preponderance" of the evidence. This standard is readily quantifiable and simply means that most of the evidence must favor the plaintiff for him or her to prevail. Thus a civil litigant can win with, at a minimum, 51 percent of the evidence.

"Beyond a reasonable doubt," the standard in criminal cases, has proved to be an elusive concept to define. It is certainly not quantifiable in terms of percentages.

Most authorities define a reasonable doubt as something concrete or a doubt based on a specific, articulable reason. Almost all judges' instructions to the jury include language that the jurors must be "morally certain" before returning a guilty verdict. However, in practice, jurors may often ignore such abstract concepts and simply decide the case based on what might be described as a rational, gut reaction.

Note that defense attorneys, particularly in closing argument, may almost appear to base their case on this difficult standard. They may argue that while there is indeed evidence against the defendant, the evidence is not strong enough to prove the defendant's guilt beyond a reasonable doubt. A particularly choice example of such an argument goes as follows:

Suppose you are a baseball umpire calling plays from behind the plate. The batter hits a tremendous drive to right field and runs, runs to third base where he slides in a cloud of dust! You can't really see the play because of the dust and the players blocking your view. But you've got to make a decision! You can't say, "I don't know"! You've got to call the runner safe or out! Well, ladies and gentlemen, in this case you don't have to make that kind of decision. You don't have to call anybody safe or out. You can simply say, "We don't know for sure." And if you don't know for sure, then the prosecution hasn't proven its case beyond a reasonable doubt and you should return a verdict of not guilty.

Case Names Generally the first name in the title of a case indicates the party instituting the action. Thus *State v. Jones* means that the state is prosecuting Jones while *Smith v. Brown* shows that Smith has filed a lawsuit against

Brown. Likewise a United States Supreme Court case titled *Black v. Ohio* indicates that it is Black who is making the appeal.

The often cryptic shorthand following the name of an appellate case is its citation—the place where the actual opinion may be found and read. Thus Black v. Ohio, 346 U.S. 917 (1984) is a decision of the United States Supreme Court in 1984 which may be found at page 917 of volume 346 of the United States Reports, a series of bound volumes containing all of the opinions of the Supreme Court.

The proper form for such citations is intricate, and the process of deciphering the citations often confusing. The answer to almost every possible citation question is to be found in *The Uniform System of Citation*, a paperback commonly known as "The Blue Book" due to the color of its cover. It is an indispensable handbook for those engaging in legal writing.

Change of Venue   A shift of the trial site, usually done only when there is substantial pre-trial publicity that would make finding impartial jurors difficult or impossible. A change of venue rarely occurs because of the cost of providing transportation and accommodations for those who must travel to the new trial site. Readers interested in the issue of pre-trial publicity might consult the Supreme Court's opinion in Gannett v. DePasquele, 443 U.S. 368, 99 S.Ct. 2898, 61 L.Ed.2d 608 (1979).

Competency   Whether a defendant is of sufficiently sound mind to be tried. Entirely separate from insanity. Insanity concerns the defendant's state of mind at the time of the crime while competency refers to one's mental state at the time of the trial.

Competency is generally determined by standards such as these: does the defendant understand the proceedings against him? can the defendant assist in his defense? is the defendant able to appreciate the potential penalties involved?

A situation could readily arise whereby there would be no question of sanity at the time of the crime, yet a defendant would be incompetent to stand trial. Where an individual is found to be incompetent, the trial will be delayed until he or she is competent. Conceivably, a trial might be postponed indefinitely until a defendant is competent.

Confessions   Although there is tremendous variance in statistics, the fact that significant numbers of criminal suspects confess their crimes never ceases to amaze people. Suspects get nothing in return for a confession and can readily invoke their *Miranda* rights to halt any interrogation. Yet they continue to confess, perhaps resulting from a desire to "get it off their chest" or perhaps resulting from the skill of the police officers questioning them.

Confessions may be suppressed—not allowed to be used at trial—for either or both of two reasons: First, a failure by the police to give the *Miranda* rights described *infra* leads to suppression of a confession under the rationale of the exclusionary rule—the best way to police the police is to take away their evidence when they have obtained it illegally. Second, any confession that is obtained as the result of coercion, threats, or force is suppressed because it is considered to be unreliable evidence.

Incidentally the term "getting it off your chest," has an interesting history. In medieval England the estates of convicted defendants were forfeited to the Crown. However, defendants who refused to plead guilty (or not guilty) could not be properly convicted, and, while they could be sentenced to death, their estates could not be forfeited. To discourage such recalcitrants the *peine forte et dure* (literally, strong and hard penalty) was adopted. According to the law of the day "the prisoner shall be . . . put in some low, dark room and there laid on his back . . . and that as many weights shall be laid upon him as he can bear and more . . . and he shall so continue till he die."

Thus the unfortunate undergoing the *peine forte et dure* could suffer and die but preserve the family estate or he could plead and "get it off his chest." This practice continued well into the eighteenth century and it was not until 1827 that an act was passed directing the court to enter a not guilty plea for those prisoners who refused to plead.

Court Systems The federal court system is perhaps the most readily explained and has the advantage of being uniform throughout the country. The system begins with the Federal District Court, the basic trial court. All cases filed in Federal Court are initially tried here. Most cases are tried by a District Court judge although some preliminary proceedings and minor matters, both criminal and civil, are referred to federal magistrates.

There are now ninety Federal Districts in the country. Some states may have only one District Court while others may have two or more depending on the amount of business. For example, there are three districts in Pennsylvania, an Eastern District (Philadelphia), a Middle District (Harrisburg), and a Western District (Pittsburgh). Currently there are approximately five hundred judges divided among the ninety districts.

After a case is decided in the District Court the losing party generally has the right to appeal to the United States Court of Appeals. The Court is divided into twelve circuits, each with a specifically defined area of the country from which it hears appeals. These courts are known as the First Circuit, Second Circuit, etc., as well as the District of Columbia Circuit. There are now some 135 Court of Appeals judges. They usually hear appeals in a panel of three.

A party who loses in the Court of Appeals may request the United States Supreme Court to hear the case. However, there is no right to have the appeal considered and the Supreme Court rarely grants such requests. The Supreme Court also considers requests to review cases decided in the supreme courts of the states.

Most states have court systems similar to the federal structure. Generally, there are two levels of trial courts. The lower court may hear misdemeanors and minor civil cases while the higher court considers felonies and, for example, civil suits where the amount in question is over twenty-five hundred dollars. Usually jury trials are available in the higher court but not in the lower court.

State appellate courts are also frequently two-tiered. Litigants will have a right to have their cases considered by the lower appellate court but, like the United States Supreme Court, the highest court will hear only a few of the many cases presented to it.

The reader should bear in mind that the structure of state courts, as well as the names given to those courts, is subject to almost an infinite number of possibilities. One would do well to contact a local court clerk in order to determine the nature of the court system in any particular jurisdiction.

Defense Counsel The role of defense counsel is, on one hand, an obvious one. Counsel represents the defendant to the best of his or her ability and, in the event of a trial, attempts to persuade the judge or jury of his or her client's innocence.

Beyond these pat responses, the role of defense counsel can be much less clear. The simple facts are that most defendants are guilty and that most defense attorneys know their clients are guilty. How then, the reader may ask, can an attorney work for the acquittal of a guilty person, particularly one who may have committed a serious crime?

The answer lies in the nature of the legal system. For better or worse, many attorneys are simply hired guns with little or no emotional involvement in the causes or clients they represent. This is not to say that some attorneys do not passionately believe in the side they represent. This is especially true in such fields as civil rights or environmental protection. However, in criminal law many lawyers do not want to become emotionally involved for to do so might rob them of their ability to dispassionately analyze the case. Furthermore, since most defendants are convicted and since many do receive prison sentences, emotional involvement can readily lead to discouraged despondency.

Thus the "I'm doing a job" outlook has become somewhat routine. This job can be severely complicated when a defendant admits guilt to defense counsel, particularly when that defendant wishes to testify and deny the crime.

Even when the defendant's guilt is obvious or admitted, the defense attorney is ethically required to force the prosecution to prove its case, to prove the defendant guilty beyond a reasonable doubt. Major problems arise however when, for example, the defendant wishes to use false alibi witnesses.

An attorney cannot knowingly use perjury. In such instances defense counsel may simply drop out of the case and new counsel is hired by or appointed for the defendant. Alternatively, a defense attorney may disassociate herself from a particular witness or witnesses by not participating in the examination of the witness(es). A judge would know why, a jury would not.

Street-wise criminals rarely admit guilt to their lawyers and frequently protest their innocence with considerable vigor. The end result is often a charade where both the defendant and defense attorney "know" the defendant is guilty, but pretend otherwise. Those defendants who do readily admit their guilt frequently plead.

The reader should realize that often the major battle for the defense counsel is not proving that his or her client is innocent, but rather getting a favorable disposition for the defendant. Many defendants, particularly those with prior offenses, think nothing of having another conviction added to their record. They are, however, reluctant to go to jail.

Thus a good attorney may spend relatively little time on the merits of a case and a great deal of time preparing for sentencing. He or she may interview family members, religious figures, friends, and employers and gain their help. Witnesses may generally testify at sentencing and a judge cannot help but be influenced by a parade of people all saying that the defendant deserves a chance. Counsel can also submit a sentencing memorandum describing the defendant in the most favorable light and incorporating statements from those who know the defendant, dwelling on his or her positive prospects for the future.

For many, the crucial battle is not to prove innocence but to stay out of jail. A dedicated defense attorney can make this happen.

Double Jeopardy   The rule of law that a defendant may not be tried twice for the same crime. An individual acquitted, or convicted, of a particular offense may not be subsequently tried for the same offense. The prosecution gets only one chance and may not avoid the rule by, for example, trying a defendant for manslaughter after he or she has been acquitted of murder.

Jeopardy "attaches," or comes into effect, once the trial begins. Thus the prosecution may not dismiss the case in midtrial and then start all over. The exception to double jeopardy occurs when the judge declares a mistrial. A mistrial might happen when a jury is deadlocked and unable to reach a decision or when a defendant falls ill and cannot be present in court. In such instances a mistrial is declared by the court, and the trial may begin all over again.

Insanity Defense   The insanity defense, although used in only a minuscule fraction of all criminal trials, has proved to be a troublesome problem when it has been raised. Much of the problem stems from the very difficulty of defining insanity.

A considerable amount of American law has its origins in British law. One of the early attempts to legally define insanity occurred in 1724 when an English court held that a man was insane if he "doth not know what he is doing, no more than . . . a wild beast." The "wild beast test," while perhaps appropriate for the early eighteenth century, proved rather unworkable as time wore on.

In 1843 the House of Lords formulated the "M'Naghten Rule": if "at the time of the committing of the act, the party was laboring under such a defect of reason, from disease of the mind, as not to know the nature and quality of the act he was doing, or, if he did know it, that he did not know he was doing what was wrong," then he was considered insane. This standard was soon exported to the United States and the ability to distinguish right from wrong became the guiding principle in this country. This test, still called the M'Naghten Rule, remains the standard in many states today.

Some states have adopted the concept of an "irresistible impulse"— whether the defendant was so overcome by such an irresistible impulse that he or she had no ability to act otherwise. This test has frequently been put in terms of whether the defendant would still have committed the crime even had a police officer been standing at the scene. If so, then an irresistible impulse was at work and the defendant was thus insane.

However, many states and the federal courts have adopted the definition found in the Model Penal Code. Under that standard a defendant is insane at the time of the crime if, as a result of a mental disease or defect, he lacked substantial capacity to appreciate the wrongfulness of his conduct or to conform his conduct to the law. The problem with that standard is that it appears to require another set of definitions. For example, a mental disease or defect has been described as "any abnormal condition of the mind which substantially affects mental or emotional processes and substantially impairs behavior controls."

As the reader will quickly realize, one definition simply leads to another. What, for example, is an "abnormal condition"? How does one quantify "substantially" affects or impairs? There is no definitive answer to these and similar questions. Insanity remains an elusive concept and in the end it is simply a matter of judgment.

Those seeking further explanation might consult two oft-cited cases in the field, Brawner v. United States, 471 F.2d 969 (D.C.Cir.1972) and Durham v. United States, 214 F.2d 862 (D.C.Cir.1954).

Jury Selection   The process of choosing a jury differs from jurisdiction to jurisdiction.   As a general rule, prospective jurors enter the courtroom in a large group.   They are questioned collectively to determine if they have knowledge, experience, or views that would bias or prejudice their ability to hear the case.

The questioning is known as *voir dire*, translated literally from French as "to see, to say."   Depending on local practice, *voir dire* may be conducted by the judge or by the lawyers.   If conducted by the lawyers, an experienced attorney can skillfully use the process to bolster his or her case.

For example, counsel might inquire, "Do any of you know the defendant, Mr. Smith?"   However, the better question would be, "Are any of you familiar with Mr. Smith through the Montgomery Hills Methodist Church, where he has been teaching Sunday School for the last ten years?"

The attorneys are also provided with lists of the prospective jurors including their addresses, age, education, employment, and like information for their spouses.   On rare occasions, where the stakes are great and the resources substantial, lawyers might employ an opinion poll or computer survey in advance of trial to determine what background indicates a potentially favorable juror.   There are also some psychologists who, for a fee, will assist counsel during jury selection by observing the potential jurors and then making suggestions based on such intangibles as facial expression and body language.   Mostly, however, lawyers base their jury selection on the information from the jury list, the answers from *voir dire* and simple gut reaction.

After questioning, the actual jury is selected.   Counsel may challenge for cause—i.e., request the court to strike, or remove, a juror because of apparent bias or prejudice.   Thereafter, attorneys may remove jurors through peremptory challenges.   Each side is given a limited number of peremptories and may exercise them to strike jurors without explanation.   This process continues until a jury is selected, often when each side has used up its allotment of challenges.

The exercise of peremptory challenges may be based on either reason or hunch.   For example, many defense attorneys will strike relatives of law enforcement officers on the belief that anyone related to the police is unlikely to believe a criminal defendant.   Oftentimes in drunk-driving cases prosecutors will excuse anyone who drives for a living, on the theory that those individuals will hestitate to convict since they realize that conviction generally leads to loss of driver's license and know that a license is a necessity for many people.

There are perhaps endless theories about jury selection.   Arguably, the end result might still be the same if the first twelve men and women were chosen.

Lesser Included Offenses   Lesser offenses that are included in the major offense.   For example, assault is a lesser included offense of assault with a dangerous weapon, as robbery is of armed robbery.   A jury considering a charge of first-degree murder could instead find the defendant guilty of either of the lesser included offenses of second-degree murder or of manslaughter. Once convicted, a defendant can be punished only for the major offense—i.e., a person could be sentenced for grand larceny but not also for petit larceny. Note, however, that a "crime" may consist of several offenses and that a defendant can be sentenced for all of the offenses committed. For example, one "crime" could consist of kidnapping, rape, and extortion. Likewise, the use of a firearm is usually considered a separate crime and often carries its own mandatory minimum sentence.

Manslaughter and Murder These crimes, in descending order of seriousness, are generally defined as follows:

First-degree murder includes deliberate and premeditated murder. A contract killing is a perfect example. In some states first-degree murder also includes murder committed during the course of another crime such as rape or robbery.

Second-degree murder encompasses deliberate and intentional murder such as where a man, annoyed at the cries of his neighbor's baby, takes a gun and shoots the baby.

Manslaughter is a killing done without malice, often with provocation and usually in the heat of passion. A common example would stem from a barroom argument, particularly if racial slurs were exchanged.

Miranda Rights A suspect under arrest must be told:

1 You have the right to remain silent.
2 Anything you say may be used against you.
3 You have the right to speak with an attorney.
4 If you cannot afford an attorney one will be appointed for you.
5 If you decide to answer questions you may stop answering at any time.

These rights were specified by the United States Supreme Court in Miranda v. Arizona, 384 U.S. 436, 86 S.Ct. 1602, 16 L.Ed. 694 (1966) and have been enforced ever since.

Motion A catchall legal term for a request. A motion for a new trial is a request for a new trial. When an attorney seeks a continuance he or she "moves" for a continuance. Similar to parliamentary procedure where one might move that a resolution be adopted.

Not Guilty by Reason of Insanity The reader should understand that defendants found not guilty by reason of insanity do not walk out the door with their freedom. Depending on the exact procedure used in each state, the defendant is then committed as an insane person to a state institution for evaluation and treatment. The defendant would not be released until certified as "cured" by the institution. This process can take anywhere from several months to a lifetime.

Note that juries are generally not told what the potential sentences are for the crimes with which a defendant has been charged. However, clever defense attorneys will often attempt to inform the jury of the above information in hopes of giving the jurors an easy out. In the Wilbur Jackson case Judge Gillis obliged the defense by spelling it out in his jury instructions.

Petition for Certiorari Commonly known as a "cert petition." A formal request to a court that it decide to consider a case. Most often used in conjunction with the United States Supreme Court although state courts may also use the terminology. It is rarely granted. During the 1982–83 term the Supreme Court received 5,079 such petitions. It granted 176 of them, a figure of 3 percent. The wording "cert. denied" in a case title indicates the Supreme Court, or a state court, declined to hear the case.

Plea Bargaining The overwhelming majority of American criminal cases are resolved through plea bargaining. In some courts, particularly those in urban areas, this figure may well exceed 90 percent. In return for a guilty plea the defendant gets a "bargain" such as a reduced charge or an indication of a lighter sentence.

In return for a plea a prosecutor might agree to, for example, reduce an armed robbery charge to a simple robbery or an assault with a deadly weapon to a simple assault. Alternatively, the prosecutor might agree to recommend a particular sentence or to make no recommendation at all with respect to sentencing.

Successful plea bargaining requires a certain amount of negotiating skill on the part of counsel and frequently results in bluffing and calling the other's bluff. In this regard it is not unlike settling a civil case.

Bear in mind that judges generally do not participate in this process and are not bound by any sentencing arguments. Thus, for example, even if the prosecutor and defense counsel both recommend a two-year sentence for burglary, a judge may still impose the maximum regardless of their agreement. This sometimes happens and while the defendant may feel aggrieved, it is simply the breaks of the game.

Most authorities would probably agree that plea bargaining is both necessary and an evil. There are simply not enough judges, courtrooms, jurors, prosecutors, etc., to try most cases, and a concerted effort by defendants in any one court system to insist on going to trial would literally bring that court system to a halt.

The reader should also realize that plea bargaining goes hand-in-hand with judge-shopping. In any given court system some judges will be perceived as lenient, some as harsh, and most in varying positions in the middle. The opportunity to appear before a lenient judge often encourages a plea while the appearance on the bench of a "long ball hitter" may well lead a defendant to risk a trial. Frequently defense attorneys faced with heavy-hitting judges will delay, request continuances, or become ill until a case comes up before a more favorable judge, at which time the defendant will promptly plead guilty.

In the Washington, D.C., court system there was a certain judge who, depending on one's orientation, was regarded as either "soft" or "compassionate." It frequently seemed that when the misdemeanor docket grew too long and the backlog of cases grew too heavy, the Chief Judge would assign this particular judge to handle misdemeanor pleas. The result was a frenzy of activity with defendants whose trial dates were weeks away rushing to the courthouse to plead guilty. Within a week the misdemeanor docket would be cleared and the backlog reduced.

Precedent Appellate court opinions that must be followed by lower courts. When, hypothetically, the California Supreme Court rules that a man may be prosecuted for raping his wife, all state courts in California are bound to follow this precedent. Courts in other states are not. Similarly, constitutional decisions of the United States Supreme Court are binding precedent for all courts in the nation.

Self-Incrimination The Fifth Amendment to the Constitution specifically provides, "No person . . . shall be compelled in any criminal case to be a witness against himself." This passage prohibits the prosecution from calling the defendant as a witness.

More importantly, it means the prosecution may not comment on the fact that a defendant does not testify. One might think that a good prosecution closing argument could include a statement to the effect that "If the defendant were innocent she would have at least told you her story. Since she hasn't, it means she's guilty." Not so. Courts have reasoned that since a person has this right not to testify, the right would be lessened if the exercise of the right could be used against the person. Hence the fact that a defendant did not testify or did not respond to police questioning after *Miranda* rights were given is not fair game for comment.

Incidentally, the question of whether the defendant will take the stand or not is probably the biggest decision defense counsel makes in a trial. Several factors often mitigate against calling the defendant. First, he or she may not be as articulate or quick-thinking as counsel might wish. This poses potential problems, particularly on cross-examination and particularly when the defendant's story might have an inherent lack of credibility.

More importantly, a defendant who takes the stand exposes himself to cross-examination about his prior convictions. This may be done as an attack on a witness's credibility. The very existence of "priors" may itself preclude the defendant from testifying. Defense counsel may then be left without a case, frequently resulting in either a plea bargain or a jury argument contending only that the prosecution has not proved its case beyond a reasonable doubt.

Sentencing The purposes to be served by sentencing a convicted defendant are complex, confusing, and open to considerable criticism. Technically, the process is generally called disposition (i.e., disposing with the case—or defendant—once and for all) while "sentencing" usually involves incarceration in a local jail or a state prison.

In some states juries may make disposition recommendations, but generally it is the judge who decides the fate of a defendant. In considering the possibilities of a fine, probation, or incarceration, the judge normally considers the following factors:

1 Deterrence. Will the punishment effectively deter the defendant from committing future crimes? Perhaps more importantly, will it deter others from criminal conduct? As much as a judge may be sympathetic to a particular defendant, a light sentence or no sentence at all might suggest to others that the potential sanctions for criminal behavior are not great.

2 Rehabilitation. Traditionally, a jail sentence was thought to help rehabilitate convicts and to give them an opportunity to see the error of their ways. Most penologists now believe that the rehabilitation aspect of incarceration is zero.

3 Protection. As long as a criminal is in jail he or she cannot commit crimes. This concept has become popular with some authorities who believe it is best to simply "warehouse" certain defendants, particularly young males, in order to keep them off the streets.

4 Punishment. Simply put, an eye for an eye. It is the thought that if one commits a wrong he or she should pay for it, and society will enforce payment with a prison term.

Obviously these factors can apply to dispositions other than incarceration. For example, judges will sentence drunk drivers to Saturday night viewing of a hospital emergency room. My personal favorite is a return of the stocks and pillories to embarrass and humiliate those convicted of nonviolent crimes.

The reader should ask himself or herself which of the four factors above is applicable to the Wilbur Jackson case.

Spousal Immunity or Privilege   This concept refers to the age-old rule of law that a person cannot testify in a case against his or her spouse. It stems from a combination of theories and traditions: a fear that a spouse could not be trusted to tell the truth in such a trial, the medieval concept that a wife was the property of her husband, and finally the belief that the sanctity of marriage should be protected.

Originally, a spouse was flatly prohibited from testifying. Gradually that rule was modified to one allowing such testimony only if the spouse on trial acquiesced. Now about half of the states and the federal system have adopted a new standard that focuses not on marital status per se, but rather on the nature of the potential testimony.

This standard, well explained in Trammell v. United States, 445 U.S. 40, 100 S.Ct. 906, 63 L.Ed.2d 186 (1980), prohibits testimony concerning confidential communications between husband and wife. A communication is considered confidential only if there is not a third party present. Thus, as Otis Trammell learned to his regret, pillow talk is protected, but group drug-smuggling discussions are not.

Subpoena   An order requiring a person to testify, and hence a method to compel reluctant witnesses to come to court. Failure to heed a subpoena may result in the offender being brought to court by the police and possibly being fined and/or jailed for contempt of court. From the Latin *sub* (under) and *poena* (penalty). A *subpoena duces tecum* is a command not only to appear but also to bring something, such as records, to court. A person subpoenaed may avoid coming to court by requesting the court to "quash" (not squash) the subpoena.

Suppression Hearing   Generally considered to be a method of policing the police. In criminal trials the defense will often attempt to suppress certain evidence, claiming that it has been illegally obtained. The theory underlying this rule is that the police will not violate an individual's rights if they know that any evidence obtained in violation of those rights will be suppressed and hence cannot be used against the defendant at trial. This procedure may be applied to many forms of evidence: an allegedly coerced confession, a suggestive lineup, or a weapon seized without a search warrant.

Conservative commentators have frequently argued that justice is thwarted in such instances and that all evidence obtained should be available for use at trial. Suggestions have been made that individual rights could be better protected by, for example, disciplinary actions against police officers who violate these rights, or by lawsuits filed by individuals whose rights are allegedly violated. However, these and other suggestions have yet to be adopted, and suppression hearings remain the standard mode of insuring that the police respect an individual's rights.

Warrants A warrant is an order signed by a judge authorizing the police to take certain action. Generally, warrants come in two forms: arrest warrants and search warrants.

Warrants should issue only upon a demonstration of probable cause to believe that the person to be arrested has committed the crime or that the place to be searched will contain the evidence to be seized.

Suppose, for example, the police have heard from two informants that Ms. Smith has a supply of cocaine in her home. The police will prepare an affidavit describing what the informants have told them and explaining why the informants are worthy of belief. The police will bring the affidavit to a judge. The judge will issue a warrant for the search of Ms. Smith's home if the judge believes that there is probable cause to believe Ms. Smith has cocaine in her home. The search warrant, and the resulting search, will be limited to the cocaine.

Note that there are exceptions to the warrant requirement. A police officer witnessing a bank robbery need not obtain a warrant before arresting a fleeing suspect. Likewise, officers inadvertently finding obvious contraband in "plain view" in an automobile do not need a warrant to seize the contraband.

The question of what can be searched and what can be seized and under what conditions is the most heavily litigated and most rapidly changing area of criminal law. In some cases the exceptions to the exceptions to the exceptions have gotten so technical that it is a wonder that judges, let alone cops on the beat, can understand them. It's hard to imagine that a police officer, with perhaps a high school education, could make sense out of the Supreme Court's latest pronouncement on searches of suitcases found in automobile trunks when that pronouncement dodges and weaves its way through several similar yet dissimilar opinions on the same subject and comes complete with three concurring and two dissenting opinions.

INDEX OF FIGURES

INDEX OF TESTIMONY

INDEX OF PHOTOGRAPHS

†